Crucicentric, Congregational, and Catholic

Crucicentric, Congregational, and Catholic

The Generous Orthodoxy
of Alan P. F. Sell

DAVID R. PEEL

☛PICKWICK *Publications* · Eugene, Oregon

CRUCICENTRIC, CONGREGATIONAL, AND CATHOLIC
The Generous Orthodoxy of Alan P. F. Sell

Copyright © 2019 David R. Peel. All rights reserved. Except for brief quotations in critical publications or reviews, no part of this book may be reproduced in any manner without prior written permission from the publisher. Write: Permissions, Wipf and Stock Publishers, 199 W. 8th Ave., Suite 3, Eugene, OR 97401.

Pickwick Publications
An Imprint of Wipf and Stock Publishers
199 W. 8th Ave., Suite 3
Eugene, OR 97401

www.wipfandstock.com

PAPERBACK ISBN: 978-1-5326-4076-6
HARDCOVER ISBN: 978-1-5326-4077-3
EBOOK ISBN: 978-1-5326-4078-0

Cataloguing-in-Publication data:

Names: Peel, David R., author.

Title: Crucicentric, congregational, and catholic : the generous orthodoxy of Alan P. F. Sell / David R. Peel.

Description: Eugene, OR: Pickwick Publications, 2019 | Includes bibliographical references and index.

Identifiers: ISBN 978-1-5326-4076-6 (paperback) | ISBN 978-1-5326-4077-3 (hardcover) | ISBN 978-1-5326-4078-0 (ebook)

Subjects: LCSH: Sell, Alan P. F. | Theology, Doctrinal | Reformed Church—Doctrines

Classification: BX6.5 P22 2019 (paperback) | BX6.5 (ebook)

Manufactured in the U.S.A.   01/31/19

To Noah and Toby

"His is a generous orthodoxy, committed to the faith once given to the saints but also willing to welcome insights from wherever they may come."

Robert Pope

Contents

Preface | ix
Abbreviations | xv

1. Introduction: The Life and Work of Alan P. F. Sell | 1
2. Doing Theology | 34
3. God | 64
4. Creation | 100
5. Jesus Christ | 122
6. Holy Spirit | 157
7. The Church | 176
8. The Means of Grace and More about the Church | 203
9. Salvation: Yesterday, Today, and Tomorrow | 238
10. Conclusion | 249

Bibliographies | 257
General Index | 289

Preface

In a review of the *Festschrift* presented to Alan Sell, a URC colleague expressed his hope that there could be "real engagement with Alan's thinking."[1] He then went on to challenge his readers as follows: "Now that [Alan] has become one of our great authorities we should pluck up courage to argue with him."[2] Like similar sets of essays, the writers had not engaged explicitly with the thought of the person they were honoring. Being one of those writers, I instinctively responded to Donald Norwood's challenge: What better way to begin my retirement from stipendiary ministry than to devote some of my time to reading the Sell corpus, with a view to writing a few short articles about Alan's work? The opportunity to mount such a project in conversation with Alan added further motivation to embark upon it. From the start, he was unfailingly generous, providing me with extensive bibliographies of his work, and quite a few of his books. What I didn't know was that he had been diagnosed with a serious illness. My intention to meet Donald's challenge to "argue with [Alan]" through a constructive conversation was dashed when Alan died in early 2016.

A major attraction of my project was the opportunity to challenge Alan's "generous orthodoxy" with my more liberal, revisionist position.[3] And, as I made my way through the vast Sell corpus, I became convinced that Alan's theological thought deserves a wider audience, not only in the Reformed world, to which we both belong, but also within the other confes-

---

1. Norwood, Review of Robbins, ed., *Ecumenical and Eclectic*.
2. Ibid.
3. I owe the phrase "generous orthodoxy" to Robert Pope. In a short pen-portrait of Alan he says this: "His is a generous orthodoxt [sic], committed to the faith once given to the saints but also willing to welcome insights from wherever they may come" (Wiseman, ed., *Colleagues*). Then, in a later tribute, he says that "Alan's was a 'generous orthodoxy', where he maintained the ancient doctrine of the church, but was also willing to see that even those with whom he might disagree might have something worthwhile to say" ("Alan Philip Frederick Sell," 524).

sional families, with whom Alan spent so much of his time in ecumenical engagement. His untimely death prompted the idea that I should attempt to present an analysis, interpretation, and criticism of his entire theology. After sharing the idea with several colleagues, a revised retirement project quickly fell into shape. It had become more extensive, and was starting to feel rather daunting: from an intention to write some short articles I found myself being challenged to write a book.

Three words describe the nature of the ensuing book. First, the work is *synthetic*. It pieces together Alan's theological position from his vast, scholarly output. He wrote extensively in the areas of philosophy and history, as well as theology. This book is only concerned with the latter, but, quite often, crucial insights about Alan's *theological* position come through in his ostensibly *non*-theological writings. Hopefully, those interested in Alan's theology will welcome having an accessible account of it, rather than have to trawl through the entire Sell corpus to formulate it. Secondly, the work is *systematic*. I have chosen to present Alan's theology under the headings usually associated with systematic theologies, and in the order the various Christian doctrines are presented in them. By so doing I am departing from the way in which Alan tended to approach theology. He was of a more Anglo-Saxon than Continental disposition, regarding the attempts of Continental theologians to encapsulate the entire gamut of doctrine within one coherent system as rather presumptuous. Systems of any sort were for him tantamount to constraints; so it is hardly surprising that we find Alan referring to systematic theology disparagingly as "the dogged plod through the 'departments' from God to eschatology."[4] While I have no intention of presenting Alan's theology as a system akin to those of the great Continentals, I still find value in following their standard conventions when discussing Christian doctrines in an orderly fashion. Hence, in outlining Alan's theology, I will start with "prolegomena" and end with "eschatology." Chapters 3 to 9 can be read in any order. Readers not at home in philosophical theology may wish to leave the material dealing with process thought in Chapter 3 to the end. Thirdly, the work is *critical*—in the complete sense of that term. Readers will find that, theologically, Alan and I share a great deal in common, but that I am led to more *revisionary* conclusions in several areas. Hopefully, they will be stimulated by two friends in effect "doing" theology together. Norwood maintains that Alan would have loved such a theological argument. He also says quite rightly that "we can all become wiser through sincere debate."[5] Even in our competitive world, though, we often have to

---

4. PHT, 260.
5. Norwood, Review of Robbins, ed., *Ecumenical and Eclectic*, 140.

settle for the stimulation and enhancement which comes from attending to our disagreements. And, when it comes to theology, it is not always a matter of whether we win or lose arguments, but, rather, whether we have bothered enough to take part in what inevitably is a never-ending discussion.

During the writing of this book two observations became crystal clear. The first concerns the vast range and depth of Alan's intellectual achievements. While my focus has been on his theology I could not avoid recognizing that what I have been addressing is part of a much wider project that included philosophy and history. Alan was just as at home producing "meticulously researched work" and "finely nuanced judgements" about the work of, say, John Locke and J. S. Mill,[6] as he was gaining a reputation for being "the current 'doyen' of studies in English Nonconformity."[7] His written output was breathtaking, and, hopefully, others will be motivated to explore the historical and philosophical aspects of it. The second observation concerns the scope of this book. Not only have issues of space prevented me dealing as thoroughly as I would have wished with several topics, but discussion of some subjects has had to be omitted entirely, e.g. the preparation of the church's representative ministers, the function of the church's ministers, Christian ethics (including the issue of same-sex relationships), liturgy, and prayer—all topics which Alan dealt with at various lengths. The necessity for such omissions points to the book's unavoidable limitations.

I have made every effort to write this book in inclusive language. I share with Alan the belief that "we should not use language which might be taken as implying that we are ignoring half the human race."[8] But Alan remained cautious in his use of inclusive language, openly fearing that "political correctness" can lead to a loss of important *theological* language. When his colleagues avoided use of the term "Lord," for example, on account of it being "unwholesomely hierarchical," he regretted that they were depriving themselves and others of a language with which Christians, "as counter-cultural agents," could tell "'the world,' on the basis of Jesus' example, that "it has not understood what true Lordship is."[9] Alan also always used masculine pronouns when referring to God, declaring that he could not "assign meaning to requests to use inclusive language when referring to God."[10] His over-riding concern was to maintain that the God-head—Father, Son and Holy Spirit—is personal. He insisted that, once we recog-

---

6. Carter, Review of JL, 122.
7. Stewart, Review of GE, 109.
8. EEE, 264.
9. NT, 169.
10. EEE, 367.

nize that God is neither male nor female, "conventions regarding inclusive language in the human context (logically) cannot apply to him."[11] When we refer to God as "Father," he maintained, we are using the term "Father" analogically, rather than employing it "univocally of ourselves and God."[12] But, while an awareness of such analogical use may be second nature to the theologically educated, the understanding of such language among rank and file Christians sometimes is one of a *literal* identification of God with what we understand as fatherhood and hence all its ensuing, unfortunate gender specifications. Alan, of course, maintained that we should call God "Father" precisely because God's self-revelation in Christ was in terms of God being our Father: "Jesus, who knew the Father as no other, taught us to address God as Father."[13] Alan maintained that an ontological claim about God's very being was being made through what is essentially analogical or metaphorical discourse.[14] But metaphors point to, rather than fully encapsulate, ontological claims. Those which are significant in one time and place may not be adequate in other times and places. Alan believed, however, that the early Christians did not have to go in search of appropriate images to use in their God-talk; they spoke, rather, of God as God had been revealed to them in Jesus; hence, he insisted, so should we address God. Alan's position, though, partly reflects the widespread idea that Jesus taught his followers to address God as "Father" in a uniquely, distinctive way.[15] This idea is now challenged.[16] The result is that many agree with Geza Vermes that "The focus of [Jesus'] concern was not God as such, but himself, his disciples, and the world, in their relation to the Father in heaven and his kingdom."[17] To put the ensuing issue succinctly: "*All* talk of God as a person . . . is at best symbolic, not literal talk. Its purpose . . . is less intellectual or metaphysical than existential, *less to describe the structure of God in itself than to express the meaning of God for us.*"[18] It follows that whenever purported *personal* language used of God hinders our hearing of the claim God makes upon our lives, we have a clear warrant to seek alternative language. If speaking about God in male categories prevents people hearing the Gospel, for example,

11. EEE, 367.
12. CCF, 244.
13. EEE, 369.
14. See CCF, 244.
15. See Jeremias, *The Prayers of Jesus*.
16. See Barr, "Abba isn't Daddy!" and Vermes, *Jesus the Jew*, 183–86; *The Religion of Jesus the Jew*, 152–83; and *Jesus in his Jewish Context*, 35–39.
17. Vermes, *Jesus in his Jewish Context*, 39.
18. Ogden, *Understanding*, 32, Italics mine.

I feel more obliged to avoid such language than to give them a lecture on God-talk.[19] I shall not only avoid gender specific pronouns when talking about God, therefore, but I will also follow other theologians in referring to "God Godself" rather than "God himself."

The subject of "language" arose for me in another context: How should I designate Alan Sell as I write about him, given that he was a ministerial colleague and acquaintance? Should I call him "Sell" and thereby evoke the specter of cold objectivity; or ought I to seek to be more personal and refer to him by his Christian name? After some thought, I chose to be personal here in the Preface, the biographical material of Chapter One, and the Conclusion, but everywhere else "Alan" is referred to as "Sell."

The following people greatly increased my knowledge of Alan through letters they wrote to me and/or conversations I had with them: Alan Argent, Clyde Binfield, Tony Burnham, Martin Camroux, Graham Cook, Martin Cope, Susan Durber, Chris Eddowes, Alan Gaunt, Carole Marsden, John Marsh, Robert Pope, Elwyn Richards, Anna Robbins, Karen Sell, Sarah Simpson, Dorothy Spence, David Tatem, David Thompson, Donald Whitehead, John Tudno Williams and David Wykes. I am particularly grateful to those who read and commented upon individual chapters or the entire book in draft form. The collective wisdom of Clyde Binfield, John Harrod, Robert Pope and Karen Sell enabled me to avoid many errors as well as sharpened up my thinking at several points.

My task in researching the book was greatly helped by the kindness and efficiency of the staff at the following libraries: The Congregational Library, Boston, Massachusetts; Dr Williams's Library, London; Highland Theological College, Inverness; John Rylands Library, Manchester; and Westminster College Library, Cambridge. The book would never have been published were it not for generous financial help received from The Marquis Fund, the URC Education for Ministry funds and the Donald Tract Fund. When quoting scripture I have used the New Revised Standard edition of the bible.

Finally, my thanks go to Caleb Shupe, Robin Parry, and the staff at Wipf & Stock for the professional way in which they brought about the publication of this book, and my family who have had to live with this particular writing project for so long. Donald Norwood, Andrew Peel, Heidi Page, David Pickering, Robert Pope, Anna Robbins, and David Thompson helped me track down some elusive bibliographic details and material. Meanwhile, Pat, my wife, played a crucial role in preparing the manuscript

---

19. I am reminded of a sharp comment of Janet Lees: "Rather than the Council of Nicea, I'm more concerned about the Council of Ikea—the thousands who spend more time in traffic jams going to out of town shopping centres on Sundays than in pews (you can't actually buy pews in Ikea—yet)" (Letter to *Reform*, 12 June 2004).

for publication. Without her help this book would never have seen the light of day. To her, in particular, I extend my generous thanks.

Abbreviations

1. ALAN SELL'S BOOKS

ACI	*Aspects of Christian Integrity*
CAC	*Christ and Controversy: The Person of Christ in Nonconformist Thought and Ecclesial Experience*
CAM	*Content and Method in Christian Theology: A Case Study in the Thought of Nels Ferré*
CCC	*Convinced, Concise and Christian: The Thought of Huw Parri Owen*
CCF	*Confessing and Commending the Faith: Historic Witness and Apologetic Method*
COM	*Commemorations: Studies in Christian Thought and History*
COS	*Christ Our Saviour*
CP	*Church Planting: A Study of Westmorland Nonconformity*
CTF	*Confessing the Faith Yesterday and Today: Essays Reformed, Dissenting and Catholic*
DAD	*Defending and Declaring the Faith: Some Scottish Examples 1860–1920*
DTLC	*Dissenting Thought and the Life of the Churches: Studies in an English Tradition*
EEE	*Enlightenment, Ecumenism, Evangel: Theological Themes and Thinkers 1550–2000*
FPA	*Four Philosophical Anglicans: W.G. DeBurgh, W.R. Matthews, O.C. Quick, H.A. Hodges*
GB	*The Great Debate: Calvinism, Arminianism and Salvation*

GE		*The Great Ejectment of 1662: Its Antecedents Aftermath and Ecumenical Significance*
GOF		*God Our Father*
HT		*Hinterland Theology: A Stimulus to Theological Construction*
JL		*John Locke and the Eighteenth Century Divines*
MOG		*Mill on God*
NT		*Nonconformist Theology in the Twentieth Century*
OMMM		*One Ministry, Many Ministers: A Case Study from the Reformed Tradition*
PDN		*Philosophy, Dissent and Nonconformity, 1689–1920*
PHT		*Philosophy, History and Theology: Selected Reviews 1975–2011*
PICB		*Philosophical Idealism and Christian Belief*
PR		*The Philosophy of Religion 1875–1980*
RECT		*A Reformed, Evangelical, Catholic Theology: The Contribution of the World Alliance of Reformed Churches 1875–1982*
RM		*Robert Mackintosh: Theologian of Integrity*
SOL		*The Spirit Our Life*
SVOC		*Saints: Visible, Orderly and Catholic*
TAT		*Testimony and Tradition: Studies in Reformed and Dissenting Theology*
TEM		*The Theological Education of the Ministry: Soundings in the British Reformed and Dissenting Thought*
TIT		*Theology in Turmoil: The Roots, Cause and Significance of the Conservative-Liberal Debate in Modern Theology*
TNM		*P.T. Forsyth: Theologian for a New Millennium*

2. OTHER ABBREVIATIONS

URC	United Reformed Church
CCEW	Congregational Church in England and Wales
CUEW	Congregational Union of England and Wales
JURCHS	Journal of the United Reformed Church History Society
WARC	World Alliance of Reformed Churches
WCC	World Council of Churches

1

Introduction
The Life and Work of Alan P. F. Sell

Theology, like all intellectual disciplines, is contextual: where we stand influences what we see; who we talk to determines what we hear; and those with whom we live and work shape our thinking. If our understanding of the building blocks of reality is bounded by "relativity" (Einstein) and "uncertainty" (Heisenberg), it ought to come as no surprise that the nature of theological claims is perspectival. We can be forgiven for thinking that theologians quite often are found speaking about God with unwarranted certainty. Some theologians are so painfully aware of the *noetic* effects of human sin, however, that they claim genuine theological insight only comes when theology is conducted within the Christian community, a body of people whose lives are in the process of being renewed by the saving presence of God. Brenda Watson claims that "The notion that *finite* human beings can encapsulate in perfect language for all time the inscrutable mystery of God and of God's believed self-revelation to human beings is inadmissible."[1] Yet there remain theological thinkers who still speak and write as if the contrary is true. Nevertheless, there are two reasons why theology is bound to be tentative, provisional, and relative: first, theology seeks knowledge of an infinite God whose nature is beyond full description by human beings; and, secondly, theology is carried out by human beings who are not only culturally conditioned, but now see only in a glass darkly.[2]

---

1. Watson, "To Know Or Not," 90. Italics mine.
2. See Pailin, *Anthropological Character of Theology*.

Recognition of the *relativity* and plurality of all theological thinking does not mean that we act as if we are caught up in a vicious *relativism* in which all theological views must be regarded as equally true. As long as human beings talk across the great divisions of race, culture, and place, distinctions can be made between "good" and "bad" theology. Through *conversation* rival claims can be tested by asking questions: Is what is being said congruent with the stream of witness flowing from the early traditions set down by Jesus' followers? What do we make of claims which depart from received orthodoxy—are they the warranted improvements which they are claiming to be, or are they merely repeating mistakes? Are these claims credible today? Do they present the truth as faithfully and arrestingly as the saints of old did in their culture, and are *their* noble aims and motives met in what is *now* said? Rival theologies can be brought into conversation with each other by addressing such questions. The wisdom of recognizing that truth is relative to context need not involve accepting a currently fashionable counsel of despair: a complete relativism in which opinion parades as fact.

It follows that we can only fully understand any person's theology if we attend to the context in which it is born and constructed. To achieve that, we can pose such questions as these: Which thinkers influenced that theology? What books were formative in its development and creation? How was it influenced by the opportunities afforded by education and subsequent career? What were the predominant questions of the age in which that theology was constructed? And, in the case of a churchman like Alan, what was the relationship between his calling to be a Christian minister and his career as an academic theologian? To answer such questions, we need to learn more about the man whose theology is the subject of this book.[3]

BIOGRAPHY

Alan described Monday 27 July 1959 as "one of the greatest days of [his] life";[4] and, as Max Boyce, the Welsh folk singer and comedian would say, "I was there!" when he was ordained as a Christian minister and inducted to serve two rural Congregational churches at Sedbergh and Dent in the Yorkshire Dales. Whatever else he was to become—Higher Education teacher,

---

3. I have been privileged to read an extensive, private memoir entitled *The Chronicles of Alan and Karen Sell*. It has been very helpful in preparing this biographical sketch. Hereafter, it is referred to as *Chronicles*. It is now located in Dr William's Library in London.

4. *Chronicles*, 123.

theological secretary of an international confessional body or university and college professor—was rooted in and defined by that particular act of worship. For that was when Alan became part of the representative ministry of the church of Jesus Christ. God had called him to this particular pastorate. It would present challenges, opportunities, and frustrations in equal measure to ministry in churches in town centre or suburban settings. It made absolute sense since Alan Sell had been brought up in *rural* Surrey. Far from being wasted at Sedbergh and Dent, he was taking up a ministry which was as appropriate for him as it was for those two Dales' churches.[5]

The Early Years (1935–53)

Alan Philip Frederick Sell was born on 15 November 1935 in Surrey, the elder of the two sons of Arthur Philip Sell, a draughtsman in the Portsmouth dockyard who became a qualified teacher, and Freda Marion, née Bushen.[6] Arthur Sell, an Anglican, married into a staunch Congregational family. Anticipating the child's later denominational affiliation, the Sells' first son was baptized at Godalming Congregational Church on 3 May 1936. When the family moved from Farncombe to Cranleigh later that year the absence of a local Congregational Church caused them to worship at the local Methodist Church. Roseacre, their new house, was large and possessed an extensive garden. It was a perfect setting for a happy childhood. Growing up in a country at war meant life was not without its risks: "a German 'Doodlebug' landed on the gas works and a German aeroplane came down in the fields next to the house."[7] Nevertheless, the Sells got through wartime safely.

Alan attended Cranleigh Infant School before going to Elstow Preparatory School in 1943. He tells us that "[his] school reports reveal that [he] was sometimes 'good,' sometimes 'interested,' sometimes 'keen,' sometimes that [he] had done 'very well.'"[8] The picture is of a bright energetic child who did everything with great seriousness and total thoroughness. It was a pattern of things to come. Much later Alan reflected on his "busy childhood":

---

5. In a society whose sense of values challenges Schumacher's conviction that "small is beautiful," it is easy to see why a *small* rural church is often conceived as weaker than, say, a *large* suburban church. However, "strength" and "weakness" can be qualities independent of numerical size: some small rural churches are strong and healthy, while some large town centre or suburban churches are decidedly weak and ailing. For Schumacher's counter-cultural challenge, see his *Small is Beautiful*.

6. Roger David Sell, Alan's younger brother, was born on 29 May 1944.

7. *Chronicles*, 13.

8. *Chronicles*, 14.

I always knew it was a happy one. I also detect an embryonic research instinct: I did not just read comics, I had to discover their histories and circulations. I did not simply go to ballroom dancing lessons: I explored the several examining boards in that field. I did not just work at the stables, I investigated the Institute of the Horse, its history and examinations. I did not just listen to dance bands, I had to find out how many players each had. And so on, and so on. And I was always working to deadlines with my newspapers and comics, radio scripts, toy theatre plays, and later, Sunday School and Guild talks and sermons. So it continues more than half a century on.[9]

In September 1946 Alan was selected for Pewley School, a well-respected grammar school in Guildford. Alongside his studies, music became an important dimension in his life. He would become a multitalented musician, proficient on piano and organ, as well as tenor banjo, saxophone and clarinet. His taste was wide: classical as well as jazz, the musical world of the dance hall as well as that of Gilbert and Sullivan. Musical ability meant that an early ambition to become a music teacher was not out of place.[10] But a musical career was not the only call placed upon this teenager. Alan was now fourteen and his Headmaster was checking on career aspirations. Alan told him that he wanted "to be a minister."[11] The Headmaster was underwhelmed: "He could not understand how anyone should wish to enter such a namby-pamby profession" and "on [his] school-leaving certificate . . . under 'Aptitudes' he wrote 'Philosophical and abstruse.'"[12]

But Alan was indeed called to become a minister of the Christian gospel. By the time he was failing his Headmaster's career interview he was already writing sermons and preaching them to his mother. His first effort on 7 May 1950 prompted a diary entry: "Mum said I had a gift for writing sermons & liked it."[13] It was not long before Alan was making enquiries about how to become a Minister. Despite having attended a Methodist Church, he made a firm commitment to Congregationalism on account of its "more settled ministry" and the centrality within it of the "Church

---

9. *Chronicles*, 55.

10. See the entry in *Chronicles* for 18 May 1950: "I have decided to be a music master at a Public School one day, I hope" (*Chronicles*, 32).

11. *Chronicles*, 18.

12. *Chronicles*, 18. In his sermon at Alan's funeral service, Robert Pope commented that "[Alan] might have been abstruse as a youth, but in later life he provided lucid accounts of intricate and subtle theological arguments" [unpublished manuscript].

13. *Chronicles*, 32.

Introduction

Meeting."[14] There began a life time of commitment to Congregational polity and practice not only in Congregationalism but also within the United Reformed Church, which latterly has been unable to maintain the settled ministry that once distinguished it from circuit ministry in Methodism, and in which the Church Meeting concept is a shadow of its former self. Alan defended both to his dying day. He did not grow up in Congregationalism, he chose to become part of it.

When the Sell family moved to Guildford on 24 October 1951, Alan worshipped at the Perry Hill Congregational Church, Worplesdon. He was received into membership on 6 January 1952. George Stanley Morgan, its minister, become "a great friend and supporter."[15] Upon Morgan's death in 1953 Alan offered his own appreciation: "Few, if any, people have impressed me more than he did, for his kindness, his humility, his utter sincerity, and the closeness of his walk with God."[16] Alan immersed himself in church life. A debut sermon at Ewhurst Congregational Church was, he recorded, "well received," and he was invited "to come again," a true Congregational accolade.[17] Alan's preparation for Christian ministry had begun.

The young Alan Sell was advised that becoming the kind of learned minister he felt called to be would entail taking a general arts degree before reading divinity. There was no question of his ability to complete such a course. On 19 April 1952 he went up to London to be interviewed by Sydney Cave, the Principal of New College, with a view to becoming an ordinand upon leaving school. He was disappointed when, early the following year, Cave informed him that New College could not offer him an arts degree as the foundation for a subsequent BD. Consequently, Alan turned his attentions to Lancashire Independent College in Manchester. After being interviewed by the Ministerial Training Committee of the Southern Province of CUEW he was accepted as a candidate for ministry, and, then, on the opening night of his denomination's May Meetings in London, he met W. Gordon Robinson, the Principal of the Lancashire Independent College. It was a memorable night: Alan was overjoyed to learn from Robinson that there should be no problem commencing his preparation for ministry in Manchester at the start of the 1953–54 session; and he was deeply moved by the atmosphere of a near-full Westminster Chapel—"made me proud to be Congy!"[18]

14. *Chronicles*, 36.
15. *Chronicles*, 40.
16. *Chronicles*, 50.
17. *Chronicles*, 47.
18. *Chronicles*, 50.

6

Crucicentric, Congregational, and Catholic

Preparation for Christian Ministry (1953–59)

When Alan travelled to Manchester on 10 July 1953 to sit the Entrance Examinations for Lancashire Independent College, it was only the second time he had been north of London. With seven other candidates he sat papers on 'English Bible' and 'Congregationalism'. He was also asked to write an essay, before being interviewed by the College Education and General Committees. On the 13 July, he was accepted as a student of the College to take the BA Ordinary Degree as a preparation for the BD Honours examinations. A six-year course would be augmented by pastoralia sessions, regular examination of the biblical books in English and weekly appointments to conduct worship in local churches. It was demanding and became even more so when Alan's application to read for the BA Ordinary Degree was rejected on the grounds that he had not passed 'O' Level English. He had actually by-passed it *en route* to 'A' Level work, but the Manchester matriculation regulations required it. As a result, he spent his first year in Manchester completing university matriculation by taking 'O' Level English, the Certificate of Biblical Knowledge and New Testament Greek. He took the set-back positively, stating that his first year turned out to be "a very good course which stood [him] in good stead for Bible studies later."[19] But, in order to avoid a seventh year preparing for ordination, Alan decided to complete the very formidable Manchester BD in two rather than three years.

Manchester provided a formative learning experience for Alan. He looked back on it with affection for the rest of his life. Illustrations of the College Building appear on the covers of two of his books, and it provided him with a template for judging the best in education for ministry.[20] A Southerner had to find his way among Northerners; the Grammar School boy had to share a study with Alan Gaunt, the Public School boy;[21] and a teetotaler had to cope with the camaraderie of those who enjoyed the odd drink.[22] His lasting appreciation of his time in Manchester, combined with the affection he always had for his College days, suggest that he succeeded. Life, however, is never without problems. This is evident in the Gaunt-Sell

---

19. *Chronicles*, 53.

20. The books are *COM* and *TEM*.

21. Gaunt was educated at Silcoates School, Wakefield, and served churches in Clitheroe, Keighley, Sunderland, Heswall, Manchester South West, and Windermere. He became well-known for writing prayers and hymn texts, many of which have been published.

22. The Lancashire Independent College had a strict no-alcohol policy. During Alan's time at the College, some students were "sent down" for bringing alcohol onto the premises.

relationship, the two Alans respectively wondering whether the other was house-trained.[23] But Alan was usually found to be as Donald Whitehead, his near college contemporary, found him, "a warm personality with a friendly disposition."[24] Alan was full of praise for the education he received at College and the University of Manchester. He was taught by some well-known scholars, as well as those who were about to make their mark.[25] Towards the end of his life, he wrote appreciatively of "those whose New Testament classes [he] attended in Manchester[26] referring particularly to the influence that T. W. Manson had upon him. Not only did Manson model "the rigorous yet joyful life of scholarship"[27] to which Alan would always aspire, but he also provided the proof, if ever it was needed, that the apostles were never "charged with transmitting their office and authority to their successors."[28] That was something every Nonconformist, Dissenting or Reformed student needed to know in an ecumenical age still dominated by debate over the necessity of an episcopal ordering of the church. Also very influential was John Heywood-Thomas who played a key role in honing Alan's philosophical sensibilities: he co-supervised Alan's later Manchester MA (1961),[29] then acted as External Examiner for his Nottingham PhD (1967), and became one of his major confidants. Looking back upon this important period, Alan lamented that "the galaxy which [he] had been privileged to have shining on [him] was progressively dimmed."[30] It was a conclusion steeped in nostalgia

23. Sell: "I sometimes wondered whether [Gaunt] was house-trained; but our friendship strengthened the further we got away from sharing a study" (*Chronicles*, 56); and Gaunt: "It was not the happiest relationship . . . he seemed to me a little precious . . . I always knew that he was clever . . . Alan was always basically respected by me, and, after all, in that first year we were both little more than schoolboys . . . He had received a far better education at Grammar School, but had not lived away from home before" (Gaunt, email to author, 16 June 2016).

24. Whitehead's time at Lancashire Independent College overlapped with that of Alan: "During my first year he would be in year 4 or 5" (Whitehead, letter to author, 24 June 2016).

25. His teachers included, for his BA: D. Emmet, E. Gilman, D. P. Henry, J. D. Jump, R. F. Leslie, A. Pollard, R. Skelton, A. Goodwin, H. Perkin, W. R. Ward, R. Western, V. Knowles, D. Leahy, A. N. Marlow and A. J. N. Wilson; for his BD: H. H. Rowley, G. Farr, J. Allegro, T. W. Manson, O. E. Evans, H. P. Owen, E. G. Rupp, C. W. Dugmore, W. G. Robinson, S. G. F. Brandon, D. H. Smith, R. H. Preston, J. Heywood-Thomas and G. Phillips.

26. See, *TEM*, 265–89.

27. *TEM*, 270.

28. *TEM*, 276.

29. The other co-supervisor was R. H. Preston, the renowned Anglican social ethicist.

30. *Chronicles*, 120

but containing truth: some changes which followed his time in Manchester involved loss (e.g., the down-grading of the Faculty of Divinity to a Department within the Faculty of Arts).

The nature of the preparation for ministry Alan received and continued to advocate has been aptly described by Robert Pope as an immersion of "candidates for ministry in the theological disciplines" with the expectation that "a genuinely theological mindset" would be sufficiently nurtured to "cope with those situations in ministry which can never be predicted."[31] But lest it be thought that this involved a total absence of practical experiences in which skills could be honed, and upon which reflection could lead to genuine practical learning, we need to recall the extensive attention to the art of preaching which took place in College, the weekly opportunities made available to students to take services in churches, and the arrangements made, often towards the end of the course, to undertake student pastorates. Alan was quickly marked out as a preacher of great promise. He enjoyed taking services in the local churches, not least the more rural ones. Bucklow Hill Congregational Church was largely "supplied" by the College and Sell suspected that "one of the reasons for [his] affection for this little church was its affinity in many ways with the Surrey village chapels from which [he] came."[32] He preached there regularly, his overall ability, stature and demeanor gaining him a somewhat dubious sobriquet for a Dissenter: "The bishop of Bucklow Hill"!

Alan did not leave Manchester as a gilt-edged academic. The BD conferred upon him in 1959 was graded as an unclassified pass.[33] Why did Alan underachieve? Two factors contributed: first, he attempted to complete in two years a degree course designed for three years; and, secondly, the time-scale was compounded when he failed the New Testament Texts paper at the end of his first year of BD studies, necessitating re-sitting the paper the following year amidst his already overcrowded examination schedule.[34] It was a great achievement to gain his BD in two years but we can sense what it must have meant when his unclassified degree was noted by the interview

---

31. Pope, "Alan Philip Frederick Sell," 525.

32. *Chronicles*, 68.

33. The University of Manchester conferred four BD degrees in the summer of 1959: two were in the Lower Second division and two were at Pass level. A well-known name, but above Alan's in the class list, is that of Michael H. Taylor, a Baptist, who became the Principal of Northern Baptist College in Manchester and then the Director of Christian Aid. Taylor gained notoriety on account of his views concerning the person and work of Christ. Alan was not impressed with those views.

34. All the students failed the course. It was incomplete due to the illness of T. W. Manson, their teacher.

panels which Alan encountered in his search for academic preferment. Any doubts about his academic standing evaporated, though, when he acquired *operis causa* DD (Manchester) and DLitt (Nottingham) degrees in addition to his PhD from the University of Nottingham. It was in Alan's nature to enjoy challenges.

Yorkshire Dales (1959–64)

During the summer vacations of 1956 and 1957, Alan was the Student Pastor at Macedonia Congregational Church in Failsworth, Lancashire. While exercising this ministry, he met Karen Elisabeth Lloyd (b. 4 June 1939). She was one of seven received into membership of the Macedonia fellowship at a service conducted by Alan on 4 August 1957. But, of perhaps greater significance, they had been dating since early December the previous year. They had music in common and enjoyed going to the theatre and cinema together. Karen attended the Moravian Fairfield High School for Girls and was later to train as a music teacher in Birmingham. They became engaged on 9 March 1957 and were married on 1 August 1959, the Saturday after Alan's Ordination and Induction at Sedbergh, at Hope Congregational Church, Oldham.

Following a honeymoon in Borrowdale, the Sells started their married life in the Sedbergh Congregational Church manse. The first pastorate is often the most memorable one in a young minister's career, partly because it is the place at which the opportunities of ministry are first exercised but also because for many it marks the start of married life and the bringing up of a family. So it was for Alan Sell as he sped up and down Westmorland hills on "Dobbin," his motorbike, to make pastoral calls and conduct worship in the chapels at Sedbergh and Dent. The three Sell children were born during this period of Alan's Christian service: Bridget Rebecca Karen (b. 18 October 1960), Judith Bronwen Amanda (b. 15 May 1963) and Jonathan Patrick Alan (b. 4 September 1964). And, whenever Alan and Karen later spent holidays in the area, they would attempt to spend some time "back home" in Sedbergh. As Martin Cope, the Church Secretary at Sedbergh says: "Clearly [Alan] had a soft spot for his first church as minister."[35] The feeling was mutual and reciprocated. During his ministry he became an important member of the local community.

Before graduating from Manchester, Alan drew up plans with Heywood-Thomas to continue his university studies. Thereafter a pattern developed in his life, one of conducting research for higher degrees while

35. Cope, email to author, 25 June 2016.

exercising full-time ministry in a pastorate. Within two years he was awarded an MA for a thesis entitled "Christian Ethics in the light of British Moral Philosophy since G. E. Moore."[36] Residential requirements in the PhD regulations at Manchester prevented Alan from moving to doctoral work, so his attention switched to the University of Nottingham, where he was awarded a PhD in 1967 for a thesis entitled "Christianity and Philosophy in Twentieth Century Britain: An examination of relationships and prospects, with special reference to the role of the philosopher of the Christian religion."[37] The attention he paid to furthering his studies within ministry did not go un-noticed. While some felt his academic interests were detrimental to his work within his pastorate, others were more encouraging. If the church's future scholars are to be produced, they argued, academically gifted ministers like Alan need all the help available to become suitably qualified.[38]

The first major innovation of his ministry at Sedburgh came with the introduction of Family Worship, in response to the denominationally led attempt to integrate children and young people more fully into the worshipping life of the congregation. Alan's approach to church life was centered upon the scriptures, and, in the positive sense of the term, "traditional," and thoroughly within the ethos of Congregationalism. He expected wholehearted commitment from the church members, or, as he preferred to call them in true Puritan style, the gathered saints. Noting that a number of those whose names appeared on the church roll had not attended worship or Church Meeting whilst he had been in post as their minister, he reminded the congregation that "A really lively church is not a church with many organisations; it is a church where the people are earnest about seeking God's will and trying to perform it."[39] Like P. T. Forsyth, his mentor, Alan had little time for churches which display a culture of "short sermons and long socials."[40] He insisted that meetings should only take place on two evenings

---

36. The thesis was examined by George Woods.

37. The thesis was supervised by R. W. Hepburn, Jonathan Harrison, and James Richmond, and was examined by John Heywood-Thomas.

38. Alan never forgot the financial help he received from CUEW in 1967 so he could take a sabbatical from his ministry in Worcester to facilitate the completion of his PhD. Through the initiative of William Simpson, Alan received £200 to reimburse Angel Street Congregational Church, Worcester for a three-month leave of absence from his church duties. In 2001, Alan himself generously made a significant sum of money available to the URC to put "towards the expenses of a minister in pastoral charge working for a doctorate in a theological discipline" (*Chronicles*, 476).

39. "Minister's Report to the Annual Church Meeting of Sedbergh Congregational Church, 20 July 1960." This minister's report and those cited hereafter are attached to the Church Meeting minutes kept at Sedbergh URC in Sedbergh, England.

40. In *Positive Preaching*, Forsyth declares that "A Christianity of short sermons is a

Introduction

of the week, thereby freeing people "to witness in the community if they so desire," and enabling him "to visit many whom it would be impossible to see during the day."[41] There was a clear, evangelical thrust to his leadership. In the wake of seismic numerical decline, it was second nature for Alan to raise expectation levels for church membership rather than lower them in the hope of attracting new members.[42] He was again echoing Forsyth.[43] The low turnout at the Church Meeting grieved him: "Our Church Meeting is drawn from about 10 people," he noted, before declaring that "This is poor."[44] As far as he was concerned, there was clearly room for improvement at Sedbergh Congregational Church![45]

Alan's ministry at Sedbergh was not universally appreciated. Some did not warm to the advent of Family Worship,[46] and, reading between the lines, some (perhaps the same people) thought he should have been doing more pastoral visiting.[47] But his detractors were in the minority. The Sedbergh

Christianity of short fibre," having earlier reminded his readers that "Brevity may be the soul of wit, but the preacher is not a wit" (75).

41. "Minister's Report to the Annual Church Meeting of Sedbergh Congregational Church, 20 July 1960."

42. See *OMMM*, 40.

43. In *Church and Sacraments*, Forsyth—in his typically robust style—opines that "We turn some of the best people away from us because our one concern seems to be to get as many as possible in. We do not present clear issues, and therefore we do not evoke sure decisions and therefore we do not appeal to manhood. We do not appeal to the strong men who have insight and decision, and who demand a faith for the mind, conscience, and the will as truly as for the heart and for the temperament" (20).

44. "Minister's Report to the Annual Church Meeting of Sedbergh Congregational Church, 1961."

45. "Apathy will take its toll sooner or later, e.g., when lax parents desire to have future babies baptised; when children who refrain from attending church wish to get married in church. Some of our members witness for Christ in daily life. One or two by back biting and jealous bickering do great harm to the body of Christ" ("Minister's Report to the Annual Church Meeting of Sedbergh Congregational Church, 1961").

46. "We regret that one of our Deacons has found it impossible as yet to attend a Family Service, and we hope this may soon be rectified" ("Minister's Report to the Annual Church Meeting of Sedbergh Congregational Church, 1961").

47. The minute book shows that Alan tried to encourage deacons to visit members more often, saying repeatedly that it was the work of them all to care. At his last Church Meeting in Sedbergh, he urged the deacons not only to visit regularly those on the lists which had been drawn up for use during the forthcoming vacancy, but also to continue doing so when the new minister arrived ("Minutes of the Church Meeting, 15 October 1964"). Some might question the wisdom of saying the following to Church Members: "It is rather annoying to be told by members that I haven't been seen for a few weeks: these members know where I am every Sunday!" ("Minister's Report to the Annual Church Meeting of Sedbergh Congregational Church, 1961"); even if Alan was without transport at that time.

church had much to be thankful for the ministry of its energetic and committed young minister.[48] Yorkshire's loss would be Worcestershire gain.

Worcester (1964–68)

It stretches the imagination to believe that Alan's need to be near Nottingham, in whose university he was enrolled as a part-time PhD student, was not a contributing factor when he accepted the call to Angel Street Congregational Church, Worcester, and the Congregational chapels of Hallow and Ombersley. He was inducted on 29 October 1964 and, following patterns which he had employed in the Yorkshire Dales, "The resourceful, determined and indefatigable Alan Philip Frederick Sell at once engaged [Angel Street Congregational Church] in a very far reaching review of its entire life and ministry."[49] But we can be forgiven for wondering whether Alan's heart—at least initially—was fully in this ministry, because less than six months into it he was interviewed for an Assistant Lectureship in Modern Theological Thought at Birmingham University. He was not offered the post.[50]

In the Preface to *Chronicles*, Alan writes of being aware of "a sense of vocation underpinning all [he had] tried to do." But learned ministers like him become easy prey to their detractors in an anti-intellectual church. Once the church's teachers were revered and placed on pedestals; now, quite often, their work is regarded as merely academic and irrelevant to the church's mainstream requirements. It is even said that "ministers close churches by degrees." At Angel Street, as at Sedbergh, there were church members who would have preferred to have seen Alan out of his study more often. What was uppermost in Alan's mind is revealed in the following statement: "I had to think seriously about how I thought God wanted me to be used in the future."[51] The ongoing need to contemplate how he could make the best use of the intellectual gifts given him would have had a more robust context if the ministerial offices advocated by Calvin had been operative in twentieth-

---

48. It is interesting that the family nature of the church involved a quarterly observation of the Lord's Supper in the presence of the children. In his "Minister's Report to the 1960 Annual General Meeting," Alan claimed that it had "proved a great blessing" with "some of the awe of the occasion" being "transmitted to the children," thereby providing "a basis upon which later understanding may grow." Nevertheless, he remained opposed to admitting children fully to the Sacrament until, by confession of faith, they testify to be believers. See chapter 8, "Sacraments" and following.

49. Marsh, *Particular Church*, 100.

50. The interview took place on 25 March 1965, and Daniel T. Hardy was appointed.

51. *Chronicles*, 161.

century British Congregationalism. Echoing Ephesians 4:11, Calvin argues that there are four permanent ministerial offices in the church: alongside the customary "minister" and "deacon" are the offices of "government" and, the one most appropriate to a man of Alan's gifts, "teacher."[52]

The review of Angel Street's life and work led to several positive outcomes which were to mark the Sell ministry. New patterns of worship were introduced: "Family Worship" was started as at Sedbergh; Word and Sacrament were integrated in the same service, and responsive prayers were adopted; an emphasis on stewardship through weekly giving eased financial pressures;[53] relationships with neighboring churches were fostered;[54] and the social, theological and spiritual life of the fellowship was enhanced. As early as 1966, Alan reviewed the situation: there was a better balance of age groups, an equal number of people below and above the age of sixty; attendances at services had improved; the Working and Study Groups had been very successful, most of their proposals having been implemented, with the notable exception of the re-development of the church site; but the position of collaboration with the Presbyterians was not too happy.[55] According to Marsh, "Minister and people evidently regarded [Alan Sell's ministry] with great happiness."[56]

After Alan received his PhD he looked for a post to fulfill what he felt called by God to become, one of those ministers Calvin called "teacher." He accepted a post at the West Midland's College of Higher Education in Walsall in May 1968. His move to a secular context raised the eyebrows of those who had become alarmed at the way the acids of the 1960s were eating away at the church's stipendiary ministers. The 1960s found many ministers leaving their pastorates to enter secular employment. With open

52. See Calvin, *Institutes*, IV.III.4–9.

53. Marsh informs us that "The necessity for extra 'Gift Days' was very soon eliminated as church members planned their giving much more effectively to meet known, understood and agreed costs" (*Particular Church*, 100).

54. Plans to enter into a closer working relationship with a neighbouring Methodist Church were halted by the Connexional Committee. Joint house groups with Christ Church Presbyterian Church subsequently led to a union of Congregationalists and Presbyterians in the Albany Terrace premises of Christ Church. It is now known as Worcester United Reformed Church. See Marsh, *Particular Church*, 100–102.

55. Marsh, *Particular Church*, 102; as the existence of Worcester URC confirms the unhappiness at the Congregational/Presbyterian interface did not prevent subsequent union of the two churches.

56. Marsh, *Particular Church*. Marsh adds that "The Church Meeting roll, which had been maintained at the level of around 150 from 1964–68, hardly reveals the extent to which new members were received, for gains were offset by deaths and removals." According to the 2018 URC Yearbook, the membership of Worcester URC now numbers thirty-four adults.

"gangways" into the "people-related" professions in place, it was *relatively* easy for the "professionally" trained minister to become part of the probation service, or turn to social work, or enter upon a media career or, as in Alan Sell's case, turn to teaching. Some of those who did were motivated by crises of faith; others were frustrated by the churches they served—their feet too firmly anchored in the past, and their eyes too firmly closed to the challenges and opportunities which an increasingly secular society presented; and yet others discovered tragically late that they were not cut out to be ministers. Inevitably friends and colleagues speculated about the reasons for Alan's apparent change of direction.

Perhaps the criticisms about him not spending enough time in pastoral work had got to him? And, as he candidly noted, there can be valid reasons to put a stop to home visits:

> I sat on a sofa, and as we spoke, I felt something nudging my ankles. I glanced down and there between my feet was an alligator's head. Sitting very still, I said, "Do you know there is an alligator in this room?" "Oh yes" she cheerfully replied. "I have to let him out because he's nearly four feet long and his tank only measures three feet; so I have to bend his tail up and he doesn't like it." I did not stay for tea.[57]

Bunyan's Pilgrim had more "bottle" than Sell the pastoral visitor.[58] But there is not the slightest doubt that Alan upheld the centrality of pastoral work in Christian ministry: "Apart from any loss to the saints, if ministers neglect the pastoral task they themselves miss so much, and their preaching is less well informed than it otherwise would be."[59]

During the latter part of the 1950s and into the early 1960s a battle raged for the soul of Congregationalism. It centred upon a proposal which invited the independent congregations of CUEW to covenant together to form a more centralized church. After heated discussions the CCEW was created in May 1966. According to Alan Argent "it marked Congregationalism's final rejection of independency."[60] Given that Sell was a committed convert to the Congregational Way could the reason for moving into secular employment have been rooted in disenchantment about the direction in which his church was heading? As Argent says, "Congregationalism had

---

57. *Chronicles*, 170.

58. Note the following lines from Bunyan's famous hymn: "No lion can him fright, he'll with a giant fight" and "hobgoblin nor foul fiend can daunt his spirit: he knows he at the end shall life inherit" (United Reformed Church, *Rejoice and Sing*, no. 557).

59. *OMMM*, 68

60. Argent, *Transformation*, 465.

begun with gathered churches from which the county unions and CUEW had emerged so, surely "To overthrow Congregational independency challenged foundational principles"?[61] It is clear that Alan, along with fellow Dales' ministers George Curry and Arnold Mee, had grave misgivings about the transition from a union to a church. They had an article published in *The Christian World* asking for more theological work to be done before a final decision was taken. A petition, signed by twenty-one persons, was sent to *The British Weekly*. It was given the headline "Anxious Congregationalists advise delay."[62] Later that year, at the May Meetings, an amendment proposed by Richard Cleaves and seconded by Alan ensured that work would be done that eventually enabled at least one of the "Anxious" Congregationalists—Alan Sell—to accept the creation of CCEW.[63] In Alan's words: "it was conceded that the use of 'church' in a denominational sense was not found in the Bible (it hardly could have been); and, more importantly, it was carefully explained that there would be no hierarchy of councils in the CCEW (as, theologically and logically, there could not be if at each focus of churchly life the mind of Christ may under the guidance of the Holy Spirit be sought and discerned); and that instead the principle of mutual *episcope* as between local and wider expressions of church life would prevail."[64] The subsequent constitutional changes facilitated the creation of the URC in 1972, among whose members Alan belonged and served from 1972 to 1983 and 2001 to 2016.[65] While he would always stand in a critical relationship with any church to which he belonged, the monumental developments within Congregationalism during the 1960s had nothing to do with him leaving pastoral charge. The bottom line was that he felt called to a ministry within theological education.

Walsall (1968–83)

From 1968 to 1983, the Sell family lived in Walsall. They settled at Broadway Congregational (later to become United Reformed) Church. Alan's role at the West Midland's college was to pioneer courses in philosophy of religion,

---

61. Argent, *Transformation*, 459.
62. The petition appeared in *The British Weekly* on 22 February 1962.
63. For a fuller account of the story see *TAT*, 299–316.
64. Sell, Review of *Transformation of Congregationalism*, 335.
65. He participated in and served URC councils at local, regional, and national levels; e.g., he had two spells on the denomination's Doctrine, Prayer and Worship Committee, served on Ministerial Training Committees and conducted and enjoyed an itinerant preaching ministry.

ethics, and the history of Christian thought. He started as Lecturer (1968–70) but was promoted to Senior Lecturer (1970–2) and Principal Lecturer (1972–83). Amidst the demands of his teaching duties, he set up a Counseling Service for the entire College, with him becoming head of the counseling team. This involved some training, and an apparent clash of perception concerning the rudiments of pastoral care. The scene is a role-play:

> We sat cross-legged on the floor, kneecap to kneecap, in the wake of [a] non-judgmental lecture, and [the teacher] said, "I shall be the distressed person, and you shall be the counsellor." With that he launched into a lengthy account of all his ailments and disadvantages (Job couldn't have put it better), and at the end he plaintively asked me? "Why has all this happened to me?" To which I cheerfully responded, "Well, I think it's because you're a rotten old sinner." You never saw a person come out of role so quickly in all your life! He burst out, "You can't say that, that's judgmental!" To which I responded, "So is that!" At which point he chose a fresh partner.[66]

This reflects the sharp, playful wit of a principled rebel. It was now that Alan's love of writing came to the fore.[67] Sometimes he wrote to introduce people and their ideas because he wanted a wider audience to discover the importance which he attached to them; at other times it was a way of sorting out his own thinking. But, according to one of his rare self-descriptions, the Walsall years marked the first-fruits of an inveterate "scribbler," a man driven to write, who might have said of himself, *"scriba ergo sum."*

The Walsall also years found Karen Sell changing career. She was a class teacher and Head of Year until greater stability in the family finances enabled her in 1980 to leave teaching for a career in singing which would blossom and gain momentum later in Geneva and Calgary. The three Sell children took steps towards their future careers: Bridget in nursing, Judith in catering, and Jonathan winning the Henney Scholarship in 1982 for study at Pembroke College, Oxford—in later life he was to become a senior lecturer in Renaissance Studies at the University of Alcala, Spain. When the Open University was launched, Alan became one of its part-time teachers on the general humanities course, covering Reformation studies and philosophy. The remuneration made a much needed contribution to tight family finances. And, amidst a crowded professional and hectic family life, he found time for qualifications in speech, drama, and public speaking that,

---

66. *Chronicles*, 183.

67. A full bibliography for Alan Sell is found in an appendix to this book.

when completed, qualified him to examine and adjudicate in that field.[68] He also became a Vice-President of the Friends of Dr. Williams's Library.

Alan was clearly making his mark, so it came as no surprise that, in the middle of his Walsall sojourn, he eyes began to focus on the next stage of his career. Failure to get a Senior Lectureship at St. Andrews (1975) and a Lectureship at Edinburgh (1979)[69] would have reminded him of the difficulty English Nonconformists have in getting Scottish university posts. If he had got the post of Chaplain at the University of Sussex (1978) would that have really been fulfilling for him? I suspect not, even though it had suited Daniel Jenkins, a respected Congregational and United Reformed theologian.[70] Alan also found good reasons not to respond to "feelers" sent to him concerning the Chaplaincy of Mill Hill School (1980) and Principal of St. Andrew's Hall, Birmingham,[71] but he did apply to become Principal of Northern College, Manchester, his beloved *alma mater*, following the retirement of Edgar Jones (1978). He was interviewed for the post, but Jack McKelvey was appointed. McKelvey had a proven academic record. He came with the strong recommendation of John Marsh, a distinguished New Testament scholar and Principal of Mansfield College, Oxford, where he had completed his doctoral studies. He offered valuable South African experience, and he had experience of preparing men and women for ministry on courses involving a period of internship training in a local church. Alan, on the other hand, was coming from a "secular" rather than "church" post, and he appeared too "academic" for those who wanted to see the practical dimensions for preparation for ministry strengthened. He rationalized his failure as follows: "At the time I did not feel sad that I was not appointed: I could not have done what they thought they needed; but was sad that they thought they needed what they thought they did."[72] As his last book shows quite clearly, Alan was critical of the way ministerial training developed after what he believed were the Manchester glory days of his own preparation

---

68. Sell's qualifications in speech, drama and public speaking were FTCL, LTCL, LGSM (SD), LGSM (PS) and LLAM.

69. Ruth Page was appointed.

70. Jenkins was Chaplain at the University of Sussex from 1963 to 1970. For Jenkins, see Taylor and Binfield, *Who They Were*.

71. Regarding the St. Andrew's Hall position, Sell said, "It would have meant living 'over the shop' and assuming a 'mine host' role for both Karen and myself, and we did not feel that we could do that" (*Chronicles*, 225). A similar situation was the case at Northern College, Manchester, concerning the role of its Principal, but Sell did apply for that particular position.

72. *Chronicles*, 214.

for ministry; he was particularly scornful of the advent of "professional ministerial" degrees.⁷³

At the end of 1983 Alan found himself in a difficult position: the College in which he worked was under the threat of closure; his job was at risk; and he needed new pastures upon which to receive fresh challenges. Martin Cressey, then the Principal of Westminster College, Cambridge and a leading ecumenical statesman, recommended Alan to Lukas Vischer, the General Secretary of WARC based in Geneva, in connection with the vacant position of Executive Secretary for Theology. Alan applied for the post, gained an interview, and, when offered the position, accepted it with a great deal of relief. He was able to take early redundancy from West Midland's College and the Sells headed for a new life in Switzerland.

Geneva (1983–87)

WARC, a worldwide fellowship of Reformed Churches, represented upwards of eighty million Christians around the world. Alan's brief as Executive Secretary for Theology was five-fold.⁷⁴ First, he was expected to network among the member churches and develop cordial relations between the various denominational offices, theological faculties and seminaries, and church congregations, paying special attention to work in the area of the history and thought of the Reformed tradition. Discussions with teachers, researchers and students on current theological and ecumenical trends, and theological education and ministerial training were at the heart of the work. Secondly, Alan organized and participated in international bilateral dialogues between the Reformed family and other Christian world communions.⁷⁵ Thirdly, he was expected to undertake and foster research in the Reformed tradition, with particular reference to its contemporary significance.⁷⁶ Fourthly, he was charged with undertak-

---

73. See *OMMM*, 70–106.

74. The following information is taken from a Curriculum vitae kindly supplied by Alan.

75. During his tenure of office, Sell was involved in dialogues between WARC and the Roman Catholic Church, the Orthodox Churches, the Anglican Consultative Council, the Lutheran World Federation, the Baptist World Alliance, the Mennonite World Conference, the Methodist World Council, and the Disciples Ecumenical Consultative Council.

76. During the Genevan period, Sell edited, on behalf of WARC, *Reformed and Disciples of Christ in Dialogue* (1985) and *Reformed Theology and the Jewish People* (1986), and published *CP* (1986), *TIT* (1986) and *SVOC* (1986), his account of the Congregational idea of the church. After he left his post in Geneva, he wrote *RECT* which, as its subtitle indicates, tracks the contribution made by WARC, and the constituent bodies

Introduction

ing and fostering theological sharing among WARC's member churches, particularly through the administration of a theological scholarship program for postgraduate students. And, finally, he represented WARC on the Faith and Order Commission of WCC. The Geneva period, therefore, provided Alan with extensive opportunities to widen his theological horizons as he travelled among the worldwide Reformed family and the ecumenical world of which it is a prominent part. Alan was able to make life-long friendships which led to invitations to lecture far and wide. His scholarship was so valued by some of the institutions he visited that they subsequently awarded him honorary degrees.[77]

London became a useful hub for Alan's travels. It enabled him to continue his research interest through the Dr. Williams's[78] and British libraries, as well as visit his mother, who from October 1987 had moved to Queen Mary Court in Bournville, Birmingham, where Geoffrey Nuttall, the distinguished historian of Puritanism and Dissent, also resided in his later years. This happy coincidence initiated extended conversations with Nuttall that Sell greatly appreciated. They had a great deal in common: a poor showing in undergraduate examinations; repeated failure to land weighty academic appointments; a life-long call to Congregational ministry; concerns about the way the URC was moving—both never becoming central to their denomination's life; and a Methodist church-going youth.[79] Such was Nuttall's prowess as an historian that when it came to Congregational history there could never have been a conversation of equals. Nuttall always suspected that Alan's work as a philosopher and theologian prevented him from the depth of involvement with history which is necessary if it is to be understood adequately. Nor did he share Alan's seeming desire to publish whatever he wrote at all costs, preferring instead the strategy of publishing work that truly cements reputations.[80] Alan dedicated *Saints: Visible, Orderly and Catholic* to Nuttall without his permission: "Though flattered, Geoffrey

---

which amalgamated to form it, from 1875–1982.

77. Debrecen, Hungary (Hon DTh, 1995) and Clus/Kolozsvar, Romania (Hon DTh, 2003). Sell also received honorary awards from Urisinus College, USA (Hon DD 1988), and Acadia University, Canada (Hon DD 2002).

78. Dr. Williams's Library is a theological library in Gordon Square, London, which was founded using the estate of Dr. Daniel Williams (1643–1716). It has always had close ties with the Unitarians and contains many items of interest to those studying English Puritanism, Dissent, and Nonconformity.

79. I am grateful to Clyde Binfield for pointing out the similarities. On Nuttall, see Binfield, "Geoffrey Fillingham Nuttall."

80. For two such books from Nuttall, see *Holy Spirit in Puritan Faith* and *Visible Saints*.

disapproved of the book and found Alan presumptuous."[81] Whether Nuttall would have wholly approved of Alan's publication of recorded reflections on Nuttall's life and career we shall never know.[82]

Alan, like Nuttall, was a member of London's Penn Club[83] and he made good use of all the available opportunities to keep in touch with friends. During the summers, the Sells typically spent their holidays in Britain, often in the Lake District; but one senses that there were stresses maintaining contact with family members, especially when tragedies occurred and there were family difficulties. Living out of a suitcase is always a trial, and, while Alan reports that he "thoroughly enjoyed the fellowship of the Alliance office,"[84] it came as no surprise when he moved on to a more settled location for teaching and research.

Heywood-Thomas once more played a role in directing Alan's career: he enquired whether Alan was interested in a Chair in Christian Thought at the University of Calgary, "one of twenty-nine University Chairs which [would] bring scholars in various disciplines to Calgary with a view to promoting post-graduate studies and research."[85] He was; he applied; and following an interview late in 1986, he was offered the post on 29 April 1987. Among the terms of reference for the new post was outreach to Christian churches. Alan's new role, therefore, found him teaching and doing theology at the interfaces of academy, society, and church. It also meant, of course, that the Sells would be even further from home. Some of the pain involved in that was compensated when Alan gained grants to fund annual research trips to England and elsewhere. By combining business with pleasure and family responsibilities Alan (and Karen) kept in touch with home. Even so, Alan wrote that "It had always been our attitude that wherever we went we would stay forever, and we could easily have envisaged remaining in Canada for the rest of our days."[86] And, indeed, just before they left Canada, they became Canadian citizens.[87]

---

81. Argent, email to author, 2 February 2017.

82. See *TEM*, 177–210.

83. The Penn Club is a private members' club in Bloomsbury, London. It has a strong Quaker heritage.

84. *Chronicles*, 321.

85. *Chronicles*, 306.

86. *Chronicles*, 384.

87. On 8 May 1992.

Introduction

Calgary, Canada (1988–92)

There are few more impressive sights than the Rocky Mountains of North America, with their snow-capped peaks, alpine meadows and turquoise lakes. And, from his office on the thirteenth floor of the Social Sciences Building at the University of Calgary, Alan had a superb view of them. The Sells enjoyed the Canadian countryside during their four-year stay in Calgary, as well as the company of academic colleagues and friends from the Varsity Acres Presbyterian Church. Karen's singing career advanced under the tutelage of Donald Bell, and even for a time Richard Miller, "the leading voice trainer in the States."[88] She became LGSM in 1988. All in all the Sells had found a beautiful and creative place in which to live and work.

Alan threw himself into his new work. It involved research, writing, consultancy, and the development of theological teaching, though the latter was in short supply. He retained a consultancy role with WARC and thus maintained his ecumenical interests,[89] played his part in university administration,[90] and accepted roles in the wider church and society.[91] Arguably his most satisfying innovation was the creation of the inter-disciplinary University of Calgary Eighteenth-Century Studies Group, not least because he "was most at home" in the eighteenth century: "There, in the history of Dissent, he found the major themes of systematic theology (Trinitarianism v. Unitarianism; Christology; Augustinianism v. Pelagianism; Calvinism v. Arminianism; Enthusiasm v. Rationalism; paedo-baptism v. believer's baptism; church order, millenarianism and eternal punishment)."[92] He joined the Canadian Theological Society, the American Academy of Religion, and the American Theological Society, while maintaining an interest in the affairs of the Society for the Study of Theology in England. This enabled him to network widely among English-speaking theologians.

True to form, Alan's flow of writings continued unabated. But, from mid-1989 onwards, his thoughts were never far from investigating possibilities to advance his career, whether in North America or the United

---

88. *Chronicles*, 329.

89. For example, by organizing an international consultation on "Baptism, Peace and the State in Reformed and Mennonite Traditions." It took place in 1989 and was jointly sponsored by the University of Calgary Institute for the Humanities, the Mennonite World Conference, and WARC.

90. For example, he chaired the University Academic Appeals Committee.

91. For example, he was Consultant to the Task Force on Theological Education of the Presbyterian Church of Canada and to Alberta Education on the Religious Studies syllabus for schools.

92. Pope, "Alan Philip Frederick Sell," 524. The list is taken from *EEE*, xiv.

Kingdom. There can be no doubting that he was quite prepared to leave his post in Calgary after only a short time. He applied for a vacant Chair at the University of Aberdeen, was interviewed for the post, but was not appointed to it.[93] By August 1990, Alan also was making enquiries about senior positions becoming vacant in the URC, but, with no suitable immediate vacancies, Alan's sights were then directed to the vacant post of Principal of John Knox College, Toronto. He had known for a few months that his name was being mentioned in connection with it and in January 1991 his local Calgary MacLeod Presbytery nominated him for the position. He was interviewed on 26 April 1992 and informed soon afterwards that his name would be taken to General Assembly in June for his appointment to be ratified. So the Sells thought that they were on the move again, this time to Canada's east coast.

What followed prompted Alan to say: "I have sometimes been tempted to reflect that I have experienced much less skullduggery and 'politicking' in secular than in Christian institutions."[94] According to his version of events, there was dissension about his nomination in the pre-Assembly caucuses. This resulted in his name being withdrawn. Among the points at issue, he came to believe, were that he was not well known, his name did not appear on the Roll of Ministers, some wanted a woman, others regarded him as anti-women, his theology was deemed too non-American and the nominating committee were held to be at fault in considering one candidate alone. We can only speculate as to where facts might make way for conspiracy theory in this story, but the bottom line for the Sells was that their nearly-sold Calgary house had to be taken off the market. Then in July 1992, while visiting mid-Wales with his mother, Alan tells us that "providence struck."[95] The Chair of Christian Doctrine and Philosophy of Religion at the United Theological College in Aberystwyth was vacant. Also vacant, and certainly more attractive to Alan, was the Chair which had been held by Heywood-Thomas at the University of Nottingham. Following interview he was offered the Aberystwyth post on 12 November, but only accepted it a week later when he learned that he had not been short-listed for Nottingham.[96] Alan had to seek membership of the Presbyterian Church of Wales, since his post was financed by that church. Academically the United Theological College was

---

93. The interview took place on the 18 December 1989. The post was awarded to "a much younger, if promising, David Fergusson" (*Chronicles*, 350).

94. *Chronicles*, 367.

95. *Chronicles*, 369.

96. Anthony Thistleton was appointed.

a constituent of the Aberystwyth and Lampeter School of Theology of the University of Wales.[97]

Aberystwyth (1992–2001)

The Aberystwyth years saw Alan Sell's academic career flourishing. In 1995 Professor Sandor Czegledy told him that in his opinion he [Alan Sell] was the leading Reformed theologian of "the generation below Tom Torrence."[98] While it is surprising that Czegledy had passed over Jürgen Moltmann, Eberhard Jüngel and even Colin Gunton when making this judgment, it is certainly true that Alan was one of the "foremost interpreters and most enthusiastic advocates" of "the English Reformed and Dissenting traditions."[99] In Wales, his rate of publication was maintained, not least with his trilogy on Christian apologetics,[100] subsequently submitted to the University of Manchester for its rarely awarded degree of Doctor of Divinity. Whether Alan was as adept at teaching as he was at writing and research is less clear. He certainly did not make a universally positive impression on undergraduates at Aberystwyth. A final year student recalls that Alan's teaching style was "very formal" and "certainly not one which encouraged questions, let alone welcomed debate."[101] It had become a widespread practice for the College teachers to have their lectures recorded, so that students could assess points that they had missed; but Alan apparently would not sanction that for his lectures. To the younger undergraduates, he came over as very aloof and "not . . . a particularly social individual."[102] He had been brought up in and largely belonged to an age in which teachers were teachers and students were students, with an asymmetric relationship between them. But Alan was renowned for his gifts and ability when supervising research students. As Director of Postgraduate Studies he enabled increasing numbers of students to gain masters degrees and doctorates. Anna Robbins, one of those students, admits that Alan's teaching style "was often less than engaging" from the perspective of undergraduates.[103] He could be found "perched on a high chair at a desk in the front of the classroom, with his black academic gown draping down over his suit and carefully-selected necktie trying to

97. The United Theological College closed in 2002.
98. *Chronicles*, 417, 451.
99. Pope, "Alan Philip Fredrick Sell," 519.
100. The three books, in order of publication, are *PICB*, *JL*, and *CCF*.
101. Sarah Simpson, email to author, 1 October, 2016.
102. Sarah Simpson, email to author, 1 October, 2016.
103. Anna Robbins, email to author, November 2016.

get students "to engage with ideas in the abstract"; it was a strategy which "didn't always resonate well as a pedagogical style in the 21st century"; and "he did not suffer fools gladly."[104] On the other hand, postgraduate students welcomed "his probing questions" beckoning them "to cut through [their] layers of presuppositions and get to the heart of theology."[105] Under Alan's guiding hand, Robbins "grew past knowledge of theology and learned to be a theologian."[106] Few theological teachers gain better testimonials.

John Tudno Williams, Principal of the United Theological College, Aberystwyth, found Alan "a reasonable and helpful colleague,"[107] one in whose "spirited company" he found great pleasure, and whose "support and kindness" he treasured during their time as colleagues and thereafter.[108] Alan could always be relied upon to keep research interests and opportunities high on the agenda at faculty meetings. He never missed a chance to encourage the rest of us in our research, forever cajoling us to "keep on scribbling."

Alan's most significant innovation arguably was not based at Aberystwyth. It was his creation in 1993 of the Association of Denominational Historical Societies and Cognate Libraries. Nuttall, speaking partly from his experience, did not think that the attempt to bring the denominational historical societies and cognate libraries together for cooperative research and publishing would be successful.[109] But he had not reckoned with Alan's powers of persuasion. With Alan as Convener, the Association thrived, its four-volume set of Nonconformist Texts representing one of Alan's foremost literary achievements.[110]

By August 1997, the Sells were actively contemplating a change of scene following Alan's forthcoming sixty-fifth birthday. They enjoyed Aberystwyth, the setting of their bungalow, and the delightful countryside of mid-Wales; but, as Alan observed, "it was so much at the end of the line that communications were difficult."[111] They had enjoyed meeting people in the Welsh Presbyterian churches but had noted with sadness the rapid decline that so many churches were facing. However, before the move arrived,

104. Anna Robbins, email to author, November 2016.
105. Anna Robbins, email to author, November 2016.
106. Anna Robbins, email to author, November 2016.
107. John Tudno Williams, email to author, 28 February 2017.
108. See "Professor Alan Philip Frederick Sell," an obituary written by John Tudno Williams in the 2017 Presbyterian Year Book.
109. See *TEM*, 205–6.
110. The four volumes are Jones et al., *Protestant Nonconformist Texts, Vol. 1*; Sell et al., *Protestant Nonconformist Texts, Vol. 2*; Bebbington et al., *Protestant Nonconformist Texts, Vol. 3*; Thompson et al., *Protestant Nonconformist Texts, Vol. 4*.
111. *Chronicles*, 439.

there were lectures for Alan to deliver at home and abroad; there was more research for him to do; and the annual trips to Acadia Divinity School in Halifax, Nova Scotia to teach their Summer School had still to be made.[112] But the time eventually came to leave the students and staff of the United Theological College, of whom they would always have fond memories, and move to Milton Keynes in Buckinghamshire. After fourteen years of membership in Presbyterian churches, the Sells were returning to the URC, albeit in a novel ecumenical setting.

The Latter Years (2001–16)

"Retirement," as a license for inertia, was a concept alien to the Sells. What happened when Alan left his position in Aberystwyth, in effect, was that he moved from stipendiary to non-stipendiary ministry. He continued to research, publish, lecture, and conduct worship, but now it could all be done at his own, if frenetic, pace. There was more time to devote to family life, to grasp the opportunity to go to London theatres and concert halls, and to enjoy travelling to places of historical, architectural, and cultural interest. And, for Alan, it was now easier to attend "Sub Rosa," of which he became President,[113] and the various meetings associated with his academic interests. But, revealingly, in the last edition of his CV, under "Current activities" he wrote "*Full-time* research and writing, interspersed with lecturing and ecumenical consultancy at home and abroad."[114] Here clearly was a man driven by his Christian vocation, determined to use fully all the gifts and graces God had given him. He was awarded honorary positions in two universities,[115] maintained his membership of learned societies,[116] continued to supervise and examine post-graduate students, and contributed to the welfare of both the Congregational and Dr. Williams's libraries.[117]

---

112. Acadia University awarded Alan an honorary Doctorate of Divinity degree in 2002. He had become a Distinguished and Life-long Fellow of the Acadia Divinity School in 2005.

113. "Sub Rosa" is a London-based meeting of Dissenting ministers which traces its origins to the eighteenth century. Alan was President from 2012–16.

114. Italics mine.

115. He was Honorary Research Fellow at the University of Wales Trinity Saint David, 2012–16, and Honorary Visiting Professor at the University of Chester, 2013–16.

116. He was a Fellow of the Royal Historical Society (1980), in recognition of publications in the history of Christian Thought, and Fellow of the Society of Antiquaries of London (1981–2000, 2009–16), in recognition of publications in the history of English Nonconformity.

117. He was President of the Friends of the Congregational Library (2013–16) and

The Sells became members of Christ the Cornerstone in Milton Keynes, attending the 9:00 am Sunday morning services and participating where appropriate in church life. With Alan in the congregation the URC element of this ecumenical church was never likely to be lost. David Tatem, one of his former ministers, notes that in debates within the life of Christ the Cornerstone Alan always "preferred to be constructive rather than destructive," and when commenting on his sermons Alan "was invariably grateful," and "if he commented it would be with relevant anecdote rather than a critique."[118] This supports the experience of Carole Marsden, who "slightly panicked as to whether her sermon would be up to scratch" when the Sells were unannounced visitors at Sedbergh URC, the church for which she had pastoral charge. Her Church Secretary recalls that "It was, and at the end of the service, Alan commended her upon it!"[119] David Tatem reports that "[Alan's] contribution to the ongoing life of [Christ the Cornerstone] was always positive, constructive and characterized by graciousness and a quiet humour."[120] And the way he worked in a local church was replicated when he was involved in the wider church. Susan Durber recalls Alan's contribution to the URC Doctrine, Prayer and Worship Committee, of which she was the Convener: "he was an incredibly useful member because he was so resolutely and unashamedly determined to think theologically at every turn and . . . he was such a passionate advocate (again with absolutely no embarrassment or shyness) about our tradition, particularly the Congregational witness."[121] Alan's collaborative style impressed her: "He was also very kind to everyone and keen that the work of a committee should reflect the way we do things—non-hierarchal, patient, listening, committed and hard working."[122] Tatem says: "The best description I can give of his presence in the church is gentle, wise and always helpful."[123]

In May 2005 Alan presented the University of Nottingham with his submission papers and three sets of books in pursuit of its DLitt degree.[124] Before the University communicated the result,[125] George Newlands, one of

a Vice-President of the Friends of Dr. Williams's Library.

118. Tatem, Free Church Minister of Christ the Cornerstone, Milton Keynes (2003–09), from notes headed "Alan Sell at Cornerstone" sent to the author in October 2016.

119. Martin Cope, email to author, 25 June 2016.

120. Tatem, "Alan Sell at Cornerstone."

121. Durber, email to author, 25 September 2016.

122. Durber, email to author, 25 September 2016.

123. Tatem, "Alan Sell at Cornerstone."

124. *Chronicles*, 531. Alan recommended that George Newlands and Clyde Binfield be asked to examine the submission.

125. They eventually did on 6 March 2006.

Introduction

the examiners, approached Alan at a meeting of the American Academy of Religion in Philadelphia to congratulate him on being awarded the degree. Alan records that Newlands was surprised that the news had not reached him: "[He] said that 'the other chap agreed' . . . it was an open and shut case, he had learned a lot, and it was a shame that solid work like [Alan's] was not better known, while drivel is."[126] And the "solid work" continued, with his publication strategy becoming one of collecting together already published essays under common themes,[127] but there still was time for a novel.[128]

On the menu for the Exit Dinner at Northern College in 1959, and in keeping with traditional practice, each of the leaving students found a quotation next to their names. Alan's came from J. Barne: "It's that damned charm."[129] It reflected the outward disposition of Alan perfectly: "He came across as a charming man, easy to talk with, and with no sense that he was intellectually superior, despite his impressive array of academic achievements."[130] His "charm" endowed him with a disarming common touch. When discussing the opinions of others in his writings he usually interpreted them fairly, finding positive things to say even about those he believed had strayed from the paths of what he regarded as orthodoxy. In that sense he displayed a "generous orthodoxy."[131] However a steely non-negotiability lurked within him that could make it hard for those who disagreed with him to feel that they had got their point heard. In that sense he could be "difficult." Robert Pope captures the contrast very well:

> In private, he could be remarkably candid and reveal frustration and even irritation. On occasion this spilt into his written work. But publicly he was generally measured, calm and irenic—essential graces for those involved in ecumenical dialogue, especially at international level; essential too for engagement in theological debate when history is often considered moot and, in some contexts at least, the Reformed and Dissenting traditions are deliberately ignored.[132]

In 2012 Alan was diagnosed with cancer. It led him "to endure several invasive procedures, operations and treatments over the last four years of his

---

126. *Chronicles*, 540.
127. See *HT*, *CTF*, and *TEM*.
128. Published under the pseudonym Isaac Owen, *A Land of Pure Delight*.
129. *Chronicles*, 121.
130. Cope. See footnote 42.
131. The term was first used for Alan Sell by Robert Pope. See footnote 3 of the preface.
132. Pope, "Alan Philip Frederick Sell," 524.

life."[133] He kept his illness to himself and his immediate family, but his colleagues realized the seriousness of it when Karen had to read his contribution to a conference honoring the 350th anniversary of the Great Ejectment. Nevertheless, he still managed to maintain his writing and keep up with his correspondence despite the constraints laid upon him. Regrettably, he never finished a book on ethics he had been working on, and he left behind several pieces awaiting publication. He died in Willen Hospice, Milton Keynes on 7 February 2015. A "Service of Thanksgiving for the Gospel on the occasion of the death of Alan Philip Frederick Sell," meticulously prepared by Alan himself, was held at the Church of Christ the Cornerstone in Milton Keynes on 3 March 2016; Robert Pope preached the sermon.[134]

WRITINGS

The first two bibliographies at the end of this book feature the writings of Alan Sell.[135] Immediately apparent is the quantity and breadth of his literary output. Others may have published as much, but few in such varied fields. Generalists are always open to accusations from specialists that they are the Jacks and Jills of all trades and the masters and mistresses of none. In Alan Sell's case, there may be some truth in that since, from the point of view of his *theology*, if he had not spent so much time researching and writing in other fields, he might have engaged more fully with continental theology and contemporary theologians. Such an engagement would have made his theology less ethnocentric and more ecumenical in the widest sense.[136]

Alan, nevertheless, eschewed the compartmentalization of modern theology, whereby the various disciplines that contribute to the *holistic* theological task gain lives of their own and are severed from their original connections with each other.[137] He found that church history, biblical studies, philosophy, and ethics all contribute to an understanding of the Christian faith rooted in the Christ event and translatable to the contem-

---

133. Robbins, email to author, 15 November 2016.

134. Before his death, Alan described Robert Pope as "a good friend, *the only real theologian* of his generation in the URC, and *the only one likely to be interested in what I have done*" (Chronicles, 535; italics mine).

135. I am grateful that, before he died, Alan Sell gave me access to both bibliographies.

136. In defence, Alan tells us that he concentrated on the English tradition in theology because it possesses "intrinsic value." He claims that his "wanderings far and wide have yielded evidence that . . . [it] is surprisingly little known—in some cases even to the English themselves" (*EEE*, xiii–xiv).

137. See my *Reforming Theology*, 10.

porary world. That is why he called himself "a borderland person who traversed the frontiers of philosophy, history and theology."[138] He found it necessary to work in a inter-disciplinary way because his "running concern" was wrapped in a "composite question:" "What is the heart of the Christian Gospel and what is its most appropriate mode of expression (theology); how may we most satisfactorily articulate it—especially in the face of intellectual challenges to it (philosophy of religion/apologetics); what happens on the ground when Christians take their beliefs seriously (history); and how may we best heal the inter-Christian divisions which our history has bequeathed to us (ecumenism)."[139] And, perhaps, the "composite question" also involves: What difference does the gospel make to the way we act and behave individually and collectively (ethics)? But a methodological point is now clear: Alan Sell's writing ranged over several disciplines because those disciplines are needed if the intellectual challenge he set for himself is to be met.

PLACING ALAN SELL ON THE THEOLOGICAL MAP

Theologians classify those with whom they engage by assigning them to "schools," e.g., conservative or liberal, Calvinist or Arminian, and so on. What we might call "family resemblances" are highlighted while "individuality" is side-lined. The practice has its virtues, but pitfalls are never far away. It is hardly surprising, therefore, that theologians prefer to be treated as Christian theologians *tout court*, rather than members of any particular school. Alan Sell was among them. Paradoxically, though, theologians continue their "labeling" of others while objecting to the "labels" which others stick on them. In Alan's early books one encounters such a surfeit of "labels" that only the theologically literate can get by without recourse to a theological dictionary; nevertheless Alan emphasized his eclecticism. This inveterate labeler of others, who knew that "the path of the labeller is perilous,"[140] turns out to be a thinker who defies labeling: "I cheerfully accept all of the following terms, when appropriately construed, as descriptive of myself: Christian, Catholic, Protestant, Reformed, Dissenter, Nonconformist, evangelical, conservative, liberal, radical and ecumenical—and I am not aware of being mentally confused or wantonly elusive."[141] Acceptance of the eclectic

138. *PHT*, 1.
139. *EEE*, xii.
140. *JL*, 206.
141. *CAM*, 99n6.

nature of Alan's theology, however, does not rule out an investigation to locate the theological thinkers who most influenced him.

As we have noted, Alan greatly valued the teaching he received in the Faculty of Theology of the University of Manchester, which, in his opinion, possessed "an ecumenical galaxy of scholarly talent."[142] Among the galaxy was John Heywood-Thomas the philosophical theologian. Heywood-Thomas was very influential in Alan's early development as a Christian thinker. Those who are accustomed to associating Alan with scholarship in the world of eighteenth-century Dissent or Christian doctrine may be surprised to know that his early training was in philosophy and, particularly, philosophical theology. Under Heywood-Thomas, Alan learned to appreciate the place of reason in theological thinking, finding a role for apologetics, which he later described as a *pastoral* as well as *theological* task.[143] He was not a narrow fideist who would intentionally flee into a "Barthian circle" whenever a great intellectual challenge confronted him. He fully regretted that "to those with serious intellectual questions about the faith . . . many churchly pre-occupation (*sic*) must appear as mightily 'in-house,' and hence as irrelevant."[144] The church envisioned by Alan is called to be more *apologetic*, not less, in its testimony.

It comes as no surprise, therefore, that there is no place for Barth in Alan's list of "the four greatest theologians of all time": his list comprises Origen, Aquinas, Calvin and Schleiermacher.[145] With the omission of Augustine we encounter Alan's distaste for the father of Western theology's understanding of divine grace; Lutherans will suspect that confessional loyalties have meant the inclusion of Calvin over Luther; but his high rating of Calvin never tempted Alan to become a scholastic hyper-Calvinist. While appreciative of Calvin's achievements,[146] Alan was appalled by the way in which Calvinism undermines God's character as love-itself:[147] "There can be no question that the Calvinistic methodological reversion to scholasticism yielded in some cases grotesque distortions of Christian truth, such that God became an oriental despot who could not be gracious until after his ever-obedient Son had suffered."[148] But he was equally critical of another kind

---

142. *PHT*, 181.

143. See *CAM*, 93.

144. *PHT*, 196.

145. *PHT*, 3.

146. See his essay commemorating the five-hundredth anniversary of Calvin's birth found in *CAT*, 147–75.

147. In this he follows Robert Mackintosh. See *RM*, 42–43.

148. *CTF*, 280.

Introduction

of theological rationalist, the one which trims down the Christian witness in order to fit it into the Procrustean bed their idealist philosophy has prepared for it. What he advocated instead was that we "begin with the claims of faith as revealed by God supremely in Christ" (echoes of Barth here) "and show where and how they endorse, and even fulfil, the best insights of metaphysics and morality" (perhaps the voice of Schleiermacher there).[149]

Among Alan's mentors we find three Congregationalists, one English and two Scottish. R. S. Franks, the Englishman of this particular trinity, was "the most learned Nonconformist divine of the twentieth century,"[150] while, Robert Mackintosh, a Scotsman, was "Britain's most incisive theologian of the twentieth century."[151] Both helped shape Alan's theology. Nevertheless, Forsyth, the second of the Scots, was, in Alan's opinion, not only "the most stimulating"[152] but also, "on the grounds of his depth and creativity" nothing less than "*The* British Reformed theologian of the twentieth century."[153] Alan even argued a case for Forsyth being *the* theologian for the twenty-first century.[154] Forsyth wrote with a unique style: "His pages are peppered with paradoxes, enlivened by epigrams, and they abound in antithesis" which "assail the mind and challenge the heart."[155] Others saw it less grandly as "fireworks in a fog."[156] Alan passionately believed that "Forsyth sounded notes which must never be absent from the score of Christian theology" and that "apart from these notes there would be no score at all."[157] What those "notes" are will become clear as we proceed. While Forsyth brings striking resemblances of Barth to the theological table, unlike Barth he had

---

149. FPA, 66.

150. HT, 499. See Sell's portrait of Franks in *HT*, 419–99.

151. CTF, 277. See Sell's portrait of Mackintosh in *RM*.

152. CTF, 6n3, 269.

153. EEE, 259.

154. TNM, 237–61. Interestingly, the cited article asked a question—"P. T. Forsyth: Theologian for a New Millennium?"—while the book's title states a fact—*P. T. Forsyth: Theologian for a New Millennium*—thereby overruling my judgment on page 184, viz. "There are good reasons to believe that the theology of P. T. Forsyth is not going to be formative for shaping our theology at the dawn of the new millennium [sic]." But it certainly did shape the judgement of Alan Sell.

155. TAT, 139.

156. Clements attributes this cruel remark to Charles Sylvester Horne (*Lovers of Discord*, 40). Clyde Binfield, though, refers us to T. Rhondda Williams telling us in *How I Found My Faith*, 94 that it was coined by J. G. Stevenson (see Binfield, "P.T. Forsyth As Congregational Minister," 189n48). Colin Gunton seems to confirm Binfield's view when tracing its origin to a letter by D. J. G. Stevenson in *British Weekly*, 31 January 1907, 22. (See Gunton, "Real as Redemptive," 37n2.)

157. TAT, 169.

a place for apologetics, found a role for reason, and maintained that both dominical sacraments have an important part to play in Christian life.[158] Alan approved of all those refinements.

INITIAL CONCLUSIONS

We are now in a position to draw out what we have learned from Alan's life and career, and the volume and breadth of his writings. Seven points are worthy of attention before we consider Alan's theological conclusions in more detail.

First, Alan's theological work is a natural consequence of not just his calling to be a Minister of Word and Sacraments but primarily of his church membership. It was a service performed for the benefit of the church, or, to put it more adequately, for the advancement of the gospel. There never was a time when Alan's feet were not firmly planted in both the ministry and the mission of the church, and the pursuit of theological understanding. It helped that theology was also his hobby; but he was a church theologian whose purpose was *apologetic* as well as *confessional*. What he had to say sought to address the situation of those outside the communities of gathered saints as well as build up the faith of those within them.

Secondly, Alan's calling impelled him to use his God-given graces to full measure. It certainly involved Godly ambition with its pursuit of qualifications and its struggles for suitable academic positions. Boundless energy, a never-say-die approach, and tremendous networking skills enabled him to achieve more than most, if less than some.

Thirdly, Alan made a conscious decision to become a Congregationalist. He entered the tradition of English and Welsh Dissent out of firm convictions. And, arguably, he became the leading spokesperson and advocate of its ecclesiology during his life-time. In one of his earlier books, Alan observes that "converts seldom move a *little* way from their formerly held position."[159] He was no exception: at times it was as if the Congregational way of being church had dropped out of heaven and had to be adopted following a divine decree. We will later consider the role of contextual factors in the adoption of our ecclesiological preferences. To what extend does contemporary ecclesiology, therefore, have to be constructed "bottom-up" rather than received "top down" in deference to past practice?

Fourthly, Alan was indebted to his teachers and those theologians who impressed him through their writings. Undoubtedly, the major influence

---

158. See Sell's biography of Forsyth in Taylor and Binfield, *Who They Were*, 68–70.
159. *GD*, 49.

upon him was Forsyth. We will discover how, at key points, Alan is found either following Forsyth or using his mentor to proof-text his own opinions. No wonder that Gabriel Fackre, one of Alan's American friends, can say that "P. T. Forsyth lives again in the witness of Alan Sell."[160] Such a level of dependency on another thinker, of course, prompts the concern that, all too easily, there can be "guilt by association." We will need to consider the adequacy of Forsyth's theological judgments if we are to engage critically with key parts of Alan's theological position. The latter very much hangs on the former.

Fifthly, Alan travelled widely and was genuinely ecumenical in outlook and disposition, but his theological interest was set firmly in the Anglo-Saxon and Reformed traditions. He seemed to find more value in steeping himself in the eighteenth century than engaging with more current issues and debates. He was prone to dismiss as "fads" what was engaging the hearts and minds of some of his theological contemporaries. It was not a strategy to court popularity. Hence Alan was never a "popular" theologian. At one point, he notes that "some theologians are adept at being children of times earlier than their own."[161] Our discussion will need to throw light on whether or not Alan was a *parochial* and *old-fashioned* theologian.

Sixthly, Alan was a Reformed theologian. Outside the Reformed world this is usually associated with standing in a tradition that finds its origins in Calvin and moves forward via Barth. Alan's theology shows this assessment of the Reformed tradition to be simplistic: it stands in a critical relationship with Calvinism; it is also critical of Barth; it recognizes the insights of Schleiermacher; and the role of experience and reason is affirmed. Alan's eclecticism offers a welcome alternative to some of the narrower expressions of the Reformed heritage.

Finally, we will need to assess the status of Alan as a theologian. He was highly thought of within his own small circle, but he was never a driving force in prominent, contemporary theological debate; he never produced a book which became a focus for widespread discussion; and his substantive theological work is not well-known. Nevertheless, Alan's theology deserves greater acknowledgement. Part of the problem is to bring his theology together from his many writings. To do so involves engagement in a synthetic, systematic and critical task.

---

160. Written in the publisher's commendation of *EEE* on its rear cover.
161. *HT*, 39.

2

Doing Theology

PRACTITIONERS AND PUBLICS

Theology faces acute challenges in the twenty-first century. Even the word "theology" has changed meaning in some quarters. Once it referred to a reflective undertaking seeking to ascertain what can be accepted as ultimate truth; but now on the lips of secularists it designates mere sophistry. So, we hear protagonists dismissing their opponents' opinions as nothing more than "theology." In the academic world, theology, once the Queen of the sciences, now is an inferior partner of supposedly more prominent disciplines. At worst, it is merely interesting; at most, it is essential for understanding human beings and the world of which they are a part; but few expect that it should have a decisive bearing on the way in which those who study it understand themselves and choose to live their lives. In the culture of individualism private opinion usurps that which was once publicly shared and commonly acknowledged, so that any existential impact which theological study may be expected to have on us is best kept to ourselves. The role of theology is questioned even in the church, where an anti-intellectual tendency has elevated the affairs of the heart over those of the head. As a result, concerns about "spirituality" now hold sway. On another level, both wings of the church view theology with suspicion: the theological right claims that it undermines faith; the theological left fears that it gets in the way of practice. We have arrived at a sorry situation in which what traditionally underpinned faith and grounded practice is considered by some to be detrimental to both.

Such challenges are met only when an understanding of Christian theology is generated which provides a *raison d'être* for its indispensible place in the lives of Christians, churches, and the academy. Sell offers some pointers towards developing such an understanding. This is only to be expected of someone who lived and breathed theology. We can move to the heart of matters by asking two questions: Who are theological practitioners, and who (or what) constitutes their audience?

First, and central to his position, is Sell's conviction that the task of thinking theologically comes with the responsibilities which Christians take on when they become church members. Insofar as they have been given the intellectual capacity required, all the gathered saints are theologians. They are called to reflect on faith in order to be in the best position to offer their testimony to others concerning the content of that faith. Sell says: "Every Christian believer who reflects at all upon God and the Gospel is, after his or her fashion, a theologian."[1] The important implication of this is that a stand is correctly being made against any attempt to restrict the practice of theology to, say, the ordained or the professional experts of the academy. Underneath it lays the realization that all the laity—the unordained as well as the ordained[2]—can show genuine theological insight. Sell reminds us that the possibility exists whereby "the saintly Christian, however unlettered, can know more than the most sophisticated theologian";[3] and with characteristic wit he can ponder the thought that an A+ in Christian Dogmatics does not guarantee admission to heaven.[4] Christians, individually and collectively, as members of the gathered church, are called to be theologians. Sell was adamant that the contemporary church suffers from a lack, rather than a surfeit, of theology.[5]

Secondly, those set apart by ordination for representative ministries within the church bear a particular responsibility to be theologians. Sell was quite clear that the church needs ministers who "conserve and explore the faith."[6] Theological awareness ought to undergird their preaching, teach-

---

1. *TAT*, 10.

2. Sell was fond of reminding those who think otherwise that the ordained are part of the *laos* and not members of a community *separate* from the unordained. That, of course, does not mean that there isn't a distinction between them. Otherwise, ordination would be vacated of meaning.

3. *ACI*, 8.

4. *ACI*, 9.

5. See *DAD*, 145.

6. *TAT*, 8.

ing, pastoral work, and leadership. Their entire approach to ministry should be understood in theological rather than managerial terms. Sell lays out a strong case for ministers as "scholar-pastors" who provide high quality theological leadership for the church.[7] Central to ministerial work is enabling church members in their theological explorations so that they grow in faith and become confident in their teaching.

Thirdly, we come to the category of theologians whom we associate with colleges, seminaries, and universities. They are accountable to those institutions; they may or may not be Christians; and very often they provide the church with critical challenges. Sell knew how divorced from the church's needs the academy can become, referring at one point to "a sometimes incestuous guild of university practitioners who write to one another through the pages of specialist journals."[8] But he welcomed the spirit of open enquiry found in the academic environment, and remained resistant to all attempts to restrict theological study to a confessional setting: "I, for one, wish theology to be studied and criticized by believers and unbelievers alike."[9] He warned against "a patronizing, falsely proud new Gnosticism . . . along the lines, 'Lack of comprehension, or of assent, is only what you would expect from the uninitiated/unsaved/unsound.'"[10] He wished to avoid at all costs a "*quasi*-Barthian ghetto protectively encircled by revelation and thereby insulated from" all the intellectual challenges posed to the Christian faith.[11]

While Christians, ordained ministers and clergy, as well as certain academics, are required to be theologians, any person who takes an intellectual interest in the content of the Christian witness of faith is also engaged in theology. In different manifestations, therefore, theology addresses different audiences: those inside and outside the church, scholarly academics as well as interested enquirers, and those of Christian commitment or none. Theology is not just "public discourse," its practitioners in their different settings speak in, for, and to their *respective* publics: "society, academy or church."[12] What is crucial, however, is that sound theology satisfies the criteria of adequacy of each public: "However personally committed to a single public . . . a particular theologian may be, each strives, in principle and in fact, for a genuine publicness and thereby implicitly addresses all

---

7. See OMMM.
8. CTF, 138.
9. PHT, 209.
10. PHT, 209.
11. CTF, 120.
12. Tracy, *Analogical Imagination*, 3.

three publics."[13] Sell was unwilling to restrict the practice of theology to the confessional community called "church." He would have agreed with John Webster that "Theology is an office in the Church of Jesus Christ"[14] and he would have concurred with Webster's view that "It is properly undertaken in the sphere of the Church, that is, in the region of human fellowship which is brought into being and sustained by the saving activity and presence of God";[15] but, unlike Webster, he would have wanted to make out a strong case for the practice of theology outside the church. He was not prepared to allow any "mythological obstacles" from within or without the church to undermine theology's public nature: "Any kind of ideological closing of doors can certainly prevent draughts, but it can also keep out fresh light and fresh air, and lead to a sectarianism of spirit which is not unknown either within Christianity or among its 'cultured despisers.'"[16] One of our ongoing concerns in this book will be to assess how open in practice Sell was to "fresh light and fresh air," or, to put it negatively, how far he begged the question of the adequacy of his own position in the light of challenging intrusions into his orthodox world.

THEOLOGY'S STARTING POINT

Early in his career we find Sell speaking from a confessional context: "My anchor is God's revelation in Christ, and my compass is the testimony of Scripture and of Christian experience ancient and modern."[17] Some years later, when reflecting upon the nature of "contemporary theology," he suggested that such theology should "be fired by the Gospel, grounded in the Scripture, nourished by the catholic faith of the ages, fertilised by Reformation emphasis, tempered by Enlightenment critiques, and . . . be applicable today."[18] Both statements reveal two facts: first, that the starting point of the Christian confession lies in the life, death, and resurrection of Jesus, interpreted as a revelation conveying good news for the human race; and, secondly, that the good news of the gospel has been re-interpreted for different times and places both within and after the biblical period. Both facts are

13. Tracy, *Analogical Imagination*, 5–6.
14. Webster, *Holiness*, 1.
15. Webster, *Holiness*, 1.
16. *CTF*, 137.
17. *GOF*, 99. Elsewhere, Sell tells us that he understands "theology to be the product of a conversation with the Bible, the heritage of Christian thought, and the current socio-political-intellectual environment" (*HT*, 1).
18. *TAT*, 3.

problematical. For example, there is a long-standing debate about whether the kind of things Christians have claimed concerning the historical events surrounding the life of Jesus can legitimately be read off from those events. Equally important is the issue of doctrinal development (or "change" as Sell would prefer to call it).[19] Sell accepts that "the balance between anchorage in the Gospel and openness to the times must ever be struck";[20] but does the ensuing conversation between the gospel handed down to us and our contemporary context involve genuine change in how we understand that gospel? If it does, what criteria help us to distinguish between acceptable and illegitimate revisionary restatements?

Questions such as these will be our concern in this chapter, but first we need to fill out Sell's understanding of his theological starting point. He tells us that it is "the confession of what God in Christ has done."[21] Following Forsyth, Sell maintains that Christianity "is founded upon a divine act of cosmic significance."[22] That "act" therefore, is the basic datum upon which the theologian is summoned to reflect. Such reflection involves various tasks: *exploration*, whereby the heart of the Christian gospel is discovered; *conservation*, whereby the Christian gospel is liberated from distortions; and *construction*, whereby the Christian gospel is presented afresh in ways appropriate to a particular context.[23] But, while the Christian gospel will always be open to fresh expressions, "all subsequent interpretations ... must be read and, if need be, corrected in the light of Jesus' words and deeds—and supremely the deed at the Cross."[24] Sell, therefore, takes his cue from "the Cross-Resurrection event,"[25] repeatedly arguing that we gain understanding of who Jesus Christ is via a consideration of what he has achieved for us and the world.[26] Hence, he maintains that the theologian should start from a revelation of God's saving activity in and through Jesus whom Christians came to call "Christ." Sell turns to Forsyth for an explanation of this saving event: it is "a radical once-for-all act of rescue on the part of the holy and merciful God."[27] Elsewhere he describes it as "the unmerited initiative

---

19. "I should rather speak of doctrinal change (which can be and is multidirectional) and then seek criteria by which to assess it" (*COM*, 272).

20. *NT*, 13.

21. *CCF*, 6.

22. *NT*, 172.

23. See *HT*, 1 and *TAT*, 7.

24. *HT*, 596.

25. *DAD*, 106.

26. See, for example, *PICB*, 194–95; *CAC*, 181; *CTF*, 127–28.

27. *PR*, 21.

Doing Theology

of God in Christ, whereby fellowship with God, disrupted by sin, becomes possible once more."[28] And what he calls "this authoritative act of God" is "the *fons et origo*" of all subsequent statements of the Christian witness of faith.[29]

Sell's position is controversial. Whereas many theologians find their starting point in Jesus' life and teaching, Sell locates his in Jesus' death and resurrection, interpreted as a divine saving act of cosmic proportions. Another way of putting the matter is to note that Sell starts with "the Christ of faith" rather than "the Jesus of history." And, further, his way of interpreting the Christ event suggests that his theological starting point ends up as Jesus Christ viewed from the perspective of Forsyth's atonement theology. Sell's decision to start where he does is not driven by any historical skepticism on his part concerning the possibility of discovering the historical Jesus from the New Testament. In fact, some will be surprised to discover that he believed "in the essential reliability of the gospels."[30] Sell was certain that we have sufficient reliable information about Jesus to ground the claims which Christians want to make about him.[31] Nor did he intend to drive a wedge between the teaching of Jesus and soteriological claims made about his death on the cross.[32] What did concern him, though, was that if we do not have a clear grasp upon what Christ did (soteriology) we will end up with an impoverished understanding of who Jesus was and is (christology).[33] And he is correct to remind us that the gist of the early Christian testimony was kerygmatic (proclamation) rather than primarily historical. Nevertheless, a nagging doubt remains as to whether or not Sell's starting point is authorized by the earliest layers of New Testament witness to Jesus.

The early Christians placed great importance upon the authority of eye-witness testimony. Apostolicity was one of the criteria they used to decide which books should belong to the canon of Christian scripture. The church was said to be "built upon the foundation of the apostles and prophets, with Christ Jesus himself as the cornerstone" (Eph 2:20). So, formally speaking, there were always going to be two types of Christians: the apostles and those who bore witness to Christ *after* the apostles, where the word 'after' has both chronological and doctrinal references. Concerning doctrinal matters, the natural question to ask was: Is what is being claimed congruent

---

28. *ACT*, 18.
29. *CTF*, 272.
30. *GOF*, v.
31. See *COS*, 7.
32. See *COF*, 11, and *PHT*, 92.
33. See *ACT*, 46 and *CAC*, 2.

with the apostolic witness? If the answer was "yes" then doctrinal claims were deemed orthodox; if the answer was "no" then they were said to be heterodox, and, hence, heresy was declared. Some theologians believe that this principle has an application today. They maintain that the appropriate question to ask is whether theological proposals meet the criterion of apostolicity; but, as Ogden has pointed out, "the whole effect of recent study of the New Testament is to disclose that none of the writings included within it is an apostolic writing in [the] strict sense of the word" since "the New Testament writings themselves are one and all precisely tradition, in that they are each a later interpretation and formulation in a changed historical situation of some earlier stage of Christian witness."[34] Does that necessitate the abandonment of apostolicity as a criterion for theological adequacy? Ogden thinks not: "the original and originating witness of the apostles, and, hence, the canon or norm of appropriateness can and must be relocated—namely, from the writings of the New Testament as such . . . to the earliest stratum of Christian witness that we today can reconstruct, using the New Testament writings as our primary sources."[35] Whereas other theologians argue that "the earliest stratum" recoverable from the New Testament provides us with "Jesus' own words and deeds," Ogden, more cautiously—some would say skeptically—insists that it "is itself witness to Jesus."[36] But whether its content is deemed to be kerygmatic or historical the principle is the same: the *earliest* stratum is the criterion which helps determine theological adequacy.

Let us now apply this criterion to Sell's proposal to operate theologically from a soteriological starting point. Ogden, for one, would find it wanting. He maintains that "one of the surest conclusions of New Testament scholarship is that the earliest Christian witness accessible to us through our own historical methods and knowledge have [sic] nothing whatever to say about the saving significance of Jesus' death," and what is to be noted is that "so far as these earliest traditions are concerned . . . what is significant about Jesus is, not his death, but his life: his own ministry of word and deed, in its immediate impact on those who encountered him and were open to his claim to bear God's decisive word to them."[37] If what Ogden says about the context of the earliest Christian witness is correct then Sell clearly is not operating from the fundamental starting point for theology. Sell's starting point understandably leads critics to say of his theology that "there is too much epistle, and not enough Gospel, not enough of the teaching of

---

34. Ogden, *Point of Christology*, 100.
35. Ogden, *Point of Christology*, 103–4.
36. Ogden, *Point of Christology*, 101.
37. Ogden, *To Teach the Truth*, 140.

the Nazarene";[38] or that it "tends to mute the voice of Jesus the teacher."[39] Conversely, of course, there are many New Testament theologians who would take issue with Ogden, arguing that full justice cannot be done to the earliest witness without some reference to atonement.

It also remains a moot point whether the earliest stratum of witness to Jesus should be allowed such an authoritative role in theology. First, on grounds provided by the practice of historical investigation, it is fallacious to assume that the earliest witness to an event will provide the interpretation of that event most likely to be correct. Distance from an event is valuable; it provides due perspective; the earliest witness is the one historians scrutinize the most, not the one whose claims they accept without further ado. Secondly, on grounds established by the development of ideas, it is fallacious to assume that the earliest formulations of claims to truth are the most likely to be correct. In fact, the reverse is usually the case since "earliest" often means "crudest." On the face of it, it is likely that the earliest witness to Jesus may have contained claims that were later refined, rather than distorted, by later traditions in pursuit of more mature expressions of truth. And, thirdly, the earliest theological tradition is not necessarily normative for future theology. As James Barr has argued, "The principle is important that status as a historical source, or nearness to the events reported, does not mean the same thing as theological normativeness."[40] Therefore, even if the earliest Jesus *kerygma* can be reconstructed from the New Testament with universally accepted precision, there are grounds for dissenting from the view that it should be assigned authoritative status for theology on account of its antiquity.

The question we are left with is this: Is Sell's atonement-laden starting point a legitimate development from the earlier expressions of the Christian witness which some believe lack such an overtly atonement-shaped trajectory? We may well agree with Sell when he says that "The underlying testimony concerning God's grace in the redemption of the world by Christ is not only the plumb line by which all interpretations are to be tested; it is the very reason for the existence of the New Testament at all."[41] But does an account of "God's grace in the redemption of the world by Christ" necessarily involve the kind of objective and particularistic atonement doctrine which Sell locates as his theological starting point? Might a more appropriate

---

38. Fabricius, Review of *CTF*, 384.
39. Jamison, Review of *CTF*, 34.
40. Barr, *Bible in the Modern World*, 80.
41. *COS*, 7.

starting point, for example, lie in an event which is not so much constitutive of the possibility of salvation as *re-presentative* of it?

Sell's starting point is a divine revelation received though an historical event, namely the life and work of Jesus of Nazareth, viewed from the perspective of his death and resurrection. Although he is adamant about "the historical particularity of the Christian claim"[42] and, hence, convinced that the so-called "scandal of particularity" must be accommodated in an adequate theology,[43] he nevertheless believes that history in the widest possible sense is "the theatre of God's gracious activity."[44] He believes that "it is supremely through the temporal acts, above all through the cross, that we are given the best knowledge available to us of God's nature and purpose."[45] He is correct to find a place for *natural* as well as *special* revelation in his theology, thereby opening up methodological distance from Barth. And the reasons he provides for taking "the *risk* of diverging from Barth"[46] are noteworthy: "On the ground of the Holy Spirit's witness beyond the bounds of the Church; on the ground of God's non-excludability from any part of his created order, and especially on the ground of the *imago Dei* (defaced but not obliterated) and the *sensus divinitatis*, I side with those who construe the proofs of natural theology as building upon insights and intimations derivative from God's general revelation, which need to be taken into account in any attempt to commend the faith to unbelievers."[47] Sell, therefore, believes that God reveals Godself in historical events in ways which are "clamant" (one of his favourite words) for human beings;[48] but he is fully aware that "a religion which claims a historical rootedness cannot distance itself from the probabilities of history."[49]

What might these "probabilities" entail? First, there is the likelihood that contemporary historians will seek natural explanations for what appear to be records of supernatural events, adopting a strategy of investigation which takes it as read that our present way of understanding the world should analogously determine our understanding of past events. Van A. Harvey declares that "the historian's canon for judgments about the past is the same

---

42. *PICB*, 202.
43. *PICB*, 232–34.
44. *GOF*, 10.
45. *CTF*, 288.
46. *CCF*, 273. Italics mine.
47. *CCF*, 273–74.
48. *CCF*, 188.
49. *CCF*, 188.

canon he uses in making judgments about the present."[50] Hence, applying this analogy to Christian claims concerning Jesus' resurrection, Harvey declares that "When dealing with an event so initially improbable as the resurrection of a dead man, the two-thousand-year-old narratives of which are limited to the community to [sic] propagating the belief and admittedly full of 'legendary features, contradictions, absurdities, and discrepancies,' how could a critical historian argue that . . . it is probably historical?"[51] Bultmann's famous declaration immediately springs to mind: "We cannot use electric lights and radios and, in the event of illness, avail ourselves of modern medical and clinical means and at the same time believe in the spirit and wonder world of the New Testament."[52] This observation was not the primary reason that drove Bultmann to propose his well-known theological program of "demythologising" and "existential" reinterpretation; a program too often dismissed as merely a strategy for reducing the Christian faith to the bare bones of what can fit into our contemporary world view, when, in fact, it was a genuine attempt to enable us to hear the Christian gospel's arresting challenge. Bultmann's intentions were evangelical rather than reductionist. In *Chronicles*, though, Sell actually admits to having flirted with Bultmann's ideas:

> I well remember an Ascension tide sermon I preached at Dent. I was passing through a Bultmannian phase, Rudolf Bultmann being the German theologian who said that in order to reach modern people we must demythologize the Bible. Accordingly, I managed to preach about the Ascension of Christ without making any spatial references. As he went out Mr Thompson [a retired Methodist minister] said what he always said, 'Well done, lad—a fine message!' but on this occasion he prodded me in the chest and added. 'But he did go up!' With that my flirtation with Bultmann came to an abrupt end.[53]

This was not Sell's finest hour as a theological interpreter. While noting the negative component of Bultmann's theological program he fails to mention its positive component of existentialist reinterpretation, thereby providing us with an overtly reductionist picture. And when were retired ministers the knock-down arbiters of theological adequacy? Here, perhaps, is an example of humor and of wit coming before sound theology?

---

50. Harvey, *Historian*, 98.
51. Harvey, *Historian*, 109.
52. Bultmann, *New Testament*, 4.
53. *Chronicles*, 117.

Elsewhere, Sell attributes to Bultmann "a process of peeling off the skins of what is to us an alien world" so that "we begin to hear [the New Testament's] word for today."[54] But that makes Bultmann sound more like Harnack than the *real* Bultmann; it does not do full justice to Bultmann's central concern to ensure that the gospel is recognized as a present *existential* address to people today rather than as a series of *empirical* claims made about events over two thousand years ago. He insisted that Christian faith in Jesus Christ is not authorized by historical enquiry concerning past events, but, rather, by whether or not it saves, or, to put it another way, gives rise to "abundant life" (John 10:10). While Sell freely admits that faith is *existential*, he follows Owen in asserting that it "is always grounded in a sure apprehension of the objective historical facts of apostolic testimony."[55] Among such facts is the resurrection which we will discuss later.[56]

Further observations about "the probabilities of history" are appropriate at this point. First, if the canon governing historical interpretation at the outset rules out any kind of supernatural interpretation of historical events, it is hardly surprising that reported events such as the resurrection are not counted as facts by those historians who slavishly employ this canon. So Gunton laments "the lack of transcendent coordinates provided by a theology of God" in some historical enquiries.[57] He is particularly critical of "the 'principle of analogy'" being employed, since it "has been used to undermine, in the name of historical method, the occurrence and intelligibility of unique and miraculous historical events such as the resurrection."[58] Secondly, while Sell would have underscored Gunton's point, I doubt if he could have accepted as true one of Harvey's observations, namely, that "faith has no function in the justification of historical arguments respecting fact."[59] What is particularly vexing, though, is when New Testament readers adopt current canons governing historical interpretation, only to abandon them when their readings do not provide warrants to underwrite their most valued beliefs. The same canons need deploying in a consistent fashion. And, thirdly, it does not seem completely unreasonable to expect such canons to be open to the possibility of divine agency being the cause of some events, or among the contributing factors that give rise to them. Even Harvey notes that "a good historian may be less sceptical of a report of a miraculous cure,

---

54. *COS*, 9.
55. *CCF*, 202. Sell is quoting Owen, *Revelation*, 49.
56. See chapter 5, "The Resurrection of Jesus."
57. Gunton, *One*, 89.
58. Gunton, *One*, 89.
59. Harvey, *Historian*, 112.

not because he believes in miracles, but because psychosomatic medicine is still in its infancy and no tight warrants are forthcoming."[60] Our current worldview may be more open to tracing divine agency in events than was earlier the case. Hard-line determinism has been overtaken by scientific worldviews underpinned by relativity theory, chaos theory, and discoveries in astrophysics which leave us gasping before "mystery" as we contemplate the origin and end of the universe as we know it. Jonathan Sacks claims that "The seventeenth century was the dawn of the age of secularisation," but he predicts that "The twenty-first century will be the start of an age of desecularisation."[61] It may be that we are now living in an age more open to hearing "rumours of angels"[62] and becoming aware of patterns of infinity within worldly events. Consequently, some historians may be required to widen the canon governing their historical interpretation.

Another feature of "the probabilities of history" concerns whether historical investigation of the events surrounding Jesus can establish the *soteriological* claims which Christians have made concerning his death on the cross? It is more likely that Christians use soteriological insights to interpret the cross, rather than receive them as divine revelations from the events surrounding Jesus' death. It seems *prima facia* clear that historians will interpret the death of Jesus purely and simply as a historical event brought about by the threat posed to the peace of Jerusalem by Jesus at the time of a Passover festival. He was executed by crucifixion on a trumped-up charge of sedition by the Roman authorities, with the collusion of the Jewish temple leaders. A historian has no *historical* reason for recording the crucifixion as anything other than a Roman execution.

The *theological* claim that the Cross-Resurrection event is the location of a decisive drama of salvation, in which God's holy love was "decisively active, audible, and visible,"[63] according to Georg Lessing, cannot be authenticated by historical means. Lessing's argument is found in an eighteenth-century essay entitled "On the Proof of the Spirit and of Power."[64] Given that all historical judgments can be no more than probable, it follows that, if conclusions are only as strong as the premises upon which they are based, Christian faith-claims based on historical events can possess no higher epistemological status than our historical understandings of those events. This led to Lessing's conclusion that "accidental truths of history

---

60. Harvey, *Historian*, 116.
61. Sacks, *Not in God's Name*, 18. Italics removed.
62. A term borrowed from Berger. See his *Rumour of Angels*.
63. *GOF*, 1.
64. See Lessing, *Theological Writings*.

can never become the proof of necessary truths of reason."[65] His rational pursuit of sure foundations upon which to base his faith-claims found him facing what he called "an ugly, broad ditch" between historical faith and the soteriological claims made about them. Lessing the believer despaired at the conclusions which Lessing the philosopher arrived at, pleading for someone to help him bridge the ditch.

Sell is adamant that any theology which severs Christian claims from their historical roots is inadequate. To avoid such heterodoxy, he believes, Lessing's argument needs challenging. Sell focuses on what he regards as Lessing's unnecessary rationalism by making four points. First, he argues that "some of the cardinal assertions of Christianity . . . are not necessary truths of reason," and, therefore, are not to be proved as if they are akin to "a truth of arithmetic."[66] If we believe them it will be because they have "been brought home to us by God the Holy Spirit."[67] The gospel comes from beyond and is not "at home" in this world. So Calvin, for example, asserts that it is the inner testimony of the Spirit which inspires faith and belief in it. But what is this if not a strategy to place Christian faith-claims beyond the reach of *public* accountability? It is difficult to see how Sell squares this with his insistence that apologetics has an important part to play in theology. Secondly, Sell protests that "history could be described as accidental only on the presupposition . . . that God is not present as creator and sustainer within it."[68] Here we find him echoing the wisdom of H. F. Lovell Cocks,[69] as well as underlining a point we made earlier. Thirdly, Sell suggests that "there is an affinity between God and humanity, traditionally characterized in terms of the *imago Dei*, which renders redundant Lessing's way of positing the logically distinct types of necessary truths of reason and accidental truths of history."[70] This observation aims to meet doubts about the possibility *in principle* of underpinning Christian faith-claims in historical assertions about past events. As David Pailin has observed: "Lessing's problem with trying to base faith on past events is . . . that since faith's understanding and past events . . . belong to distinct logical orders, there is no valid way of deriving the former from the latter."[71] Lessing's supporters will ask whether hard evidence can be put forward to support the notion of the *imago Dei*. If

---

65. Lessing, *Theological Writings*, 53.
66. *CCF*, 195.
67. *CCF*, 195.
68. *CCF*, 196.
69. See *CAC*, 160.
70. *CCF*, 196.
71. Pailin, *Probing the Foundations*, 151.

it cannot then we arrive at the situation of one faith-claim being put forward to warrant another faith-claim. Fourthly, Sell tells us that our knowledge of Christian faith-claims is mediated to us through "God's gracious initiative" whereby God "enables a personal response to his grace in Christ."[72] He claims, therefore, that "the interpretation of the Christ event is given in and with the event itself."[73] This does not take us very far, since, as the history of Christian doctrine reveals, there is not one but many purportedly definitive accounts of the Christ event in the Christian tradition. What we find is a multitude of sometimes competing christologies and soteriologies. The question then becomes: Which *theological* account of the historical events is the most adequate? And the answer to that will not be found by recourse to historical investigation.

Pailin points out that Lessing's problem can be solved "so long as faith is admitted to be an assent guided by probabilities, not the entertainment of necessary truths demonstrated with the rigour and indisputability of geometrical theorems."[74] And, granted the nature of faith as trusting assent, that may be sufficient for some; but confronted with a plurality of soteriological interpretations of the cross and resurrection we are justified in wanting a means whereby we can come to know which, among the competing christologies and soteriologies, are the most adequate. That "means" will not be found in the past; it will be discovered in the present. It concerns whether or not the story being told about Jesus can be shown to be credible through the use of theological rather than historical arguments, and it involves a fundamental practical issue: Does what is said place the hearer before the life-transforming presence of God, who graciously makes a claim on all our lives and invites our love, not least through the neighbor who makes a claim on our life? Hence, what is vital to belief is God, "the actuality in which theistic faith puts its trust and by which it is orientated."[75] Hence the insights which we glean from the Christ event cannot be "verified by the tests for historical accuracy" but will need to be examined for adequacy by "the tests for metaphysical actuality."[76] This conclusion implicitly calls into question the exclusivity and particularity which Sell assigns to the Christ event.

---

72. *CCF*, 196.
73. *CCF*, 197.
74. Pailin, *Probing the Foundations*, 150.
75. Pailin, *God and the Processes*, 196.
76. Pailin, *God and the Processes*, 196.

THEOLOGICAL RESOURCES

As a Reformed thinker and "unrepentant theologian of the cross,"[77] Sell places the Bible at the heart of his theology. It is the primary source of the earliest Christian witness to Jesus Christ, viewed from the perspective of his death and resurrection. But, for Sell, two secondary theological resources also warrant the theologian's attention, namely, the Christian tradition and the contemporary context. We turn now to consider each in turn.

The Bible

According to Sell, "The Bible is the book of the people of God, and its authority is derived from that to which it is the chief earthly witness, the redemptive grace of God in Christ."[78] It follows that the canon of the Bible is not authoritative for theology, because the Bible's status is itself authorized by a "canon within a canon," namely the Christ event. Hence, for Sell, the supreme rule for Christian faith and practice is not the Bible *per se*, but, rather, "the saving deed" of which it is "the primary earthly witness."[79] Elsewhere he offers us something akin to a definition: "the Bible is the record of God's mighty deed to effect our salvation and to show us ourselves in the light of his holy love, which both judges, forgives and guides us to our eternal home."[80] It is a definition which invites thought concerning the possibility of God's saving work taking place outside of, as well as in, the Christ event. That invitation will be taken up in due course.[81]

The Bible is the means by which God reveals Godself to us, so, Sell believes, its books must be read according to their unique *genre*. While it is crucial that they are studied "against the background of their times," it is also vital that they should be attended to "in the light of what God has supremely said and done in Jesus Christ."[82] What Christians are called to do, therefore, is "discern the word of God in the Bible . . . and to view it all in the light of God's self-revelation in Jesus Christ."[83] The Bible ought not to be handled as if it is "a resource book for aesthetes or elocutionists";[84]

---

77. *CTF*, 224.
78. *COM*, 29.
79. *COM*, 29.
80. *CAM*, 95.
81. See chapter 5, "Sell's Doctrine of Atonement."
82. *OMMM*, 72.
83. *OMMM*, 72.
84. *EEE*, 143.

nor can we be satisfied with reading it merely as literature, since it was not designed to be read that way.[85] But, in saying this, Sell is stretching a point since, historically, one of the criteria used to decide which books should make up the New Testament was their appropriateness for being read publicly in the church.[86] It is unfortunate, therefore, that Sell should take a pot-shot at the more recent literary approaches to the Bible, since some have found them "immensely enriching and liberating in preaching," and a refreshing complement to the historical-critical approach in which they were schooled.[87] One gets the impression that Sell was not fully aware, nor adequately appreciative, of ways of reading the Bible which either challenge the historical-critical approach or complement it. Nevertheless, he always regarded the historical-critical method as a bulwark against biblical fundamentalism. The Bible is no paper-Pope, and he recoiled at tendencies within Protestantism towards bibliolatry and "all its legalistic ugliness."[88] He was also saddened that an unfortunate alliance between pulpit and pew should too often ensure that the results of biblical scholarship do not get a hearing in church congregations.

As a student of John Locke, Sell knew that scripture can become "like a nose of wax, to be turned and bent, just as may fit the contrary orthodoxies of different societies."[89] It has become as much a battleground as was the composition of the historic creeds. Sell admits that no one comes to the Bible "psychologically or philosophically . . . neat."[90] As Bultmann convincingly argues, there is no such thing as biblical exegesis without presuppositions.[91] But, Sell argues, crude *eisegesis*—"the art of finding in a text what no reasonable person of integrity could possibly find in it"[92]—must be eschewed. Sell notes three factors which carry weight for Christians who sensitively and openly come to the scriptures in search of truth. First, their reading will be under the guidance of the Holy Spirit. In *The Basis of Union of the United Reformed Church*, the Church of which Sell was a member when living in England, we find stated: "[The United Reformed Church] acknowledges the Word of God in the Old and New Testaments, discerned

---

85. See *OMMM*, 72.

86. See Bruce, *New Testament Documents*, 26–27 and *Books and the Parchment*, 111–12.

87. Thompson, Review of *OMMM*, 569.

88. *COM*, 28.

89. In *JL*, 95, Sell quotes Locke's famous saying found in "Second Vindication," 295.

90. Sell, "John Wyclif," 295.

91. See Bultmann, *Existence and Faith*, 342–51.

92. *OMMM*, 59n47.

under the guidance of the Holy Spirit, as the supreme authority for the faith and conduct of all God's people."[93] Secondly, one should factor in the claims placed upon an interpretation by the reader's conscience. What may have been appropriate and acceptable in the cultures of biblical times need not in all conscience be necessarily always binding for us today. Thirdly, our readings of scripture can be ameliorated by the wisdom of the Christian tradition. Christians need not read the Bible in individualistic isolation, since, as church members, they are part of a community which possesses experience of reading the Bible over two thousand years. Therein lies the possibility that, through a process of "checks and balances supplied by the fellowship of saints,"[94] inappropriate readings of scripture texts can be avoided. Sell believes that those who have sought to hear God's word within "the communal nature of the people of God . . . have in fact been less liable to heresy than others who have preferred to say 'It's in the Book,' or 'It's in the creeds,' or (pointing emotionally—and sometimes inaccurately!—to the heart) 'It's in here.'"[95] But the overriding point to note is that for Sell the gospel rules over the Bible.

On several occasions Sell makes a point about the Bible which has significant ecumenical implications. The Protestant emphasis upon the authority of the Bible, he argues, can so easily lead to "an excessive bibliolatry which overlooks the fact that if Christians are the people of the Book, the Book is also the compilation of the Church."[96] The Bible may be said to contain the *primary* traditions of the Christian faith, but being "primary" does not alter its status as tradition. The Reformers, of course, appealed to the Apostolic Fathers, whom they believed had correctly interpreted the Christian faith from the scriptures, rather than cry "*Sola Scriptura*." Hence, the old Protestant cry of *Sola Scriptura* is muted, the ancient battle between scripture and tradition concerning theological authority is ended, and a fresh notion of what constitutes authority in the church is required. This leads us forward to a consideration of what we can call the secondary traditions of the Christian faith.

Tradition

By the term "tradition" we mean three distinct but inseparable types of Christian witness: the historic creeds agreed at Ecumenical Councils, the

---

93. Found in Thompson, *Stating the Gospel*, 251.
94. *TAT*, 249. See also *EEE*, 68.
95. Sell, "John Wyclif," 295–96.
96. *SOL*, 54. See also "John Wyclif," 295, and *RECT*, 69.

Doing Theology

confessions of faith formulated by churches, and the witness, by word and through deed, made by Christians, whether as individuals or corporately. The point now to be explored concerns the fact that tradition so understood is a valuable source for Christian theology. Past expressions of faith provide markers for future articulations of the gospel. We do not have to construct the Christian witness entirely anew, though we do well to recognize the possibility and likelihood that some translation, amendment, and revision may be needed if the past formulations of Christian witness are to be heard by contemporary ears.

Sell maintains that, given their status as tradition, the written creeds and confessions of faith, as well as the recorded witness of the saints, all refer to a higher authority: Jesus Christ, understood from an Easter perspective. He believed it important that theology should recognize the importance of such tradition. The Creeds as well as "the formulations and declarations" set down what Sell calls "secondary standards"[97] presumably because they represent the *secondary* witness of tradition rather than the *primary* witness of scripture, though both of course are subject to the higher authority of Jesus Christ. He provides a much needed warning: "If we forget that confessions of faith are subordinate we are on the way to idolatry; if we forget that they are standards, heresy may beckon."[98]

Sell found great value in his Separatist heritage. We can note the following by way of example: "My forebears, in peril of their lives, refused to subscribe to the words of men, especially when those words were legally enforced by governmental authorities bent on securing ecclesiastical comprehension as an aid to national cohesion in the face of enemies."[99] Their reason for doing so was that "They upheld the church's right and duty to submit to the Word of God alone," and they possessed "a profound sense of the continuing guidance of the Holy Spirit and felt that to elevate, or fossilize, a specific form of words might in time constrain their response to the Spirit's contemporary address to them through the Word."[100] We find Sell standing upon the shoulders of martyrs when he opposes the use of confessional documents as "tests of faith or criteria of church membership."[101] He gives five reasons why he was opposed to any form of "subscription." First, it can lead to the substitution of "cerebralism for faith, *assensus* for *fiducia*."[102]

---

97. *CTF*, 9.
98. *CTF*, 9.
99. *CTF*, 12.
100. *CTF*, 12.
101. *CTF*, 13.
102. *CTF*, 13.

Secondly, it "may foster the myth of the saving *system*"[103] when, in fact, it is God's grace revealed in Jesus Christ that saves. Thirdly, it "plays into the hands of ecclesiastical agents of a controlling disposition."[104] They may be tempted to make life tough for those whom "our present-day politicians call 'off-message.'"[105] In a manner reminiscent of Forsyth, Sell thunders: "The Church is a fellowship of believers, called by grace, before it is a corporation bound by trust deeds."[106] Fourthly, it inevitably leads to "sectarianism . . . the offspring of authoritarian, legalistic ecclesiasticism."[107] And, fifthly, confessional documents can never protect the faith, only witness to it. Sell wisely suggests that "it would be a usurpation of the role of God the Holy Spirit, the guardian of the faith, to suppose that were particular confessions to fall the gospel would fall with them."[108]

Creeds, confessions, and doctrinal standards are inherently contextual, arising as responses to theological debates at different times and places. Sell notes that they do not aim "to be comprehensive and systematic statements of Christian faith" since "they are concerned to bar the exit to current heresies, or to major on doctrines deemed to have been neglected."[109] The former was the case at Chalcedon, while the latter explains the emphasis upon justification by grace through faith in the Reformation confessions. It becomes clear, therefore that the theological context of theologians, whether implicitly or explicitly, plays an important role in their theologizing.

Context

Theologians respond to the deep and vexed questions of their day and utilize the conceptual resources available in their culture. So we find, for example, Aquinas employing Aristotle's philosophy, Barth and his fellow neo-orthodox theologians responding to the crisis of World War, Schleiermacher addressing the intellectual question of the cultured despisers, and the Liberation Theologians responding to the cry of the oppressed. In each era, theologians seek to correct what they regard as the mistakes or deficiencies in the theologies bequeathed to them, and, although they seldom anticipate this, their successors will pay them the same compliment.

103. *CTF*, 13.
104. *CTF*, 14.
105. *CTF*, 14.
106. *CTF*, 14.
107. *CTF*, 15.
108. *CTF*, 16.
109. *CAM*, 136.

Doing Theology

Theology, therefore, ought to be a humbling discipline. As Maurice Wiles has reminded us: "We see through a glass darkly and every attempt to speak sensibly and appropriately about God and God's relation to the world is bound to be partial and provisional, in need of correction in the light of some other approach, some other aspect of the matter to which our formulation of the question has failed to do full justice."[110] It follows that sometimes theologians need to show "godly agnosticism"[111] rather than utter the "thunderings of a pretended omniscience."[112] They ought to engage in a creative dialogue between past and present formulations of the Christian witness of faith. Since their context belongs to but one of the many cultures on earth, they also must be open to receiving wisdom from cross-cultural encounters. Sell shows that he is alive to the first requirement in the way he utilizes his historical work in his theology, and he stood on the international ecumenical stage long enough to know that "however we define our personal, local or regional contexts, they are inextricably interwoven into the fabric of the global context."[113] It follows that "The context into which the good news comes is a continuum at one end of which is the individual Christian, at the other, the whole of humanity."[114] This must never be forgotten if theological parochialism is to be avoided.

Wiles notes that, "Over a period of time the particular lack or imbalance inherent in the dominant theology of the day comes to be felt with increasing strength; a reaction sets in, and the imbalance is redressed—more often than not over-redressed—in the opposite direction."[115] Viewed with hindsight, he likens it to a swinging pendulum. It helps him explain the passages from "conservative" to "liberal" (and vice versa) in theology over the years, but it can very easily be deployed in other ways, to account for, say, emphases on transcendence or immanence in speaking about the God-World relationship, or focusing on objective and subjective theories of atonement, or talking about the humanity and divinity of Jesus. We will be wise if we look for theological insight at the point where the pendulum rises and falls, not just at some middling position which we have chosen to stake out.[116] To put the point another way: theologians cannot avoid being contextual, but, in pursuit of theological adequacy, they must take steps

---

110. Wiles, "Theology in the Twenty-First Century," 409.
111. *EEE*, 298.
112. *DAD*, 86.
113. *EEE*, 332.
114. *EEE*, 332.
115. Wiles, "Theology in the Twenty-First Century," 409.
116. See Peel, *Encountering Church*, 99–102.

to widen their given context as much as possible. They need to hear from "strangers" who can spot lacunae and locate mistakes.

Sell's theology was rooted in the world of English and Welsh Dissent which he counted as his rich heritage. And, as we have seen, it centers on an understanding of the Christ event viewed primarily as an act of redemption. Sell's view of the Christian gospel comes from a cultural environment which formulated the human predicament in terms of sinful human beings standing empty handed before a God of holy love. The resolution of the sinner's plight is predicated in terms of redemption: an atonement for sin, brought about through Jesus' self-sacrifice on the cross. The central problem which the gospel addresses with its good news, therefore, is that of being a sinner. But, it is reasonable to ask, what if the central problem which individuals face in another context is not so much that they are sinners but that they are "the sinned against"? What if the *angst* destroying the human spirit is caused by oppression? The Latin American liberation theologians answered this question by writing theology from *their* context, with a stress on Jesus as the Liberator, and, in the process, provided a critique of what they regarded as the one-sidedness of Western theology's emphasis on Jesus as the Redeemer.[117] Using Sell's reaction to liberation theology as a test case we can gain some insight into how open he was to cross-cultural challenges to his particular way of doing theology.

It is tempting to think that Sell regarded the various liberation theologies as passing fads. Whereas some of us found ourselves profoundly challenged by them, a similar response from him was unforthcoming: what he agrees with in liberation theology he has already learned from elsewhere, and what he disagrees with he finds adequately corrected in his own position. Sell believes that "one of the strengths of liberation theology is its anti-docetic thrust."[118] It insists, as he does, that "Christ is at work in history, and the saved are working therefore, and with him, sustained by an eschatological hope."[119] Also he has no trouble acknowledging that the Christian gospel has social and political dimensions, though he doubts whether the liberation theologians always hold together "liberation" and "redemption" adequately in their soteriologies. In fact, he maintains, they often prioritize the former over the latter, thereby succumbing to the danger of "elevating a socio-political programme above, or regarding it as an alternative to,

---

117. For Latin American Liberation Theology, see Guttierrez, *Theology of Liberation*; Segundo, *Theology for Artisans*; and Sobrino, *Christology at the Crossroads*.

118. EEE, 319.

119. EEE, 319.

the Gospel."[120] He insists that the gospel is not concerned *essentially* with liberation from particular injustices; it *primarily* concerns God-in-Christ's universal redemption of human beings from sin. This makes one wonder whether he has committed in reverse the mistake he sees in liberation theology?

We ought to be in a world of "both and" rather than "either or" at this point, having recognized the unfortunate Western theological tendency to address the questions of the sinner at the expense of the equally important questions of those we can refer to as "non-persons," through the result of their being sinned against by others. But Sell's repeated criticism of the liberation theologians' purported failure to give full attention to Christ's atoning work not only gives the impression that he has not fully heard the challenge to the Western theological tradition's emphasis upon *theoretical* matters of faith and belief at the expense of *practical* issues of social justice, but it also re-enforces a one-sided view of God's saving activity. God is *both* the Redeemer and the Emancipator; there is one, holistic, divine saving activity:

> . . . the one process of liberation whose necessary ground is God comprises two quite different, if closely related, processes that can and must be distinguished respectively as redemption and emancipation, God himself understood correspondingly as both the Redeemer and the Emancipator.[121]

When considering the ultimate purpose of being human, Sell juxtaposes Segundo's emphasis upon humanization and the answer of the *Westminster Shorter Catechism*, "Man's chief end is to glorify God, and to enjoy him forever," before asking what he regards as an essential question: 'How, if at all, are these answers related—and does it matter if they are not?'"[122] Well, as the New Testament makes clear, they *are* related: we should note the Synoptic Gospel story which finds Jesus declaring that our human duty is not only to love God, but that it also concerns all those who place a claim upon our lives and love (Mark 12:28–34; see also Matt 22:34–40 and Luke 10:25–28). And, in what counts among the most challenging stories which Jesus is reported to have told, we learn that our love of God is demonstrated according to whether or not we serve the need of "the least of these who are members of [Christ's] family" (Matt 25:40).

---

120. *EEE*, 319.
121. Ogden, *Faith and Freedom*, 36.
122. *PHT*, 263.

No context is a privileged context for a theologian. Sell, therefore, is correct to rail against what he calls "contextualization gone parochial."[123] He will not countenance attitudes which suggest that because we are not, say, black, gay, female, or poor we cannot do theology legitimately.[124] Such attributes lead to "sectarianism" and "the 'unchurching' of others who belong to different contexts."[125] Meanwhile, every context requires examination to ascertain its strengths and weaknesses. Sell was aware that the Western context in which he was living was far from perfect. He spoke of writing in "relatively rudderless times."[126] Outside the church he deplored the rugged individualism and consumerist outlook, while inside it he lamented "a creeping and troubling anti-intellectualism . . . unanchored, impressionistic and self-serving spirituality . . . some theologians [evincing] only the slightest grasp of the heritage of Christian thought."[127] But he would have nothing to do with the "back to the future" theologians who put all our contemporary ills down to the Enlightenment. The Enlightenment, he believed, "is too varied and too interesting to be either utterly denounced or uncritically lauded."[128] Sell regarded it as "a legitimate protest against the imposition of conscience–denying authorities"[129] and "a moral protest against expressions of Christian doctrine which turned God into a tyrant or human beings into automata."[130] Hence, it is hardly surprising that, peddling "stereotypes of the Enlightenment some writers are oblivious to the victories it brought home.[131] One of those victories was the recognition that reason has an important role to play in theology.

THE IMPORTANCE OF REASON

Sell's theological starting point calls forth from human beings an existential commitment grounded in objective facts, both historical and metaphysical, which are open to rational exploration. Although Sell accepts that "the

---

123. *RECT*, 195

124. *EEE*, 124.

125. *EEE*, 124.

126. *PHT*, 91.

127. *CCC*, 1.

128. *EEE*, 110.

129. *COM*, 344n7. Elsewhere Sell suggests that "It may be that even Enlightenment rationalism is preferable to the sectarian violence which so often preceded it" (*PHT*, 266).

130. *EEE*, 107.

131. *PHT*, 118.

essential feature of religion is its non-rational side"[132] reason plays its part in the reflection leading to our encounter with God through the Christ event, as well as in our attempts to gain a fuller understanding of the God revealed to us. Given the dynamic involved in this, he wishes to avoid any rigid "compartmentalization" between natural and revealed theology.[133] But unlike many Reformed theologians he insists upon the role of natural theology in our theological explorations.

Sell recognizes the destructive, *noetic* effects of sin on our ability to reason clearly. He is fully aware of the way in which, on the basis of Romans 1:18–23, many have declared that we are so blinded by sin that reliable, rational reflection concerning God is impossible. But, eschewing Calvinist notions of total depravity, Sell insists that sinners remain beings born in God's image. On the basis of the *imago Dei*, we can claim that our vision is *blurred* rather than blind. We still need revelation to redeem and re-orientate our reasoning, to "clear our minds and harness our wills";[134] but, while natural theology can never provide us with "a copper-bottomed demonstration of the existence of the Christian God"[135] it can access "a general revelation of God in nature."[136] One way of viewing its competence is to say that it leads us "to the threshold of revelation."[137] Sell is skeptical, however, about the so-called accumulative proof for the existence of God. This claims that while each single argument for the existence of God fails, the *combined* impact of them carries credibility. Flint said that "whilst you can easily snap one rod, you cannot so easily snap a bundle of rods"; but, Sell suggests, "sadly, if we change the metaphor we can see that six broken signposts do not point the direction any more clearly than one!"[138] He notes that while the natural theologian sometimes sees things which a skeptic has not seen, the Christian often gains new eyes for seeing through the work of the Holy Spirit. The basic difference between natural and revealed theology, therefore, largely concerns the perspective from which the respective enterprises are conducted.

Sell studied philosophy of religion as an undergraduate when analytic philosophy was in its heyday and when challenges to the meaningfulness of religious discourse were plenty. He relished the opportunity to come to

132. *PR*, 154.
133. *DAD*, 61.
134. *JL*, 84. See also *FPA*, 106.
135. *CCF*, 276.
136. *CTF*, 270.
137. Words used by Sell in describing the position of Mackintosh in *RM*, 65.
138. *GOF*, 6.

a more sophisticated awareness concerning the cognitive status of theistic language. It made him think hard, so much so that he commended it to others: "there is nothing like a dose of linguistic analytical rigour to encourage theological precision and scupper theological opacity."[139] Whether he learned its lessons fully may be open to question, but it led him to hold a correspondence view of truth and affirm that Christian claims intend to impart knowledge.[140] He was certain that the theologian is concerned with facts that are every bit as reasonable as scientific data: "We need to defend an idea of facticity which will admit not only the facticity of such 'phenomena' as faith, repentance, forgiveness, agape, and the like, but which will at least raise the question whether, apart from the presupposition of God, we may properly apprehend any facts at all."[141] Philosophy helps us understand the logical status of our theological language. It teaches us that theistic claims cannot be understood properly if they are simply treated as references to *physical* phenomena; God talk is inherently odd and must be understood in language appropriate to "God": *meta*physics.

All theologians are indebted to philosophy: the fundamental question concerns not whether but *what* metaphysics provides the conceptual framework for their theistic claims. Sell recognizes that some will not admit that they are making metaphysical claims in their theology;[142] he ruefully observes that "the theologian who is afraid of philosophy is almost certain to be unconsciously dominated by it;"[143] and he laments the fact that some thinkers eschew all contact with metaphysics only to end up unknowingly operating with a redundant example of it.[144] It is a fundamental feature of a viable Christian theology that it is metaphysically sound. But the crucial challenge is to find "a *Christian* philosophy . . . which is adequate to the claims of the Gospel."[145] Sell recognizes that this challenge has to be taken up whenever fresh conceptual systems appear in the philosophical window.

What must be avoided is a choice of metaphysical conceptuality which makes it impossible to say what needs saying from a Christian point of view. Sell wants to avoid "the philosophical shoe" pinching "the theological foot."[146] He seriously doubts, for example, that "idealism" or "process philos-

---

139. *CAM*, 25–26.
140. See *CCF*, 145, 98.
141. *DAD*, 55.
142. *CTF*, 257.
143. *COM*, 317.
144. He gives "latter-day positivists" as an example (*RM*, 58).
145. *DTLC*, 117. Italics mine.
146. *PICB*, 228.

ophy" can provide the conceptual framework in which to speak adequately of the Christian God. He believed that they provide alien categories which distort the Christian witness. As a theologian he wished to retain his Christian integrity: he did not come empty-handed to any metaphysical system which he felt useful for his theological purposes; he recognized, rather, that he had to come to all of them as an Anabaptist and not a poacher![147] Recognizing the necessity of metaphysics for theology is one thing, but finding the *right* metaphysics for *theological* purposes is something else, as we shall discover later.[148]

THE VOICE OF EXPERIENCE

Christian faith is not just a concern of the head, it also involves the heart. Hence, it comes as no surprise to be told by Sell that personal experience, as well as rational reflection, is a channel through which we can arrive at an awareness of God.[149] What is more, religious experience can yield knowledge which not only grants us understanding of God but, in principle, can be verified in ways appropriate to its genre.[150] Religion starts from experience but points beyond it. For Sell, all claims to know God are autobiographical (and, hence, experiential and thereby subjective).[151] A vicious subjectivism can be avoided, though, if we allow that to which our Christian experience testifies and points to be authoritative for us. What makes such experience genuinely Christian is that it is generated through the Spirit's work. A repeated emphasis upon the Spirit's activity in individual lives, society and the world ensures that, as far as Sell is concerned, we are never out of touch with God. He may be a theologian of the cross but, following hard on the heels of that designation, he can also be called a theologian of the Holy Spirit.

Sell is concerned to give due attention to the *super*natural at the heart of natural events. Otherwise, theology ends up being nothing more than anthropology. Since theology ought to be grounded in God's gracious gift of holy love, Sell accepts what he calls "The standing challenge . . . to rehabilitate the supernatural . . . without exchanging faith for gullibility, or

---

147. Sell uses the poacher/Anabaptist distinction very often. See *PR*, 31; *ACI*, 19; *PICB*, 123; *CCF*, 371; *HT*, 585; and *CAC*, 181–82. This all goes to show that, if we have a good song, it deserves being sung often!

148. See chapter 3.

149. See *CCF*, 6.

150. See *CAM*, 84–85.

151. See *PR*, 166, 202.

succumbing to deism."[152] This involves "human reason, neither demeaned nor deified" being treated "as the servant of God."[153] Does this mean that he gives priority to reason over experience in the formulation of his understanding of God? If it does he runs the risk of taking us back to a view of religion dominated by arid dogma, the very outlook Schleiermacher challenged when he argued that the heart of religion is contained in "feeling."[154]

Sell is one of the better British interpreters of Schleiermacher. He knows that, when using the term "feeling," Schleiermacher is using a *relational* term. "Feeling" is not a totally subjective term, but one which links the human being with an objective God.[155] Fully expressed, it is the feeling of absolute dependence *on God*, or, to use another definition, without the emotive word "feeling," it is "sense and taste for the Infinite."[156] Sell points out that "In the eighteenth century 'feeling' connoted more than 'having an emotion'":[157] it referred, for Schleiermacher, to an *existential* knowledge of the One who stands over and against us. Sell was very critical, therefore, of Owen[158] and Littlejohn[159] for failing to take account of the cognitive element in Schleiermacher's notion of "feeling." But for Sell, of course, experience, like reason, is at best a means of discerning our final authority, "God's authoritative, saving act at the cross."[160]

APOLOGETIC METHOD

Christians are encouraged to "always be ready to make [their] defense to anyone who demands from [them] an accounting for the hope that is in [them]" (1 Pet 3:15). Their testimony needs backing up with a reasoned account to defend it: dogmatics should evolve into apologetics. The Christian witness of faith needs defending against those within the church who are guilty of distorting it or reducing it to what they find believable or comfortable. Primarily, of course, apologetics is directed to those who reject the Christian faith, or have doubts about its validity. In many cases, that will mean addressing those who do not (or, indeed, do not expect to) find God

152. *DTLC*, 505.
153. *DTLC*, 505.
154. For Schleiermacher's position, see *Christian Faith* and *On Religion*.
155. See *CCF*, 337.
156. Schleiermacher, *On Religion*, 39.
157. *CCF*, 338. See also *FPA*, 64n338.
158. *CCC*, 15.
159. *PHT*, 231.
160. *CTF*, 144.

anywhere. But, alongside the inhabitants of the age of "the eclipse of God," there also are atheists whose non-belief is rooted in current philosophical predilections. Sell's approach to apologetics, therefore, recognized the challenges posed to Christian faith by "classical foundationalism," which, "by narrowing the scope of rationality" seems "to rule out from the start the kind of reasonableness which can accommodate what has happened in Christ and to believers"[161] as well as the challenge posed by "positivism," which tends to erect barriers that preclude the articulation of Christian claims *ab initio*.[162] This led him to claim that "With many of the intellectual opponents of the faith it is well to investigate the degree in which their presuppositions are allowing them to mark out, and construct, the territory of the meaningful, justifiable or rational, with the result that they discount important facts of human experience."[163]

We can note some ground rules which Sell laid out for his apologetics. First, he declares that he does not belong to those "who spurn the allegedly-antiquarian";[164] thereby he flagged up the importance of giving proper attention to the insights of the Bible and Christian tradition. This involves, secondly, developing a knack of distinguishing "between irreconcilable contradictions, and those paradoxes of faith to which we must cling with all the tenacity we can muster."[165] Sell is perfectly aware that it is all too easy for theologians to baptize their muddles as mysteries, but, he maintains, some paradoxes enable us to transform our problems into genuine insight. Thirdly, he does not want to risk trimming down the Christian faith to what the contemporary age deems acceptable or relevant. In the necessary conversation between Christian faith and contemporary culture two risks are involved: one of not taking the issues of culture seriously enough, thereby rendering our statements of the Christian faith largely irrelevant to our age; the other of using the presuppositions of contemporary culture as a Procrustean bed upon which to lay out Christian claims, thereby ending up with a reductionist theology. Sell typically is found pointing out the dangers of the latter rather than the former. We find him advising us to avoid doing "such obeisance to the God Relevance that ideas of the recent past are dismissed as 'old hat,' passé"[166] or pointing out that it is only when we "distinguish carefully between rationality and rationalism, science and

---

161. *CCF*, 251.
162. See *CCF*, 88, 211–12.
163. *HT*, 586.
164. *DTLC*, 576. See also *CCF*, 3.
165. *COM*, 249.
166. *CCE*, x. See also *PICB*, 229.

scientism, the experiential and the empirical"[167] that we will be able to do justice to the givenness of the Christian witness of faith. Nevertheless, he still wishes to avoid a methodology that sets out "from a given revelation in disjunctive, 'either-or' terms, with the attendant risk of an Olympian, even an imperialistic failure to communicate."[168]

Sell describes his apologetic method as "eclectic reasoned testimony"[169]—"reasoned" or "reasonable eclecticism."[170] As we should by now expect, it starts from the Christ event viewed from the soteriological perspective of the cross and Resurrection; and it then involves reflection upon it in the light of individual and corporate Christian experience as well as the intellectual challenges posed to the Christian from inside and outside the church. A wide terrain is involved: "a texture of historical, existential, theological, metaphysical, ethical, aesthetic, liturgical assertions" will require a "hospitable" method to enable what, from a Christian point of view, needs saying in the ensuing testimony.[171] Sell's intention is that the "context and manner" of his method "will not utterly disgrace that holy, redeeming love, supremely active at the Cross, which is its mainspring."[172] It starts from a *confession* which, through reflection upon it, involves *construction* of a fresh statement of the Christian witness of faith, and leads to *commendation* of it through *conversation* with its detractors. A defense of the Christian witness of faith, therefore, takes place in the context of attempting a constructive rather than "offensive" engagement with "alternative theories and world views."[173] Sell's methodology tries to make room for "a reverent agnosticism before ultimate mystery"[174] as well as take an irenic attitude to opponents of the Christian faith.

However laudable Sell's attempt to avoid ending up in a theological ghetto, serious doubts concern the genuine openness of his theology to development and change. Although his apologetic involves construction does it have a place for revision? His final authority appears to be nothing other than his chosen starting point: "our final authority is not our little accounts of what the mighty God has done, but God's saving act at the cross."[175] He

---

167. *CCF*, 136.
168. *JL*, 277.
169. *JL*, 277.
170. *CCF*, 88, 257.
171. *PICB*, 235.
172. *CCF*, 370.
173. *HT*, 584.
174. *CCF*, 370.
175. *CTF*, 17.

appears to be operating within an all too familiar theological circle. That said we must bear in mind two factors. First, the passage from confession to commendation via construction does, at least, in principle, allow for the kind of development and/or change which entails revision. Whether that occurs in Sell's theology, in practice, is a moot point. Most of the time, he gives the impression of being a theological conservationist rather than revisionist. That is very much the flavor of his "9.5 Theses," offered at the end of *Confessing the Faith Yesterday and Today*.[176] Nevertheless, secondly, we should not undervalue the holistic nature of the Christian witness of faith: it involves our "practices, values, experiences" as well as our intellectual apprehension of Christian doctrine.[177] In certain ways and to a certain extent, the truth of the Christian witness of faith is *shown* by those who adhere to it. We discover who we are by living; we develop values by living them. It is all about "walking the walk," not just "talking the talk." To know the truth, as they say, is to do the truth. A key question is: Are lives of genuine gratitude to be found in those "called by grace to be pilgrims on a way"?[178] It remains a concern that Sell's starting point does not appear to be *fully* open to critical scrutiny; thereby the adequacy of his theological proposals is at risk. Another way of putting this is to say that, using Ogden's terms, while Sell strives hard to ensure that his theology is *appropriate* to the Christian witness of faith, he is not so convincing when it comes to establishing the *credibility* of his Christian claims.[179] It comes as no surprise therefore that doubts are raised about his success in avoiding the "ghettoization" of the Christian faith. The question of the credibility of Sell's theology will be in our minds in what follows.

---

176. See *CTF*, 268–90.
177. *CCF*, 88.
178. *EEE*, 202.
179. For Ogden's criteria of theological adequacy, see his *On Theology*.

3

God

Sell believes that "it is difficult to see how Christians could, or would wish to, testify to their understanding of God without adverting to the Cross."[1] When he claims that "distorted theology has its origin in a distorted view of God,"[2] he is flagging up a fundamental conviction, namely, that any doctrine of God which does not do justice to God's self-revelation as holy love is inadequate. Let us first learn more about Sell's conception of God.

THE GOD OF HOLY LOVE: CREATOR AND REDEEMER

Sell is extremely critical of what he regards as the "sentimentality concerning God's love," which accompanies a lot of liberal theology.[3] He maintains that many theologians wax elegantly about a loving God, forgetting that "his love is holy, righteous, love in the presence of which sin cannot stand."[4] God's love is welcoming and inexhaustible, but it is also holy and righteous. A juridical element, therefore, belongs to the divine nature. It is imperative, Sell argues, to give due weight to both "holiness" and "love" when conceiving God as holy love. If the stress is placed solely on "holiness" we run the risk of so envisaging God that God is conceived as exercising "malice or vindictiveness"; meanwhile if the emphasis is one-sidedly placed upon "love"

1. *CCF*, 165.
2. *PHT*, 249.
3. *TIT*, 83. See also *TNM*, 245.
4. *HT*, 294.

our concept of God easily slips into "sentiment and antinomianism."[5] The former constitutes the mistake of Calvinists, the latter that of liberals like Ritschl. Sell repeatedly rounds on those who do not do justice to what he calls God's "high-and-lifted-up-ness."[6] It is essential that due weight is given to God as a *moral* being: "His nature is moral, his purpose is moral, and his methods are moral."[7]

While it is inevitable that we seek concepts and images in which to conceive God appropriately, it is important to remind ourselves that the early Christians were able to speak of God as they believed they had found God in Jesus. It is crucial that the concepts and images we choose reflect the early witness to God in Christ. Sell insists, therefore, that we are living in the presence of a gracious, non-coercive God:

> He will not compel submission to his will; he does not coerce the mind, or violate the freedom he has given to us. He is no oriental despot. He is a Good Shepherd. His character determines his ways with us.[8]

God acts, therefore, according to the divine character. Sell shares Calvin's view that "all events are governed by God's secret plan"[9] but, while God is "working all the time some divine acts are more dramatic than others."[10] He argues that if "the one God cannot change in the sense of acting out of accordance with his nature . . . his holy, loving nature is such that he cannot but act responsively according to the divine moral and existential situations of persons created in his image and the fluctuating condition of the created order."[11] Amidst the *general* divine activity there is room for *special* divine acts, the supreme example of which is the Christ event. It is "a dramatic and victorious rescue bid which entails [God's] utter self-giving . . . grace at work."[12]

Sell is aware of the difficulties of talking coherently and credibly about divine activity given scientific accounts of how the universe works.[13] But

---

5. *FPA*, 135.
6. *CAM*, 132.
7. *GOF*, 101.
8. *GOF*, 101–12.
9. Calvin, *Institutes*, I.XVI.2. See *GOF*, 84.
10. *GOF*, 74.
11. *FPA*, 112.
12. *COS*, 15.

13. For some attempts to offer explanations of how God might be said to act in the world see Ogden, *Reality of God*, 164–87, Wiles *God's Action*; Ward, *Rational Theology and Divine Action*; Pailin, *Probing the Foundations*, 100–115.

he is *assertive* rather than explanatory when speaking of God's activity in creation and redemption. Both are works of God's love: "Creation is the free act of a personal God"[14] and redemption is the way in which "In face of man's sin and alienation the creator God proceeds with his gracious work of re-creation."[15] In terms of their similarities as acts of gracious love, creation and redemption belong together, but, given the specific, purposeful intent of God's action in Jesus Christ, Sell envisages the Christ event as a *once-for-all* divine act which constitutes rather than re-presents the possibility of salvation. Just how such assertions fit into the current scientific world picture of "a long, slow development of rational conscious life from inorganic matter by natural processes, of humanity as evolving and surviving by lust and aggression as well as by love and friendship"[16] is difficult to fathom. When some serious apologetics is called for, we get confession.

THE GOD-WORLD RELATIONSHIP

There are three formal ways of construing the God-world relationship: classical theism, classical pantheism, and panentheism.[17] In classical theism God and the world are considered to be so distinct that there is an asymmetrical relationship between them. God is the wholly necessary cause of a wholly contingent world which cannot affect God: "there cannot . . . be any way of linking the two in *mutually* enriching ties."[18] The logical structure of classical theism makes it very difficult for theologians to say what they want to say about God since it inhibits talk of God acting in response to events which take place in the world. Indeed, as Pailin points out, "its conception of the intrinsic perfection of the divine fundamentally undermines any faith that suggests the divine is aware of, incorporates, and responds to the contingent events of the world."[19] Needless to say, theologians in pursuit of theological adequacy have tried to marry the classical theistic conceptuality with talk which recognizes that God has a reciprocal relationship with the world. Pailin believes that the resulting theologies "struggle to maintain that uneasy compromises are not hiding fundamental contradictions."[20]

14. *GOF*, 67.
15. *GOF*, 68.
16. Ward, *Living God*, 33.
17. See Pailin, *God and the Processes*, 76–95.
18. Pailin, *God and the Processes*, 79.
19. Pailin, *God and the Processes*, 80–81.
20. Pailin, *God and the Processes*, 81.

If there are question marks over the suitability of classical theism as a conceptual system for use in Christian theology, the same can be said for classical pantheism, its logical opposite. In pantheism there is no distinction between God and the world: God is the world and the world is God. Given that God and the world are indistinguishable there is no *real* relationship between them. The world at best is a mere emenation of the divine. Everything is in the grip of strict necessity, and the supposed "freedom" of the world is an illusion. Pantheism cannot do justice to what Christians want to say about God, the One, the unique individual who, as creator, redeemer and sustainer, is distinct from the world but genuinely related to it.

The third of the formal ways of modeling the God-world relationship is that of panentheism. Pailin informs us that "panentheism is not a new position but a new appreciation of the proper conceptual structure of a dominant tradition of religious faith in God."[21] Usually associated with the so-called "process" philosophers and theologians, it is also employed by theologians as diverse as Tillich[22] and Garvie.[23] Panentheism shares similarities with both classical theism and classical pantheism, but is equally different from them. Garvie found it enabled him to steer "the straight middle course" between the Scylla of deism and the Charybdis of pantheism.[24] It provided him with a concept of God which distinguishes between but does not separate God and the world. Panentheism relates God and the world, derived from God and dependent upon God, so that "no reality above or beyond God will be possible for our thought."[25] God includes the world but the world does not exhaust the divine reality. Hence, as Garvie puts it, "the God in and through all" is also "over all."[26] The transcendence and immanence of God, therefore, are held together conceptually as "complementary truths."[27] A popular model for understanding panentheism is that of the human self-body relationship: as the self is to the body, so God is to the world. And, as Pailin puts it, "God incorporates within the divine being all the experiences which constitute the world while having an identity as a self-conscious being which is significantly separate from and accordingly able to respond to the contingent processes of the world."[28]

---

21. Pailin, *God and the Processes*, 81.
22. See Tillich, *Systematic Theology*, 3, 420–22.
23. See my "Alfred Ernest Garvie," 18–22.
24. Garvie, *Christian Certainty*, 10.
25. Garvie, *Christian Belief*, 437.
26. Garvie, *Christian Doctrine*, 188.
27. Garvie, *Christian Doctrine*, 188.
28. Pailin, *God and the Processes*, 81.

The immediate question concerns where Sell fits on this map of the God-world relationship. Without any hesitation we can say that he will have nothing whatsoever to do with pantheism. God is not to be collapsed into the world; God's transcendence over the world must be maintained at all costs. He repeatedly castigates thinkers who fail to pay sufficient attention to the *distinction* between God and the world, thereby becoming "in real danger of vitiating the gospel."[29] So-called "immanentists" are opposed, since, by eschewing the transcendence of God, and hence undermining genuine possibilities for divine relation, they turn to "reason, conscience or . . . religious experience . . . as the arbiter of truth."[30] Sell's final "arbiter" is God's revelation in Jesus Christ as holy love. That revelation arose from a free decision by God taken *outside* the world, not one which occurred due to any *necessary* divine involvement *in* the world. Sell sets his face, thereby, against all "pantheistic immanentist automaticism, which was ever the peril of those in Hegel's wake."[31] Taken to task are the post-Hegelian idealists of the eighteenth and nineteenth centuries,[32] some nineteenth and twentieth century Scottish divines,[33] the Cambridge Platonists,[34] R. J. Campbell,[35] and Ferré.[36] The latter generates Sell's critical ire because he is among those who have bought into "process thought excesses."[37]

There is a *distinction* between God and the world because the latter is the product of the free creation of the former. A separation is not involved, though, because, as Sell acknowledges, "between Creator and creature there cannot be an absolute ontological distinction if the life of the latter is derived from the former."[38] The world is wholly dependent upon God for its existence: Sell maintains it was created *ex nihilo* by God. Hence he warns against all pantheistic attempts to merge God with creation. Only when the God-world distinction is maintained, he argues, will human beings be afforded their real identity as free individuals. Without it, it becomes all too easy for us to regard ourselves as God. The doctrine of creation not only guarantees the God-world distinction, but also ensures our human

---

29. *TIT*, 32.
30. *TIT*, 33.
31. *TAT*, 189.
32. See *PICB*.
33. See *DAD*.
34. See *EEE*, 1–45.
35. See *HT*, 274–75.
36. See *CAM*.
37. *FPA*, 113.
38. *PICB*, 133.

status: we are distinctively who we are because we stand "right down to the innermost core and essence of [our] being, in the profoundest possible relationship to God all the time in an order of persons."[39] If we were not in a Creator-creature relationship with God we would not be truly *human*. Hence, for Sell, the God-world distinction guarantees the proper status of both God and human beings.

There is, of course, a world of conceptual difference between saying that God and the world are "distinct" rather than "separate." While Sell resolutely wishes to maintain the former, he denies the latter. The God-world relationship is guaranteed from God's side: "There is the pneumatological consideration that all are in some way accessible to, and reached by, the Spirit."[40] But we are immediately warned by Sell that this should not be allowed to foster a "false immanentism . . . which would blur the Creator-creature distinction and construe the Spirit's work in terms of genial intellectual accord rather than dramatic rescue on the ground of Christ's atoning work."[41] Sell's picture of the God-world relationship is now opening up: a perfect God in need of nothing freely decides to create a contingent universe; this transcendent God decides to rescue the world from the mess in which it has got itself by intervening in its affairs and effecting a process of atonement on its behalf through the incarnation; after the incarnation God chooses to be immanent in the world by way of the divine presence in the shape of the Holy Spirit. The picture raises a number of questions: What motivated a perfect God who already had everything to engage in external creative activity? What kind of loving God is it that, from Creation to Incarnation, is essentially absent from the world in either a creative or redeeming capacity—if, that is, those terms can rightly be separated in an adequate understanding of divine activity? How can a divine "rescue" in the death and resurrection of Jesus Christ be of use to those who had lived and died before the Christ event—why did it come so late?

Questions like these raise the concern that Sell's "God" is in need of more "immanence" in the world. It needs to find expression not just in terms of the Christ event, but also before and outside of it. Sell asserts the standard claims of classical theism. But how can One who essentially transcends time be said to be involved in time, whether on a 'rescue' mission let alone in intimate and ongoing ways?[42] Sell informs us, nevertheless, that "immanentism" and "transcendence" do need holding together. While God

39. *COS*, 89.
40. *EEE*, 297.
41. *EEE*, 297.
42. See *GOF*, 49: God "transcends time."

and the world are not "correlative terms," Sell argues that, according to the paradigm of "Christ the God-man," transcendence and immanence most certainly are to be so conceived.[43] He quotes David Jenkins: "Transcendence without immanence makes nonsense of God; immanence without transcendence makes nonsense of man. Both are quite untrue to the givenness of Jesus Christ."[44] For Sell, "the givenness of Jesus Christ" is the supreme revelation of "the *transcendence* of *immanent* holy, active love."[45] But if that "givenness" is paradigmatic of the God-world relationship, is not the nature of the God-world relationship revealed through the *particular* Christ event that which *universally* has been in place since God created the world? Sell thinks not—his theology is far too rooted in the *particularity* of the Christ event to allow for that. He does not believe what is revealed of the God-world relationship in the Christ event is *re-presentative* of what has been the case since the creation of the world; rather God's immanence is rooted in the Christ event and the ensuing work of the Spirit.

Sell argues that God's "rescue" act in Jesus Christ is *supernatural*. First, "its provision is not from nature, least of all from human beings, but from the holy God of all grace."[46] And, secondly, "it has to restore nature, especially ours" since it "has gone awry."[47] What is at the heart of the Christian faith, therefore, is "a supernatural act of regeneration and re-creation, and a supernatural power for living."[48] Once that is fully recognized, Sell argues, it becomes clear that the really important feature of the Creator-creature relationship turns less on ontology than morality. So he is critical of what he calls the "ontological drag" in Ferré's theology which gives "precedence to ontology ... over morality" and thereby reveals a "methodological neglect of the moral in favour of the ontological"[49] and he takes Tillich to task for doing theology disproportionally in response to "ontic" rather than "moral" shock, our "consciousness of sin and guilt before a holy God."[50] It follows that, for Sell, the term "'transcendence' may in Christian doctrine be said to find its supreme place in reference to the holiness of God *vis-a-vis* the sin and alienation of humanity."[51] The basic human problem is not that we

43. *CCF*, 180.
44. *CCF*, 180. The Jenkins quotation comes from *Glory of Man*, 104.
45. *CCF*, 151. Italics mine.
46. *CCF*, 180.
47. *CCF*, 180.
48. *CCF*, 182.
49. *CAM*, 2, 56.
50. *PR*, 174. See also *EEE*, 304–6.
51. *PICB*, 129.

are finite but that we are in rebellion against God.[52] Sell argues that this is where the New Testament emphasis falls.[53] The fundamental issue, therefore, does not involve "the transcendence of geographical location, but of holy purity:[54] it is "a matter of God's character as holy" far more than "a matter of the quasi-geographical distance between him and human beings."[55] But, even if this is true, the ontological issues surrounding the God-world relationship remain and need addressing in adequate ways. That will not be achieved by any of the variations of classical theism. What is entailed will become clear as we continue our discussion of the ontological ramifications of the God-world relationship through a consideration of Sell's critique of process thought.

SELL'S CRITICISMS OF PROCESS THEOLOGY

Introduction

By "process" thought we mean the work of philosophers like Whitehead and Hartshorne, who employ a neoclassical metaphysics in which the primary category of reality is understood as "becoming" rather than "being" and the thinking of those theologians who make use of such philosophies for strictly theological purposes. The safest way of offering a critique of any so-called "process" thinker is to treat him or her as an individual thinker rather than as a member of the school to which they are purported to belong. That said, we are on safe ground when we say that, at the very heart of process theology lies a commitment to a *panentheistic* view of the God-world relationship and the employment of some form of a *dipolar* conceptual structure for the divine attributes. These commitments are made in response to what are taken as fundamental difficulties in classical theism's concept of God; they constitute a purported solution to problems found in "the classical metaphysical—theological tradition of the Western world."[56]

From his earliest philosophical explorations to his later mature theological writings, Sell was a severe critic of process thought. We will suggest that he presents a very one-sided, and sometimes misleading, view of it—a not altogether unusual occurrence in British theology, and that his criticism of it brings into question the adequacy of his own theology, which is

---

52. *COS*, 92.
53. *CCF*, 205.
54. *SOL*, 4.
55. *CCF*, 167.
56. Ogden, *Reality of God*, 16.

presented as if it is *the* orthodox position. Sell's criticisms were heavily based upon the conclusions of his teachers and theological friends. The names of Richmond,[57] Owen,[58] and Gunton[59] are important to note in this connection. Sell gives the impression that process thought is a passing theological fad rather than something of more lasting value. Perhaps it was so foreign to the British mind and experience that he felt it could be discounted? This might explain why he notes that Pailin is "one of *the few* British philosophers of religion to have been influenced by process thought,"[60] thus implying that majorities are always right. The clear inference, though, is that process thought is of little consequence. Then, convinced that process thought "seems to" have rendered God's transcendence "inconsequential," such that "it is quite impotent to serve any longer as the bulwark between the process thinker's desiderated pan*en*theism and . . . full-blown pantheism," very patronizingly he remarks that "*Undeterred*, such scholars as Schubert Ogden and Norman Pittenger *persist* with process thought."[61] The reason why persistence is still in order is that Sell has weighted "transcendence" incorrectly vis-á-vis "immanence" in process thought's conception of panentheism.[62]

We need to know more about process thought's aversion to classical theism before getting too involved in its defense. It arises because the metaphysics upon which such theism is based reflects an outlook that all our thought and experience contradicts. Everything known to us is subject to change and is in a process of becoming. But classical metaphysics asserts that "being" is the "primary" interpretative category of reality, not "becoming": the static is superior to what is developing. Hence "the time-honored

---

57. Richmond co-supervised Sell's PhD at the University of Nottingham. His criticism of process thought is found in "God, Time and Process Philosophy," 234–41.

58. Owen taught Sell briefly at the University of Manchester. Sell wrote *CCC* to "salute the memory of the Welsh theologian-philosopher" (ix). Owen's major criticisms of process thought are found in *Christian Knowledge*, 105–97 and *Concepts of Deity*, 75–89. Also of interest is Owen's review of Ogden's *Reality of God*, Pittenger's letter in response ("Letter," 456–57), and Owen's reply ("Letter," 513).

59. Gunton and Sell were both members of the URC. For Gunton's critique of process theology and, particularly, Hartshorne, see *Becoming and Being*. Also of interest is a debate with Pittenger, started by Gunton's "Process Theology's Concept of God," enjoined by Pittenger, "Process Theology," with a reply from Gunton, "Process Theology: A Reply." See also Ogden's critique of Gunton's criticisms of process theology: "Christian Theology and Neoclassical Theism."

60. *CAM*, 46n4.

61. *PR*, 228. Sell's treatment of process thought in *PR* is repeated in a slightly rearranged way, with minor amendments and additions, in *CCF*, 166–70. From *PR* in 1988 to *CCF* in 2002, there is little evidence of change in Sell's opinion about process thought.

62. For a defense of the neoclassical metaphysics of Hartshorne and its application in Ogden's theology, see my "Is Schubert M. Ogden's 'God' Christian?"

premise of the Western theistic tradition" is "that God, as in all respects the perfect or unsurpassable individual, must also be strictly immutable or unchanging and wholly absolute or incapable of relation to others."[63] It follows that the world cannot be accredited with being of consequence to God since nothing taking place within it counts for anything with God. With or without the world, God is God, incapable of being moved by both the world's joy and delight, or pain and suffering. Needless to say, theologians who stand in this metaphysical tradition recognize that they still need to speak of God in keeping with the biblical witness. That witness everywhere implies that God possesses real relations with the world: God hears prayers, responds to needs and is engaged with creation. But theologians who build upon the foundations of classical theism cannot do justice to what they are obliged to say about God. They end up facing either utter contradictions or unresolved compromises in their theology.[64] The honest alternative is to accept that the classical metaphysics presupposed by their theology is obsolete and in need of exchanging for a more adequate conceptual system.

The process thinkers believe they have such a system, namely, neoclassical metaphysics. We have already outlined the panentheistic model for the God-world relationship at the heart of it. To be sure, there are those who seem unable to understand it. Owen, for example, recognizes that panentheists hold that "God includes and penetrates the world" but also "maintain that he and the world are substantially distinct."[65] Given that neoclassical theists maintain that "God's individuality is constituted by his inclusion of the world," Owen asks, "how does panentheism differ from pantheism?"[66] It should be obvious: in pantheism God's individuality is constituted *wholly* by the world, while in panentheism God's individuality contains the world but is *not* wholly constituted by it. God can make judgments over against the world. As Hartshorne makes clear, there is "the quite essential distinction between "God and all things" and "God includes all things or between pantheism and panentheism."[67]

---

63. Ogden, "Faith and Secularity," 36.

64. Ogden puts it like this: "They generally contend not only that God is the metaphysical Absolute, whose only relation to the world is wholly external, but that he is also the loving heavenly Father revealed in Jesus, who freely creates the world and guides it towards its fulfillment with tender care. The difficulty, however . . . is the obvious incoherence of these two contentions, which both deny and affirm that God's relation to the world is real and that he is relevant to its life because it is relevant to his" (*Reality of God*, 18).

65. Owen, *Concepts of Deity*, 76.

66. Owen, *Concepts of Deity*, 85

67. Hartshorne, *Reality As Social Process*, 120.

The Concept of Dipolarity

In Hartshorne's version of *dipolarity* we are provided with "a formal structure in terms of which the material qualities of the divine are to be understood."[68] A distinction is made between "existence" and "actuality." Pailin helps us understand what is entailed through an analogy: our knowledge of the existence of a table in the next room.[69] Without going into the room we know *abstractly* what is there: a flat topped object with legs capable of having objects placed upon it; but until we enter the room we have no idea of its *concrete actuality*, whether it is round or square, has three legs or more, is made of metal or wood etc. Therefore, to say that the table *exists* is only to assert the *abstract* presence of an object with the properties expected of a table. The *essence* of being a table does not specify its *concrete* actuality. That occurs when, as it always must, the essence of a table is exemplified in a specific way. Applying this analogy enables us to talk about the necessary and absolute features of objects (in their *existence*) as well as their contingent and relative features (in their *actuality*). Then, following what Pailin refers to as Hartshorne's "great insight," we can, in the case of God, suggest that "the nature of the divine existence does not entail that the divine actuality must have the same formal properties."[70] The *actuality* need not be necessary and absolute, but indeed can be contingent and relative.

When this formal structure is applied to "God" a way is opened up for talking about God which does justice to what classical theists hold to be of supreme importance when developing a doctrine of God: in terms of the divine *existence*, "we can think of God only as a reality whose relatedness to our life is itself relative to nothing and to which, therefore, neither our own being and actions nor any other can ever make a difference as to its existence."[71] But the dipolar structure also enables us to assert that in *actuality* God can "be conceived as a reality which is genuinely related to our life in the world and to which, therefore, both we ourselves and our various actions all make a difference as to its actual being."[72] This enables us to talk of God in ways which do justice to the divine nature as both absolute and related. In some respects God's character reveals qualities that are necessary and absolute (the divine *existence*), while in other respects we are shown qualities that are contingent and relative (the divine *actuality*). Since we are

---

68. Pailin, *God and the Processes*, 70.
69. Pailin, *God and the Processes*, 66–68.
70. Pailin, *God and the Processes*, 69.
71. Ogden, *Reality of God*, 47.
72. Ogden, *Reality of God*, 47.

dealing with *polar* opposites, a complete picture of God only appears when both sides of the conceptual structure are firmly held in place.

It will be helpful to provide some examples of the way this dipolar structure can be applied. Let us, first, consider God's knowledge. Viewed in respect to the divine existence it is necessary and absolute: God will always know everything there is to know. When viewed from the perspective of divine actuality, however, it is contingent and concrete: God knows what can be known at a certain time. God's knowledge, therefore, is relative to what there is to be known. New events will take place in the cosmic process which will further advance God's knowledge at a later stage; but God will never be ignorant, since God always possesses full and complete knowledge of what can conceivably be known. The attribute of divine love is similarly understood. God necessarily loves: in principle, the divine *existence* reveals an absolute love, untarnished by competing instincts or passions. God's love, therefore, is infinite in that nothing, literally nothing, falls outside its range; it is also eternal since God never stops loving. But, in practice, viewed from the perspective of the divine *actuality*, God's love is contingent, being relative to what at a particular time there is to love. At a future time in the cosmic process there will be new calls upon God's love. Also the nature of God's love will always be appropriate to each concrete situation: at different stages and times in our lives God's love will be appropriately contextual. A final example is God's reality itself, that which makes "God" God. In principle, viewed in respect to the divine existence, God is the ground of all that exists, wholly self-explicable and in no way dependent upon anything outside God for existence; in practice, viewed in respect to the divine actuality, God is the ground of what happens to exist at any particular time as a result of the divine creation and our decisions. On the one hand, then, God's reality is absolute and unchanging (in God's existence), but, on the other hand, that reality is relative and changing to fit whatever is the present state of the world (in God's actuality). It will now be clear that *pace* Sell, the dipolar formal system is not analogously akin to "the frowned upon substance and accidents of (Lockean, not Thomist) tradition—that is, between God as he is in himself and God as he appears to us."[73] God is, as God is in Godself, *as well as* God as God appears to us, in some respects necessary, absolute, and unchanging and in other respects contingent, relative, and changing.

We turn now to some of the interpretative problems Sell has with neoclassical metaphysics' prevailing structure of dipolar panentheism. First, in some of his statements, it appears that process thought is interpreted as being pantheistic when, in fact, as we know, it advances panentheism, a concept

---

73. *CAM*, 45.

as different from pantheism as it is from the kind of theistic view Sell favors. He regards pantheism, in its "varying guises," as "those most resilient of intellectual tendencies," and there seems little doubt that he found such a tendency in process thought.[74] But we have a right to expect that panentheism be understood on its own terms, rather than through a classical theistic lens which views any model for the God-world relationship other than its own as incipiently pantheistic. Nor, secondly, should we accept negative interpretations of thinkers on the basis of assertion rather than argument. Sell accuses Whitehead, for example, of so conceiving God that God "is *in* . . . *danger of* becoming imprisoned within the process."[75] No evidence is given for this claim, but given the nomenclature of the panentheistic model upon which Whitehead builds his philosophy, it would hardly *prima facia* seem likely. If all things are somehow to be envisaged *in* God, with God the unique, supreme individual to whom all things are internally related, then, there is little possibility of God "becoming imprisoned within the process." One senses a failure to grasp the way in which "transcendence" as well as "immanence" is bound together in the panentheistic model for the God-world relationship. When Sell claims that "the emphasis" in process thought "is found in its immanentism" we can be forgiven for wondering which purported process thinker(s) he has in mind. Indeed, with his concept of "dual transcendence" Hartshorne has challenged the adequacy of traditional understandings of transcendence: "God is the self-surpassing surpasser of all, transcending not just all others but also Godself as new experiences are received into the divine being during the cosmic process."[76] Then, thirdly, when Sell tells us that part of the inspiration of process thinkers resides in "the doctrine of emergent evolution"[77] we sense that he thinks less of them for so doing. Arguably the reverse ought to be the case: praise needs giving to theologians who, searching for credibility in their claims, take into account advances in scientific knowledge. The real problem comes when theologians continue to work as if such advances haven't taken place.

Sell's acceptance of Owen's criticism of neo-classical metaphysics as authoritative rides on the back of the assumption that the theism they support is not only adequate but is also the *Christian* theism. Dipolar panentheism is significantly different from the classical theism they believe valid, so, in Owen's words, "dipolarism is beyond doubt non-Christian."[78] Nowhere,

---

74. EEE, 219.
75. PR, 74. Italics mine.
76. See Hartshorne, *Creative Synthesis*, 227–44.
77. PR, 228. See also *CCF*, 167.
78. Owen, *Concepts*, 89.

however, does Owen work through the rigorous criticism of classical theism's logical consistency and religious adequacy which Hartshorne, for example, has made. He simply regards it as self evident that classical theism is the only valid theism there is and, consequently, uses it as the yardstick by which to judge the adequacy of the other candidate theisms, in general, and neoclassical theism, in particular. Consequently, neoclassical theism is deemed to be invalid, because it denies or fails to affirm that God's life is "self-sufficient";[79] that "nothing that creatures do, and nothing that happens to them, can cause any increase (or decrease) in [God's] desire and knowledge";[80] that God "is changeless and self-sufficient Love"[81] yet also is "pure act, and . . . cannot be enriched by any creature";[82] that "the most perfect form of spiritual being would be one from which these conditions [change and growth} are absent";[83] that God responds to us but "'response' does not imply 'change'";[84] and, finally, though not exhaustively, that "the world is created totally by God."[85] That such things are claimed by classical theism is true; that they are mutually coherent, consistent and what an appropriate and credible theism needs to say is something else.

Asserting that an adequate theism requires such statements is rather different from making it clear why the monopolar prejudice is to be preferred over the dipolar alternative. In fact, Owen brings into question the adequacy of his own theism and Sell runs the risk of following suit. In a roundabout way Owen even admits it. He tells us that the idea of a suffering God is hard to square with classical, monopolar theism, but he assures us that "we cannot form an adequate idea of the manner in which God's sufferings are transfigured in his joy."[86] Of course, he could have been more frank had he admitted the logical impossibility of classical theism's wholly necessary and perfect deity ever meaningfully doing anything!

There is a tendency for critics of process theology to assume that all so-called "process thinkers" say so much in common that they can be treated as a group, with the result that the way in which they differ is hidden. This problem becomes acute when the notion of dipolarity is under consideration. Owen, for example, falls into the trap of assuming that what

79. Owen, *Concepts*, 86.
80. Owen, *Concepts*, 87.
81. Owen, *Christian Knowledge*, 86.
82. Owen, *Concepts*, 86.
83. Owen, *Concepts*, 85.
84. Owen, *Concepts*, 87.
85. Owen, *Concepts*, 86.
86. Owen, *Concepts*, 87.

Whitehead and Hartshorne say about dipolarity is identical. He tells us that dipolarism in Hartshorne and Ogden "consists in distinguishing between an aspect of God's being (*corresponding* to Whitehead's "primordial nature") that is necessary, and an aspect (*corresponding* to Whitehead's "consequent nature") that is dependent."[87] But, as David R. Griffin points out, while both Whitehead and Hartshorne agree that "God" is dipolar, their two concepts of dipolarity are quite different.[88] Owen is incorrect to criticize Hartshorne on the basis of what Whitehead is supposed to have said (or vice versa) since the two thinkers have quite different ways of conceiving dipolarity. One reason why Owen has problems with neoclassical metaphysics is that sometimes he attributes Whitehead's locutions to those of Hartshorne, and, thereby, fails to understand the basic logic of Hartshorne's position. It is true that "dipolarism is self-contradictory" when solely viewed through the lens of some of Whitehead's looser statements rather than Hartshorne's more coherent position.

Owen is particularly prone to misunderstand Hartshorne's distinction between "abstract existence" and "concrete actuality." After declaring dipolarity in "God" to be "a sheer self-contradiction"[89] he admits that neoclassical theism "is given a semblance of intelligibility only by the distinction between God's 'abstract identity' and 'concrete existence.'"[90] But he shows little evidence of understanding that distinction when employed. He fails to understand the relationship in neoclassical metaphysics between "essence," "existence," and, "actuality," seemingly incorrectly suspecting it to deny the identity of "essence" and "existence" in God, and thereby ending at a loss as to what the distinctions employed in dipolar theism really mean. Ogden reminds us that "'Existence,' in short, properly functions as an abstract constant always implying 'actuality' as an abstract variable. Hence to say that anything 'exists' requires that the variable 'actuality' have some specific value."[91] Or, as Hartshorne says succinctly, "essential integrity and

---

87. Owen, *Concepts*, 83. Italics mine.

88. See Ford, *Two Process Philosophers*, 35–36.

89. Owen, *Christian Knowledge*, 105. In *Concepts*, Owen later confirms his view that "dipolarism is self-contradictory" (82).

90. Owen, *Christian Knowledge*, 105. Owen is referring to a passage in Ogden's *Reality of God* where Ogden, confusingly, describes what Hartshorne and he usually refer to as "abstract existence" and "concrete actuality" as "abstract identity" and "concrete existence." I shall use Hartshorne's and Ogden's usual way of putting the matter. The doctrine of dipolarity depends upon the distinction between "existence" and "actuality" being crystal clear.

91. Ogden, *Reality of God*, 48.

connectedness is an abstraction from the total reality of the individual."[92] It is necessary that God exists in some actual concrete state which conceivably could have been some other state among a range of possibilities open to God. However, in whatever state God exists with creation God's "essence" will be fully manifested because, for God "essence" and "existence" are identical. The necessary character of God's "existence" implies that God's actuality must be manifest in some appropriate form.

One further charge from Owen warrants a firm response. He opines that "the ground on which panentheists posit dipolarity in God . . . is surely a piece of gratuitous anthropomorphism."[93] Sell, the faithful follower of Owen concerning everything to do with process thought, does not demur. We must note carefully what Owen says:

> Because change and growth, in response to environment characterise human personality, it does not follow that they also characterise the personality of God. On the contrary, their presence in our form of personality is an obvious sign of our finiteness. They are not essential to the spiritual qualities of which they are (in the finite case) conditions. The most perfect form of spiritual being would be one from which these conditions are absent.[94]

Why so? Because Thomism declares so, with its negative outlook on change and growth demanding it![95] Ogden openly admits that neoclassical theism is anthropomorphic and he congratulates Hartshorne for "working out a frankly 'anthropomorphic' view of God."[96] He argues that Hartshorne "convincingly shows that the traditional prejudices against such a view spring, not from commitment to the understanding of God attested by Scripture (with which understanding, on the contrary, this view is perfectly compatible), but rather from the tacit assumption of the premises of classical metaphysics."[97] Only a classical theistic prejudice against "change," in favor of "static being," can, in the end, make Owen's charge of anthropomorphism a negative rather than a positive virtue. God should be considered in strict analogy to the human self.[98] Categories from the world of persons are more

---

92. Hartshorne, *Creative Synthesis*, 233.

93. Owen, *Concepts*, 85.

94. Owen, *Concepts*, 85.

95. See Hartshorne, *Man's Vision*, 85–141.

96. Ogden, *Reality of God*, 175.

97. Ogden, *Reality of God*, 175.

98. See Hartshorne, *Man's Vision*, 174–211; Hartshorne, *Natural Theology*, 97–101; Hartshorne, *Logic of Perfection*, 133–147; and Hartshorne, *Divine Relativity*, 32.

fitting to use analogously for "God" than those from the inanimate world of objects.

Sell's Criticisms of Nels Ferré

Sell is critical of Ferré's use of process thought. He argues that "Ferré, for all his cautions against tying theology to "alien" philosophies, actually gives precedence to ontology (with process thought adhesions) over morality and, as a result, offers "an attenuated account of the doctrine of the atonement."[99] As far as he is concerned process philosophy is an outstanding candidate for being an "alien" philosophy. He offers five major strands of criticism.

The first concerns the tenets of classical theism. Along with other members of the process school, Ferré displays an "implacable opposition to classical theistic ontology."[100] It does not allow Christians to conceive God appropriately and coherently, posing the question concerning how it is possible to talk of the self-sufficient, static absolute of classical theism as a God of love. Sell believes that Ferré's attack on the substance ontology of classical theism is "too unspecific to be more than an emotional reaction to a general notion that appalled him."[101] That notion was that Sell calls "substance staticism," which Ferré wished to replace with the dynamic conceptuality of neoclassical metaphysics. Sell, however, argues that Ferré was over-reacting to what is a pseudo-problem. Turning to Coppleston and Curtin, he suggests that "there is more dynamism in Thomism . . . than the personalist and process thinkers allow."[102] Curtin is quoted: "the whole tone of the [*Summa Theologica*], the emphasis upon the efficient and final causality as against occasionalism, convey[s] *an impression of* dynamism and activity."[103] There is a world of difference, however, between creating an "impression" and coherently and adequately underpinning a credible doctrine of God.

Sell, nevertheless, makes an important point which is not lost on others. Gilkey, for example, questions whether "there has been a dominant conception of God in Christendom characterized by Thomist attributes and claims that "what process philosophers of religion call 'classical theism' is a strange hodgepodge that bears little historical scrutiny; and . . . they seem to think that it has been scholastic philosophy that dominated the religion and piety of almost all Western Christendom until finally a new philosophy

---

99. *CAM*, 2.
100. *CAM*, 33.
101. *CAM*, 38.
102. *CAM*, 47.
103. *CAM*, 47. The quotation comes from Curtin, "Process Philosophy," 237.

appeared in Whitehead."[104] Ogden typically tells us that "most of us today . . . are determined in our thinking about God by a common intellectual tradition that has served throughout Western history for the conception of his reality."[105] He believes "traditional theism" has been "in the process of breaking down under the cumulative weight of experiences and reflections that run counter to its basic premises" and "even where these premises are denied, they continue to exert an influence scarcely less profound than where they are still affirmed."[106] But most today are more likely to speak of God according to conceptuality derived from the Bible than obtained from classical theism. Generally speaking, theology has been more influenced by the biblical picture of God than scholastic philosophy.

Ferré believed that the inherited approaches to conceiving God have been dominated by certain axioms derived from the scholastic period, in general, and the thought of Aquinas, in particular, e.g., a denial of change in God; the absence of real relations between God and the world; a static view of divine perfection etc. Not only have critics queried whether Western theologies are as influenced by these axioms as thinkers like Ferré suggest, but some Thomist experts clearly feel that a pejorative interpretation of Thomism has been given by the process thinkers. Tracy takes many of the insights of neoclassical metaphysics into his theology, but still believes that "Hartshorne and others are too often satisfied with accepting some outdated neo-scholastic interpretations of Aquinas' meaning when more accurate and more contemporary formulations can be found."[107] While he is satisfied that "the basic dipolar criticisms of Aquinas' monopolar position may well still hold," he insists that "an adequate criticism of these more modern and accurate interpretations of the subtle and complex position of Aquinas cannot . . . be found in the process corpus."[108] Burrell, one of the "modern and accurate" interpreters of Aquinas referred to by Tracy, suggests, *pace* Ogden, that "a more sensitive probing to discover what the medievals were getting at would certainly be more sportsmanlike."[109] He points out that Aquinas attempts "to locate the parameters of discourse concerning God so that these very parameters display what cannot be stated," and he claims that thinkers like Ferré misunderstand the position since they take "the 'formal features'

---

104. Gilkey, "Theology in Process," 449.
105. Ogden, *Reality of God*, 16.
106. Ogden, *Reality of God*, 17.
107. Tracy, *Blessed Rage*, 188.
108. Tracy, *Blessed Rage*, 188.
109. Burrell, Review of *Reality*, 608.

indicated by the parameters as offering a description of the object."[110] They, thus, confuse an enquiry into what God is not (Aquinas' intention according to Burrell) with an explanation of the divine nature (Aquinas' intention according to process thinkers). Once it is recognized that Aquinas uses predicates like simple, good, limitless and unchangeable "prescriptively but never descriptively" and, therefore, maintains a distinction between grammatical prescription and direct statement, Aquinas, in Burrell's opinion, "appears no more subject to monopolar prejudice or philosophical tenets derived from the Greeks than Hartshorne who insists upon God's abstract divinity."[111] Ogden, following Hartshorne, has criticized a conception of God—"a self-sufficient, all-powerful icon of divinity, set off in solitary splendor"—that is a popular interpretation of Aquinas' position but not the one actually held by Thomas himself.[112] When correctly interpreted, Burell argues, Aquinas' position is remarkably similar to Hartshorne's!

Students of the work of Aquinas must decide upon the adequacy of Burrell's interpretation of that work as "a grammar of divinity,"[113] but Sell is correct to echo the conviction that some process thinkers have not fully acknowledged what the medieval theologians were actually trying to achieve. What Ferré and others give voice to, though, is a conviction that the scholastics were not able to achieve their intentions and have left us with theology beset by fundamental incoherence. Burrell argues that just because Thomas asserts that we cannot speak of God having a real relationship with creatures this in no way implies that he says God has no relation with creatures: "All Thomas wants to say is that God is not causally dependent upon us. It is the gratuity of God's action which is at stake."[114] While denying that God has real relations with the world, Aquinas argues that, through intellect and will, God is *intentionally* related to the creation. God is not *naturally* (and, hence, necessarily) but *freely* related to the world. Process thinkers, however, simply note that Aquinas everywhere assumes that God is a *wholly* necessary being, and then they ask: How can a *wholly* necessary God logically be said to be *freely* related to anything? Because that question cannot be answered satisfactorily, there is good reason to share Tracy's conclusion that the process tradition is more adequate than that of Thomas for interpreting the Christian claim that God is love. This holds even if process thinkers have been rather wooden in their interpretation of Aquinas. That God is a

110. Burrell, *Aquinas*, 79.
111. Burrell, *Aquinas*, 82.
112. Burrell, *Aquinas*, 83.
113. See Burrell, *Aquinas*, 1–11.
114. Burrell, Review of *Reality*, 608.

wholly necessary being is one premise among others to which Aquinas is tied in such a way that it prevents him from fulfilling his theological aims. He cannot give an adequate account of a loving God who is involved with God's creatures because there is no logical reason for the existence of those creatures in the first place, let alone an adequate account of how God is related to them.

A second area of critical concern about Ferré's theology concerns God's ultimacy. Sell asks: "Can there be a becoming apart from a being that becomes?"[115] He maintains that process thought compromises God's self-sufficiency. If "self-sufficiency" implies completeness, is it not the case that in process thought God is "developing" and hence imperfect? Process theism's "God" changes as God is enriched by the events in the world, so Sell concurs with Owen in maintaining that it is "impossible to conceive how 'the most excellent being' (*ens perfectissimum*) could achieve a more excellent state, or how any being could achieve a superior state without thereby becoming a superior being."[116] He agrees with Richmond "that absolute faith, trust and commitment can only be invoked by a Being who is himself absolute in the way described by classical theism."[117] There are two issues here: first, is neoclassical theism's "God" complete and, hence, perfect? And, secondly, is process theism's God capable of evoking "absolute faith, trust and commitment" from us?

The process theism advocated by Ferré insists that, in Ogden's words, "God is 'completely perfect' *in whatever sense these words have any coherent meaning.*"[118] It does not conceive "perfection" in terms of completedness but as unsurpassability or maximum value. Consequently, since God always possesses maximum value or is unsurpassable, save by Godself in future states of God's becoming, neoclassical theism's God is perfect. When critics like Sell suggest that process theism's "God" is incomplete, they are begging the issue concerning whether or not completedness is a property we should predicate of God. Part of the genius of neoclassical theism is the way in which it has challenged the classical "God." Ogden reminds us that it has questioned "whether the very idea of *actus purus*, of the simultaneous actualization of *all* (even incompossible) possibilities of being and value, is not an incoherent idea, given what we mean by 'actuality' and 'possibility.'"[119] At any moment, God is perfect and, hence *ens perfectissimum*, where, of

---

115. *CAM*, 48.
116. Owen, *Christian Knowledge*, 106–7. See also Owen, *Concepts of Diety*, 86.
117. Richmond, "God, Time and Process Philosophy," 240.
118. Ogden, *Reality of God*, 59–60, n97.
119. Ogden, *Reality of God*, 59–60, note 7.

course, "being" is understood dynamically. God always possesses maximum value, but, in future states, God may have acquired more value from the world. God can only be surpassed by Godself: that is "a matter of principle, not simply of fact."[120] To change, grow and increase in value is a positive conception, therefore, which does not threaten God's perfection. When Sell, *pace* Ferré, suggests otherwise his case rests upon a conviction successfully challenged by neoclassical theism, namely, that "change" is a property inappropriate to predicate of God.

But Sell presses the charge that process theism's "God" is not ultimate on the grounds that it is God's "creativity" rather than God's "being" which is ultimate in such theism. He joins Richmond in suggesting that "it appears impossible to attribute real ultimacy to God, because God appears to be at least partly locked within a process for which he is not totally responsible."[121] Richmond seems to be saying that, in Ogden's theology, the process within which God is "at least partly locked" is ultimate, and not, as an adequate theism most hold, God. But Richmond phrases his criticism in a way which suggests a considerable misapplication of the basic tenets of neoclassical metaphysics. For example, he says that Ogden holds that "God is essentially temporal" without taking into account that dipolar theism enables Ogden also to say that God is eternal.[122] Secondly, Richmond describes Ogden's "God" as "moving towards as yet unrealized perfection" implying that until God reaches that "perfection" God is lacking in some way.[123] But, as we have already noted, neoclassical theism asserts that god is "completely perfect" in whatever sense those words possess real meaning. Thirdly, Richmond ought to know that neoclassical theists do not conceive God "locked within a process for which he is not totally responsible." He uses qualifying words like "partly" and "at least," thereby suggesting that he knows Ogden, the subject of his attention, says something far more subtle: God is related necessarily to *some* world of creatures but the particular world to which God is related is the result of God's utterly free decision. The contingency of this world is preserved because there was no necessity that God create *this* world.

Having addressed three fundamental misapplications of the basic tenets of neoclassical theism in Richmond's criticisms of process thought— misapplications neither recognized nor corrected by Sell when bringing forward Richmond as an advocate for his argument—we need only point

---

120. Ogden, *Reality of God*, 59.
121. Richmond, "God, Time and Process Philosophy," 240. Quoted by Sell in *CAM*, 50.
122. Richmond, "God, Time and Process Philosophy," 240.
123. Richmond, "God, Time and Process Philosophy," 240.

out that "creativity" functions in neoclassical theism *as per* "being" in classical theism, and, thereby, show that ultimacy remains with God in process thought. In classical theism "being" is not ontologically prior to God; it is of God's essence. *Mutatis mutandis* "creativity" is not ontologically prior to God in neoclassical theism; it is part of what it means to be God. God is creativity-itself, the chief causative agency of anything and everything. Richmond fails to understand neoclassical theism: talk of God being "locked within a process" suggests pantheistic monism rather than panentheism. In neoclassical theism, the world is contained in God, rather akin to the way cells are included in an organism. The world never exhausts God's being or creativity. To be sure, process theology's "God" is not ultimate if "ultimacy" implies God's complete independence from any and all worlds. Process theists do insist that God necessarily must have *some* world, but they also deny "that there is any being or principle save God alone which is the necessary ground of whatever exists or is even possible."[124] Hence, there are good reasons to suggest that Ferré could defend his position against Sell's charge that it undermines divine ultimacy.

Thirdly, Sell believes that "the idea of a "becoming" God is problematic where worship and devotion are concerned," since "it is hard to worship a God conceived as less than absolute, or ultimate."[125] But it is arguable that Ferré's "God" is far more capable of evoking "worship and devotion" from people than the "God" of the classical alternative defended by Sell, since it is hard to see how the Absolute of classical metaphysics is worthy of evoking any positive religious feelings at all. Classical theism's "God" is completely devoid of real relations with God's creatures, remaining aloof and impassive towards the world, with nothing happening in the world promoting any divine response. God's being and experience is complete. My suffering matters not to God; my joy makes no difference to God. Surely, it is this "God," rather than the "God" of process theism, which is not capable of evoking positive religious feeling in people? As Ogden says curtly, classical theism's God is existentially repugnant.[126] Neoclassical theism, on the other hand, presents a "God" who has real relations with the world. God is not only active but also passive when dealing with the world. Creation makes a difference to God. Hartshorne suggests that perfection means "completely worthy of admiration and respect," before going on to ask whether "such complete admirableness" is "infringed by the possibility of enrichment in

---

124. Ogden, *Reality of God*, 62.
125. *CAM*, 49. See also *PR*, 231.
126. See Ogden, *Reality of God*, 17–19.

total value"?¹²⁷ His answer is correct: "I say it is not.... If God rejoices less today than he will tomorrow, but ideally appropriately at both times, our relevance for him should in no way be affected by the increase in joy."¹²⁸ Neoclassical theism's "God," in envisaging "a God in process of becoming" is "worthy of worship."¹²⁹ There is more to be said for Ferré's "God" than Sell allows.

Sell's criticisms of Ferré reveal rather one-sided and, at times, mistaken interpretations of the neoclassical metaphysics Ferré uses, as well as provide evidence of his begging the question concerning the adequacy of his own position, one which sometimes is found resting upon the premises of classical theism. Nowhere is this more obvious that in Sell's fourth area of concern concerning the adequacy of Ferré's doctrine of God. He asks a very important question: "Does process thought abolish the Creation-creature distinction?"¹³⁰ His own answer is clear, not least because he finds Ferré also departing from what he believes process theologians claim on this issue. Sell credits "process theology" with the claim that "there is no originating creator from whom creation can be distinct."¹³¹ He is not alone, of course, in being critical of process theology concerning the doctrine of creation.

Gunton observes, for example, that "there can . . . be no doctrine of *creation ex nihilo*" in process theology because clearly the world process did not possess a beginning.¹³² If creation is described as the event whereby God, who, up to a particular time, had existed in total solitude, suddenly gave rise to a world of creatures, and, if this is entailed by "a recognizably Christian doctrine of creation,"¹³³ a thinker like Ogden, for example, clearly cannot affirm an important Christian doctrine. But Aquinas himself never insisted upon *creatio ex nihilo* requiring a time before creation. Rather, as Ogden asserts, "what is at stake in [the doctrine of *creatio ex nihilo a deo*] . . . is not the claim that God once existed in lonely isolation, as the Creator of no actual world of creatures" but the denial of the claim "that there is any being or principle save God alone which is the necessary ground of whatever exists or is even possible."¹³⁴ Ogden denies that there was a time when God had no world of any sort; but he insists that, nevertheless, he is affirming the

---

127. Hartshorne, *Divine Relativity*, 47.
128. Hartshorne, *Divine Relativity*, 47.
129. *CAM*, 50.
130. *CAM*, 50.
131. *CAM*, 52.
132. Gunton, *Becoming and Being*, 103.
133. Gunton, "Process Theology's Concept of God," 292–96.
134. Ogden, *Reality of God*, 62.

genuine insight of *creatio ex nihilo a deo*. He insists that God alone exists as the universal necessary cause of all other existence which, being wholly contingent, depends upon God for its being and worth. Of course, according to neoclassical theism, God is not the sole creative agency in the process. The real potentiality of any world lies "in the conjoint actuality of God and of the creatures constituting the precedent actual world (or worlds)."[135] Therefore, while it is impossible for God to exist without *some* world, God, nevertheless, is the source of creative advance, since each occasion, to a greater or lesser degree, actualizes the potential of God by prehending God's subjective aim and making it wholly or partly its own. Fundamentally, the *creatio ex nihilo* formula, according to thinkers like Ogden, is primarily concerned with a universal claim about God which applies to each and every Creator-creature relationship. But this will not satisfy Sell who insists that the idea that God was once without a world is essential for Christian doctrine. Given the limitations of our experience of time, though, it is naïve to assume that "ontological dependence" requires "temporal beginning."

There are, perhaps, three reasons why traditionally theologians have insisted that God created the world out of nothing. First, it is argued that unless there was a time when God existed without any kind of world the existence of the world cannot be accounted for. While process theism can account for the existence of new worlds which arise out of preceding worlds, it cannot account for the existence of the "first" world God must have had at the start of things. All it can say is that *that* world is necessary. The traditional doctrine of creation has always claimed, the argument runs, that the world is the result of the free creation of God. By making it necessary that God even has some world of creatures it is being denied that God is the sole necessary cause of the contingent world, and it is to assert an infinite regress of past events, thereby denying that creation had an absolute beginning in time. But the whole basis of the neoclassical position rests upon a conviction that, in Pittenger's words, "the notion of a 'before creation,' when God existed entirely alone in majestic isolation from some world in which he might creatively work, seems a bit of cosmological nonsense that ought to be dismissed for the absurdity that it is."[136] Gunton struggles to convince us that neoclassical metaphysics is wrong to say that the idea of a beginning of time is self-contradictory.[137] But the idea of a *timeless* deity who is a *wholly* necessary being creating a *wholly* contingent world *in time* remains the problem he leaves us with but never adequately resolves.

135. Ogden, *Reality of God*, 63.
136. Pittenger, *Picturing God*, 69.
137. See Gunton, *Becoming and Being*, 101–5.

Either we accept a neoclassical revision of the Christian doctrine of creation or we solve the problem of saying logically that a wholly necessary being creates a wholly contingent world. Sell is unwilling to do the former, as we shall see more fully later,[138] but moves to achieve the latter in a way which takes us to the heart of the neoclassical case for revision. He tells us that God "willed to create because he is love, and because he desired fellowship with us."[139] Elsewhere he agrees that "it may well be a requirement of God's character as love to *condescend* to sinful humanity" before impressing upon us that "this is far from saying that were there no human beings . . . God could not be."[140] We start to sense that Sell accepts the possibility that within the character of God there exists a divine attribute which necessitates God entering into a relationship with what is other to God. That attribute, of course, is love. Sell even leads us to the point of suggesting that Owen might also have arrived at a similar conclusion, when he sums up Owen's position as follows: "But [God] is also perfect and must therefore be perfect in love, and *this implies an object of love external to the lover.*"[141] Owen, though, seeks to resolve the contradiction of a self-sufficient God who needs "an object of love" in his exposition of the doctrine of the Trinity. But that resolution turns the need for God having an object to love *external* to God into God needing to have self-love totally *internal* to God. Just how that can be squared with the biblical witness to God as love is anybody's guess.

This takes us to a second reason why critics of neoclassical theism maintain that God was once without a world: God's creativity is a product of divine, gracious love and not a matter of necessity. Traditional theologians have always maintained that God creates because of want not need. So Gunton argues that "if love is to be described as love, it must be given freely" and, consequently, he claims that neoclassical theism makes this impossible because God "is bound to be related to all that happens."[142] With Sell, he believes that an adequate Christian doctrine of creation is one which conceives God having no need to create any world. It maintains not so much a Creator-creature distinction as a separation until the first creative act takes place. On the one hand, we have to do justice to the divine self-sufficiency. Sell quotes Owen approvingly: "As pure Spirit [God] does not require any further medium for his self-expression. We cannot call the material world

138. See chapter 4, "Creation, Redemption, and Science."

139. *GOF*, 67. Sell quotes Martensen in making his point: "In a certain sense one may say that God created the world in order to satisfy a want [i.e., lack] in Himself; but the idea of God's love requires us to understand this want as quite truly a *superfluity*."

140. *PICE*, 135.

141. *CCC*, 47. Italics mine.

142. Gunton, *Becoming and Being*, 193.

(even by metaphor) his body; for he made the world out of nothing, and does not need it to complete his being."[143] Therefore, on the classical view, God once existed in isolation from any world, thus guaranteeing that God is not related necessarily to any world since God needs nothing outside God to be God. This supports a view of "love" in which the Cosmic Lover has no need of gain from the act of loving. Hence, God's love is totally free of self-interest because God receives nothing from it. But, on the other hand, an adequate theology must do justice to the conundrum of a perfect self-sufficient God creating graciously and freely. That can be done, *pace* Sell et al, by focusing upon the nature of "love."

When God's love is conceived upon the basis of analogy with human love, it becomes clear that "love" is a *relational* concept. A lover both gives and receives in return; reciprocity is implied. By analogy, God's love is "pure personal relationship" and as such God receives as well as gives.[144] God's love is the perfect coincidence of the maximum benevolence of others and the maximum acceptance of those others as they contribute value to the divine life. Love is a necessary attribute of God; it defines who and what God is: "God is love" (1 John 4:8, 16). If God *is* love, and if love *is* a relational term, it follows that there never could have been a time when God did not have some world to love.

Sell objects to this idea on the ground that God's love is devoid of self-interest. But, Hartshorne argues, such a position "is not good religion but bad metaphysics" claiming that "To will the good of others is the entire positive side of benevolence, and it adds nothing to this to insist that one must *not*, in willing the good of others, find in this good *also* good for one's self."[145] The problem with human love occurs when self-interest determines other-interest, but since God is the perfect co-incidence of both dimensions of love this problem cannot occur for God. It is love, the central feature of God's life, which being relational requires that God have *some* world. A God who could have existed in lonely isolation cannot be the God of whom Scripture speaks. Strange as it may seem, it is Sell and other traditional theologians who are in danger of making it impossible for God to act lovingly and graciously by denying God at *every* moment the only necessary condition God requires for his character being fleshed out—*some* world to love.

A final reason why critics of neoclassical theism maintain that God was once without a world rests upon a claim that the Bible teaches *creatio ex*

---

143. CCC, 47n67.
144. Ogden, *Reality of God*, 68.
145. Hartshorne, *Reality as Social Process*, 139.

nihilo. Psalm 90 opens as follows: "Lord, you have been our dwelling place in all generations. Before the mountains were brought forth, or ever you had formed the earth and the world, from everlasting to everlasting you are God." Supporters of *creatio ex nihilo* might argue that Psalm 90 is one of several biblical passages which presuppose that at one time God existed without a world. It remains debatable, however, whether this particular passage of scripture necessarily implies that doctrine.[146] Persistent critics, however, may refer to the P story of creation (Genesis 1–2:4a), claiming that this passage gives clear evidence that a biblical doctrine of creation presupposes the doctrine of *creatio ex nihilo*. Gerhard von Rad accepts that *bārā'* ("create") in Genesis 1–11 "contains the idea" of *creatio ex nihilo*; but he acknowledges that "the theological thought [of the P story] moves not so much between the poles of nothingness and creation as between the poles of chaos and cosmos."[147] Nevertheless, he insists that it would be wrong to say that the idea of *creatio ex nihilo* was not present at all in the P creation story because "v.1 stands with good reason before v.2!"[148] Sell, though, places his emphasis upon a passage from the Apocrypha, where Maccabeus' mother is found speaking to her son: "I beg you, my child, to look at the heaven and the earth and see everything that is in them, and recognize that God did not make them out of things that existed" (2 Macc 7:28). It leads him to "a summary statement: creation is *ex nihilo*. It is the free work of the sovereign God of holy love whom we know in Christ. It did not involve the shaping of already existing materials; it is not a question of emanation, or of teamwork."[149] But, in view of von Rad's caution, I venture the alternative suggestion made by Pittenger that, "in the Genesis creation myth," as well as in other parts of the Bible, "talk about some aboriginal chaos might very well be interpreted as a poetic statement of an early Hebrew insight which refused ever to think of God as without a world."[150]

Westermann makes two important observations regarding the Genesis creation stories. First, he reminds us that those narratives do not address intellectual questions asking after a first cause to account for the universe's existence, but rather seek to answer the *existential* questions facing people living in a hostile environment.[151] Actually, the idea of God as first cause, Westermann informs us, was read into and not out of the Bible

---

146. See Anderson, *Book of Psalms*, 650 and Bultmann, "Idea of God," 93.
147. von Rad, *Genesis*, 49, 51.
148. von Rad, *Genesis*, 51.
149. *GOF*, 65.
150. Pittenger, *Picturing God*, 69.
151. See Westermann, *Creation*, 11.

"under the influence of medieval philosophy."[152] The Genesis stories cannot *in principle* provide normative theological evidence to support the idea of a wholly necessary God who freely decides to break out of lonely isolation to create a wholly contingent world. Those narratives are concerned with human existential plight and not questions concerning the universe's origin. And if this is not enough of a riposte to those who advance the notion of *creatio ex nihilo* on biblical grounds, Westermann's second observation puts the matter beyond reasonable doubt. He asks us to recognize the plurality of the Old Testament's statements concerning creation: "The conclusion is that the Old Testament did not limit itself to one definite way of presenting Creation which was the only correct one, but allowed different ways of presentation to stand side by side."[153] Even Sell has to admit that the doctrine of *creatio ex nihilo* "is not taught in so many words in the Bible" though he offers the qualification that "*many* scholars believe that it is clearly *implicit* there."[154] Whatever the strength of the word "many," it is at least doubtful whether that doctrine is *explicitly* taught by scripture. Further, other strands of scripture (e.g., the J creation story [Gen 2:4b–25] and the Prologue of John's Gospel [John 1:1–3]) actually suggest models of creation that support process thought's alternative position. The Bible, therefore, does not offer *conclusive* evidence one way or another to give an authoritative basis for Sell's position. In any case, a doctrine needs to be credible as well as appropriate to scripture. We will consider the *credibility* of Sell's classical understanding of creation later in this study.[155]

The fifth and final strand of criticism Sell makes of Ferré's use of process thought centers upon the question: "Is transcendence displaced by immanence in process thought?"[156] We have already discussed at length the way in which transcendence and immanence are held together as polar opposites in the dipolar panentheism of neoclassical metaphysics: God is *always* the self-surpassing surpasser of all. If Sell had interpreted neoclassical theism in an even-handed way he would have had to acknowledge that transcendence is *not* displaced by immanence in the best examples of process thought. Process thinkers are as concerned as he is to hold together divine attributes which need keeping together. But whereas process thinkers work out the relationship between them *ontologically*, Sell insists that they must also be understood *morally*. He believes that "The process theolo-

---

152. Westermann, *Creation*, 22.
153. Westermann, *Creation*, 115.
154. *GOF*, 63. Italics mine.
155. See chapter 4, "Creation, Redemption, and Science."
156. *CAM*, 52.

gians have not . . . succeeded where all others failed in bringing God near" because they have failed to understand God's transcendence "as a matter of his character as holy."[157] It is in the Christ event that the true model of the Creator-creature relationship is found: it is a unique revelation of "the immanence of the transcendent holy God, who graciously redeems in an act which nature (including humanity) could neither have imagined nor undertaken."[158] Once again we encounter the way in which Sell's soteriology underpins the rest of his theology. The adequacy of Sell's theology always turns on the adequacy of his understanding of God's saving work.[159]

THE DIVINE ATTRIBUTES

Sell admits that our attempts to conceive God will fall short; but, unless we are to remain silent concerning the One before whom we live and who alone warrants our ultimate devotion, we are bound to make an attempt. All our *theo*logical work is underpinned by the rather sobering fact that "our analogies fail in the last resort because Godhead is unique."[160] For Sell, the most important claim to be made about God is that God is holy love. This particular divine attribute plays a crucial role in Sell's account of Christ's person and work. But Sell also conceives God by using many of the traditional attributes of the classical theological tradition. In *God Our Father*, for example, he lays out a collection of them: "The one God is self sufficient, or independent . . . he requires nothing in order to make him complete";[161] "God is eternal and immutable";[162] "God is omnipresent";[163] and "God is omniscient."[164] And, as we have learned, Sell resisted invitations to re-envisage such divine attributes using the tenets of neoclassical metaphysics. He was thoroughly committed to the view that "the absolute is psychologically and ontologically necessary to Christian faith."[165] We, in turn, have put forward reasons to doubt the wisdom of such a commitment. Given what has already been said about the divine attributes, we can restrict this particular discussion to three areas: one raises acute issues concerning

157. *CCF*, 167.
158. *CCF*, 181.
159. See chapter 5, "The Work of Christ."
160. *SOL*, 100.
161. *GOF*, 47.
162. *GOF*, 48.
163. *GOF*, 51.
164. *GOF*, 52.
165. *PICB*, 118.

Sell's commitment to the classical tradition, while the other two provide us with examples of the way in which he is not *totally* bound by that tradition.

Sell accepts the classical view concerning God's omniscience: "Since he is eternal, he knows all things from eternity (Acts 15:18). He knows past, present and future; he sees the end from the beginning."[166] This, as he readily acknowledges, presents him with a puzzle concerning "God's omniscience *which, it would seem, must include his foreknowledge,* and our freedom to act or not to act."[167] If God knows my every move from my birth to death in what real sense of "freedom" can I be said to be a human being? Sell's response to this puzzle starts with him inviting us to recognize that "If we speak of God's foreknowledge . . . we must realize that we are drawing an analogy from our experience, and that this analogy, while it enables us to avoid utter silence, does not entirely encompass its object."[168] Being outside time, God lives in the eternal "now" of past, present and future, so strictly speaking, *fore*knowledge is inapplicable. It is not unusual, though, for philosophers to maintain that it is possible to hold together divine foreknowledge and human freedom without contradiction. Amidst his work on J. S. Mill, Sell records Mill replying to W. G. Ward: "I am not aware of having ever said that foreknowledge is inconsistent with free will. That knotty metaphysical question I have avoided entering into, & in my Logic I have even built upon the admissions of free will philosophers that our freedom be real though God foreknows our actions."[169] This matter, as we shall see, is of great significance in the doctrine of election.[170] But Sell is quite prepared to leave the puzzle unresolved. After pointing out that denial of divine omniscience to protect human freedom only results in "a free-wheeling universe" which "needs no God"[171] he lamely admits that it is beyond human ken how to hold together divine foreknowledge and human freedom without tension. It is surprising that he does not critique a fellow URC theologian's treatment of this issue. John Hick argues that the compelling power of divine love will in the end win over everyone, thereby putting a modern twist on the old idea of God's "irresistible" grace. But the universalism entailed by Hick's position would not have found favor with Sell.[172] Of course, if Sell had allowed for genuine, *internal* relations between God and the world in his

---

166. *GOF*, 53.
167. *GOF*, 53. Italics mine.
168. *GOF*, 53.
169. *MOG*, 42.
170. See chapter 9, "The Doctrine of Election."
171. *GOF*, 53.
172. See Hick, *Death and Eternal Life*, 242–46.

construal of the Creator-creature relationship—and, most of the time, in his theism, that relationship appears to involve "separation" rather than to rest upon a "distinction"—then the puzzle can be resolved. "Omniscience" is a pseudo-concept: God has knowledge of all things at any one time, but, given that there will be more to know as the cosmic process evolves, the divine knowledge will be more extensive in the future that it is now. Nevertheless, at all times, God's knowledge is perfect because God will know all that it is possible to know. My free decisions contribute to God's life, mostly bringing God pain due to my sinful ineptitude and activity but hopefully at times some modicum of joy. Since I reside in a *two-way* relationship with God my life has "ultimate meaning."[173]

Moving to the second issue, we must remind ourselves of Sell's methodology. He maintains that to understand God we should first and foremost turn to God's self-revelation in Jesus. Paul quotes an ancient Christian hymn which asserts that Jesus Christ, "though he was in the form of God, did not regard equality with God as something to be exploited, but emptied himself, taking the form of a slave, being born in human likeness" (Phil 2:6–7). The word "emptied" comes from the Greek *kenoō*. It has given rise to a distinctive understanding of the incarnation called *kenotic* christology, whereby the condescension of God to become a human being in Jesus is explained. God "empties" Godself of divine attributes to take on a human nature. In keeping with Forsyth, Sell affirms that it is "difficult to conceive how kenoticism . . . can be left out of any satisfactory Christology."[174] He acknowledges that some varieties of kenoticism must be avoided, but he remains committed to the concept.[175] In Jesus Christ, we see evidence of God limiting Godself so that God can appear in the world of time and space. A divine self-renunciation, therefore, is at the heart of the incarnation. It follows that "this entails [the Lord's] willing curtailment of certain aspects of his divinity."[176] The Incarnate Son of God, *in some sense*, is not omnipotent, omniscient or omnipresent. Whether such attributes were literally "given up" or merely "veiled" during the incarnation is a contested issue among practitioners of kenotic christology. But, at the very least, Sell's position involves him accepting that *kenotic* love is of the very essence of God. If that is correct, it is very difficult indeed to see how this supreme theological truth can be expressed adequately by the conceptuality of classical theism. Its static concepts ill serve talk of real, mutual love.

---

173. Hartshorne, *Omnipotence*, 27.
174. *DAD*, 189.
175. Sell's christology will be developed more fully in chapter 5.
176. *DAD*, 191.

God

Following on from this we turn to the matter of God's impassibility. The early church Fathers condemned what became known as *patripassianism*, a modalist view of the divine Trinity which states that, if Christ is God, and therefore identical with the Father, since Christ suffered on the cross, the Father also suffered. They insisted that God was unable to suffer due to the divine impassibility, maintaining that distinctions within the Godhead between Father, Son and Spirit must be made. This enabled a prevailing orthodox view to emerge which, while admitting that the Son suffered, claims the Father did not. More recently *patripassianism* has come to refer to views which maintain that God takes the sufferings of the world into the divine experience and, thereby, is affected by them. Classical theists like Owen, for example, regard this as heretical. He argues that "All Christians can agree on these propositions: that God, out of his infinite love for us, suffered in our nature on our behalf; that if he suffers in his divine nature his sufferings, being wholly imaginative and vicarious in relation to a created order that is wholly distinct from him, cannot change him . . . for better or worse; and that, if he thus suffers, what finally matters for us is the transfiguration of his sufferings by his eternal joy."[177] This leaves us with the grotesque picture of a God who sends his Son into the world on *the* redemptive mission, but for whom the Son's suffering on the cross is either imaginary or vicarious. Throughout God the Father continues to enjoy eternal bliss.

Sell, for once, disagrees with Owen and classical theism on this matter. He suggests that "there is much to be said for the view that God is not impassible."[178] While he makes no mention of this in his treatment of the divine attributes in *God Our Father*,[179] it is very clear from later books that he departs from the classical tradition in holding that God can and does suffer.[180] He applauds Duthie's attempt to center theology upon "a God who suffers and triumphs through suffering," believing that it is due to "this later fact, *and because God knows all things from the beginning*," that we have no "need to fear that God's passibility ultimately interferes with his external bliss; on the contrary, it is his chosen route towards the securing of his own and his people's ultimate happiness."[181] Sell knows that "there is widespread agreement" that "God the Son suffers" but he adds the all-important rhetorical question: "if the Father is not suffering alongside him, how can we any longer maintain that in a deep sense each person of the Trinity is involved

---

177. Owen, *Christian Theism*, 111. Quoted by Sell in *CCC*, 52.
178. *TEM*, 141.
179. See *GOF*, 48–51.
180. See *CCC*, 48–53; *HT*, 606–10; and *TEM*, 139–41.
181. *HT*, 609. Italics mine.

in the acts of all?"¹⁸² God *qua* God, not just God *qua* Son, suffers. Sell is applying a basic principle of Trinitarian theology: "each person of the Trinity is involved in the acts of all."¹⁸³ He clearly centers his conclusions about God's suffering on the Christ event. But, we may ask, what of God's suffering before and after it? When Bonhoeffer declared that "The Bible directs man to God's powerlessness and suffering; only the suffering God can help,"¹⁸⁴ many believe that he was speaking about a general feature of God on the basis of the particular incident of the cross. This theme has been taken up by theologians as diverse as Moltmann, Küng, and the process theologians. They all point to the suffering of God on the cross as *paradigmatic* of the divine nature concerning the entire world's suffering. And, it can be argued, such thinkers go much further than Sell in presenting *conceptually* how we can coherently speak of whom Whitehead calls "the fellow sufferer who understands;"¹⁸⁵ what Garvie refers to as God's "omnipatience," God's sympathy with our experiences;¹⁸⁶ or, more generally, what is involved in talking about God in terms of the divine response to the world's life. Be that as it may, Sell is wise to resist the temptation to use an *essentialist* Trinitarian distinction to reconcile the reality of Christ's suffering with the doctrine of patripassianism.

GOD: ONE IN THREE AND THREE IN ONE

The doctrine of the Trinity is of fundamental importance in Sell's theology. As we have seen, he was extremely critical of theologians who find it impossible to do full justice to crucial Christian doctrines like the Trinity and atonement due to the constraints imposed upon them by their adoption of "alien" philosophies like idealism or empiricism. One senses Trinitarian doctrine becoming more explicit in Sell's theology when reading his work sequentially. This may have been a response to the way in which the doctrine of the Trinity became central to the work of a group of English theologians towards the end of the twentieth century. He acknowledges that "No Nonconformist theologian did more in the last two decades of the twentieth century to place the Trinity in the centre of theological debate than Colin

---

182. *HT*, 610.
183. *CCC*, 53.
184. Bonhoeffer, *Letters and Papers*, 361.
185. Whitehead, *Process and Reality*, 351.
186. See Garvie, *Christian Doctrine*, 246: "God feels with and in all His sentient creatures. It is thus the whole of God as personal which is wholly present in the universe."

Gunton."[187] And, with an important reservation we will note later, Sell approved of Gunton's achievement of putting the Trinity at the center of theological discussion.

Sell finds the root of the doctrine of the Trinity in Christian experience rather than metaphysical speculation.[188] He tells us that "the doctrine was only developed and defended because it speaks of those practical realities of which Christians are bound to take into account."[189] He develops his point by asking some rhetorical questions:

> Who else could save sinners but a gracious *God*, and who else would feel the need to save them but a holy *God*? Who but *God* the Son could offer once and for all, on the stage of history, the "full, perfect and sufficient" sacrifice which we could never make? And who but *God* the Holy Spirit could take the scales from our eyes, import new life, and keep us in fellowship with the Father through the Son, and with all Christ's people, eternally?[190]

Sell's reflection upon the atonement drives him to affirm that it is "the glorious work of the one holy and undivided Trinity."[191] While Trinitarian doctrine therefore is the *culmination* of reflection upon Christian experience, it is also the very *presupposition* of Christian theology.[192]

Trinitarian doctrine grew out of the early Christians' testimony that God had made Godself known to them in Jesus Christ through the work of the Holy Spirit. As Sell puts it, "the doctrine of the Trinity grew out of the experience of the Trinity."[193] While there are "pointers" or "clues" to the doctrine in the New Testament, it only became more fully worked out conceptually through subsequent theological debate in the church's life. The doctrine is "not contrary to reason" but "fully to comprehend" it "is beyond our reasoning powers."[194] When considering "the inner life of the Godhead" Sell remains on "the side of godly agnosticism."[195] Our Christian experience may well drive us to affirm the *economic* Trinity, God as God reveals Godself

---

187. *NT*, 81. For Gunton's position, see, in addition to works already cited, *Enlightenment and Alienation*.

188. See *CAM*, 147.

189. *SOL*, 100.

190. *SOL*, 100.

191. *SOL*, 100.

192. See *SOL*, 97 and *PICB*, 221.

193. *SOL*, 98.

194. *HT*, 24.

195. *HT*, 185.

to us; and we will want to say that as God is revealed to us so God is in God's inner life (the *essential or immanent* Trinity); but beyond that important inference reason cannot take us. When it comes to knowledge concerning the inner relations of the Godhead, Sell avoids speculation. We have no means of knowing what is going on in God's inner life. In acknowledging that we can truly experience and apprehend God, but never fully understand God, Sell is rehearsing "the theme so popular among Puritan writers."[196]

Sell is on firm ground in his account of the origins of the doctrine of the Trinity. As he reminds us, "Experience, rather than debate and cognition, was at the bottom of it all."[197] It was a discovery of believers rather than the work of professional theologians who sat down to lay out a treatise on the doctrine of God. Secondly, Sell is correct to warn us about the inadequacy of the traditional analogies used to explain the doctrine of the Trinity. Whether they come from human experience (e.g., the analogy of body, mind and soul in an individual), or nature (e.g., the three petals of a clover leaf), or mathematics (e.g., the three sides of a perfect triangle), they all finally break down: "These illustrations speak of three parts which together make a whole, but they do not speak of a common essence which is completely present in all the parts."[198] And, of course, the belief that all *three* members of the Trinity are present in the activity of *each* member is an essential feature of Christian orthodoxy. Nevertheless, those who remain mystified by the intricacies of Trinitarian theology will be relieved to learn from Sell that "competence in Trinitarian exposition has never been a condition of entry to the kingdom of heaven."[199] Thirdly, and finally, Sell is wise to advocate the shrewd policy of "godly agnosticism" concerning what we can know about the workings of God's inner-life. He chides Vine, for example, with seeming to know "more about things divine than I [Alan Sell] think are knowable;" and he finds "present-day expounders of the Trinity" similarly at fault: they "seem to project upon the Trinity those characteristics of the divine community that they deem appropriate, and then proceed to draw inferences therefrom regarding the right workings of the empirical Church."[200] Sell quotes Gunton as an example: "The Church is called to

---

196. *FPA*, 125.

197. *SOL*, 98.

198. *SOL*, 97.

199. *NT*, 177. This soteriological observation may go some way to accounting for the extent to which Sell delves into Unitarianism in his historical forays, as well as the even-handed way he deals with it; so much so that contemporary Unitarian historians counted him among their friends.

200. *CAC*, 171n226.

be the kind of reality at a finite level that God is in eternity."[201] But Sell is adamant that it is inappropriate to "extrapolate, or draw analogies, from the inferred inner fellowship of the members of the 'social' Trinity to the fellowship of the Church."[202] Then casting a wry smile in Gunton's direction, he says: "I very much welcome the renewed attention to the Trinity, though I am made to feel very inferior by those writers who know so much about the inner workings and relations of the persons of the Trinity that they can draw analogies as to how the empirical Church should be conducting itself."[203]

---

201. The quotation is from Hardy and Gunton, *On Being the Church*, and is used by Sell in *HT*, 590.

202. *HT*, 411.

203. *CTF*, 287.

4

Creation

We turn now to an analysis, interpretation and criticism of Sell's doctrine of creation.

CREATION, REDEMPTION, AND SCIENCE

What is very striking about Sell's theological writings is the lack of references to creation compared to the voluminous attention paid to redemption. This is surprising in view of his commitment to having *general* as well as *special* revelation play a role in his theology. Sell maintains that creation *was*—note the tense—"an act of grace."[1] It was the wholly gratuitous gift of a self-sufficient divine Being. Although God had no need of a world, God freely created one, not for Godself's benefit, but the world's. It was created by God *ex nihilo*. Other than this Sell has surprisingly little to say about creation.[2]

This is quite remarkable given that the origin and nature of the created order has been a battleground upon which the conflicts between religion and science have raged over the centuries. When theologians turn a blind eye to knowledge that compromises their claims they are at the top of a slippery slope which often leads to those claims subsequently being dismissed as untrue. Consider the unease with which the discoveries of Galileo and Darwin were received by some parts of the Christian community and quite often its theologians. This is hardly surprising given what was at stake: in

---

1. *GOF*, 16.
2. The only place where Sell deals with creation substantively is in *GOF*, 57–71.

Creation

Galileo's case a threat was made to the Aristotelian framework upon which contemporary Christianity was based; while Darwin's discoveries led to questions concerning biblical literalism, the authority of Christian revelation, and the nature and dignity of human beings. And, if simplifications of complex stories are allowed, each instance led to significant revisions to the prevailing theological orthodoxy. It proved impossible to keep science apart from religion, not least because both are concerned with the same reality—the *natural* or *created* order (depending upon whether one is a secular scientist or Christian theologian respectively). Although they approach it from different angles, science and religion share a concern about a world they hold in common.

It is Sell's conviction, though, that "The Christian doctrine of creation cannot conflict with natural science."[3] They are concerned with different lines of enquiry which potentially at least can be seen to overlap. Science deals with "the when and how of creation,"[4] while religion is concerned with its ultimate cause and purpose. He tells us that "Science deals with causal relationships within the natural order, and that is precisely what the doctrine of *creation* is not about."[5] But if God's creativity is not just conceived in terms of "once upon a time," but also includes recognition of on-going and current involvement in the world, then, arguably, it can best be thought of as a divine engagement with the "causal relationships within the natural order." We can agree with Sell that "Evolution presupposes the existence of something that evolves; it does not tell us the origin of that something."[6] But, given the way in which nature evolves through self-creation, we are caught up in Deism unless we posit some measure and form of divine activity *within* the world. Sell's construal of the relationship between religion and science is, therefore, inadequate. The "what is the case" concerns of science regarding the *structure* of reality have a direct bearing upon how theologians can most adequately conceive God's involvement in the world. Religion therefore needs to take scientific findings into account lest some of its claims be dismissed as incredible. The theologian should seek to provide an "overall understanding" in which "scientific discoveries are to be regarded as part of the data which it has to examine critically and then seek to incorporate in that overall understanding, together with other data provided by more commonly accepted sources of religious insight."[7]

3. *GOF*, 61.
4. *GOF*, 61.
5. *GOF*, 62.
6. *GOF*, 62.
7. Pailin, *Groundwork*, 123.

Some might have wished, therefore, to have seen Sell joining those "late nineteenth and early twentieth-century Nonconformist theologians" who, he records, came to use the concept of evolution as a model for "God's providential method of working."[8]

The basic reason Sell is reluctant to do this concerns his insistence that a fundamental distinction between the Creator and creation must be maintained. Otherwise, he believes, anthropocentric rather than theocentric factors come to dominate the doctrine of creation, and, in this case, evolutionary ideas usurp those of religion. The result, of course, is that he ends up operating within a framework for the God-world relationship which prioritizes "disjunction" rather than "connectedness" between God and the world. Gordon Kendall questions whether disjunction should have "the ultimate word . . . If God is in control, and if our hope in ultimate victory is assured, there is inescapably a sense in which for Christian experience unity must be prior to difference."[9] A caveat is in order here lest we fail to recognize the gravity of sin: complete unity will be unknown this side of eternity.

We noted earlier Sell's commitment to the doctrine of *creatio ex nihilo*. Keith Ward reminds us that "Aquinas noted, quite correctly, that this idea does not entail that the world had a beginning in time, or that it will have an end in time."[10] What it does teach us, though, is that whatever world exists depends "solely and at every moment upon the power of God for its being, whereas God depends upon nothing, but is self-determining."[11] Like me, and *pace* Sell, Ward challenges the traditional concept of God's self-sufficiency. He argues that "the perfection of the Divine nature lies, not in its infinite self-satisfaction, but in its self-giving love."[12] Elsewhere he tells us that "if [God] is the infinitely dynamic creator and eternal lover, he must create some finite world of persons" and "there must always be some such world, or perhaps an endless succession of such worlds."[13] God possesses *positive* freedom to create world A rather than world B, but not the *negative* freedom which would allow God not to create *some* world. Having chosen to create a world which has self-determination built into it, and that has evolved to include rational creatures, it is clear that God has been involved in an act of *self*-limitation.

---

8. *PDN*, 203
9. Kendall, Review of *PICB*, 775.
10. Ward, *Rational Theology*, 72.
11. Ward, *Rational Theology*, 72–73.
12. Ward, *Rational Theology*, 82.
13. Ward, *Divine Action*, 36.

Creation

We can detect here echoes of that theological language usually associated with *kenotic* christology. Sell recognized that it is "difficult to conceive how kenoticism . . . can be left out of any satisfactory christology."[14] Given that Sell regards the incarnation, understood in terms of its soteriological significance, as the paradigm for understanding God, ought not the concept of *kenosis* be applied to God: the Creator as well as God: the Redeemer? Garvie, for example, postulates an eternal activity of self-limitation in the Godhead which becomes the necessary condition not only for the incarnation but also for God's manifestation in the whole cosmic process. Therefore, "the Incarnation is the supreme instance of an activity of God which is illustrated by all creation; it is only by self-limitation that the Infinite can create within time and space a finite and changing world."[15] Then, using the concept of *plerosis* (Eph 1:23), Garvie argues that the divine self-emptying leads to a form of self-expression in the world which is God's self-fulfillment. Not only does God achieve the divine purpose by self-emptying rooted in love, the Deity also derives joy when that love is returned. Garvie is critical of understandings of love which eschew the thought that God desires a response in personal relationship from those loved. For him love is a relational term, "a personal interchange, a giving as well as a receiving, a finding as well as a losing oneself in another."[16]

Forsyth also attributed *kenosis* to the creative as well as the redeeming activity of God.[17] It is not clear whether Sell followed his mentor here as elsewhere.[18] But this position is not universally accepted in Reformed circles. Gunton, for example, believes that "the continuity of redemption with the act of creation is not . . . best expressed by the concept of kenosis, which concerns rather the shape God's saving involvement in *fallen* time and space must necessarily take."[19] I prefer to avoid making such a sharp disjunction between God's creative and providential activity. It is much better to view

---

14. *DAD*, 189. In *CCF*, he declares, "The Christological teaching derivable from Philippians 2 comes to mind as being among the sublimest statements of the truth I am seeking, however falteringly to express" (180).

15. Garvie, *Christian Doctrine*, 20.

16. Garvie, *Christian Ideal*, 204.

17. See Forsyth, *Person and Place*, 314. For discussion of Forsyth's use of kenotic christology, see Floyd, "Work of Christ."

18. Floyd tells us that Forsyth's kenotic christology "attempts to explain the mystery of the incarnation and the inner workings of the atonement without using the metaphysical language of which he was so suspicious." ("Work of Christ," 148.) Sell, of course, refrained from eschewing metaphysics.

19. Gunton, *Christ and Creation*, 85.

creation as "continuing creation." Once this is done any sharp disjunction between the divine creative and redeeming activity is out of place.

Gunton maintains that God is essentially defined by self-giving love of others, while at the same time affirms God's self-sufficiency and hence denies that some world of others is necessary for God. He is caught up in what Keith Ward calls "the old dilemma" which "has been sufficient to impale the vast majority of Christian philosophers down the ages."[20] He seeks resolution of it in God's triune love of others, whereby the necessary "others" God loves are the members of the Trinity rather than anything outside God's triune life. But all such attempts to meet an insistence upon there being a time when God existed without a world are subject to serious objections. Ogden puts them as follows: "For either God's love of Godself as triune preserves the essential truth of the fundamental presupposition of radical monotheism, in which case God is one and God's love of Godself is merely self-love rather than also love of others; or else God's love of Godself as triune really is love of others and not merely of self, in which case the essential truth of radical monotheism is lost by affirming a monotheism that is only verbally distinguishable from tritheism."[21]

By way of a conclusion to this stage of our exploration of Sell's doctrine of creation three points are worthy of being underscored. First, Sell unnecessarily drives a wedge between "creation" and "redemption" when they are better viewed as different ways of talking about one holistic divine activity. Another way of making the point is to eschew talk of a *qualitative* difference between God's *general* revelation through the *natural* created order and God's *special* revelation through the *super*natural Christ event. Sell was determined to avoid any "ghettoization" of the Christian faith, but to achieve his aim he ought to have placed as much emphasis on creation as he did on redemption. Secondly, Sell remains tied to a view which prevents him overcoming "the old dilemma" associated with positing appropriately both freedom and necessity to God. Once God's self-giving love is regarded as an essential property of God, it follows that self-sufficiency cannot, in one sense, be predicated of God: God always needs *some kind of* world to love. But, of course, just what kind of world God freely chooses to create is not bound by necessity. Given God's respect for the autonomy of creation, a world created through evolution is precisely the kind of world which fulfills God's purposes. Therefore, as Ward says, "God's actions will be constrained immensely by his antecedent decision to leave relevant human freedoms intact, and to permit . . . millions of creaturely decisions to play a large part in

---

20. Ward, *Rational Theology*, 73.
21. Ogden, *Understanding of Christian Faith*, 41.

determining what happens in the world."²² Thirdly, the evolutionary nature of creation suggests not only a requirement to dispense with a view of God's creative activity centered upon a fixed moment in the past, but also that we conceive it as ongoing within the natural order. This involves avoiding any unnecessary demarcations between what was traditionally referred to as "creation," "preservation" and "redemption" or "re-creation."

THE NATURE AND VOCATION OF HUMAN BEINGS

When theologians have reflected upon the nature, position, and place of human beings in the world their starting point has usually been the Genesis account of creation. They have derived their understanding of human beings and the relationship of men and women to God, each other, and the natural world from that story's account of God's creative activity on the sixth day (Gen 1:27–28). From this profoundly suggestive myth particular attention has been paid to the claims that human beings have been created in God's image (*imago Dei*) and that God has given human beings the responsibility to "subdue" the earth and "have dominion over" all the living creatures. The former set of reflections provides us with insight into the nature of human beings, while the latter set helps us come to an understanding of their vocation. We will deal with each in turn.

The Nature of Human Beings

The Genesis witness to people being born in God's image is central to Sell's understanding of human beings. He says that we will not "get our thinking straight on humanity unless we see people as creatures, children, and potential sons and daughters of God."²³ Stamped at birth with the *imago Dei* human beings are graciously given a distinctive nature, one which means that every person ought to be treated as having more than instrumental value. They are special to God and uniquely precious in God's sight. As Jesus said: "And even the hairs of your head are all counted" (Matt 10:30). In other words, human identity is shaped by men and women being born in a relationship with God. What happens to the status of that relationship through human sin is a question that will concern us shortly, but we get a hint of Sell's answer when he asserts that "man is only distinctively man at all be-

---

22. Ward, *Divine Action*, 132.
23. *COS*, 89.

cause—whether he knows it or not, whether he likes it or not—he stands right down to the innermost core and essence of his being, in the profoundest possible relationship to God all the time in an order of persons."[24]

Two further insights concerning the nature of human beings flow from Sell's reflections on the *imago Dei* theme. First, given that human beings are created in God's image, they can have knowledge of God. Sell says that "although God is distinct from the things he creates, not least from us, he is not utterly divorced from us."[25] All human beings can know God. This is the basis upon which a natural theology can be pursued. It provides for "epistemological" continuity between Christians and those of other Faiths or none.[26] Sell believes that a *sensus divinitatus* exists in all human beings; it is "non-expungeable."[27] Secondly, Sell argues that being created in God's image carries with it an awareness of God's claim upon our lives.[28] In response to God's graciousness in creating us only "a little lower than God" (Ps 8:5) we are summoned to live lives of gratitude to God. Such lives are engendered in us by the work of the Holy Spirit. We learn to live in response to God's gracious love towards us, the obedient children of a loving Parent; or, as the Apostle Paul puts it, "When we cry, "Abba! Father!" it is that very Spirit bearing witness with our spirit that we are children of God" (Rom 8:15b–16).

Just what we make of human nature through focusing upon the *imago Dei* motif, of course, depends very much upon how we perceive God. The range of options for envisaging God is vast. Whitehead reminds us that in the history of Christianity we have seen God pictured after the image of "the ruling Caesar, or the ruthless moralist, or the unmoved mover."[29] He contrasts such perceptions with what he calls "The brief Galilean vision of humility" which has "flickered throughout the ages, uncertainly" and "dwells upon the tender elements in the world, which slowly and in quietness operate by love."[30] Sell, of course, was no Whiteheadian, but he would have recognized the contrast being made. For him, the proper way to understand God is to center upon God's self-revelation in Jesus Christ. In the life, death, and resurrection of Jesus we witness "the proper man," the perfect example

---

24. *COS*, 89.
25. *COS*, 91.
26. See *CCF*, 299 and *EEE*, 297.
27. *CCF*, 222. See also *CTF*, 135.
28. See *DAD*, 192–93.
29. Whitehead, *Process and Reality*, 343.
30. Whitehead, *Process and Reality*, 343 and 344.

of a person born in the image of God.[31] God is disclosed to us in Jesus as holy love. We are drawn, therefore, to a perception of God based on parenthood, one in which nurture, care, guidance, and responsibility carry great weight, while conversely control, domination, and rule by fiat are eschewed. Such a vision of God has not universally held sway in Western Christianity. Its absence may have contributed to the way human beings have treated one another and the natural world, which has often left a great deal to be desired.

The Vocation of Human Beings

As we have become more aware of global warming, ecological disasters, and the environmental threat caused by humankind's often selfish and cavalier use of the natural world, it is hardly surprising that theologians have pointed to the dangers of grounding a Christian anthropology in biblical injunctions to "subdue" the earth and have "dominion over the fish of the sea and over the birds of the air and over every living thing that moves upon the earth." It is a moot point whether such biblical commands actually played a totally dominating role in establishing the anthropocentric view of creation which has underwritten the way some human beings have exploited the natural order to the point that the planet's very survival is now threatened. But, at the very least, they will not have helped. Nor must we forget that for many people down the centuries life has been a struggle for mere existence in the wake of nature's uneven provisions and often frightening terror. Those who claim that ecological concerns are a privilege of the well-to-do who are in a position to respond to the call to live more simply make an important point. What is certain, however, is that the full potency of human hubris is displayed in the way Western civilization has so emphasized the "specialness" of human beings that the earth has been demeaned. Sell knew all this full well. What is now required is a fundamental change of outlook: from an anthropocentric to a theocentric Christian anthropology.

The starting point for such an anthropology lies in an exegesis of Genesis 1:1—2:4b which establishes beyond peradventure that earlier assumptions about the meaning of "dominion" are utterly erroneous. This involves challenging previous homocentric interpretations. Westermann and Brueggemann, for example, suggest that the Genesis creation narratives witness as much to the symbiotic unity of human beings and the rest of the created order as to their important differences. Westermann asserts that in Genesis 1 "humanity was created by God to rule over the rest of creation."[32]

31. COS, 78.
32. Westermann, *Genesis 1–11*, 157.

The only question concerns the nature of this "rule." We are drawn to an appropriate answer when we accept that "Dominion over the animals certainly does not mean their exploitation by humans.... The second part of v.26 gives us to understand that it is the attitude of humans towards other living beings that should characterize the human attitude to the world about them; and this means a markedly *personal* attitude."[33] Both Westermann and Brueggemann set the term "dominion" in the context of the Old Testament picture of a shepherd king.[34] Hence "the task of 'dominion' does not have to do with exploitation and abuse"; rather, "It has to do with securing the well-being of every other creature and bringing the promise of each to full fruition."[35] The one who rules does not lord it over others since "Lordship means servanthood."[36] Brueggemann actually attributes to the Genesis text "an inverted view of humanness. *This* man and woman are not the chattel and servants of God, but the agents of God to whom much is given and from whom much is expected."[37] One could say, using language which would resonate with Sell, that human beings and God are set in a *covenantal* relationship, albeit one frequently broken from the human side.[38]

Moltmann argues that while, in the first Genesis creation story, human beings are created last, and thus are "the apex of created things," they are not "the crown of creation."[39] That accolade properly belongs to the Sabbath. He reminds us that God's instruction to "subdue" the earth "means nothing but the injunction to eat vegetable food."[40] And what Moltmann says about the nature of human beings very much echoes Sell:

> As God's image, human beings are God's proxy in his creation, and represent him. As God's image, human beings are for God himself a counterpart, in whom he desires to see himself as if in a mirror. As God's image, finally, human beings are created for the Sabbath, to reflect and praise the glory of God which enters into creation, and takes its dwelling there.[41]

While Sell would agree that the meaning and purpose of human beings—like that of all created things—is to be found in God, unlike Moltmann,

33. Westermann, *Genesis 1–11*, 157. Italics mine.
34. See Ezek 34.
35. Brueggemann, *Genesis*, 32.
36. Brueggemann, *Genesis*, 188.
37. Brueggemann, *Genesis*, 188. Italics mine.
38. See *COS*, 16.
39. Moltmann, *God in Creation*, 187.
40. Moltmann, *God in Creation*, 188.
41. Moltmann, *God in Creation*, 188.

he never developed his theological anthropology to specifically address the great ecological and environmental concerns of the age. One would have thought that a theologian so committed to Christian apologetics as he was would have felt a need to do so.

The human vocation is to rule over the societies and cultures of which men and women are a part and it is to be modeled upon God's rule of the cosmic process. It involves a responsibility for the environment in which societies and cultures find themselves. And it is impossible to conceive how that rule can be exercised effectively without political activity. Politics, therefore, not only involves working with, among, and on behalf of people to promote human flourishing; it also includes commitments to ensure that the well-being of the environment in which they live is maintained in a healthy state. But, lest we remain imprisoned in a narrow homocentric mind-set, our Christian vocation must also include a concern for the non-human world beyond the utilization of its instrumental value to humans. The well-being of the human world depends upon the well-being of the natural world—and, of course, vice versa. Thomas Berry, consequently, has argued that "We need a way of designating the earth-human world in its continuity and identity rather than in its discontinuity and difference."[42] He calls for "a new spiritual and even mystical communion with the earth, a true aesthetic of the earth, a sensitivity to earth needs, a valid economy of the earth."[43] Regarding "the fish of the sea . . . the birds of air . . . every living thing," Tom Regan argues that we should acknowledge that, "since we share a biographical presence in the world with these animals, it seems arbitrary and prejudicial in the extreme to insist that all humans have a kind of value that every other animal lacks."[44] An adequate doctrine of creation, therefore, will affirm the value of all creatures, not only extrinsically to the ecosystem but also to God.

Sell says that "we are challenged to be responsible stewards," but the stewardship he has in mind concerns the God-given "talents and possessions" we have "on loan" from God, in whose image we are created.[45] What we might have wished for is a more extensive treatment of the theme of "stewardship," one which includes reference to our responsibility to be wise stewards of the created order. An adequate theology of creation will move in the direction of taking a *sacramental* view of the world. It is a world created by God through evolution; its ownership will always be in God's

---

42. Birch et al., *Liberating Life*, 154.
43. Birch et al., *Liberating Life*, 154.
44. Regan, "Christianity and Animal Rights," 78.
45. *COS*, 88.

providential hands; and, ultimately, it will find its fulfillment in God. When we treat it irresponsibly we sin against God. With that sobering thought we move on appropriately to the next stage of the discussion.

THE HUMAN CONDITION

Sell is acutely aware of the gravity of sin. He maintains that it has a detrimental effect on all our thought and activity. Indeed, he is extremely critical of those liberal theologies which he believes are "soft" on sin. Nevertheless, while he often refers to the nature, effects, and resolution of sin he says precious little about its origin in "the Fall."

Sell's understanding of the relationship between God and human beings is rooted in the idea of "covenant." God has made a covenant with human beings in which God took the initiative; it was an act of grace. God's covenant love for human beings is shown in God's dealings with Israel which are witnessed to in the Old Testament and supremely in the Christ event of the New Testament.[46] Sell insists that the covenant relationship should be viewed primarily as a gracious act of a holy God: "if ever we divorce the concept of God's will from those of his holiness and grace, then God is on the way to becoming an arbitrary despot, and we are nothing more than robots."[47] Sin appears when human beings do not fulfill their responsibilities within the covenant relationship; it is the result of the mis-application of their freedom.

Traditionally, the origin of sin has been explained via an exegesis of Genesis 2:4b—3:24, with particular reference to those parts of the primeval story which describe events in the Garden of Eden. This text is part of a story proclaiming "that all corruption, all confusion in the world, comes from sin; but it also testifies that the continually widening cleft between God and man is matched by a secret increasing power of grace."[48] The apostle Paul belonged to a tradition which used the Garden of Eden story to explain the origin of evil, sin, and death.[49] Brueggemann, however, argues that the primary purpose of the text does not lie in what he calls "false, escapist questions," but, rather, it focuses upon "the summons of this calling God for us to be his creatures, to live in his world on his terms."[50] The text is a story about God's way of relating to a recalcitrant world; it illustrates the way in which

46. COS, 16–17.
47. COS, 16.
48. von Rad, *Genesis*, 24.
49. See Rom 5:12–21.
50. Brueggemann, *Genesis*, 43–44.

human beings break their covenant responsibilities. What then is God to do about the ensuing state of affairs? The answer, in Brueggemann's words, is that "When the facts warrant death, God insists on life for his creatures."[51] In other words, the story about Adam and Eve's disobedience of God is not so much concerned with the origin of sin as testifying to the grace of God. It reminds us that we live before the graciousness of a God who gives us a second chance, calling us anew to play our part in the covenantal relationship. For, as Brueggemann says, "To trust God with our lives is to turn from the autonomous "I" to the Covenanting "Thou," from our invented well-being to God's overriding purposes and gifts."[52]

Such a generous view of God's reaction to human sin is hardly reflected in the picture of sinners painted by many thinkers in the Reformed tradition, particularly those who have maintained that, as a result, of "falling" into sin, men and women are *totally* depraved. Calvin, reading the Garden of Eden story literally, asserts that Adam "infected all his posterity with that corruption into which he had fallen."[53] The "infection" is total since "whatever is in man, from the understanding to the will, from the soul even to the flesh, has been defiled and crammed with . . . concupiscence."[54] The corruption of sin, Calvin maintains, is all pervasive: "the whole man is overwhelmed—as by a deluge—from head to foot."[55] The *imago Dei* in human beings has been completely wiped out by sin. Barth comes to a similar judgment about post-fallen human beings. He tells us that human pride "is radical and in principle . . . total and universal and all embracing, determining all [human] thoughts and words and works, [the] whole inner and hidden life, and [the human being's] visible external movements and relationships."[56] Lest we have not heard the depressing message clearly, he goes on to say darkly that "at every point . . . we are dealing not merely with any *corruptio*, but with the *corruptio optima* . . . the selling and enslavement of the good man and his nature and all the activations of his nature to the service of evil and the work of his pride."[57] Our fallenness, to use Sell's distinction, is "total" both in "extent" as well as "depth."[58]

---

51. Brueggemann, *Genesis*, 50.
52. Brueggemann, *Genesis*, 54.
53. Calvin, *Institutes*, II.I.6.
54. Calvin, *Institutes*, II.I.8.
55. Calvin, *Institutes*, II.I.9.
56. Barth, *Church Dogmatics*, IV.1.3.
57. Barth, *Church Dogmatics*, IV.1.3.
58. *CCF*, 67.

Concerning the meaning of "total" in the concept of total depravity Sell refers us to the well-known debate on the matter between Barth and Brunner, reminding us that "Brunner thought that, despite sin, a point of contact remained" between sinners and God.[59] Barth, of course, disagreed. Sell sides with Brunner: "Indeed, were it otherwise any approach of God would be a further instance of divine sovereignty gone arbitrary; it would be far removed from the loving, personal, approach of a heavenly Father to whom a free, albeit graciously enabled, response is due."[60] Sell quotes O. C. Quick approvingly: "God created man's spirit to mirror his love, and never has the glass been completely darkened by sin."[61] Sell agrees that the sinners' depravity is total in that "none of our actions and motives is untainted," but he did not believe that "all our actions and motives are utterly worthless."[62] He gave conceptual precision to the matter as follows: "My way of construing 'total' in 'total depravity' is to say that it is extensive rather than intensive."[63] This conclusion reflects the Eastern theological tradition which, following the initiative of Irenaeus, argues that, while sinful men and women find themselves bereft of being in the "likeness" of God, they nevertheless retain their status of being in God's "image." This particular understanding treats "image" and "likeness" in Genesis 1:24 as if they are referring to a "natural" and "supernatural" likeness to God respectively, when, as Sell observes, most likely they are "synonyms."[64] Thereby we witness an example of arriving at a correct solution by false reasoning!

Sell's position on the gravity of sin, therefore, centers upon a conviction that in sinful human beings the *imago Dei* is defaced but not obliterated.[65] He shrewdly concluded that "it is hard to see how people could ever become new creatures apart from something of worth in them to which God's love could appeal."[66] Also "the defaced-yet-not-obliterated *imago Dei*" possesses epistemological significance in so far as it witnesses to a common ground upon which dialogue can take place across cultural, racial and religious divides.[67] And, lastly, but by no means less important, is Sell's perceptive observation that totally depraved persons, whose sin has robbed them of

---

59. *HT*, 575.
60. *HT*, 575.
61. See *FPA*, 176. The quotation is from Quick, *Doctrines of the Creed*, 152.
62. *CTF*, 129.
63. *TEM*, 171.
64. *CCF*, 65.
65. See *PR*, 165; *COS*, 95–96; *EEE*, 38.
66. *CCF*, 321.
67. *CCF*, 79

both the "image" and "likeness" of God, are not in a position to sin at all. Sin has become a necessary feature of their lives, so they cannot freely rebel against God.[68]

Earlier we saw how crucial it is to hold together "freedom" and "necessity" in our understanding of the Godhead; it is equally important when considering the human condition. If our sinful condition makes it impossible for us not to sin, it is difficult to see how we can be held morally responsible for our actions. But, on the other side of the coin, reflection upon our best efforts to live appropriately before God and with others forces us to acknowledge that the law Paul found operative applies to us as well: "when I want to do what is good, evil lies close at hand. For I delight in the law of God in my inmost self, but I see in my members another law at war with the law of my mind, making me captive to the law of sin that dwells in my members" (Rom 7:21-24). The paradox is that we are free not to sin but always find ourselves falling short of what we know deep down we should be saying and doing. Reinhold Niebuhr expressed this paradox by saying that while sin is *inevitable* it is not necessary. Being born into a sinful world it is inevitable that we will fall short: "the situation of finiteness and freedom would not lead to sin if sin were not already introduced into the situation."[69] But, not only are we free to decide which way to act, but we are also freely able to recognize our ensuing failures. Somewhat solemnly Niebuhr tells us that "Man is most free in the discovery that he is not free."[70] Regrettably, Sell did not provide us with a clear indication of his alternative to the classical Christian doctrine of sin which maintains what Niebuhr calls "the seemingly absurd position" that we sin "inevitably and by a fateful necessity" but nevertheless are "to be held responsible for actions which are prompted by an ineluctable fate."[71] But, given that Sell recognized the "common ground to which the doctrine of sin points" in our experience of often knowing the correct thing to do, but somehow not always doing it, he would have wanted to honor the paradox Niebuhr went on to explore. And it must not be forgotten that he eschews the Calvinist suggestion that Adam's guilt was imputed to his descendants: "Such a doctrine would encourage us to transfer our wickedness and sin to a wrong cause, Adam, whereas we ourselves are culpable when we freely sin."[72] He cannot accept a view in which human freedom is usurped

---

68. See *TEM*, 170.
69. Niebuhr, *Nature and Destiny*, 270.
70. Niebuhr, *Nature and Destiny*, 276.
71. Niebuhr, *Nature and Destiny*, 256.
72. *PDN*, 83.

and God's equity and justice undermined.[73] But neither can he tolerate any view of the human condition which does not take seriously the fact of sin. "We are not sinners because we do wrong," he announced, "we do wrong because we are sinners."[74] That we are each born into a state of sin would seemingly entail that, to use Niebuhr's terminology, we will "inevitably" do wrong.

Sell follows what he calls "a strong line in Reformation theology" in believing that "people generally only begin to be aware of their needy condition as sinners when they begin to grasp what God has done to rescue them."[75] He maintains that we do not completely understand sin "until we have seen something of the costliness of God's act in Christ to deal with it."[76] It is upon hearing "the Gospel of grace" that we "experience a sense of sin."[77] We discover our true nature when we appropriate what the Christ event means for us. While we become aware of our sin, we even more have pressed home to us that God reaches out to us to renew the covenant relationship. Hence we learn that "the first word of the gospel is grace."[78] As with his doctrine of God, Sell's Christian anthropology takes its bearings from the Christ event. The essence of humanity is revealed in the *sinless* Savior, so sin is a characteristic of *fallen* humanity.[79] Sell speaks of a cosmic "out-of-sorts-ness" in the world to which sin contributes. It is "a witness to alienation from God";[80] it reveals that "we are at odds with the holy Father who loves us";[81] and it reflects our willful determination to reject God's reign over us. Elsewhere, he insists that sin is not just "an outward cause of alienation" from God but actually "willful abuse" of "the personal divine-human relationship."[82] Make no mistake about it, sin is an extremely serious matter for Sell: "It is the state of rebellion against God in which we are all implicated."[83] In essence, it is idolatry, the placing of trust in and giving loyalty to something other than God. But, regrettably, Sell never attends to the feminist critique of sin which shows how the traditional view is one-

---

73. See *HT*, 601.
74. *COS*, 97–98.
75. *CTF*, 259.
76. *TAT*, 352. See also *HT*, 578 and *NT*, 178.
77. *EEE*, 313.
78. *RECT*, 43.
79. See *COS*, 24.
80. *GOF*, 90.
81. *SOL*, 20.
82. *TEM*, 140.
83. *COS*, 96.

Creation

sided. For some, the primary sin is not that of rebellion but of "the failure to take responsibility for self-actualization."[84]

Let us now reflect upon Sell's claim that we get in a mess because the world is "out-of-sorts" due to human sin. If Sell's comments to his counseling teacher are to be taken at face value,[85] we could be forgiven for thinking that Sell regards the Job-like misfortunes which afflict some people as just deserts for their sin. But, we might object, such misfortunes fall upon people indiscriminately, with the good and not just the wicked being the recipients. We should not forget that suffering is no respecter of persons. Can people be held responsible for their actions if they are living in a world beholden to sinful systemic forces? Sell's answer is crystal clear. Whatever the provenance and pervasiveness of such forces—and I suggest it is greater than Sell allows—Sell opines that "language concerning 'structural sin' . . . should not encourage any to seek to evade moral responsibility by lamenting, 'What could I do—I am embroiled in sinful structures?'"[86] While Sell correctly wants to block any route which tempts individuals to evade responsibility for their actions, he fails to do justice to the way in which countless people, particularly those who live in the two-thirds world, suffer Job-like misfortunes due to structural sins imposed upon them. The mess they find themselves in is less to do with them being sinners than with them being sinned against. We also need to deal with the issues raised to traditional Christian understanding of the human condition by the way in which some psychological conditions and mental illnesses which undermine human freedom, and, hence, responsibility are rooted in physical conditions in the brain beyond human control. Some we once treated as "bad" were in fact "ill."

While it is quite true that "Structures cannot obey, or disobey, the law—still less can they repent and turn from their wicked ways,"[87] and, hence, that those who run them are responsible for them, Sell does not do justice to the complexity of "structural" sin. Missing is the profound subtlety on the matter evident, for example, in the work of Reinhold Niebuhr.[88] Niebuhr reminds us that "there are collective forces at work in society which are not the conscious contrivance of individuals."[89] This explains why the well-intentioned actions of seemingly good individuals so often lead to bad

84. Plaskow, quoted by Hampson, *Theology and Feminism*, 123.

85. See chapter 1.

86. *FPA*, 116. Note also Sell's claim that "to explain how one has come to be the sort of person one is is not the same as providing sustainable arguments for one's nonculpability in a particular situation" (*RECT*, 228).

87. *RECT*, 225. See also *FPA*, 116 and *EEE*, 318.

88. See Niebuhr, *Moral Man* and Niebuhr, *Children of Light*.

89. Niebuhr, *Children of Light*, 11.

and even wicked collective outcomes. All too often, however, people appear "to be unconscious of the basic difference between the morality of individuals and the morality of collectives, whether races, classes or nations,"[90] and, I must add, churches. Individualistic views of sin lead to an individualistic ethic which then is unable fully to deal with social and political problems. It is, in Niebuhr's opinion, "one of the tragedies of the human spirit" that it cannot "conform its collective life to its individual ideals," since "as individuals, men believe that they ought to love and serve each other and establish justice between each other," while "As racial, economic, and national groups they take for themselves, whatever their power can command."[91] Sell's understanding of sin and, hence, as we shall see in due course, salvation is far too individualistic to deal with the "out-of-sorts-ness" in which we find ourselves. And, of course, theologians also have to meet the objection that an all-powerful and all-loving God ought to have been able, if so inclined, to create human beings less prone to commit sin and perpetrate evil.

THE PROBLEM OF EVIL

Sell follows Christian orthodoxy in claiming that God is both omnipotent and omnibenevolent. But how can such a God be worthy of belief and worship given the horrendous amount of suffering and evil in the world? Like every Christian, Sell faced a vexed issue. If God is able to prevent evil and will not, then, God is not omnibeneficent; if God is willing to prevent evil but cannot, then God is not omnipotent. The ensuing "problem of evil" has been notoriously difficult to solve. Many people, on the basis of the degree of human suffering in the world, have concluded that God is not worthy of worship. Given that "the problem of evil" is a serious inhibitor of Christian believing we would expect that, out of apologetic concern, Sell was concerned to address it. And address it he most certainly did, albeit not wholly satisfactorily.

Sell follows traditional practice in isolating two types of evil: "moral" and "natural." Moral evil represents the pain and suffering which is inflicted upon human beings as a result of the free decisions of others. It is wholly the responsibility of human beings, and its cause ought not to be laid at God's

---

90. Niebuhr, *Moral Man*, ix. Note Niebuhr's reason: "In every human group there is less reason to guide and check impulse, less capacity for self-transcendence, less ability to comprehend the needs of others and therefore more unrestrained egoism than the individuals, who compose the group, reveal in their personal relationships" (Niebuhr, *Moral Man*, xi–xii).

91. Niebuhr, *Moral Man*, 9.

door. It stems from human sin. Natural evil, on the other hand, comes in the form of pain and suffering inflicted by phenomena such as fire, flood, earthquake, and drought. While the effects of global warming remind us that such natural phenomena can have human causes, it has traditionally been thought that the cause of natural evil does not lie in our hands. It can hardly be blamed totally on human beings. Natural evil is a problem for Christian believing because people "are outraged by its apparent randomness and by the inequitability of its distribution."[92] The cry goes out: "If God is all-good and all-powerful God would not allow evil to happen." And, contrary to the advice Sell gave to his counseling tutor, he admits that "it is often necessary to allay any fear on the part of a sufferer that his suffering *is* a direct consequence of his sins."[93]

Sell rules out three purported answers to the problem of evil. First, he rejects dualism, which posits "evil" alongside and in opposition to God, either as a competing deity or malevolent matter. He reminds us that "many thinkers . . . refused to allow that evil had any independent existence at all" regarding it as "a privation of good" and hence "the absence of a good which ought to be present."[94] It was argued that, while it has real *existential* impact upon individuals, *theoretically* it has no lasting status. Secondly, Sell rejects pluralism which teaches that God is in competition with "other and alien beings" and "the first among equals."[95] Such a view undermines what Christians need to say about God's sovereignty. Then, thirdly, Sell will not countenance views which suggest that evil is illusory. He tells us that "Christianity affirms the reality of pain and suffering, and sin."[96] Indeed, at its heart lies an evil act which led to Christ's suffering and painful death on the cross. It is via testimony to the Christ event, soteriologically conceived, that Sell's discussion of the problem of evil is advanced. Not only does he maintain that "the doctrine of the providence of the Fatherly God of holy love whom we know in Christ is preferable to alternative theories" to explain the problem of evil, but he also is convinced that "it is the only view which makes the agonies of life tolerable, and offers ground for hope."[97]

What Sell offers is a *practical* rather than theoretical solution to the problem of evil. Indeed, "the theoretical problems concerning the suffering of the righteous, and random and apparently quite unmerited natural

---

92. *GOF*, 90.
93. *GOF*, 90.
94. *GOF*, 91.
95. *GOF*, 91.
96. *GOF*, 92.
97. *GOF*, 85.

disasters in relation to a God deemed to be both loving and omnipotent" are left unanswered by him.[98] He accepts that "the fact of the divine providence cannot rationally be demonstrated to an unbeliever."[99] All that can be offered instead, he maintains, is "a practical answer which takes its bearings from the Cross-Resurrection event."[100] It will not "remove all the intellectual problems . . . nor will it remove our sense of outrage against evil and inequity";[101] but, Sell insists, it is adequate. His proposed Christian answer "builds upon the Old Testament experience of Job" who "after his ordeal . . . was in an intellectual sense, none the wiser."[102] Nevertheless, he came to know God, resolved to trust God, and accepted that "fellowship with God was enough."[103] Sell then turns to the New Testament witness to the Christ event: "The Christ bears the worst that sin could do, and vanquishes all by holy love."[104]

Sell delights in paraphrasing what he calls the brave answer to the problem of evil Forsyth offered during the Great War: "If there is a God of *holy* love, and if people willfully and persistently thwart him, what else would you expect but all this?"[105] Not only does this remind us of the "what's befallen you is the result of your sin" conclusion questioned and rejected earlier, but it also fails to address the issues posed by the ongoing presence of *natural* evil. Sell's own approach is modeled on that of Forsyth: "The only final theodicy is that self-justification of God which was fundamental to His justification of man."[106] It involves three "practical implications." First, since Christ has vanquished evil, Sell claims that "Christians may believe in the ultimate victory of good over evil."[107] The cross, therefore, is the ground upon which our confidence in God's providence is established. It is in God's nature to bring victory out of the jaws of defeat. Secondly, since Christ has vanquished evil, Christians "may glorify God in their sufferings, knowing that they will not have the last word with us."[108] And, thirdly, following the Cross-Resurrection event, "Christians may, even in suffering, experience a

---

98. *MOG*, 135.
99. *GOF*, 85.
100. *MOG*, 135.
101. *GOF*, 92.
102. *GOF*, 92.
103. *GOF*, 92.
104. *GOF*, 93.
105. *GOF*, 93.
106. Forsyth, *Justification of God*, 122.
107. *GOF*, 94.
108. *GOF*, 95.

'peace which passes understanding' (Phil 4:7), and exult in the hope of an inheritance which 'nothing can destroy or spoil or wither' (1 Pet 1:4)."[109] Christ's resurrection enables us to believe with Paul that "because . . . Christ was raised we shall be raised."[110] Sell, therefore, affirms wholeheartedly the "come-what-may gospel of eternal union with the Saviour who has vanquished sin and death."[111]

It is rather noticeable that Sell's "three practical implications" underscore the basis upon which John Hick's very popular, Irenaean inspired theodicy is based. In his theory of "eschatological verification" Hick maintains that "The good that outshines all ill is not a paradise long since lost but a kingdom which is yet to come in its full glory and permanence."[112] What awaits the faithful in the future, then, outweighs and fully compensates for any pain and suffering in this life: all's well that ends well. While such a view may well bring some comfort and satisfaction to a person of faith, the skeptic is more likely to dismiss it as "pie in the sky when you die." It resolves one problem—the problem of evil—by introducing an equally contentious issue, that of whether there is an after-life. Perhaps the truth is that the good which triumphs over evil is located neither in a past paradise nor a future utopia, but in the *present* joy and delight God receives from a processive world which unfolds ever more sophisticated configurations of life? And might it not be the case that our redemption is not something created for us by Christ's death and awaiting us in the future, but rather is found in God's ongoing activity? God is always receiving what is taking place into the divine life, making dross into gold, and laying down the material out of which fresh patterns of creativity can evolve.

If the *kenotic* principle is fundamental to God's creative as well as redeeming activity, it follows that the "omnipotence" of God is compromised by the freedom God has endowed to the creative order. God could not at one and the same time create a world of creatures possessing freedom as well as ensure that they always act according to God's wishes. Having chosen the route of self-emptying, God gives *permission* for the existence of the kind of world which gives rise to sin and evil. Presumably that involves a measure of risk on God's part, but the risk of creating a free world carries greater benefits to God than that of a wholly determined world in which God would be akin to a puppeteer pulling all the strings. Keith Ward, working within the conceptual framework of traditional theology, contemplates the possibility

109. *GOF*, 96.
110. *MOG*, 135.
111. *CAM*, 124.
112. Hick, *Evil and the God of Love*, 297.

that God could revoke the divine permission upon which divine kenotic activity is based: "Why should an almighty being not allow real freedom and independence to creatures, on condition that their power is finite and could be annulated at any time by him?"[113] But as long as God's permission holds the conditions exist for sin and evil to be manifested. Within the logic of the kenotic principle the beginning of a possible theoretical solution to the problem of evil is located. Had he followed it up, Sell would have had a theodicy of greater apologetic appeal to those outside the Christian community.

After the divine *kenosis*, the divine attribute of omnipotence is compromised by creatures given powers to act freely by God. But, if we focus on the meaning of "power" we discover that "omnipotence" turns out to be a *pseudo*-concept, and that from a theoretical point of view the problem of evil is "a *pseudo*-problem."[114] Ogden notes, following Hartshorne, that "anything actual both freely creates itself in response to the self-created others already actualized and belonging to its past, and then contributes itself, along with others, to be responded to by still other self-creations, not yet actualized and belonging to its future."[115] As a result, nothing whatever—not even God—can wholly determine the existence of another actuality. Hartshorne's concept of power is social through and through. It follows that omnipotence means possessing all the power there is to be possessed while there are other beings that possess power. God has the power to set up the conditions whereby the maximum opportunity is created for the free decisions of finite actualities—and that is all the power God could possibly have. It is inconceivable that all that happens in the universe is to be laid at the door of divine responsibility. An adequate solution to the theoretical problem of evil involves questioning the classical notion of omnipotence. It says that the notion that God can ever have all the power there is, and can in fact be, in the strictest sense, omnipotent, quite simply is bad metaphysics.

If the classically conceived omnipotent God chooses to place a limit on divine power, God can still be indicted for failing to eradicate evil, when omnipotence is understood in the traditional manner, because classical notions of God's omnipotence assume that God *could*, if God wants, coercively overcome other powers at work in the world. It follows that traditional theology does not really consider the "other powers" as *real* powers because it is conceivable that they could make no difference to what comes to pass. God could overrule them; only God declines to do so. But, in neoclassical theism, it is not a matter of God having all the power (classical omnipotence)

---

113. Ward, *Rational Theology*, 82.
114. Ogden, *Understanding of Christian Faith*, 47. Italics mine.
115. Ogden, "Evil and Belief in God," 32.

and then choosing to limit Godself by devolving power to the created order; rather it is a matter of God *always* having the power that the eminent Individual called God can have while there *always* exists a powerful world of *some* kind with which God is related. God so creates Godself, in an endless procession of self-creation, as to lay Godself before whatever world exists to optimize the possibilities of others. Since all entities are not *totally* determined by God, they are responsible for their self-creation, even those entities in the sub-human world. And Hartshorne reminds us that "our having at least some freedom is not an absolute exception to an otherwise total lack of freedom in nature, but a special, intensified, magnified form of a general principle pervasive of reality, down to the very atoms and still further."[116] When power is understood neoclassically the problem of evil becomes a pseudo-problem because God conceptually cannot be held responsible for all that happens. It is a metaphysical fact that risk is involved in the creative process: the greater the possibility of joy, the greater the chance of evil.[117] The possibility of genuine evil, therefore, is located in the necessary characteristics of God and the world. Therein lays the reason why the problem of evil has a theoretical solution, as well as the crucial practical one to be received in faith from the Christian witness to the Christ event.

---

116. Hartshorne, *Omnipotence*, 13.

117. As Ogden says: "Although God is unsurpassable in both power and goodness, and thus is all-powerful as well as all-good in the only coherent senses of the words, evil can be and is real because of the real power of creatures, also, to make decisions—decisions that God does not make and cannot make, not because God's power is somehow limited, or 'finite,' but solely and simply because to be at all and to have some power, however, minimal, are simply two ways of talking about one and the same thing" [*Understanding of Christian Faith*, 47–48].

5

Jesus Christ

We have arrived at the pivotal chapter of this book. Not in the sense that we are now at its midpoint, but because we are about to consider Sell's doctrine of the atonement. Sell follows Forsyth in making Christ's work his starting point: while *logically* "Christology takes precedence over soteriology: Christ can only do what he does because he is who he is"; historically, and through Christian experience, we arrive at "an understanding of who Christ is via what he has done."[1] When Jesus' followers were coming to terms with the implications of "the Good Friday-Easter-Pentecost events" Sell maintains that they had a burning question on their minds: "Who alone can save us?"[2] When the stress was placed upon the word "save" their answer was "God alone"; when the emphasis was on "us" their answer was "A perfect representative of humanity only."[3] An understanding of who Jesus is followed from their conclusion about what he had achieved for them. But not only that: "until we have seen what God in Christ has done we do not *really* know who we are—for Christ is *the* Man."[4] So, christological investigations also have anthropological implications.

---

1. *PICB*, 194–95.
2. *NT*, 176.
3. *NT*, 176.
4. *COS*, 4.

THE PERSON OF CHRIST

Classical christologies possess a distinctive genre in which Jesus is understood as "uniquely *God in man*, God Godself uniquely present in and as a human being."[5] More recent revisionary christologies, on the other hand, have focused on Jesus "as uniquely *man of God*, a human being uniquely open to the gift and demand of God's love."[6] Sell's approach belongs to the classical genre. Theologians are apt to approach their christological understanding boldly, some would say cavalierly, given the nature of our sources—gospels rather than what we would recognize as histories—and the manifold problems of knowing the innermost intentions of any human being, even those closest to us, let alone one who lived two thousand years ago. Sell is not among them. He says that "in treating the subject of Christ's person we cannot avoid the fact that we are thereby confronted by mystery."[7] An old adage warns us that "theologians baptize their muddles as mysteries," but Sell insists that he is not "sanctifying irrationalism."[8] Indeed, one senses reverence on his part when discussing the person of Christ. Sell regards it as "encouraging to the humble believer as it is humbling to the sincere scholar" that "no creed, no confession, no individual theologian, can completely solve, still less dissolve, the mystery of Christ."[9] Nevertheless, Christian theologians are duty bound to attempt their particular answer to the question Jesus is reported to have asked: "But who do you say that I am?" (Mark 8:29 and parallels). They will be wise to tread cautiously since, as Sell reminds us, "the shape of ecclesial life" in many places has "had more to do with differing views of the person of Christ within the broader context of Trinitarian debate than with any other Christian doctrine."[10]

The Self-understanding of Jesus

Sell recognizes that "The history of the doctrine of the person of Christ is in large part the history of attempts to answer [Jesus'] question" on the way to Caesarea Philippi.[11] Whether this story is to be treated as "legend"[12]

---

5. Ogden, *Understanding of Christian Faith*, 63.
6. Ogden, *Understanding of Christian Faith*, 63.
7. *CAC*, 4.
8. *CAC*, 4.
9. *CAC*, 81.
10. *CAC*, 88.
11. *CAC*, 4.
12. See Bultmann, *History*, 257.

or "based on sound historical tradition"[13] is a moot point, but Sell accepts the latter. First, he claims that Jesus understood himself as the Messiah, not in the then contemporary, militaristic, and political understanding of that term but reinterpreted on the model of the Suffering Servant central to Isaiah 40–66.[14] Secondly, he maintains that "Jesus . . . was quite convinced of the inevitability of his death at the hands of those who would not accept him and his kind of Messiahship."[15] Thirdly, he is confident that Jesus' death was "in accordance with the divine plan" and "a prelude to his victory."[16] He anchors this claim in passages found only in Luke: Luke 24:25–27 (part of "the Road to Emmaus" story, which Bultmann classifies as "legend"[17] though others regard as rooted in eye-witness testimony), and Luke 24:44–47 (the opening of a story concerning the appearance of the Risen Jesus to the disciples, which Bultmann regards as "a quite late achievement of Hellenistic Christianity (if not also in part of Hellenist Jewish-Christianity)"[18] but C. F. Evans accepts as "a solid foundation for apostolic faith in, and preaching of, the resurrection.")[19] Fourthly, Sell tells us that Jesus knew the purpose of his suffering and death. He bases his argument on Mark 10:45, a text which divides scholars as to whether it is genuine or fed back onto the lips of Jesus.[20] Jesus knew, Sell asserts, that he was "*the* ransoming sacrifice."[21] Fifthly, Sell concludes that the cross is the place where human sin and evil is overcome and defeated. It is the place of triumph, a victory underscored by the resurrection. Sell insists that "we cannot think of the cross apart from the Resurrection and still have the gospel."[22] Indeed, without it there would be "no Church at all."[23]

Sell can only establish these claims on the basis of interpretation of key texts shared with some scholars but not others. The peril of authorizing Christological claims on such texts was not lost on hm. He perhaps chose

13. See Cranfield, *Gospel According to Mark*, 267.
14. See *COS*, 31.
15. *COS*, 31.
16. *COS*, 32.
17. Bultmann, *History*, 286.
18. Bultmann, *History*, 289.
19. Evans, *Saint Luke*, 921.
20. While Nineham voices the opinion that "probably the majority of scholars are against" originality (*Saint Mark*, 280) we note that Vincent Taylor and Cranfield were among the minority. (See Taylor, *Gospel According to St. Mark*, 446 and Cranfield, *Gospel According to Mark*, 343–44.
21. *COS*, 33.
22. *COS*, 33.
23. *COS*, 33.

to read them the way he did because his soteriological convictions about Christ presupposed such a reading. But there are many cautious readers of these texts who are not as confident about being able to get inside the mind of Jesus through reading largely evangelical writings about him. Their reason need not be that they share skeptical conclusions about the Gospels' historicity, though that may have a bearing on the matter; it is, rather, a challenge to face up to the difficulties involved in making claims about Jesus' innermost intentions even on the fullest, most pristine historical evidence. I fail to see how we can do anything other than *surmise* about a person's self-understanding, or personal aims in life, on the basis of our *first*-hand knowledge of them, let alone from two-thousand-year-old documents of the gospel genre. Sell's confidence in the claims he makes about Jesus' self-knowledge is controversial.

The Resurrection of Jesus

While talk about Jesus' self-understanding as the Messiah born to suffer and die as part of God's saving plan for the world certainly stretches biblical exegesis to, and arguably beyond, its limits, the same need not be said for Jesus' resurrection from the dead. Sell shares the Pauline conviction that, "if Christ has not been raised, [our] faith is futile" (1 Cor 15:17). He insists that the basis of this claim lies in a historical event, rather than either an appeal "to 'the intuitions of the disciples of all ages,' or to some sort of existential encounter now," although both of the latter are clearly part of a full appreciation of the meaning of "resurrection."[24] Nor is the resurrection "merely an interpretation which Christian individuals place upon ancient texts"; it is actually "a revelation from God brought home by the Spirit."[25] The resurrection claim entails that Jesus "ever lives, that sin and the grave are vanquished and that God's final victory is assured."[26] More is involved than the notion that "he was resuscitated."[27]

Sell offers evidence for Jesus' resurrection. First, he endorses Denney's view that "The real historical evidence for the resurrection is the fact that it was believed, preached, propagated, and produced its fruit and effect in the new phenomenon of the Christian Church."[28] Sell was convinced that without the resurrection there would have been no Christian gospel and,

24. *DAD*, 225.
25. *CCF*, 189.
26. *CCF*, 189.
27. *CCF*, 189.
28. *DAD*, 206–7. Sell is quoting from Denny, *Jesus and the Gospel*, 107, 111.

hence, no church. Secondly, he focuses on the change which came over the disciples: the disillusioned and devastated were overcome with joy and once again exuded confidence.[29] Such a change would not have occurred had not the crucified Jesus been raised to life. Then, thirdly, he notes how the first Christians—a sect within Palestinian Judaism—began to worship on the first day of the week. This was "a considerable departure from tradition for the disciples."[30] It is best accounted for, Sell maintains, by the historical fact of the resurrection. But, given the heated debate surrounding the *factuality* of the resurrection, it is interesting to observe that Sell's understanding of the resurrection concerns "not so much the empty tomb" but rather more the fact that "The disciples *experienced* the risen Christ and proclaimed their good news to all who would hear."[31] This sits neatly with the scholarly consensus which concludes that the appearance stories pre-date the empty tomb traditions. If historical factuality is required it will most likely be discovered by paying particular attention to the former rather than the latter. Sell insists that Jesus' resurrection was a *bodily* resurrection. This was necessary, he believes, if his death was sacrificial.

During the 1980's, David E. Jenkins, the then Bishop of Durham, was involved in an infamous debate concerning Jesus' resurrection.[32] Bishop Jenkins argued that "people are not put on to God by exterior evidences but by internal and shared experiences."[33] Up to a point, Sell endorses such a view: "Christian belief in the resurrection is not just a matter of agreeing that once, nearly two thousand years ago, Jesus was, as a matter of historical fact, raised from the dead. To what we might say, 'How odd!' or 'How amazing!' or even, 'Bless my soul!'"[34] But, presumably, problems arise if what Jenkins refers to as "internal and shared experiences" get contradicted by "exterior evidences"? Nevertheless, as Jenkins affirms, "Miracles do both evoke faith and indicate faith and develop faith, but they do not compel faith and certainly do not compel faith in public and external ways."[35] One senses that Sell has this in mind when grounding the resurrection in the disciples' *experience* of the risen Christ rather than explicitly in the empty tomb traditions. He invites us to prioritize the claims of those disciples. When we do we are placed before two astounding facts: first, because of the resurrec-

---

29. CCF, 189.
30. CCF, 189.
31. CTF, 256.
32. For a popular account of the debate, see Harrison, *Durham Phenomenon*.
33. Jenkins, *God, Miracle and the Church*, 31.
34. COS, 35.
35. Jenkins, *God, Miracle and the Church*, 31.

tion "our eternal hope is secure, and our deepest present needs are met;" and, secondly, "the ultimate consummation of God's purposes is assured."[36] These facts ought to hold our attention rather than the empirical details of an event long ago. If we find them credible through our contemporary experiences of God's gracious promises it is debatable whether their historical validation is necessary; and, conversely, if we have experiential reasons to render them incredible no amount of historical investigation is likely to give them credibility. In any case, given that the resurrection is clearly rather more than simply a matter of the resuscitation of Jesus' corpse, it was not merely an *historical* event.

The resurrection clearly is a *supernatural* occurrence. We now see why Sell is adamant that a place be left open for the supernatural in theology. For him, the essence of the gospel is at stake. He claims that the gospel is supernatural in two ways: "first, its provision is not from nature, and least of all from man," and, "secondly, it has to restore nature—especially man's."[37] But Sell then tells us that the resurrection in fact is "the most 'natural' thing in the world," given that nothing could be "more 'natural' than that God should raise his Son and give him glory (1 Pet 1:29)?"[38] What is supernatural to us is natural to God.

The Orthodoxy of Chalcedon, 451 CE

Sell follows orthodox Christianity in asserting that there was "an eternal purpose in the mind of God in which his Son was intimately involved."[39] The notion of Christ's pre-existence is one of the givens of his trinitarian theology. Sell, therefore, insists that the incarnation is best conceived as the Word (the eternal *logos*) becoming *flesh* rather than human. He points out that, in the Godhead, "God the Son was ever present with the Father," and, hence, "humanity was ever present."[40] Sell is very critical of those who "concentrate exclusively upon Christ's incarnation" since they tend to "minimize not only his pre-existent life, but also the atoning work he did while he was on earth, and the continuing work he does now."[41] So Christ initially belonged in eternity; then, through divine *kenosis,* became incarnate in human flesh; and, finally, following the crucifixion and resurrection, returned to eternity. Such

36. *COS*, 38, 39.
37. *DAD*, 225.
38. *COS*, 39.
39. *COS*, 15.
40. *COS*, 19.
41. *COS*, 20.

descriptions of the divine economy are clearly mythological. They presuppose an understanding of the universe quite foreign to modern cosmology, and reflect the metaphysics of early Christianity. Not surprisingly they have been challenged by theologians seeking to talk about Jesus' significance in ways which carry contemporary credibility *for us*, rather than in terms of the Second Person of the Trinity, God incarnate, living a human life on earth.[42] The contemporary theological task involves finding ways of doing justice to Chalcedon's intentions in language that resonates with modern people.

Sell remains within the bounds of orthodoxy in his christology. He believes that "the rationale of the incarnation is in the Atonement,"[43] and he was fond of quoting Forsyth on the matter: "The doctrine of the Incarnation . . . grew up (very quickly) in the Church out of the doctrine of the cross."[44] He suspects that theologians come to stress the incarnation over the Atonement partly due to "a reaction against soteriology gone legalistic and externally transactional."[45] He notes a tendency for some even "to employ 'incarnation' almost as an atonement-avoiding concept."[46] But we need to ask whether Sell's criticism of such theologians is built on the inadequacy of his own atonement theology. Young, for example, argues that: "It is not by accepting traditional formulations as God-given and unquestionable that we join the band of witnesses in the New Testament and the early church, but by wrestling with the problem of expressing intelligently in our own contemporary environment, our personal testimony to the redemptive effect of faith in Jesus of Nazareth."[47] Sometimes one feels that Sell is critical of those "wrestling with the problem" but oblivious to the way in which those problems impinge upon the adequacy of his position. His christology remains very much one of Chalcedonian orthodoxy, but his emphasis on the atonement means that the places where it is outlined are few and far between.

Sell believes that the Chalcedonian divines made a very important attempt to answer the question of Jesus' followers: "Who do you say that I am?" They stopped short of "elucidating the mechanics of the incarnation,"

---

42. See Hick, *Myth of God Incarnate*, for views of those seeking alternative Christologies to those of traditional incarnationalism, and Green, *Truth of God*, and Harvey, *God Incarnate*, for views defending a more orthodox position.

43. COM, 271, quoting from Denny, *Christian Doctrine*, 65. See also COS, 6; EEE, 394; DAD, 208, 226.

44. See CCC, 108; PHT, 234; NT, 175. The quotation comes from Forsyth, *Cruciality*, 50n.

45. COM, 264.

46. RECT, 36.

47. Hick, *Myth of God Incarnate*, 30.

since "They knew when they were confronted by mystery"; and, as a result, "their Formula was a confession, not an hypothesis, still less a full-blown explanation."[48] But Chalcedon, Sell maintains, still "enshrines many of the Christological issues that . . . remain alive to this day."[49] He very helpfully points out the way in which its Definition attempts to block pathways to heresy,[50] and recognizes the importance of following Chalcedon in order to maintain that Jesus was "truly God and truly man." He is less interested in asserting *how* that claim can be made than with insisting, on soteriological grounds, that it *must* be made. I would also insist that the essential Chalcedonian insights not only can, but need to, be expressed in language which resonates today rather than the language and thought forms of a bygone age. After quoting several passages from Forsyth, which claim that the road to christology necessarily passes through the land of soteriology, Sell announces that, "Christology begins when we grasp the fact that only if Jesus is divine can he *save* us, for salvation is God's work alone; and only if he is human can he save *us,* for we, being sinners, cannot satisfy God's holy love: hence the Mediator."[51] His belief that human and divine are present in Christ's person is non-negotiable, but when it comes to the virgin birth he is more flexible.

The Chalcedonian Definition affirms that Jesus was born of "Mary the Virgin." Whereas many rule out the possibility of a virgin birth in principle, Sell remains unsurprised that "the birth of this Saviour should be supernaturally marked."[52] He is not prepared, however, to speculate upon how the virgin birth took place: "We can no more resolve that issue than we can finally explain the innermost constitution of the God-man's personality, or the mechanics of the Resurrection."[53] Neither does he countenance a suggestion put forward by some Evangelicals that "those only who assent to the dogma of the Virgin Birth may be saved."[54] His generous orthodoxy does not permit him to "elevate assent" to this particular doctrine "into a rigid test of faith."[55] And he is clear that overt concentration on the virgin birth risks making Jesus so "special and unusual" that his humanity is compromised.[56]

48. *CAC*, 5.
49. *CAC*, 5.
50. See *CAC*, 5.
51. *CAM*, 141.
52. *COS*, 85.
53. *COS*, 85.
54. *COS*, 85.
55. *COS*, 86.
56. *COS*, 85.

Nevertheless, he suggests that "if Jesus is who Christians believe him to be, the dogma of the Virgin Birth is less than absolutely incredible."[57]

Sell believes that "there is something to be said for the view that the Virgin Birth tradition as appropriately marks the entry of the Christ into history as the ascension tradition marks his departure from our physical sight."[58] But, arguably, what needs saying can be conveyed quite adequately by treating the virgin birth as a *myth* rather than as an historical fact. Ogden, for example, treats the doctrines of the virgin birth and ascension as myths, claiming they affirm that "Jesus himself as a historical person . . . is the decisive self-revelation of God, whose primal source and final end, therefore, are nothing in the world, but are nothing other or less than God Godself."[59] But I know of no public statement in which Sell comes down one way or another on the question of the historicity of the virgin birth. While he is often found giving short shrift to theologians who treat mythologically what the Gospel tradition purportedly claims are historical occurrences in Jesus' life, or who play down the historical basis of an objective atonement, he does not present us with a defense of the historicity of the virgin birth. He is agnostic about the matter, in contrast, say, to Cranfield who argues in its favor.[60]

Sell was never agnostic, however, about the clause in the Chalcedonian Definition which asserts that Jesus was "like us in all respects, apart from sin." He defends the view that Jesus was sinless. First, he argues that had Jesus shown real evidence of sinfulness, the detractors of the Jesus movement would have made a great deal of it.[61] Since all our information about Jesus comes from his followers, though, it is not too difficult to see how "unfortunate" information about Jesus could and would have been filtered out of what was bequeathed to subsequent centuries. Secondly, Sell admits "we cannot absolutely demonstrate the sinlessness of Jesus."[62] Only God is in a position to do such a thing. What can and indeed must be said, however, is that "sinlessness is all of a piece with what we do know about him," and, most important of all, that "it was an essential characteristic if he was really to do the work he came to do."[63] Once again we find Sell establishing his christological claims by inference from his soteriological commitments. His argument is simple: If Jesus was not sinless, "How else could he have made a

---

57. *COS*, 85.
58. *COS*, 85.
59. Ogden, *To Teach the Truth*, 66.
60. Cranfield, *Apostles' Creed*, 26–30.
61. See *COS*, 24.
62. *COS*, 24.
63. *COS*, 24.

'full, perfect and sufficient sacrifice?'"[64] But, thirdly, we can ask: What does Sell make of the argument that, given sin is a feature of being human, Jesus, being sinless, could not have been human? We touched on his answer in the previous chapter. What it is to be human is defined by Jesus, not by us: "Jesus is the Man, and . . . the rest of us betray the description."[65] So while Jesus, in principle, could have sinned, in practice, he did not. Thereby, he retained his humanity while we fall short of ours. Fourthly, Sell notes that even Christianity's "most sceptical of critics have been impressed by the moral goodness of Jesus."[66] Jesus shows no evidence of "feeling guilt" or requiring to ask for forgiveness, and he never needs "to claim that he is sinless."[67] To believers and unbelievers alike, "His positive goodness shines out."[68] Consequently, the importance of Jesus' sinlessness is twofold: it becomes the mirror in which we see our sin; and it is one of the presuppositions upon which our salvation is made possible.[69] With that claim we move from Sell's christology to the center of his theology.

THE WORK OF CHRIST

Central to Sell's theology is his belief that the primary purpose of Christ's mission was not so much educative as redemptive. The incarnation is "a decisive divine act with a view to the redemption of the world."[70] God has produced the decisive solution to our predicament in the Easter event. Once and for all, at a definable point in human history, and through the obedient sacrifice of Christ on the cross, God has taken the necessary steps to deal with our sin. A drastic action was taken to remedy a grave situation.

Sell recognizes "the tragedy of alienation" from God;[71] he talks about the "hideousness"[72] and "exceeding sinfulness"[73] of sin; and he regards sin as nothing less than "willful rebellion against a holy, righteous, loving Father."[74] It is "a most serious affront to God's holiness and repudiation

64. *COS*, 24.
65. *COS*, 24.
66. *COS*, 25.
67. *COS*, 25.
68. *COS*, 25.
69. See *COS*, 25.
70. *PICB*, 205.
71. *TIT*, 25.
72. *COS*, 4.
73. *TIT*, 70 and *ACI*, 43.
74. *TIT*, 19.

of his love."⁷⁵ He maintains that God's remedy for sin is equally drastic: it enables God to be God while enabling people to be truly human. Christ's sacrifice on the cross was as much for God's satisfaction as it was necessary for sinners. This makes Sell critical of those who affirm the latter while remaining silent about the former: "How dare any preach half a doctrine of atonement—as if the sacrifice of Christ were for humanity alone?"⁷⁶ Sell envisages God as well as sinners needing atonement. He maintains that the need for atonement would always have been envisaged by God, who, due to divine omniscience, knew about human sin and, therefore, envisaged what would be required to tackle it. Hence, according to Sell, God "graciously willed to send his Son into the world" from eternity to effect the salvation of sinners: "The coming of Christ was no expedient hastily thought up when things had gone awry."⁷⁷

The key texts for Sell, when talking about Christ's work, are: "in Christ God was reconciling the world to himself, not counting their trespasses against them." (2 Cor 5:19); and "In this is love, not that we loved God but that he loved us and sent his Son to be the atoning sacrifice for our sins" (1 John 4:10). He recognizes that these and other similar texts have been fertile soil in which quite different atonement theories have grown. So, for example, Sell claims that "from the East we hear much of humanity's education and gradual, grace-assisted development" but "from the West the accent is much more upon the need of dramatic rescue."⁷⁸ Some will think that both East and West have a point, but for Sell there was a reluctance to "open the door to salvation by education or social improvement rather than by radical rescue."⁷⁹ While he could venture the thought that the *fact* of atonement was greater than the *theories* which have been brought forward to illustrate it, we must be in no doubt that he eschews many of those theories on account of their inadequacies. What we understand as the "fact" of atonement, however, is largely determined by the theory we put forward to explain it. Sell's understanding is determined by the "fact" of atonement as understood by Forsyth.

---

75. *PICB*, 176.
76. *TAT*, 45. See also *TAT*, 351.
77. *COS*, 14.
78. *CCF*, 68.
79. *TAT*, 176.

The Mistakes of Two Classical Atonement Theories

Sell's understanding of Christ's work starts to become clear when we consider his criticisms of the atonement theories of Calvinistic and liberal theology. He attempts to steer a middle course between the two predominant theological positions with which he grew up. We will deal with each in turn.

Sell shared with Dale the view that if "the faith of Calvinism" could be set free from "its speculative theology" there would be "immeasurable" gain.[80] Calvinism is rooted in the conception of the sovereignty of God and an insistence that human beings are totally dependent upon God for their salvation. Sell regretted that Calvin is "unjustifiably the whipping boy of so many who have not read him."[81] Calvin's strengths ought not to be ignored because his followers dwelt too much on the less acceptable points of his teaching, e.g., total depravity. Sell is often found attempting to rescue Calvin from the worst of Calvinism. And that is clearly the case when it comes to atonement.

The roots of Calvin's understanding of the work of Christ are to be found in the theology of Anselm (1033–1109), who argues that sin is a failure to give God due honor: "He who does not render . . . honor which is due to God, robs God of his own and dishonors him, and this is sin."[82] The background to this lay in medieval feudalism, where stability was believed to be achieved by individuals pledging their loyalty to their superiors in a hierarchical society. It was accepted that "everyone who sins ought to pay back the honor of which he has robbed God."[83] Anselm called this "the *satisfaction* which every sinner owes to God."[84] When applied to atonement theology, he recognized that "the honor taken away must be repaid, or punishment must follow; otherwise, either God will not be just to himself, or he will be weak in respect to both parties; and this it is impious even to think of."[85] He went on to argue that Jesus became our penance, an offering through life but supremely in death, given to God in the wake of sin. This was good news for sinners and it was also satisfying for God.[86] The emphasis in Anselm's atonement theory, therefore, is on what Jesus, the God-man, does on behalf of sinful human beings to satisfy the honor of a deeply offended Deity.

---

80. *RECT*, 63.
81. *COS*, 17.
82. *Cur Deus Homo*, I.12. Found in Anselm of Canterbury, *St. Anselm: Basic Writings*.
83. *Cur Deus Homo*, I.12.
84. *Cur Deus Homo*, I.12. Italics mine.
85. *Cur Deus Homo*, I.14.
86. See *Cur Deus Homo*, II.20.

Calvin's treatment of the doctrine of the atonement is formally similar to Anselm's. The material difference comes when Calvin replaces "honor" with "justice" as the divine requirement needing satisfaction. Human beings have broken God's laws and, if the moral order is to have meaning, justice must be carried out. A penalty has to be paid if the divine-human relationship is to be restored. The required penalty, Calvin maintained, has been paid by the crucified Christ.[87] Through the work of Christ, therefore we "escape the imputation of our sins to us—an imputation bringing with it the wrath of God."[88] At the heart of Calvin's *penal substitutionary* theory of atonement lies the biblical idea of sacrifice: Jesus voluntarily offers himself to God as a vicarious sacrifice for sin. The blood of the Hebrew sacrificial system was believed to wipe away people's sins, so, *mutatis mutandis*, Christ's death is understood to be a *representative* sacrifice on behalf of sinful humanity. The shedding of Christ's blood, therefore, was not just the means by which satisfaction was achieved; it was also what Calvin called "a laver . . . to wash away our corruption."[89] In contrast to purely *expiatory* ideas of sacrifice, however, Calvin insists upon there being a *propitiatory* dimension to Christ's death. While that death was an act through which God graciously forgave sins, it was also an act performed by Jesus to get God to act. Therefore, God is both the subject and object of a transaction: at the cross, God's wrath is appeased and God accepts Christ's sacrifice as a substitutionary punishment for sin. The penalty due to us was borne by Jesus. Calvin maintains that, at the cross, God wipes away our sin and liberates us from the stranglehold of death; while, in the resurrection, "righteousness was restored and life raised up, so that . . . his death manifested its power and efficacy in us."[90]

Sell was impressed by the way in which Calvin takes sin with utter seriousness; he also approved of Calvin's insistence that the focus of salvation is placed well beyond anything we can achieve for ourselves; and he agreed that its location is in the death and resurrection of Jesus—a particular event in history therefore being of its essence. He also was happy to embrace the idea of "substitution," going so far as to claim that "we cannot really avoid the concept of substitution and still retain the Christian gospel."[91] But, notwithstanding such points of agreement, Sell identifies with the "searching criticism" launched by Robert Mackintosh at Calvin's atonement theory.[92] First,

---

87. Calvin, *Institutes* II.XVI.3.
88. Calvin, *Institutes* II.XVI.3.
89. Calvin, *Institutes* II.XVI.6.
90. Calvin, *Institutes* II.XVI.13.
91. *COS*, 47.
92. *RM*, 75.

while punishment may be said to "vindicate justice, or reassert it against the law-breaker," Mackintosh doubts whether it may be said to "satisfy" it.[93] Secondly, Mackintosh questions whether the notion of penal substitution has biblical support. He suggests that Old Testament notions of sacrifice do not involve it, and he argues that, while "the sacrificial metaphors of the New Testament testify to the fact of Christ's atoning death" they "do not define a theory concerning it," be it that of penal substitution or any other.[94] Thirdly, Mackintosh suggests that Calvin's theory "offends our religious consciousness" in that God is presented as being necessarily just while only being "accidentally or contingently loving, gracious, redemptive."[95] God's need for justice appears more important than God's compassion and mercy, with the result that Calvin's "God" seems more vindictive than loving. This is unfortunate since, according to Sell, the gospel for Calvin resides in the glorious fact that "despite all sins and difficulties, sovereign grace prevails."[96] Fourthly, Mackintosh argues that Calvin's atonement theory "cannot explain how forgiveness leads to a life of obedience."[97] A new life *today* is generated by the Holy Spirit not by the fact that long ago "a substitutionary arrangement has been made on our behalf."[98] And, in any case, given that the notion of vicarious punishment is unjust, why should we be grateful that the moral order has been shelved just for us? Fifthly, "the penal substitutionary theory raises many logical difficulties,"[99] not least of which concerns the Father being set against the Son in God's Trinitarian life: the Father is found condemning the innocent Son, while the Son pleads for sinners through his sacrificial death.

The doctrine of penal substitution arose at a time of precarious stability when order was enforced by punishment. Perhaps it is not surprising, therefore, that theologians at that time suggested that the seriousness of sin must be addressed by the necessity of punishment? At one point, Sell raises the question whether Christ, the sinless one, could morally be punished? He acknowledges that "he entered into the agony of separation from God which sin entails, but he had not sinned, and therefore he could not be punished."[100] The penal element in Calvin's atonement doctrine is impos-

93. *RM*, 75.
94. *RM*, 75.
95. *RM*, 75.
96. *CTF*, 36.
97. *RM*, 75.
98. *RM*, 75.
99. *RM*, 75.
100. See *COS*, 47.

sible to maintain, along with the requirement that as Son of God Jesus must have been sinless, if normal understandings of justice are to be maintained. Sell acknowledges the difficulty: "There is mystery here, and [I am] quite unable to plumb the depths."[101] He finds himself following Forsyth's paradoxical view that the sinless Christ submitted himself to God's judgment of holy love on sin. Sell, thereby, advocates maintaining a *juridical* element in his atonement doctrine while denying that what took place on the cross had a penal dimension. As he puts it: "God's nature as love—indeed, as holy love, is by the victory of the Cross (juridically yet non-penally) satisfied, vindicated and placarded before the world."[102]

Many Christians find it difficult to believe that their relationship with God has been made possible by God inflicting punishment, suffering, and death upon God's Son as a substitutionary penalty for their sin. Sell knew that "The burden of the anti-Calvinist position was that the doctrine of imputed sin and guilt removed freedom and responsibility from human beings, and assaulted the principle that one individual may not be responsible for the actions of another, with the consequences that the divine equity and justice were called into question."[103] But he refused to join the ranks of those who have turned to more subjective atonement theories which trace their origins back to Abelard (1079–1142). Sell is committed to an *objective* view of the atonement free from Calvinist error.

Whereas many of the classical theories deal with humanity as a whole and attempt to explain how the entire human race is made right with God through Christ's work, Abelard's focus is upon the individual within society. Further, Abelard drew upon a "profound psychological insight" which, according to Dillistone, enabled him to recognize that "nothing is more powerful to move the will from its apathetic acquiescence in some sinful habit than the sight of the One who actually suffered on account of our sins and bore their penalty in His death."[104] For Abelard, therefore, the major result of Christ's death on the cross concerns its demonstration of the depth and extent of God's love for men and women. Once God's "pure unbounded love" (to annex Charles Wesley's phrase) is seen and accepted we will be so moved to respond reciprocally to love God and our fellow human beings that we will be empowered to establish and practice new patterns of behavior. He believes that, through the example of Christ, God has provided a particular act of grace which, if we respond to it appropriately out of grati-

---

101. *COS*, 47.

102. *HT*, 349.

103. *HT*, 601.

104. Dillistone, *Christian Understanding*, 325.

tude, will establish for us a new relationship with God. Hence, in Abelard's own words, "our redemption through the suffering of Christ is that deeper love within us which not only frees us from slavery to sin, but also secures for us the true liberty of the children of God, in order that we might do all things out of love rather than out of fear—love for him who has shown us such grace that nor greater can be found."[105]

It is important to remember that Abelard had no intention of suggesting that, as Dillistone puts it, "the sight of Christ's obedience even unto death would simply evoke sympathy and pity and a general sentiment of gratitude."[106] Dillistone endorses Moberly's interpretation of Abelard's thought: "The emphasis . . . is not really so much upon Calvary as a picture exhibited before our eyes, as it is upon Calvary as a *constraining and transforming* influence upon our characters. It is not so much really upon the love of God *manifested to* us as upon the love of God *generated within* us."[107] Nor should we be led into thinking that Abelard did not recognize the gravity of sin or that Christ had paid the penalty for it. Just because he disagreed with the way in which divine justice was often said to be established in alternative atonement theories, e.g., in terms of a *quid pro quo* or the satisfaction of honor, we should not conclude that he sat lightly upon the need for justice. He looked for it elsewhere in what Dillistone describes as "the willing service of love by man to his neighbour, the reflection in humanity of the very nature of God Himself."[108] Abelard claims that this was achieved in the Christ event and can now be replicated by those inspired by Christ's sacrificial act at Calvary. The problem as Abelard saw it was this: How can sinful human beings be liberated from their fear of God and respond personally to God's love? The answer he gave was: It is made possible by the presence of God's sacrificial love in the Christ event, which can grasp people's imaginations, light up their minds and move their wills in a way not adequately articulated by alternative atonement theories.

Abelard's theory finds favor with many who believe that penal atonement theories contradict God's character as love-itself. It has provided the model for a great deal of liberal theology. But it finds little favor with Sell, who, one-sidedly, regards it as "more aesthetic than realistic."[109] As far as he is concerned, the theory does not take sin with radical seriousness, since "it

---

105. From McGrath, *Christian Theology Reader*, 184.

106. Dillistone, *Christian Understanding*, 326.

107. Dillistone, *Christian Understanding*, 326. Italics mine. Dillistone quotes from Moberly, *Atonement and Personality*, 381.

108. Dillistone, *Christian Understanding*, 327.

109. *EEE*, 380.

underestimates what needed to be done at the Cross to break the power of sin and death and reconcile sinners to God."[110] An over-optimistic view of human beings loses the belief that "man is something more than unable"[111] and it "overlooks the full significance of the fact that we are sinners."[112] Sell believes, further, that all variations of moral influence theories emphasize the *subjective* over the *objective* dimensions of atonement. They make salvation "too dependent upon our response, our self-identification with Christ" and neglect the transaction which took place at Calvary.[113] Sell even claims that they "can become perilously close to a doctrine of salvation by works."[114] They are clearly reductionist in his opinion: the cross becomes "the place where something is merely shown, not done,"[115] and the atonement ends up as "an example given rather than a price paid."[116] He maintains that for sinners to be made "willing and rendered able" to gain salvation two things are required: first, "externally" there needs to be "the expiation of our sins," and, secondly, "internally" there must be "the regenerating work of God the Holy Spirit."[117] Neither requirement, in Sell's opinion, is adequately met by what critics, often pejoratively, call "moral influence" theories.

Stepping Stones to an Adequate Understanding of the Work of Christ

Sell's understanding of Christ's work owes a great deal to a theological tradition which originates in the work of John McLeod Campbell and reaches a climax in the atonement theology of Forsyth. It will help set Sell's soteriology in context, as well as prepare the way for our discussion of his atonement doctrine, if we consider what these two theologians had to say on the work of Christ.

---

110. *EEE*, 380.
111. *TIT*, 128.
112. *COS*, 60.
113. *COS*, 60.
114. *COS*, 60.
115. *MOG*, 32.
116. *TIT*, 128.
117. *COS*, 60.

John McLeod Campbell: The Perfect Amen to the Judgment of God

Campbell presented an alternative atonement theology to that of the Calvinism in which he grew up. It involves a powerful and persuasive rejection of the penal doctrine of atonement.[118] The starting point comes from the claim that Christ, in atonement for human sin, must either have endured an equivalent punishment for those sins or offered God a required amount of repentance. The first option underpinned the Calvinist view he wanted to reject, so Campbell constructed his atonement theology around the latter option. He believed that love was the cause rather than consequence of Christ's work;[119] he was critical of accounts of Christ's work which made use of all too human ideas like honor, justice, and punishment; and he insisted that Christ's work should be viewed "in its own light."[120] In opposition to more subjective theories, Campbell maintained that Christ has done something at the cross which we are unable to do for ourselves. He focused upon Christ's self-sacrifice: through Christ's suffering we have a revelation of the extent of human sin, and the height, depth, and length of God's love. Christ honors the Father before human beings with a perfect display of suffering love, while, viewed retrospectively, Christ's work also involves Christ dealing with God on behalf of sinners by offering God the perfect confession of our sins. The vicarious punishment of Calvinistic atonement theory, therefore, has been replaced by vicarious repentance. In Campbell's oft quoted words: "This confession . . . must have been *a perfect Amen in humanity to the judgment of God on the sin of man.*"[121] Christ's sacrifice—the suffering of a sinless one for the sins of all others—was not only vicarious but also expiatory.

Campbell's treatment of Christ's work utilizes a higher, more excellent, and more spiritual form of satisfaction. Sell, for example, tells us that he wishes "to side with all those of the English Enlightenment who lodged a moral protest against expressions of Christian doctrine which turned God into a tyrant or human beings into automata."[122] It comes as no surprise,

---

118. See Campbell's *Nature of Atonement*. Macquarrie regards this book "as probably the best theological treatment of atonement to be found in modern writing on the subject" (*Jesus Christ*, 420).

119. As, of course, did Calvin: "For how could [God] have given us in his only-begotten Son a singular pledge of his love to us if he had not already embraced us with his free favour" (*Institutes*, II.XVI.2).

120. Campbell, *Nature of Atonement*, 113.
121. Campbell, *Nature of Atonement*, 134.
122. *EEE*, 107.

therefore, that he approved of Campbell making "God's love in Christ's Incarnation and Atonement the first word of his preaching."[123] He regarded this as "a most welcome and healthy emphasis,"[124] since 'The grace of God, not the sin of humanity, must be the first word of the Gospel and of the Christian 'system.'"[125] Sell shares Campbell's view of "the idea of redemption as spiritual rather than as mere deliverance from punishment."[126] God "did not need to be provoked or cajoled into being loving by a penal substitutionary atonement."[127] The atonement was the *consequence* not the cause of God's love. Sell also shares Campbell's belief that "atonement mattered from the point of view of God's holiness, as well as of man's need."[128]

Sell is critical, however, of Campbell's proposals in three areas. He wonders why the idea of vicarious repentance is ultimately free from the problems which beset the idea of vicarious punishment. Should we expect someone else to do for us what we really should be doing for ourselves? As Cunliffe-Jones points out, in the final analysis there seems to be a contradiction at the heart of Campbell's position.[129] Campbell argues that Christ's confession contains "all the elements of a perfect repentance in humanity for all the sin of man . . . excepting the personal consciousness of sin."[130] But Sell reminds us that Christ does not and cannot repent for us, and he certainly is not in need of repentance himself.[131] Quoting Franks, he argues that the idea of Christ making a vicarious confession of humankind's sins "violated the fundamental principles of moral personality."[132] It is illogical to say that someone can repent of a sin of which they are incapable of committing. Sell's way of resolving the ensuing conundrum is to follow Forsyth in saying that our repentance was latent in that holiness of Christ which makes it subsequently manifest. Secondly, Sell maintains that "Campbell's critics were right to observe that he did not pay enough attention to the judicial aspect of Christ's work: the fact that something had to be done; that

---

123. *ACI*, 37.

124. *ACI*, 37.

125. *HT*, 184. Sell also *CCF*, 85; *TAT*, 135–36, 236; and *EEE*, 390.

126. *EEE*, 161.

127. *PHT*, 245.

128. *DAD*, 215.

129. See Cunliffe-Jones, *Christian Theology*, 91–92.

130. Campbell, *Nature of Atonement*, 135–36.

131. "Christ lives and acts on behalf of humanity; we cannot confess our sins and repent as we ought, but can Christ, the guiltless one, do that for us? Can anyone repent on behalf of another? How could the virtue of a vicarious repentance he [sic] transferred to a sinner?" (*PHT*, 246).

132. *HT*, 482n317. The quotation comes from Franks. *The Atonement*, 184.

a costly offering had to be made if God's holy law and holy love were to remain inviolate."[133] Sell agrees with Forsyth that "The juristic aspect is a real element in Christ's death" which cannot be lost "without discarding the moral order of the world."[134] Sell always feared that "if the juridical does not have its due place we may launch ourselves from the top of a slippery slope into that sentimental view of God which remembers that he is love but conveniently forgets that his love is holy, righteous, love in the presence of which sin cannot stand."[135] Thirdly, Sell believed that "it has fairly been claimed that Campbell did not link his theory of the atonement with a doctrine of the Holy Spirit."[136] If sinners have to take hold of the fruits of Christ's sacrifice by their own efforts, Sell believes they are "uncomfortably close to a doctrine of salvation by works."[137] What is required is a Spirit-enabled response.

Our discussion of Campbell's atonement theology has revealed two things. First, we have seen how appreciative Sell is of Campbell's attempt to work out an alternative to the more objectionable features of Calvinist atonement theology. Secondly, we have seen why Sell, in criticizing Campbell's theology at three strategic points, turned to Forsyth for a more adequate alternative view.

P. T. Forsyth: The God of Holy Love

Forsyth's theology impressed Sell because it drives "decisively to the heart of the Gospel" in the work of Christ.[138] Forsyth maintains that "some real apostolic belief in the real work of Jesus Christ" is essential to the existence of the church.[139] He warns against any devaluing of the work of reconciliation, but his concern is much less with the church's survival than with the world's salvation. He believes that God's reconciling work in Jesus Christ is the only basis upon which "human society can . . . continue to exist in final unity."[140] For Forsyth, the Christ event is constitutive of the world's salvation.

Forsyth laments the way in which liberalism "beclouds" and "robs" Christianity of "the power of moral conviction by reducing the idea of sin

---

133. *COS*, 52.
134. Forsyth, *Work of Christ*, 228. Quoted by Sell in *CCC*, 66–67.
135. *HT*, 294.
136. *COS*, 53.
137. *COS*, 53.
138. *CCF*, 373. See also *EEE*, xii, 259 and *NT*, 163.
139. Forsyth, *Work of Christ*, 4.
140. Forsyth, *Work of Christ*, 9.

and dismissing the note of guilt."[141] He maintains that we must recognize that we stand as sinners before God's holiness, guilty and at the mercy of divine justice. He wants theology to stress God's holiness and duly recognize that human guilt stirs "the anger of a holy God" and produces separation from God.[142] Forsyth describes our sinfulness in lurid detail: it is "active hostility" to God and "enmity against God."[143] Sin so penetrates the human condition that even our ability to respond to Christ has to be created afresh. Since God by nature is holy, sin causes offence; the moral order has been thrown out of kilter; and, if any sense of justice is to be maintained, God's justice must be satisfied. Forsyth insists that God's judgment upon human sinfulness cannot be sidestepped; it is just as much part of the divine character as God's love: "The judgement of God is perfectly compatible with His continued love, just as a father's punishment is perfectly compatible with his love for his children."[144] Those who hold that the idea of God's judgment is morally repulsive, Forsyth argues, forget that God does not possess the power to overturn the divine nature. God is holy and, if eternal righteousness and holiness is to be maintained, God must exercise judgment over all contrary forces. What else should we expect?

> The holiness of God was God as holy. When that holiness is wounded or defied, could God be content to take us back with a mere censure or other penance and the declaration that He was holy? We would not respect a God like that. Servants despise indulgent masters.[145]

So how is God to be satisfied? How is the penalty for the human race's sin—what Forsyth calls "solidary sin"[146]—to be met? Where can our pardon be found?

We can clear a way for a description of Forsyth's understanding of Christ's work by noting some of the ideas often associated with atonement theories that he flatly rejects. He refuses to accept the notion that the atonement placated an angry God,[147] or that it is "the touchy honour of a feudal monarch that was to be dealt with at the head of the world."[148] Nor is recon-

---

141. Forsyth, *Work of Christ*, 229.
142. Forsyth, *Work of Christ*, 80.
143. Forsyth, *Work of Christ*, 19, 20.
144. Forsyth, *Work of Christ*, 119.
145. Forsyth, *Work of Christ*, 131.
146. Forsyth, *Work of Christ*, 189.
147. Forsyth, *Work of Christ*, 89–90.
148. Forsyth, *Work of Christ*, 231.

ciliation between God and human beings to be conceived as occurring due to "some third party coming between us and God, reconciling God on the one hand and us on the other."[149] Forsyth insists that since the atonement was made by God it is objective.[150] He rejects the idea that Christ's work was merely "an object-lesson of God's love";[151] it was rather "the divine initiative as an act" whereby God's justice is met and God's mercy is bestowed on the cross.[152] Forsyth also rejects the notion that atonement involves "a change of affection" in God.[153] He believes that "Reconciliation is not the result of a change in God from wrath to love," since "it flows from the changeless will of a loving God."[154] Nor does Forsyth sanction the classical substitutionary view of atonement: "we are not disposed to speak of substitution so much as representation. But it is the representation by One who creates by his act the Humanity He represents, and does not merely sponsor it."[155] Christ takes "the penalty of sin but Forsyth, forging a distinction between *penalty* and *punishment*, refuses "to speak of His taking its punishment."[156] And he also rejects the notion the Christ suffered an equivalent of the punishment due to the whole human race.[157]

In certain respects, Forsyth follows Campbell, but where Campbell speaks of Christ as a representative who vicariously confesses our sin before God, Forsyth argues that he confesses "God's holiness in His judgment upon sin."[158] The context in which this takes place is a meeting between persons, and the act by which reconciliation between the sinner and the holy God is achieved involves change by *both* parties. If the classical theories tend to express an objective change in God, more subjective alternatives move toward the other extreme by emphasizing the change which occurs in the sinner. Forsyth argues that both emphases are required in any adequate doctrine of Christ's work. To be sure, some critics suspect that Forsyth ends up stressing the "one event in the past" at the expense of "the salvation we experience," but Forsyth might be forgiven this if we remember that he was trying to counter what he considered to be the mistaken, one-sided, subjec-

---

149. Forsyth, *Work of Christ*, 88.
150. See Forsyth, *Work of Christ*, 93.
151. Forsyth, *Work of Christ*, 101.
152. Forsyth, *Work of Christ*, 69.
153. Forsyth, *Work of Christ*, 105.
154. Forsyth, *Work of Christ*, 180.
155. Forsyth, *Work of Christ*, 182.
156. Forsyth, *Work of Christ*, 162.
157. See Forsyth, *Work of Christ*, 181–82.
158. Forsyth, *Work of Christ*, 149.

tive emphasis found in much of the prevailing liberal theology of his day.[159] In the circumstances, it is not surprising that he stresses the sense in which "the moral adjustment of man and God" takes place "in one, holy, loving, mighty, final, and eternal act."[160] His priorities become clear when he argues that Christ's work on God is the prerequisite for his work on sinners. He suggests, for example, that "we could not have full security except by trust of an objective something, done over our heads, and complete without any reference to our response or our despite."[161]

But what was the "objective something" which, Forsyth believes, achieves the reconciliation between God and sinners? The heart of the matter lies in God's act by which the divine judgment on sin fell upon the sinless eternal Son of God. It was essentially a case of God reconciling God with no third party involvement. At his crucifixion, Christ as "the representative of the whole race" presented to God "a perfect racial obedience."[162] Another way Forsyth puts this is to say that "He presented before God a race He created for holiness."[163] But Forsyth not only looks back, he also looks forward. He tells us that Christ "represents before God not a natural Humanity that produces Him as its spiritual classic, but the new penitent Humanity that His influence creates."[164] As our representative, Christ made confession for us in an act of self-sacrifice and obedience through his life and death. This act found God making Christ to be sin for us and us righteous in Christ. Therefore, according to Forsyth, "The real ground for our forgiveness is not our confession of sin, and not even Christ's confession of our sin, but His agonized confession of God's holiness, and its absorbing effect on us."[165] Christ took our guilt upon him and "spread it out as it is before God," thereby experiencing the reality of sin "as only the holy could, as God did."[166] His obedience involved a *penal* sacrifice, but Forsyth argues this was not in the sense that "God punished Christ" or that "Christ was in our stead in such a way as to exclude and exempt us";[167] it was, rather, a matter of Christ bearing "God's penalty upon sin."[168] Forsyth's discussion

---

159. Fiddes, *Past Event*, 106.
160. Forsyth, *Justification*, 69.
161. Forsyth, *Work of Christ*, 187.
162. Forsyth, *Work of Christ*, 129.
163. Forsyth, *Work of Christ*, 129.
164. Forsyth, *Work of Christ*, 193.
165. Forsyth, *Work of Christ*, 214–15.
166. Forsyth, *Work of Christ*, 159.
167. Forsyth, *Work of Christ*, 146.
168. Forsyth, *Work of Christ*, 147.

of Christ's work, therefore, centers upon "solidary reparation" and not the idea of "substitutionary expiation."[169] Christ makes an adequate confession instead of receiving a punishment equivalent to that deserved by the whole human race.

Forsyth understands the atonement as the means by which the whole of humanity was reconciled. A change of relationship takes place, a new sense of community results — the church is born. Forsyth is very dismissive of individualism in religion. The collective sin of the race calls for what he calls "a collectivist redemption."[170] We enter into salvation, therefore, as we join the body of Christ and become part of what has already been achieved for us: "What He brought . . . was the Church, and not any aggregate of isolated souls."[171] The work of Christ is final in both nature and effect. What we all discover that we most need has in fact already been done for us. As Forsyth claims, "The last judgment is past."[172]

Sell was utterly convinced that Forsyth presents the most important account of Christ's work in recent theology. Forsyth presents the cross in such a way that, as Gunton puts it, it becomes "a way to express theologically a living relationship between God and the world."[173] Nevertheless, even a sympathetic supporter of Forsyth's position such as Gunton is forced to admit that Forsyth's proposal "may appear to lack a grounding in actual human life."[174] Many have concluded that Forsyth is strong on rhetoric but weak when it comes to setting out the way by which God's justice becomes real in human life. Indeed, there is something almost mystical and mysterious in the way Forsyth speaks of us being "absorbed" into the effects of an event from over two thousand years ago. And skeptics will press the point that the current state of the world hardly warrants Forsyth's confidence about the "finality" of Christ's work. They will want to know how a past event has a bearing on the present, rather than only hear assurances that a new order will be fully effective in some long-awaited future. But criticism of Forsyth is not our primary object, even if, given Sell's dependence on Forsyth's thought, criticism of Forsyth is also criticism of Sell.

---

169. Forsyth, *Work of Christ*, 164.
170. Forsyth, *Work of Christ*, 114.
171. Forsyth, *Work of Christ*, 114.
172. Forsyth, *Work of Christ*, 160.
173. Gunton, *Actuality of Atonement*, 107.
174. Gunton, *Actuality of Atonement*, 109.

Sell's Doctrine of Atonement

Our treatment of Sell's doctrine of atonement focuses upon ten points which are related to one another in a consecutive manner.

First, the need for atonement arises, Sell argues, because human sin has caused a breakdown in our relationship with God. We were created by God for fellowship with Godself, but the covenant relationship has been undermined because of our idolatry. A sense of "brokenness" and "disruption" results as we discover how the world has become out of kilter. We sense how we have fallen short of our intended relationship with God and become estranged from our true selves. The relationship we were to have with our Creator has been corrupted, but we are powerless to set matters right. Indeed, we may even need God to show us that things have gone awry.

Secondly, the redemptive initiative lies with the Triune God.[175] Sell eschewed all those "grotesque explications of the atonement"[176] which, taking their "point of departure from the sin of humanity rather than the grace of God,"[177] end up making immoral religious claims. The atonement does not involve an angry, outraged, holy God being placated, bought off or bribed in order that the wrathful God is "cajoled into being loving."[178] The cross did not "cause" God's love; it was rather the "effect" of it.[179] Sell was very fond of using a quotation from Forsyth to make this point: "The atonement did not procure grace, it flowed from grace."[180] He claimed that this was "the single most important sentence in the whole of *British* theological literature of the twentieth century,"[181] or, even, "the most important single sentence in *the whole of twentieth-century theology*."[182] But, as we have seen, it is far from original.[183] Put another way, Forsyth reminds us that "Reconciliation is not the result of a change in God from wrath to love. It flows from the changeless will of a loving God."[184]

---

175. See *RECT*, 81.

176. *MOG*, 32.

177. *ACI*, 37. See also *HT*, 184, 578; *CCF*, 34.

178. *COS*, 29. See also *ACI*, 37; *HT*, 538; *NT*, 172.

179. *COS*, 12.

180. Forsyth, *Cruciality*, 41. Sell quotes it at *HT*, 184; *CTF*, 285; *NT*, 172.

181. *CTF*, 285.

182. *NT*, 172.

183. See n119 above. It does, however, confirm how central "atonement" is to Sell's theology. Indeed, those of a more liberal disposition may be prompted to say that Sell is fixated on "sin" and "atonement."

184. Forsyth, *Work of Christ*, 180.

Jesus Christ

Thirdly, the work of the atonement belongs to the Triune God, with Father, Son and Spirit each involved in a unified way. Sell was insistent that "any view of the work of Christ which proceeds as if a wedge may be driven between the Father and the Son should be eschewed."[185] The atonement does not involve an "allegedly tyrannical Father" requiring the death of "the allegedly docile Son" before being able to be gracious and loving.[186] The key text here is "*in Christ* God was reconciling the world to himself" (2 Cor 5:19, italics mine). Sell was clear that "the Father is actively involved in the sacrifice of the Cross: he is not remote from it or untouched by it . . . the Father is not punishing the Son, but on the contrary he takes the weight and offers Christ to the world, with the promised Comforter standing by."[187] Sell recoiled from objective atonement theories being rejected *per se* on account of the wrong-headedness of their worst examples. It is also significant that he believed that the "unsystematic" Forsyth failed to show fully how "the entire Godhead is implicated in the work and reception of redemption."[188]

Fourthly, Sell advises us to avoid overtly forensic models for expressing the nature of atonement. We are wise to use metaphors based upon the interactions between human beings rather than those of the law-court. This does not mean, though, that Sell has no place for a juridical dimension in his doctrine of atonement. On the contrary, he affirms that, "as our *representative*, Jesus Christ paid to the full the penalty of our sinful refusal to honour God's law, to obey his will and to receive his grace."[189] Christ "humbled himself, suffered, died, rose again and ascended," and "the outworking of this . . . continues till now" though the work of the Holy Spirit.[190]

Fifthly, the atonement is more than exemplary: at the cross something was done. Sell declares that "at the Cross God in Christ did not merely *show* us something about his love, or our need, or both, but *acted* . . . for the salvation of the world by vanquishing sin and death and all that could keep us from him."[191] What took place on the cross, he tells us, was "a radical . . . act of rescue on the part of the holy and merciful God,"[192] and, hence, "a divinely initiated atoning act wrought in the midst of human history by one

---

185. *EEE*, 380. See also *COS*, 28; *MOG*, 332; *HT*, 610.
186. *HT*, 610. See also *EEE*, 380.
187. *HT*, 610.
188. *TAT*, 152.
189. *EEE*, 383. Italics mine.
190. *HT*, 293.
191. *EEE*, 385.
192. *PR*, 21.

who is God incarnate."[193] The act was supernatural: it could not have been conceived or carried out by nature; and its essential purpose was nature's restoration.

Sixthly, the atoning act was unique. Sell claims that "in the Cross-Resurrection event God acted *once and for all* for the redemption of the world."[194] He stresses the "once-for-allness" of God's initiative in the Christ event, thereby introducing a decidedly exclusivist interpretation of the soteriological significance of Jesus' life and work. The so-called "scandal of particularity" is embraced by him. It must be accommodated,[195] it cannot be by-passed;[196] and it "may not be obliterated."[197] Something different in kind from anything before or since happened on the cross: What took place was crucial for the whole human race. Sell's exclusivist stance raises acute issues concerning the salvific status of the non-Christian world Faiths and their relationship with Christianity.

Seventhly, God by nature cannot behave as if sin does not matter: the divine justice needs satisfying. Sell claims that there must be a propitiatory element in sound atonement theology unless we are to lose contact with the fact that God is not just love but *holy* love. He argues that "it is God in Christ who renders satisfaction and reconciles the world to himself."[198] While the Father gave up the Son to suffering and death on the cross, the Son accepted his role voluntary. Sell acknowledges that this brings him to "an aspect of the mystery of the cross which must forever elude out attempts to 'explain' it."[199]

Eighthly, God's action in Christ-crucified enables God to accept sinners as righteous. The atoning sacrifice has been made and accepted: "A broken relationship is restored, the penitent are forgiven and a new quality of life is bestowed."[200] God has done what human beings could not do for themselves. Through a stupendous and gracious act—the Christ event—the broken relationship between God and human beings has been mended. Men and women can know, through a Holy Spirit engendered faith, that their sins will not be counted against them. As they reflect theologically upon their renewed status before God they will become aware that "the tri-

---

193. *PICB*, 188.
194. *ACI*, 118. See also *COM*, 267; *EEE*, 385; *PR*, 21.
195. See *PICB*, 232.
196. See *RECT*, 196.
197. *RECT*, 238.
198. *TNM*, 245.
199. *RECT*, 31.
200. *CCF*, 35.

umph at the cross" includes an interactive mixture of "holy love, sovereign grace, [and] righteous mercy."²⁰¹ But, it ought to be asked, was the possibility of our forgiveness *constituted* by the cross? What about the witness to the forgiveness of God in the Old Testament (e.g., Jer 31:34; Ps 86:5)? What about Jesus, prior to the cross, welcoming sinners and offering forgiveness? It is more theologically coherent to claim that what is witnessed to in Jesus' religious tradition, as well as in his life and work, *re-presented* rather than constituted God's offer of forgiveness to sinners.

Ninthly, what God has achieved through the triumph of the cross does not provide those who have benefitted from it any grounds for triumphalism. Those who have been drawn into the community called "church" on account of their faith may well know the way but they have not yet reached the goal. They may well have been justified by God but the Holy Spirit engendered process of sanctification is a life-long vocation. Sell is quite clear that "the Cross does not legitimate Christian triumphalism."²⁰² And he reminds us that "Jesus was first called Lord over against the Caesars of this world; that his Lordship is that of one who takes a towel and does slave's work by washing his friend's feet; that to a large extent the Gospel concerns the condescension of this Lord; and that he, and no one else—and no ideology either—can claim our absolute loyalty."²⁰³ But while the church must seek to avoid triumphalism, there will always be a place for it to proclaim the triumph of the cross. To fail to do so, Sell maintains, is to lose the gospel. But, I regret, when it has done so it has often displayed an imperialistic attitude to other world Faiths.

Finally, Sell insists that commitments to social justice ought not to be allowed to usurp a proper emphasis upon the atonement. He was certainly not against Christians doing everything in their power to make the world a more just and peaceable place; but he was concerned lest we forget what he took to be an essential truth. In Forsyth's words, "We shall never get permanent justice done to human nature till we are concerned before that about having justice done to God."²⁰⁴ But just how such a claim can be squared with the witness of Jesus will be taken up within our later consideration of whether Sell's atonement theology is authorized by Jesus' life and teaching.

It is important to remember the contextual nature of our understanding of Christ's work. Within the period of the New Testament churches theories to explain Christ's work were well established. As Christianity

201. *EEE*, 391.
202. *EEE*, 386.
203. *EEE*, 386.
204. Forsyth, *Faith, Freedom and the Future*, 38. Quoted by Sell at *EEE*, 388.

developed various metaphors drawn from everyday experience were exploited as atonement theologies took shape. From the world of the Jewish sacrificial system came the idea that Christ was the perfect sacrifice that wiped out human sin. Experience of military conflict provided the notion that the cross represented Christ's defeat of the Devil. From the slave market came the idea of Christ paying a ransom to set free sinful people. The law-courts provided the motif of Christ paying the penalty and undergoing the punishment for human sin. A feudal culture's acceptance of the need to honor superiors in a hierarchical society contributed the idea of satisfaction. Meanwhile the medical word threw up metaphors of healing and restoration. As we study the history of Christian thought we often find these atonement models operating side by side. There never has been a time when there has been one agreed means of talking about Christ's work. Indeed, it takes a kaleidoscope of metaphors even to get close to doing it justice, and even then we will never penetrate the mystery.

The models of atonement with which we are familiar all arose as Christians reflected upon, and tried to make sense of their experience of forgiveness. Groves reminds us that "Models of God's redemptive act begin with the Christian experience of grace and forgiveness and not with something which happened long ago."[205] All images of the atonement "come after the fact . . . as attempts to give content to the Christian life of transformation by grace."[206] As different people, at different times, and in different cultures, have reflected upon their experience of forgiveness soteriologies reflecting their contexts emerged. Forsyth is no exception. In Chapman's opinion, he is "a theologian with a fixation on the holiness of God, the justice of the cross, and obedience to God's will."[207] From our standpoint, it is relatively easy to spot "the highly patriarchal and authoritarian character of Forsyth's language."[208] Forsyth invariably associates "the heroic features of faith" stereotypically with male strength, power, and assertiveness, and what he considers distortions of true faith are linked by him to the "feminine."[209] Bewailing the lack of men in the Congregational congregations of 1917 he applauds the women of those churches in a back-handed way: "It is not so much that we have now more female Christianity, but that we have less male. The Christianity of the men has ebbed, and left the godliness of the women

---

205. Groves, "Atonement," 27.
206. Groves, "Atonement," 29.
207. Chapman, Review of *Justice the True and Only Mercy*, 58.
208. Chapman, Review of *Justice the True and Only Mercy*, 58.
209. Forsyth, *Rome, Reform and Reaction*, 14.

more conspicuous. It is realized much has always been due to them."[210] Given what was happening in Western Europe at the time it was hardly surprising that the churches were down in their male membership figures. But we can ask: "What constitutes "female Christianity" and "the Christianity of men"? Forsyth's answer is clear: the former is a religion of "the heart and the temperament" with a preponderance towards sentimentality, the latter "a faith for the mind, the conscience, and the will."[211] There are few better examples of sexual stereotyping in Christian theology. It reflects what we now regard as an impaired understanding both of people and the composition of Christian churches.

Forsyth cannot be faulted for being a child of his time, but we might have expected Sell, from his different standpoint, to have provided a critique of the patriarchal and sexist nature of Forsyth's theology. Forsyth belonged to the Victorian/Edwardian era with its distinctive take on law and order. The overriding concern was punishment rather than rehabilitation, the so-called regime of "hard bed, hard board and hard labour." To his credit, Forsyth attempted to avoid a *penal* element in his atonement doctrine, but one senses that his hard language about the gravity of sin, and his insistence that Christ voluntarily paid the *penalty* for sin, reflects the era in which he lived. Pailin laments the fact that "the reality of divine salvation" is often interpreted in "a mainly negative way—as a matter of being saved *from* something nasty" instead of being affirmed more positively as being set free *for* something good.[212] But, for Sell, the possibility of the latter appears to depend upon the achievement of the former. While moral codes change over time the church has a habit of clinging on to aspects which are well past their sell-by dates. An account of Christ's work so heavily dependent on notions of "satisfaction" and "sacrifice" will hardly ring bells in today's world.[213] Sell is to be congratulated, though, for being determined to avoid any *overt* suggestion that God's saving love of sinners is dependent on God being somehow cajoled into turning from judgmental anger to accepting love by a propitiatory sacrifice. But, following Forsyth, he insists that there is a *double* atonement, one which not only recognizes the benefit accrued to sinners but also specifies that Christ's voluntary sacrifice on behalf of his

210. Forsyth, *Church and Sacraments*, 19.
211. Forsyth, *Church and Sacraments*, 21.
212. Pailin, *Probing the Foundations*, 178.
213. But, as Robert Pope has pointed out to me, the ideal of redemptive violence is present in the music of modern culture, notions of people needing to receive due punishment for their crimes is deeply embed in the human psyche, and the hero willing to die for the good of others is celebrated. Such ideas may be analogous to some Christian atonement teaching whatever we make of its appropriateness and credibility.

fellow men and women satisfied God's need for justice and righteousness by his hallowing of God's name. Thereby he retains in his soteriology a feature which stresses that God's saving love is in *some* sense conditional. Others, rightly to my mind, will stress that Christ's voluntary sacrifice was that of a Godly life, and his death the consequence of living such a life in a brutal world.

This leads me to ask whether Sell's understanding of the atonement is underscored by Christ's life and teaching? His atonement model is rooted in the image of a holy God in whose presence sin cannot stand. But Jesus does not seem to have exercised a similar taboo: there is no stand-off with sinners as far as he is concerned. He not only accepts their company, he seeks it out. It gains him a reputation: "Look, a glutton and a drunkard, a friend of tax-collectors and sinners!" (Luke 7:34). He also told stories which inferred that the likes of tax-collectors and prostitutes would be going into God's kingdom ahead of "the priests and the elders of the people" (see Matt 21:23–32). And, then, there was that most revealing story which left everyone who heard it knowing that God's love is unconditional (Luke 15:11–32). It is very difficult to see how the Father's reaction to his prodigal equates with Sell's insistence that an adequate understanding of Christ's work involves the Father having the Son *somehow* satisfying a need for justice and righteousness. Sell's critics can be forgiven for wondering what more is needed for atonement than true repentance and wholesale openness to God's redeeming grace? A fundamental flaw in Sell's theology, I believe, centers upon the way that he prioritizes Christ's work over his person to such an extent that he loses touch with the way Jesus' person and life offers us guidance concerning the nature of his saving work. Sell is sometimes too Forsythian for his own good. Mark Chapman, for example, claims that "the greatest gap" in Forsyth's theology is that "there is no room for a God who refuses holiness."[214] But, if the earliest traditions about Jesus are to be believed, such an insistence on God's holiness would mean "that the God who is in Christ is no longer God."[215]

However much he seeks to avoid Forsyth's tendency to state one truth at the expense of another truth, Sell falls victim to it. One example is the way in which, following Forsyth, he repeatedly thunders that the cross involves an *act* of God rather than being merely an *example* of God's salvific action. But why cannot it involve both? Sell is reluctant to accede to such an idea for to do so might compromise his commitment to the cross as a "once-for-all" event constitutive of salvation. If, however, we hold "salvation" in

---

214. Review of Hart, *Justice the True and Only Mercy*, 58.
215. Hart, *Justice the True and Only Mercy*, 58.

Jesus Christ

much closer relation to "creation" than Sell does, it is possible to regard the Christ-event as the decisive re-presentation of God's universal offer of salvation instead of the one *constitutive* presentation of it. God is *always* creative in salvific ways, not just in the Christ event. While there are many who follow the *exclusivist* stance favored by Sell, others can no longer support such a contention. First hand encounter with non-Christians in our multiracial society has left them with a deep appreciation of religions other than Christianity. They find it difficult to believe that there is no salvific value in them. Rather than accept an *exclusivist* attitude of Christianity towards other religions, they want to be more affirming of those religions. This may involve people in continuing to affirm that the Christ event *constitutes* the possibility of salvation, but making the added claim that the work of Christ can be seen *anonymously* in other great religions;[216] or it could involve people arguing that the Christ event is *representative* rather than constitutive of the possibility of salvation;[217] or it might even mean that people travel across the theological Rubicon to a *pluralist* view which sees all the world's faiths as different but, in some degree, legitimate means of offering salvation.[218] Whichever position such people adopt they will demur at statements like this: "It is only by Christ's holy work, translated into the holy society of the Churches, that Society at large can be converted into the holy Kingdom of God."[219] Unfortunately, this exclusivist assertion unnecessarily limits God's redemptive activity, even though it clearly points to the church's missionary mandate.

In Shakespeare we find Lear saying, "I am a man / More sinned against than sinning" (*King Lear* 3, 2). One can sense the vast majority of the world's population wanting to say something similar in the wake of the Forsyth/Sell take on salvation. Its agenda will be deemed parochial when set in the global context. For the Forsythian it is sin which causes the offence of which the human race is guilty before God. However, as Fung has observed, the primary problem which besets the inhabitants of the "Two-Third's World" is not that they are sinners but rather that they are repeatedly and systematically sinned against by a global economic and political system which maintains them in grinding poverty and merciless dependency.[220] Their problems

---

216. See the work of Rahner, *Theological Investigations*, Vols. 5, 6, 14 and 16, for a sophisticated treatment of the "inclusivist" position.

217. For a sustained defence of "pluralistic inclusivism" (as distinguished from Rahner's "monistic inclusivism") see Ogden, *Is There Only One True Religion?*

218. See Hick and Knitter, *Myth of Christian Uniqueness*.

219. Forsyth, "Holy Church," 33.

220. I owe my understanding of the distinction between being a "sinner" and being "sinned against" to Fung's series of letters on evangelism published by the WCC.

are not self-inflicted but imposed by others; they are political rather than personal; social and not simply individual. From the perspective of the underside of history, therefore, Forsyth's prescriptions for human ills will appear to be merely palliative, and dismissed as naïve, since few today can seriously subscribe to a view that the simple and straight-forward way to establish justice and equality in society is to work on changing the lives of individuals. And yet this was Forsyth's strategy: "Set that right in every man by what sets right also the race, and right views and right relations will follow as the night the day."[221] Robert Paul acknowledges that "Forsyth was perhaps too optimistic at this point."[222] It is always tempting in a Western sitting room, though, to wax eloquently about the world becoming a better place, as more and more people turn from their personal sin through their encounter "with the event which has seen the destruction by God in Christ of sin's guilt and sin's distrust, and sin's blocking of the sky."[223] But, as Reinhold Niebuhr has taught us, sin is a most complex phenomenon; and it is found in its most virulent form in social, economic, and political manifestations which are immune to the individualistic strategies advanced by a lot of Western theology.[224]

Gunton, for example, insists that "the Church's being, acts and words ... fulfil its responsibility to society" when they are directed to the basis of "all human social life ... in redemption."[225] This leads him to assert that "The primary task is not to organize the world, but to be within it as a particular way of being human, a living reminder of the true basis and end of human life."[226] But, we ask: Is the basis of "all human life" found "in redemption" alone? Is there not a further injunction, one that flows from Jesus, that we love our neighbor as ourselves—as well as loving God with all our heart and mind? Is not the theme of "emancipation" also to be brought into view if we are to give an adequate account of God's liberating work? If that liberating work involves the "emancipation" as well as the "redemption" of sinner and sinned-against alike, it is legitimate to conclude that the church is called to do more than "remind the state that political and moral programmes are secondary to and depend upon redemption."[227] In obedience to the One whose liberating work encompasses both "redemption" and "emancipation"

---

221. Forsyth, *Positive Peaching*, 40.
222. Paul, "P. T. Forsyth," 51.
223. Forsyth, *Positive Preaching*, 40.
224. See Niebuhr, *Moral Man*.
225. Gunton, *Actuality of Atonement*, 193.
226. Gunton, *Actuality of Atonement*, 193.
227. Gunton, *Actuality of Atonement*, 193.

the Church ought to be engaged in social and political activity to establish "political and moral programmes" that become the context in which "the creative transformation of relations" *does* take place.[228] Christ's work is prophetic: the cross has social implications and a political dimension. As Brueggemann argues:

> The cross is the ultimate metaphor of prophetic criticism because it means the end of the old consciousness that brings death on everyone. The crucifixion articulates God's odd freedom, his strange justice, and his peculiar power. It is this *freedom* (read religion of God's freedom), *justice* (read economics of sharing), and *power* (read politics of justice) that break the power of the old age and bring it to death ... The cross is the assurance that effective prophetic criticism is done not by an outsider but one who must embrace the grief, enter into the death, and know the pain of the criticized one.[229]

It is surprising that Sell never engages with such a seminal thinker as Brueggemann.

Sell takes a more balanced attitude than Gunton to the incorporation of "emancipation" alongside "redemption" in a holistic view of Christian liberation. He notes that the liberation theologians have reminded us that "there is no genuine liberation of persons which does not have a sociopolitical dimension and that, where the oppressed are concerned, it is necessary to be for them and against the oppressors."[230] But it remains the case that Sell is never found challenging theologians for not paying enough attention to "emancipation" in their soteriologies. Instead, he is invariably found taking to task those he perceives are so emphasizing "emancipation" that proper concerns for "redemption" are not being met. At one point he quotes Garvie approvingly: "Man's self-sacrifice for the good of society has sometimes been so insisted on as to obscure God's self-sacrifice on behalf of man, in which alone is a motive potent enough for the moral task to which man is called."[231] But I know of no instance where Sell criticizes someone for failing to take the emancipatory dimensions of salvation seriously enough.

While some will remain suspicious about whether Sell is fully committed to a holistic view of Christian liberation, the apologetic strength of his soteriology is questioned further by the prevailing mood of the Western world. Stanley Russell claims that Forsyth will not be "the cutting edge for

---

228. Gunton, *Actuality of Atonement*, 193.
229. Brueggemann, *Prophetic Imagination*, 99.
230. *EEE*, 314.
231. Garvie, "Limits of Doctrinal Restatement," 94. Quoted by Sell at *EEE*, 315.

our evangelism today."[232] In a world dominated by the culture of "life-style choices" it is no longer the accepted view that "morality is the nature of things."[233] Ours is a world without a clear sense of sin, so the need for atonement does not arise in people's minds. The doctrine of Christ's work according to Forsyth the teacher and Sell the pupil, therefore, may well be "a great resource for the spiritual refreshment of the faithful" but it is less likely to become a successful Christian apologetic in our contemporary environment.[234]

---

232. Russell, Review of *P. T. Forsyth*, 95.
233. Russell, Review of *P. T. Forsyth*, 95.
234. Russell, Review of *P. T. Forsyth*, 95.

6

Holy Spirit

At the beginning of *The Spirit Our Life*, Sell writes what he describes as "the longest and clumsiest sentence in this book."[1] It goes as follows: "By God the Holy Spirit I mean the fatherly God of holy love whom we know in the victorious Christ of the Bible, as generously active in the world; as life-givingly active in us; as drawing out and enabling our response of faith, love, and service; as uniting us to Christ and therefore to each other in his Church; as ever renewing and refining our life in this world; and as holding us in fellowship with himself eternally."[2] Long it certainly is; clumsy it may well be; but the sentence neatly encapsulates the content of Sell's doctrine of the Holy Spirit. It demonstrates the Trinitarian context within which he sets this doctrine.

THE SPIRIT OF PENTECOST

The doctrine of the Holy Spirit deals with the way in which God is active in the created order and the means by which God's love is forever being expressed in God's ongoing relationships with the world. As we read the New Testament witness about the way in which Jesus' followers experienced God working in their lives, we are confronted with mighty claims about the renewal of people's lives. Our attention is drawn also to life-changing and sometimes spectacular occurrences in the experience of Christian people.

---

1. *SOL*, 1.
2. *SOL*, 1.

But, as Sell points out, "there were some loose ends" in that witness.³ He notes the way in which the Spirit is described variously as "the Spirit of Jesus," "the Spirit of Jesus Christ," "the Spirit of God's Son," and "the Spirit of God"; he observes the way in which sometimes the Spirit is said to be active in Jesus' ministry, while at other times the texts suggest that the Spirit was a post-Easter gift to an embryonic church; and, hence, he concludes that, "It is certainly no surprise that those who came afterwards had to contend with differences of emphasis within the texts as they sought to hammer out doctrine."⁴ As later generations of Christians sought clarification of doctrine and attempted to offset heresies, they discovered that the provisionality attached to all Christian claims applies particularly to those concerning the Spirit. Given God's sovereign freedom, who can possibly determine the exact outworking of God's gracious love? The Spirit blows where the Spirit wills and that may be beyond our wildest imagining.

Sell emphasizes that "the earliest Christians did not simply believe in God the Holy Spirit—they *experienced* him."⁵ Then they interpreted their experience through categories within a cultural understanding dominated by the Hebrew concept of *ruach* and the Greek word *pneuma*. *Ruach* originally referred to elemental "wind" or "breath" but, as Sell reminds us, following the Babylonian exile it "came to denote the human being's rational and emotional centre."⁶ From being conceived as an external force, *ruach* evolved into the description of an internal phenomenon akin to what we now understand by conscience. This phenomenon was known by the early Greek-speaking Christians as *pneuma*. Sell points out, however, that both Old and New Testaments refer to both good and evil spirits, thus posing the crucial need always to "test the spirits to see whether they are from God" (1 John 4:1).

While Sell acknowledges that the Spirit was at work prior to the Christ event, until that event he could not have been "understood as Christians understand him."⁷ The Old Testament, of course, contains prophecies concerning the Spirit coming into the world (Joel 2:28–29; Ezek 37), and in the New Testament John the Baptist is the herald of God's Spirit coming into people's lives (Mark 1:8). Sell insists, though, that "There was no sure knowledge of God the Holy Spirit as the agent of *re-creation* as of creation until Jesus associated him so clearly with himself and made it clear that the Spirit

---

3. SOL, 4.
4. SOL, 4.
5. SOL, 1.
6. SOL, 2.
7. SOL, 3.

Holy Spirit

was to continue *his* work in the world."[8] Following the Christ event, the Spirit is no longer an occasional visitor, but the very presence of God living among Christ's friends. Pentecost marks the moment when the role of the Spirit comes fully into view: bringing new life to the world; enabling people to live saintly lives; creating and sustaining the church; bringing salvation to individuals; and generating eternal hope amidst the temporal world. Sell is making a bold statement by suggesting that God's activity within creation is different in kind after Jesus' death than before it. That is how it may seem to Christians, but how do we know that is the case? A measure of holy reticence is in order lest unwarranted triumphalism is to set in.

Sell is concerned that the Spirit be understood in *personal* categories. The Spirit is known and experienced as the one who continues the work God started in the Christ event. As the third member of the Trinity, the Spirit's relation to the world is identical to God's relation to the world. Sell puts it as follows: "The Spirit is the personal God as transcendent over us in challenge and demand, and as immanently at work in us as guide and sustainer."[9] The Spirit is the "Spirit of Jesus . . . not some kind of anonymous 'world soul.'"[10] When we test the spirits to discern whether they are of God, Jesus is the yardstick. Nor must we equate the Spirit to "'the spirit of the age,' 'the spirit of progress,' the evolutionary principle, or blind force"[11] since the third member of the Trinity is transcendent as well as ceaselessly present and active. Sell is determined to give due weight to both transcendence and immanence in his doctrine of the Holy Spirit, but we have already expressed concern over whether the conceptuality he uses enables him to do this adequately.[12]

The Nicaeno-Constantinopolitan Creed (381) states that "We believe in the Holy Spirit, the Lord, the giver of life, who proceeds from the Father."[13] But at the Third Council of Teledo (589) the king recited a version which contained an addition that implied a *double* rather than single procession of the Holy Spirit.[14] This addition, called the *filioque* clause, had become fully part of the Western version of this Creed by the eighth century, even though it took some time to be accepted in the Roman church. Its insertion was always bitterly resented by the Eastern Church and the *filioque*

---

8. *SOL*, 3.
9. *SOL*, 4.
10. *SOL*, 7.
11. *SOL*, 4.
12. See chapter 3.
13. Found in Thompson, *Stating the Gospel*, 9, and Bettenson, *Documents*, 37.
14. See Kelly, *Early Christian Creeds*, 361.

issue remains an unresolved point of contention between the Eastern and Western branches of the church. In an ecumenical spirit, Sell acknowledges that "There is growing agreement that the implications of the addition of the *filioque* must be faced, and the underlying theology analysed afresh."[15] But Sell never tells us what might emerge from such an analysis. He does remind us, though, of the reasons for the addition of the *filioque*: it underscores the strand of New Testament witness which asserts that the Spirit is the Son's gift to his followers; it accommodates the New Testament witness to the Spirit being the Spirit of *both* Father and Son; and it testifies to the way in which "equality with the Father and the Son is roundly attributed to the Spirit."[16] But there are reasons to suggest that the addition of the *filioque* was a mistake.

Moltmann and Gunton, for example, provide several reasons to support the view that the addition of the *filioque* was a basic error. First, when the Spirit is said to proceed from the Father and the Son, it is difficult to see how it is possible to avoid subordinating the Spirit to the Son.[17] The Western view allows Christological concerns to dominate, thus tending to reduce the Spirit's work to its focus in Jesus. At a time when there is a greater awareness of the existence and worth of the world religions it becomes increasingly implausible to understand the Spirit's work exclusively through the lens of the Christ event. Secondly, Jesus' life would seem to indicate that the Spirit stands over and against him. This suggests that the Western view fails to do justice to the biblical evidence. Moltmann puts it like this: "If Christ was conceived by the Holy Spirit, baptized with the Spirit, then he presupposes the Spirit, and the Spirit precedes him."[18] But this cannot be expressed adequately when it is claimed that the Spirit proceeds from the Father *and* the Son. Gunton, meanwhile, also notes that the Gospels show that "the Spirit is portrayed as over-against Jesus, driving him into the wilderness to be tempted, supporting him through temptation and empowering the ministry that follows."[19] The evidence of "the otherness of the Spirit" requires "a doctrine of the personal distinctness of the Holy Spirit in relation to both Son and Father" which, in turn, demands "the abandonment of the Western *Filioque*."[20] Sell insists, nevertheless, that "the divine Spirit" be understood

---

15. *SOL*, 6.
16. *SOL*, 6.
17. See Moltmann, *Spirit of Life*, 295.
18. Moltmann, *Spirit of Life*, 295.
19. Gunton, *Promise*, 134.
20. Gunton, *Promise*, 134.

"in terms of God's supreme revelation in Christ."[21] The Holy Spirit does not bring a new revelation but bears witness to Christ: "he is not just any spirit. He is God the Holy Spirit, and we know him in Christ."[22] The key to "testing" the manifold spirits which claim people's allegiance, therefore, is whether they are "Christlike."[23]

The Holy Spirit is "by no means exclusively inward and private"; nor does the Spirit come to people "*incognito*"; but, rather, the Spirit bears the nature of Christ.[24] Sell would have agreed with Moltmann that, when affirming that the Spirit proceeds from the Father, what is being claimed is that the Spirit proceeds from the *Father of the Son*. Moltmann tells us that, "The Son is the logical presupposition and actual condition for the procession of the Spirit from the Father; but he is not the Spirit's origin, as the Father is."[25] This is a way of seeking a *via media* between East and West concerning the *filioque* controversy. Against the West, Moltmann denies that the Spirit proceeds from the Father and the Son, while, against the Eastern view, he insists that "the Spirit proceeds from the Father in the eternal presence of the Son, and . . . therefore the Son is not uninvolved in it."[26]

Following Calvin, Sell wishes to hold together Word and Spirit in his theology.[27] He reminds us that Calvin was "fighting on two fronts."[28] On the one hand, against Roman Catholicism's claim that authority rests with the Pope and his bishops, he argues that God's word revealed in Scripture is "the supreme authority for faith and practice."[29] On the other hand, "Against the fanatics with their claim to be in receipt of extra-biblical, often eccentric, revelations [Calvin] is no less severe."[30] The objective Word protects us against all "subjective whims and fancies while "the subjective work of the Spirit" ensures the Word never degenerates into "a dead letter."[31] Sell maintains that "the Spirit confirms and brings home the Word, he does not contradict it or supplement it."[32] While the Spirit may blow where the Spirit

21. *SOL*, 8,
22. *SOL*, 9.
23. *SOL*, 8.
24. *SOL*, 8.
25. Moltmann, *Trinity*, 184.
26. Moltmann, *Trinity*, 184.
27. See *SOL*, 9–10.
28. *CTF*, 155.
29. *CTF*, 155.
30. *CTF*, 155.
31. *SOL*, 10.
32. *CTF*, 155.

wills, it would seem that the direction of travel is mapped out by Christ. But this does not imply that the work of the Holy Spirit is confined to the Christ event and its outworking in the church and the world.[33] Sell insists that, while the Holy Spirit is "supremely" found at work in that event, the third member of the Trinity is also found at work prior to and beyond it.[34] He acknowledges that this work may be "unknown or unacknowledged" but it is of "tremendous importance."[35] Sell is particularly insistent, therefore, that we acknowledge that the Holy Spirit's work is not confined to the church. He joins those who think that "some Pentecostals are not Pentecostal enough" chiding them for talking a great deal about "the Spirit's gifts to the individual" but being rather silent about "the Spirit in relation to creation, the world or even the Church."[36] It is a feature of Sell's generous orthodoxy that he tells us that "The essential nature of the Spirit is to be learned from Christ, but his work may not be restricted to the sphere of things Christian."[37] It does not follow, therefore, that those who remain outside the stream of influence which flows from Jesus are necessarily "beyond the love, the influence, the reach of God."[38] What this means for the relationship between Christianity and the other world faiths, and how it contributes to answering the question concerning whether salvation is to be found outside Christianity, is never made clear.

REGENERATION: BRINGING NEW LIFE

Christians, according to Sell, are called to a new way of life. By God's grace they are drawn into a union with Christ which is at the heart of Christian experience. This new relationship is made possible by God who, through the work of the Spirit, takes the initiative in redemption. Our response to the gift and demand of God's love is motivated by the Spirit. Sell, therefore emphasizes "the inward, effectual, powerful call of the Spirit" without which "nothing moves."[39] Sinners are moved to the throne of grace by God's help; it is the Spirit who ensures they arrive and respond.

Sell reminds us that the Spirit's activity is a unified work appearing in several forms, but he rejects the idea of those "older theologians" who "gave

---

33. See *EEE*, 296–97.
34. *SOL*, 11.
35. *SOL*, 11.
36. *SOL*, 76.
37. *SOL*, 11.
38. *SOL*, 11.
39. *SOL*, 17.

the impression that the "different works of the Spirit" could be placed "in temporal succession."[40] They conceived an order of salvation (*ordo salutis*) which formed "a linear route" over which believers in turn passed—covering, in sequence, "effectual calling, justification, adoption, sanctification, saving faith and repentance."[41] Sell argues instead that "these grand old words" refer to multiple aspects of the one experience of finding new life in Jesus Christ. Nor will Sell countenance the Spirit's work being described as the "application of redemption."[42] He maintains that such ways of speaking convey the impression of an *external* agent of redemption who "in some way violates our freedom as he operates upon us from without."[43] But, he insists, nothing is further from the truth.

Sell delineates three principal features of the process which leads to a person becoming a Christian.

Called by Grace and Born Again

Sell testifies that the calling to be a follower of Jesus is special: "Those who are called are highly privileged and richly blessed."[44] But what is the nature of this call? Sell tells us that it has both *external* and *internal* dimensions. God's *external* call is addressed to all who have been born in God's image. It is directed to everyone in the preaching of the gospel when individuals are challenged to repent from their sins and believe anew in God. But ministers, preachers, and evangelists can only do so much. Sell quotes Watson: "Ministers knock at the door of men's hearts, the Spirit comes with the key and opens the door."[45] He argues, therefore, that the *internal* work of the Spirit accounts for the motivation of sinners to seek forgiveness. But our freedom is never violated: we are drawn not dragged into a relationship with God. It is "truly a miracle" that those called *inwardly* receive new life: "the first creation was amazing enough; the re-creation of the sinner is more amazing still, and it is all of grace."[46] Sell stresses the dramatic nature of regeneration: it involves the bringing to life of those who are spiritually dead; it entails a new birth by God's grace; and it can even be likened to being raised from the

40. *SOL*, 15.
41. *SOL*, 15.
42. *SOL*, 16.
43. *SOL*, 16.
44. *SOL*, 16.
45. *SOL*, 16–17.
46. *SOL*, 18.

dead (Rom 5:4). Through the work of the Spirit, the Father calls us through the Son and renews us in God's image.

Convicted of Sin, Brought to Repentance, and Granted Forgiveness

Sell is never reticent to emphasize his belief that we have to reckon with the gravity of our sin and the fact that we cannot do anything about it on our own. He invites us to focus our attention on Romans 7:14–25, where Paul confronts us with both law and gospel. His exegesis of the passage is as follows: the law of God tells us how far away from God we are; it sets us unattainable standards; and it leaves us without excuse since we know what God expects of us but are utterly unable to do what is required. This hapless predicament causes Paul deep anguish: "Wretched man that I am! Who will rescue me from this body of death?" (Rom 7:24). As Sell puts it: "It is not more instruction, more advice that [we] need. It is power, ability."[47] And as soon as we recognize that true fulfillment cannot be gained from *self*-sufficiency, *self*-determination or *self*-righteousness, we are on the cusp of being open to hearing the gospel message: "Thanks be to God through Jesus Christ our Lord!" (Rom 7:25). We will now explore that message further as we comment on each component of the section heading.

First, the process of regeneration starts *for some* with the conviction of sin but for others, I believe, it begins with their simply being among the followers of Jesus. Sell tends to underplay the implications of Jesus' first call on people being to follow him when he argues that, through the proclamation of the gospel, we realize that our sinfulness is an affront to God and hear God's claim on our lives. We learn, as Sell puts it, that our primary concern ought not to be "for our own condition" grave though it is, "but for his honor and glory."[48] Both our hearing of the good news concerning the steps God has taken to forge a new relationship with us, as well as learning to put God and others before self, are the result of the Holy Spirit's work upon us.

Secondly, Sell tells us that, "By humbling us the Spirit prompts and enables our repentance."[49] If we believe in God's gracious gift to us in Christ, we will recognize the enormous gulf which separates sinners from God. The Spirit will then enable us to renounce sin and commence a new life. As Sell puts it: "Repentance *is* a turning—a complete turning around of the whole person."[50] This turning *from* sin and *to* God represents a radical change

---

47. *SOL*, 20.
48. *SOL*, 20.
49. *SOL*, 20.
50. *SOL*, 21.

in a person's life. Some Christian converts proudly can state a date, time and place when such an about-turn initially took place in their lives; other Christians cannot, or they decline to locate the origin of their Christian discipleship in such a precise way. But, whatever the nature of the way we become Christians, Sell reminds us that "repentance must be a continuous work."[51] While none of the believers' sins are imputed to them by God, they still sin and therefore must always be on their guard for the rest of their lives concerning their propensity to sin.

Thirdly, Sell affirms that those who truly repent of their sins enter into a renewed relationship with God. To put it another way, they are *reconciled* with God. God's forgiveness of sinners makes that reconciliation possible. Sell emphasizes that "God's forgiveness is full and free and has no strings attached."[52] It is never the case that we get back into God's good books if we repent enough. If it were, we would be departing from the world of "justification by grace through faith" and entering that of "salvation by works." But how can we know that believers know forgiveness? The answer, Sell observes, is whether a believer in turn forgives others: there are no sins which God cannot forgive; so it must be with the believer. While it is the Spirit's work which enables our repentance, we still have to make it our own through a commitment to make an about-turn in our lives. Conversion, therefore, is radically experiential. Sell, however, warns believers against making their conversion experience the yardstick by which every other purported believer is to be judged for authenticity. He tells us that "None of us may regard other Christians as 'second class' because their route to Christ has been different from ours."[53] Nor will Sell countenance the religious hypocrisy which stems from judging others according to outward appearance rather than inner disposition: "it is the worst kind of pharisaism to imagine that so long as the externals are presentable the inner motives and attitudes can remain in their unrenewed state (Matt 23:25)."[54] Only God fully knows who are "the children of light" and "the children of darkness."

Sell outlines the blessings of the reconciled life graciously given by God. First, believers receive "a new status as an adopted son or daughter of God."[55] We can describe the Holy Spirit, therefore, as "the Spirit of

---

51. *SOL*, 21.

52. *SOL*, 21. See also *RM*, 72: "the sole condition of forgiveness is that we confess our sin."

53. *SOL*, 23.

54. *SOL*, 23.

55. *SOL*, 24.

adoption."[56] Secondly, believers are led into "a new outlook, new motives, and new attitudes."[57] Their entire disposition is changed from selfish concerns to generous attitudes towards others. They strive to follow the example of Christ and give God glory through their daily lives. Thirdly, believers are granted "new power."[58] With the help of the Holy Spirit they are enabled to keep on fighting to be rid of a former life, as well as continually testifying to God's saving love revealed in their crucified, risen and ascended Lord, with conviction and fearing no one. Fourthly, believers gain "new friends and a new task."[59] Their new friends are found within the household of faith or, as we know it, the church. Believers are elected *from* others *for* the service of others. The real privilege they inherit is one of being part of the church's evangelism, mission, and service. Finally, Sell tells us that believers are enabled to sing a new song: "Instead of worshipping ourselves, our possessions—or any conceivable idol, we now sing with the saints of the ages: "Worthy is the Lamb, the Lamb that was slain, to receive all power and wealth, wisdom and might, honour and glory and praise" (Rev 5:12)."[60] They are thus led into a vibrant God-centered spirituality.

Justified by Grace through Faith

Although we play our part when responding in faith to God's gracious love towards us in the Christ event, Sell insists that ours is an *enabled* response. He cannot stress enough that "Our salvation is all of grace."[61] Echoing Donald Baillie, he asserts that "the paradox of grace" is the backbone of his theology.[62] An important text for him, therefore, is Ephesians 2:8–9: "For by grace you have been saved through faith, and this is not your own doing; it is the gift of God—not the result of works, so that no one may boast." He argues that the experience of being "justified by grace through faith" is fundamental to Christianity: "This was Paul's experience; this was the rallying cry of the Reformation; this has been at the heart of evangelical preaching in every age."[63] Let us discover how Sell understands this pillar of Christian doctrine.

56. *SOL*, 24.
57. *SOL*, 24.
58. *SOL*, 24.
59. *SOL*, 25.
60. *SOL*, 25.
61. *SOL*, 27.
62. *SOL*, 27. See Baillie, *God Was in Christ*.
63. *SOL*, 27.

We begin with the term "justification." The term was taken from the law courts, but, as Sell points out, Paul had the *heavenly* assize in mind when using it theologically. Sell refers us to a key passage to illustrate his point: "all have sinned and fall short of the glory of God; they are now justified by his grace as a gift through the redemption that is in Christ Jesus" (Rom 3:23-24). Sinners have no way of achieving righteousness before God by their own efforts. Sell reminds us, therefore, that "the heart of the Christian gospel" rests upon the fact that God set us right with Godself when we were still sinners (Rom 4:8); and, hence, God "justifies the ungodly" (Rom 4:5).[64] How does God achieve this? In framing his answer, Sell repeats one of his fundamental theological convictions. Since "God will never let us pretend, or act as if, sin does not matter we can be certain that "He will not glibly justify us."[65] This conviction risks, as we have already seen, placing undue qualifications upon God's unconditional love.[66]

When Sell claims that, "What [God] does is to declare us righteous, and to treat us as righteous on the basis of Christ's finished work" he is clearly making the Christ event constitutive of our salvation: "God *constitutes* a new relationship as he makes us sharers in the righteousness of Christ."[67] Sell declares that "The righteousness of Christ, *supremely* displayed in the Cross-Resurrection event, is a righteousness which engages with sin and vanquished it once and for all."[68] He calls this "a miracle."[69] We are enabled to stand before God because we are benefactors of God's "condescending mercy."[70] But, *pace* Sell, it is perfectly possible to regard that mercy as universally operative in the world rather than constituted by the Christ event. This alternative and less exclusive position cannot be readily dismissed by claiming that it reduces the Christ event to "a divine 'visual aid.'"[71] It is every bit as much a saving *act* as are all the other conceivable saving acts of which God has been, is and will be the agent, but it is also a *decisive* re-presentation of God's saving love. We can share with Sell his conviction that "Justification does not mean that at a stroke bad men have become good" as well as his realization "that sinners have been acquitted and fellowship with God

---

64. *SOL*, 28.
65. *SOL*, 28.
66. See chapter 5, "The Work of Christ."
67. *SOL*, 28–29. Italics mine.
68. *SOL*, 29. Italics mine.
69. *SOL*, 29.
70. *SOL*, 29.
71. *SOL*, 29.

is restored."[72] And we can also, with Sell, continue striving "to be humble enough to realize that where our relationship with God is concerned we are in a position only to receive."[73] But we can see little virtue in tying God's grace down to one particular historical event, thereby possibly opening the doors for Christian triumphalism and courting attitudes to other world religions which belittle their ultimate significance and worth. I say "seemingly" because, as we have also seen, Sell does not want to restrict the work of the Holy Spirit to the Christ event. What then is the status of that work? Logically, for Sell, it cannot be salvific, given his commitment to the notion that salvation came into the world uniquely through the Christ event and his acceptance of the ensuing "scandal of particularity."

We turn, secondly, to the term "faith." We are justified *through* faith. But what does faith entail? Sell answers that faith is "both God's gift to us and our act of trust and commitment to God through Christ."[74] Faith is, first, "the instrument by which God justifies sinners (Rom 12:3; 3:30)."[75] But faith is also "a decision . . . an act of commitment" on our part.[76] It is the instrument, if never the currency, through which we are saved. Sell recoils at the thought that "saving" faith is merely a matter of giving assent to propositions. He reminds us that, "while the Christian witness is not well served by haziness of proclamation, undue preoccupation with ecclesiastically-approved doctrinal formulae can lead to a 'Pelagian' cerebralism which prompts us to forget that the Christian evangel primarily concerns a saving *act*; that Christianity is a Way, not a doctrinal system; and that the gate to the pilgrim pathway is opened by God's sovereign grace, to which we respond by a faith which is truly ours but also a gift, and not by assent to a set of prescribed dogmas by whomsoever authorised."[77] It is wise when speaking about "faith," therefore, to make a clear distinction between faith understood as belief, or giving intellectual assent to purported truths (*assensus*), and faith in the sense of trust or loyalty (*fiducia*). It is the latter that is the *instrument* through which we are saved. Sell reassures those who are floundering with their theology that "doctrinal puzzlement, and the attempt to dissolve it by reasoning, does not necessarily diminish a person's psychological certitude concerning the faith."[78] And also he reminds them that

---

72. *SOL*, 30.
73. *SOL*, 30.
74. *SOL*, 31.
75. *SOL*, 31.
76. *SOL*, 32.
77. *EEE*, 167.
78. *FPA*, 286.

"there is rather more in the New Testament concerning the contrast between faith and sight, than about the alleged contrast between faith and reason."[79] Nevertheless, faith incorporates intellectual content and involves the will: "it is a life-commitment" in which "propositions are never far away."[80] Faith essentially is an act of existential commitment for which we are responsible; but Sell insists that we are enabled in making our faith commitment by the Spirit. He rejects, consequently, "bald evangelical Arminianism ('God will save you if you let him')" as well as "hyper-Calvinism ('If your name is written in the Lamb's book of life you have nothing to do; if it is not, you cannot do anything')" and echoes "Paul's paradox, 'I, yet not I but Christ'" which, he maintains, "lies at the heart of the Gospel."[81] Sincere believers should look away from their sinful selves to Christ for the grounds of their faith. Weak their faith may be, but their justification is sure. And, as they tread the pilgrim way under the influence and guiding of the Spirit, there is reason to believe that their confidence and trust in God can increase.

While faith is the instrument through which we are saved, the agent of our salvation is the grace of God. Grace therefore, is "the first word of the Gospel."[82] It is, arguably, the most important concept in Christian theology since it refers to the free, unmerited activity through which God reconciles a wayward creation to Godself. Sell, as we discovered earlier, holds that "the grace of God, most fully active in the Cross-Resurrection event" is the trigger for people coming to see their need "most clearly."[83] Grace comes first, not only in the sense that it makes possible the reconciliation of estranged sinners with God, but also because it makes sinners aware of their sinful state. Some have argued that God's grace is "irresistible," thus opening up the thought that, through God's benevolence, all will one day be drawn into a lasting relationship with God. This might suggest that God ultimately could exercise coercion to achieve divine ends. Sell demurs at such a thought; "'irresistible grace' need not be construed as sheer force: it can mean that God's grace is so winsome that none who experience it would resist it."[84] But, leaving to one side for a later discussion the question whether one day all

---

79. FPA, 286.
80. TAT, 158.
81. FPA, 261–62.
82. HT, 184. See also HT, 300.
83. ACI, 55n89.
84. FPA, 179.

will be saved,[85] it is certainly the case that, as Sell says, "it is only when they are under the authority of grace that people are truly free."[86]

Sell has nothing to do with the idea that the primacy of grace in our regeneration means that effort on our part is unimportant. As far as he is concerned, "good works" are "the evidence that our new life has begun."[87] He cuts through the supposed conflict between Paul and James on the relationship between "faith" and "works" by reminding us that the two Apostles were addressing different contexts. This accounts for their apparent differences: "whereas James is criticizing Christians who wrongly thought that once saved they could live as they pleased, Paul is denouncing all who think that they can contribute in any way to their salvation."[88] Sell maintains, therefore, that "Taken together they sum up the biblical teaching on the matter."[89] The benefits and privileges which flow from a faith expressed in Godly commitment to do good works are manifold. Sell tells us that "all that God has to offer becomes ours."[90] He offers us a list of the Christian's God-given gifts: "Christ becomes precious to us (1 Pet 2:7)"; "We have fellowship with the Father through the Son by the Spirit"; we have fellowship with God's people in the church; we can approach God confidently through faith at all times (Eph 3:12); Christ comes to live in us in love (Eph 3:17); we can walk by faith (2 Cor 5:7); and, finally, "we triumph by faith (1 John 2:4–5)" and "by faith we are kept to the end (1 Pet 5, 9)."[91] The ultimate goal of our faith lies ahead: meanwhile there is the work of believers being fashioned into God's likeness to be completed.

SAINTHOOD: LIFE IN THE SPIRIT

Sell reminds us that the Spirit who justifies us is also the One who empowers us to sainthood. The Spirit restores us to a vital relationship with God and then drives us forward to a new Christ-like life. Christianity is not a faith which resides in endless prohibitions; though it does eschew the worst of antinomian tendencies. It should always be positively concerned with engendering an enhanced life. Sell rightly recoils, therefore, at the way in which some Christians tend to make their faith burdensome, thereby

---

85. See chapter 9, "The Doctrine of Election."
86. *CTF*, 102.
87. *SOL*, 33.
88. *SOL*, 33.
89. *SOL*, 33.
90. *SOL*, 33.
91. *SOL*, 33.

Holy Spirit

suggesting that the quest for sainthood is a most fearful task. He rightly reminds us that "We have not been liberated from sin or order to be enslaved by duties."[92] Christians, he believes, must "preach sanctification as a work of grace, as God's good news."[93]

The term "sanctification" is based upon the Latin word *sanctus*, which means "holy." It refers to the process whereby the Spirit endows believers with new life, liberates them from sin's power, and enables them to love God and serve all those who place a call upon their lives. Sell reminds us of Thomas Watson's definition: "Holiness is the badge and livery of God's people."[94] For those who do not resonate with the imagery of a seventeenth-century Puritan, we offer the thought that striving for holiness is part and parcel of the Christian "brand." It is very much a life-time work and is made possible by the Spirit. Sell speaks of the Holy Spirit as "the strengthener" who "comes alongside to make possible a quality, a depth, a freedom of life which by ourselves we could never attain."[95] He provides us with a most helpful analogy to describe the way in which the Spirit aids Christians on the road to holiness. We are given "the picture of an experienced mountain guide roped to a novice," which "emphasises the dependence of the novice, the closeness of the relationship, the frequent difficulty of the path to be traversed."[96] The Holy Spirit helps Christians not only to meet the challenges of daily life but also what Sell calls "the constant down-drag of our sinful nature."[97]

According to Sell, there are two strands to our sanctification. First, it is a finished work: "we *are* sanctified; we *have* passed from death to life."[98] Sell draws our attention to Paul's witness: "you were washed, you were sanctified, you were justified in the name of the Lord Jesus Christ and in the Spirit of our God" (1 Cor 6:11). He insists with Paul that, since Christ has been victorious, the sanctification of Christ's followers is also certain. They know that they are benefactors of God's grace. Does this mean that Christians are already perfect? Sell accepts that, in one sense, they are indeed perfect since, as he puts it, "the work of grace is done."[99] He argues that "There is a perfection, a wholeness, about the Christian's standing which cannot be

---

92. *SOL*, 36.
93. *SOL*, 36.
94. See *EEE*, 225–26.
95. *SOL*, 37.
96. *TAT*, 230.
97. *SOL*, 37.
98. *SOL*, 39. Italics mine.
99. *SOL*, 38.

improved upon: we cannot be partially regenerated, partially justified, or . . . partially sanctified."[100] But, on the other hand, Christians know that they are far from perfect: they may be on the road to holiness, but have yet to fully reach their destination (Rom 7:19; Phil 3:13). As Sell says, "The new life that Christians enjoy is not absolutely new—as if there were an absolute disjunction between what they were before and what, by grace, they now are."[101] They continue to sin, but, through the gospel, they know that their sin no longer rules over them since they "cannot 'sin unto death' (1 John 5:8)."[102]

It follows that in a second sense, therefore, sanctification is a work in progress to which we have a contribution to make: "we *are being* sanctified."[103] With the help of the Spirit we are called to "work out [our] salvation with fear and trembling" (Phil 2:12). All Christians, as Sell puts it, must "progress *in*, rather than towards, sanctification."[104] There is an important sense in which prior to becoming Christians we are on a journey *towards* faith; but once we confess our faith in Christ we commence our journey *in* faith to sainthood. We do not make this journey alone since we travel with fellow church members. This means that the process of sanctification has corporate as well as individualistic dimensions, with all the checks and balances that are provided by being part of the church. Sell emphasis that this journey is "a great leveller."[105] The standards set for each traveler are identical. All are called to model their lives on Jesus. Sell tells us that, when we seek the mind of Christ with others in the church, "our prayers will come alive; our attitudes will be appropriately adjusted; our love of our Lord and of others will deepen, and we shall bring forth a harvest of fruit to his praise."[106] Before we discuss the nature of that "harvest of fruit," it is worthwhile noting that the spirituality Sell envisages being central to the journey in *and* towards holiness is fundamentally different from the "rampant and sometimes self-serving spirituality" so typical of the contemporary Western world.[107] It is firmly anchored in the work of God, and its calling card is a love of God and neighbor rather than any "self-serving" motivations.

---

100. *SOL*, 38.
101. *CCC*, 69n177.
102. *SOL*, 39.
103. *SOL*, 39. Italics mine.
104. *SOL*, 40.
105. *SOL*, 40.
106. *SOL*, 40.
107. *HT*, 261. In *CCC*, Sell talks of our living "at a time when frequently unanchored, impressionistic and self-serving spirituality swirls all around us" (1).

When talking about the qualitative nature of the Christian's new life in the Spirit, Sell unsurprisingly turns to Paul's classic statement on the matter; "the fruit of the Spirit is love, joy, peace, patience, kindness, generosity, faithfulness, gentleness, self-control" (Gal 5:22). The characteristics of the sanctified life together represent "one many-sided fruit of the Spirit."[108] They are not produced by us but are "part of one cluster" of fruit which owes "its total existence to the sanctifying work of the Spirit of God."[109] We will note briefly what Sell has to say about them.

Love, arguably, is the key thread of the Christian gospel. Quoting Henry, Sell reminds us that the word "love" in the Christian faith covers "God's love to us, ours to him, and one to another."[110] The "others" we are called upon to love include not only our fellow church members (Gal 6:10) and those outside the household of faith who place a claim upon our lives (1 Thess 9:22), but even our enemies (Rom 12:20). The model is Jesus himself (Matt 5:43–44; cf Luke 6:27–31). Our "neighbour," of course, "is defined not by race, religion, or status, but by need."[111] In the context of Christian love no one is beyond the pale. Crucial to the process of sanctification is learning by experience the height, length, and breadth of love. Sell tells us that, "As the Spirit works within, Christians make a beginning in the art of loving as they have been loved."[112]

The second characteristic of the fruit of the Spirit is "joy." Sell affirms that "The gracious life is the Spirit-filled life is the joyous life."[113] He believes that when people are in the presence of a Christian they should be aware of joy radiating from them, or, to put it another way, "no matter what a person's circumstances . . . he or she should feel uplifted."[114] *Christian* joy is not any kind of joy. It is "holy joy."[115] Sell claims that it is "irrepressible" and, as it "bubbles over to others," he says that "it consoles, it cheers, it strengthens."[116] But how can this be so when there are so many dreadful things happening in the world? Sell's answer to this question takes us to Jesus' "Farewell Discourse" in John's Gospel: "Who would have thought that a man on the point of going out to face the ugly, cruel death by crucifixion would have made joy

---

108. *SOL*, 41.
109. *SOL*, 41.
110. *SOL*, 41.
111. *SOL*, 42.
112. *SOL*, 42.
113. *SOL*, 42.
114. *SOL*, 42.
115. *SOL*, 42.
116. *SOL*, 42.

the theme of his farewell speech to his friends?"[117] Nothing that can happen to Christians in the world ought to rob them of their joy in the Lord.

Thirdly, "peace" clearly designates far more than merely the absence of war, conflict, and violence. Sell defines the term as "peace with God, peace in all circumstances . . . peace with our fellows—not least within the church," and "peace with oneself."[118] We are at peace when we experience God's presence in us; we experience peace when we take hold of the fact that, due to the death and resurrection of Jesus Christ, our relationship with God is restored; we are sustained in our service in the world, with any conceivable hardship it might entail, by God's peace; and peace is beyond all human understanding (Phil 4:7). Not only does Sell believe that "If the peace of God reigns within a church because all the members live in peace, that church prospers and can be used by God," but he also reflects experienced realities when he sadly confesses to having "sometimes felt, however, that strife within the household of faith has done more harm to the cause of Christ than all the assaults of the godless."[119] When it comes to Christians being at peace with themselves, he accepts that "we have apostolic authority for the practice of self-examination (2 Cor 13:5) but, wisely, he cautions us against "the wrong kind of soul-searching" which makes people "morbid and neurotic" and "self-obsessed."[120] He admits, though, that "it is by no means unknown in Reformed circles" for Christians, in attempting to take their "spiritual temperature" to seek evidence from personal experience as a guarantee of their salvation.[121] But our inner-peace does not depend upon our experiential feelings, powerful as they may be and reassuring as they often are, but upon "the promises of God given for us in Christ and brought home to us by the Holy Spirit."[122] Sell is certain that God will never turn away from us in our hard times (Rom 8:16–17).

Fourthly, Sell reminds us that "patience is not a matter of doing nothing, of biding time" but, rather, is "a way of doing everything."[123] It is a way of living which takes the measured view, seeks the opinion of others, and looks for consensus. Patience requires us to recognize that some problems are not solvable and to accept that sometimes seemingly insolvable issues simply have to be left with God. This does not mean that Christian patience

---

117. *SOL*, 43.
118. *SOL*, 44.
119. *SOL*, 44.
120. *SOL*, 45.
121. *EEE*, 233.
122. *SOL*, 45.
123. *SOL*, 46.

is "spineless" since, as Sell says, true patience "will not stand by and see injustice done, or God dishonoured, or the fellowship marred."[124]

Sell, rather optimistically, claims that "The remaining parts of the one harvest of the Spirit are more straightforward."[125] "Goodness we are simply told, "will shine out" of Christians.[126] Christians will be "faithful," he matter-of-factly asserts, since they will be "faithful to God and trustworthy in their dealing with others."[127] He says that they will also be "gentle"—"the opposite of being brash and arrogant."[128] And finally he claims that Christians will possess "self-control." This also is not easy to maintain. He refers to 1 Corinthians 10:23: "'All things are lawful,' but not all things are beneficial. 'All things are lawful,' but not all things build up" in order to draw our attention to the fact that "Christian freedom is not licence."[129] The final criterion for Christian living is that everything has to be done "in the name of the Lord Jesus, giving thanks to God the Father through him" (Col 3:17). Every Christian, however, knows that they will never come up to the mark of what is required of them. Sell is going with the evidence, therefore, when he informs us that, "The end of our sanctification is not yet."[130] This certain fact, however, should not be allowed to suppress something more important. Sell tells that, for Christians, "the end is assured" even though "We can scarcely imagine what it will be like."[131] The Holy Spirit is "*the* guardian of the faith."[132] Sell insists, therefore, that "in the deepest sense the faith is conserved and Christians are kept by the [sic] God Holy Spirit, to whom we owe any truth, and any ability to articulate the truth which we have."[133] Christians are not being arrogant, consequently, when they confidently confess their faith, since the hope to which they are testifying does not come from them but from God. And, when they are true to what they know of themselves, they will be thankful for the church in which they ought to find a worshipping community engaged with the task of growing up into Christ.

---

124. *SOL*, 46.
125. *SOL*, 46.
126. *SOL*, 46.
127. *SOL*, 46–47.
128. *SOL*, 47.
129. *SOL*, 47.
130. *SOL*, 47.
131. *SOL*, 47.
132. *CTF*, 16.
133. *TAT*, 18.

7

The Church

Alan Sell was a staunch advocate of an ecclesiology whose roots are found in the Separatist, Dissenting, and Congregational traditions: he wrote about it many times, and he offered its principles as signposts on the road to greater ecumenical understanding and agreement. Three of those principles stand out: first, that Christ alone is Lord of the church; secondly, that the church is made up of the gathered saints; and, thirdly, that all sectarianism which divides Christians at the Lord's Table is to be opposed.[1] Sell believed that such principles are rediscoveries by the Reformed churches of genuine marks of the catholic church. They are not new inventions, but are, rather, the outcome of Christians applying the maxim of *semper reformanda* to their church life. The Reformers, as Sell puts it, "sought to reform the existing church according to the Word of God, and to encourage its continual renewal under the Spirit; and all of this in the interest of *catholic* truth."[2] They were employing a process of self-assessment as relevant today as it was at the Reformation.

Any contemporary application of this process has to recognize two factors that would not have been widely apparent during the Reformation. First, with the advent of biblical criticism has come the realization that "there is no one fully developed pattern of Church order in the New Testament."[3] Sell uncompromisingly concludes that "the restorationist hope of finding a specific church polity (namely one's own) in the New Testament is doomed

---

1. See *HT*, 628.
2. *RECT*, 129. See also *TAT*, 238.
3. *SOL*, 53.

to disappointment."⁴ Then, secondly, the contextual factors which shape church polity and practice have become increasingly recognized. While Sell acknowledges that "Church order has unquestionably been influenced by biblical clues," he also admits that other factors have been involved, such as "the diverse socio-political circumstances in which Christians have found themselves" and "even . . . sometimes idiosyncratic personalities."⁵ Whether he takes sufficient account of the contextual factors which gave (and continue to give) shape to the various competing ecclesiologies is a question we need to explore, but Sell was never found lacking confidence in the adequacy of his own ecclesiology. He believed that his church tradition had received "an understanding of catholicity and of church order which is of great value for the whole Church."⁶ The problem is that other members of the Christian confessional family also regard their ecclesiologies in similar ways.

Even Sell's closest ecumenical friends could be permitted a wry smile when Sell's proposal to break the logjams in "faith and order" turns out to be a declaration of his own particular ecclesiology, rather than, say, a carefully constructed *via media* between opposing positions. Aside from the imperialist overtones, one could be forgiven for thinking that Sell believed that the Congregational Way had actually been given as God's gift to the whole church. While it is debatable whether any ecclesiology ought to be credited with divine origin, Sell is on firmer ground when he asserts that the church is a God-given community, and when, in a statement which reflects a carefully nuanced position, he declares that the work of the Holy Spirit "is church-creating *no matter by which confessional body it is processed.*"⁷

GOD'S GATHERING OF THE VISIBLE SAINTS

The substance of Sell's ecclesiology comes into view when we consider the following statements:

> . . . on the ground of Christ's saving work, God the Holy Spirit, the original hunter-gatherer, both pursues sinners with grace, transforms them into willing saints, and gathers them into one catholic ecclesial fellowship which is both eternal and visibly embodied in the world, and over which Christ is the sole Lord.⁸

---

4. *CTF*, 177. See also *TAT*, 295.
5. *CTF*, 177.
6. *EEE*, xiv.
7. *GE*, 228. Italics mine.
8. *GE*, 270. See also *CCF*, 35–36.

> ... the Church is the gathering of the Lord's saints, a holy priesthood for his praise, and competent under the guidance of the Spirit—interpreted Word to seek his will for service and witness—all of this in fellowship with the wider family.[9]

The first, and arguably the foundational, point to be made about Sell's ecclesiology is that it is rooted in pneumatology. To put it another way, he recoils at the thought that the church should be considered as just another human organization. He provides two reasons for this. First, "Christ is present in its fellowship."[10] Matthew 18:20 has profoundly influenced followers of the Congregational Way: "For where two or three are gathered in my name, I am there among them." Then, secondly, Sell emphasizes that church membership, unlike that of other organizations, is "by divine calling."[11] Far from being "a club for the promotion of the interests of the like-minded" he reminds us that "the Church comprises people who may have very little in common, except that by grace they have been called together and they have been enabled to respond."[12] Church members—the saints—"are gathered by the Spirit, to whose call they are enabled by grace to respond, and with whom, together with the saints around them, they are in communion."[13] The proclamation of the gospel—"The Gospel of God's free, Church-convoking grace"[14]—has created and will continue to create the church. It is in keeping with Sell's *crucicentric* theology, therefore, that he locates "God's Christianity-founding act" in "the Cross-Resurrection event"[15]—though to be more accurately Trinitarian he might have preferred to say "the Cross-Resurrection-Pentecost event."

Secondly, Sell is convinced that there are "twin and inseparable acts of God" which "constitute the Church."[16] In addition to the act of redemption, he refers to "the calling of a renewed people into being."[17] God's elected saints are called out by divine sovereign grace to become the Christian fellowship. They are incorporated in Christ and "grafted . . . into his family" in "response to God's redemptive initiative."[18] Penitence on their

---

9. *DTLC*, 609.
10. *FPA*, 126.
11. *FPA*, 126.
12. *FPA*, 126.
13. *GE*, 238.
14. *TAT*, 253.
15. *CCC*, 95.
16. *RECT*, 51.
17. *RECT*, 51.
18. *SVOC*, 1. See also *EEE*, 294.

part is fundamental, with the emphasis upon "enabling grace" rather than "human ability."[19] Sell speaks of "the Spirit's call of grace" being "a constraining, drawing call" to become a church member.[20] No compulsion is implied; men and women remain free to reject the call; but those who respond positively are ever aware of "the 'I, yet not I, but Christ' that is the *sine qua non* of response to the gospel."[21] Joining the church is to become a Christian. It is not a matter of individuals with a common interest coming together to form a mutual benefit society or special interest group. On the contrary Sell argues, "God often comes to us when we are not interested in him at all— even when we are in rebellion from him. He calls us; he takes the initiative; we are his people."[22] But the bottom line is that "Christian fellowship is first a 'vertical' matter."[23] He uses well-known biblical analogies and metaphors to make his point: "God takes the initiative, he engrafts us into Christ as branches are engrafted into the vine";[24] "God calls his Church into being by the Spirit through the Word and gives it to his Son as bride";[25] and "God's gracious call is not to individualism, but into a household of faith, a body with many limbs, a *covenant* people."[26] His overall aim is to articulate what he calls "a genuinely Trinitarian ecclesiology; that is the idea of the Church as a people graciously called out by the Father, through the Spirit, and given to the Son as Bride."[27] And Sell is probably correct to lament that "In relation to such an ecclesiology prevailing Church-state relations, the para-church movements, the practice of mission, the fact of consumerism in much Western Christianity, and all 'sectarianisms' whether of the doctrinal, ecclesiological, methodological or issue-based kinds, could not legitimately pass unchallenged."[28] But, even more certain, is the possibility that Sell's "high" understanding of the church provides fertile ground in which church reformation can take root in any age or place. Once it is acknowledged that the church is constituted by Christ's sovereign presence among the saints, duties and demands are placed upon the membership which prompts questions

19. *CAM*, 131.
20. *CAM*, 131.
21. *CAM*, 132.
22. *SOL*, 51.
23. *ACI*, 131.
24. *ACI*, 131. See also *CTF*, 18, 226, and *CAM*, 130.
25. *PHT*, 259.
26. *EEE*, 290. Italics mine.
27. *DTLC*, 164.
28. *DTLC*, 164.

like: "To observers, do we seem more like passengers on a holiday cruise than pilgrims on the way of the Cross?"[29]

Thirdly, Sell places emphasis upon the church being made up of people who, through confession of their faith in Christ, are active in the church fellowship. The gathered saints are "in Christ" and together they are "a visible presence, an embodiment in the world."[30] They have turned their backs on an old way of life.[31] Whereas Presbyterians in the eighteenth century held that formal subscription was sufficient to admit a person into church membership, Congregationalists at that time expected a personal confession of faith from their membership candidates. While, clearly, it is the latter whom Sell holds up as "best practice," he ventures the thought that the Congregationalists may have remained more orthodox than the Presbyterians, who tended to lapse into Unitarianism, because of the requirement to make personal testimonies: "Could it be that the risk to orthodox doctrine posed by the possibility of stereotyping was less than that posed by the unfettered reason with its avant garde attractiveness?"[32] As David M. Thompson has suggested, this is an argument "which must be taken seriously."[33]

Fourthly, Sell was fond of declaring that one cannot be "a Christian 'in general," only ever "an enrolled and locally anchored saint."[34] Or, to put the point another way, he believed that "To be in Christ is to be of the church; it is to be a visible saint . . . the church comprises Christians."[35] He draws a distinction between members and non-members of the church, and, therefore, between the church and the world. Guided by the Separatist tradition, Sell holds fast to the maxim that the church is called to be *in* but not *of* the world. He tells us that the church is "a visible sign and foretaste of God's kingdom"[36] and, hence, "the advance party of the kingdom"[37] but his own roots in rank and file churches made sure that he never confused the local out-cropping of gathered saints with that kingdom. He knew full well that "while the Church is called to witness to God's kingly rule it is not co-terminus with the kingdom."[38] Christian triumphalism is never an op-

---

29. *EEE*, 240.
30. *SOL*, 53.
31. See *CCF*, 35.
32. *DTLC*, 23.
33. Thompson, Review of *DTLC*, 504.
34. *EEE*, 41.
35. *OMMM*, 44.
36. *EEE*, 343.
37. *SOL*, 79.
38. *PHT*, 234.

tion because "empirical Christianity displays a sufficiently large multitude of blemishes to keep it in repentant mood to the end of time."[39] What he found particularly galling was the way in which the catholic intentions of the Reformed churches so often are undermined by what he termed "the sectarian demon."[40]

Fifthly, central to Sell's ecclesiology is the idea that "the Church is a covenant community"[41] brought into being by God to fulfill Old Testament promises (Jer 31:31–34). It is composed of "regenerate saints whom Sell, not being afraid to use "a term so sadly hijacked by a particular brand of Christianity," calls "born again."[42] Upon profession of their faith they join the church by "covenanting with Christ's people in the church."[43] Sell drives to the heart of his ecclesiology with his emphasis upon membership being grounded and fulfilled in the corporate, covenanted life of a gathered congregation. He insists that the church can only be conceived adequately when due emphasis is placed upon it being essentially an ecclesial *body;* it is always more than a granular aggregate of individual Christians. Sell's commitment to the corporate dimension of church membership, though, may seem rather anachronistic in a post-modern era dominated by individualism. Zygmunt Bauman claims that, in contrast to the passing age of "solid modernity," we are now moving into an era he calls "liquid modernity" in which "Everything . . . is now down to the individual" and "'we' is nothing more than an aggregate of I's, and the aggregate . . . is not greater than the sum of its parts."[44] It is a world favorable to more fluid forms of association than the corporate, membership patterns of the passing age of "solid modernity." Unsurprisingly, therefore, Pete Ward invites us to embrace the idea of a "liquid church."[45] Sell, with some justification, felt that current trends in society make the church's "counter-cultural" nature more important than ever. But due fidelity to our Christian origins can indeed support a return to viewing the church more as a movement than an institution. Nevertheless, the concept of "covenant" remains a crucial key to unlock the nature of commitment to Christ. What the gathered saints believe in common is crucial if local church witness is to have credibility. Sell puts great emphasis upon local covenants hammered out and agreed by congregations, going as

39. *CTF*, 108.
40. *TAT*, 238.
41. *COM*, 343.
42. *GE*, 225.
43. *CAM*, 128.
44. Bauman, *Liquid Modernity*, 62, 63.
45. See Ward, *Liquid Church*.

far as declaring that "major declarations have no more status than the local covenant."[46] While many will admire his great effort to develop a "bottom-up" rather than "top-down" ecclesiology, some will suspect that it results in his being unable to give due recognition to the church's catholicity.

We begin our sixth area of consideration by recognizing that Sell was fully aware of the isolationist tendencies of churches in the Congregational tradition. He admits that "the saints have not always understood that what they are visibly gathered into is the church catholic in one of its numerous local expressions" and he bewails the "granular independency" which has resulted.[47] It has to be acknowledged also that sometimes the councils of the Reformed churches have served the purposes of their own local congregations rather more than the wider catholic church, thereby adding the sin of denominationalism to the isolationist tendencies. Daniel Jenkins argued that "one of the first conditions of re-union and of the establishment of a "Church genuinely Catholic" in this country is the rediscovery by the Reformed Churches of their own true foundation and the bringing of their whole Church Order into conformity with God's ordinance for His Church."[48] His observation may seem dated now that all possibilities for reunion appear thwarted, and we may well be living in a climate more open to Christian diversity, but his central assumption holds good: at the heart of the Reformed tradition lies an understanding of "catholicity" which is as coherent as it is convincing. It is to Sell's credit that he refuses to allow his church tradition's isolationist and denominational tendencies to hide its deep catholic foundations. Returning to the earliest Nonconformists, he locates "the root of catholicity" in the church's pneumatological origin. God calls out one church comprising all those who confess Jesus Christ as their Lord and Savior. Sell insists that "the evangel is inherently catholic";[49] he stresses the "inclusivity in the Gospel" which "breaks down barriers, transcends localities and cultures, calls out the one Church, and meets our deepest need of salvation";[50] and he argues passionately that fellowship in the catholic church is entered locally.[51] The one catholic church, therefore, is located in all its manifestations.[52] A Reformed ecclesiology does not necessarily lead to an individualistic view of the church; rather it directs us to an

46. *DTLC*, 47.
47. *GE*, 231.
48. Jenkins, *Nature of Catholicity*, 154.
49. *TAT*, 336.
50. *EEE*, 324.
51. See *EEE*, 324.
52. See *SOL*, 52; *PHT*, 269 and *HT*, 617.

understanding of catholicity rooted in the gathered saints, "who, being severally grafted into the vine" are "necessarily related to *all* of the branches."[53] It follows that the one catholic church is "logically prior" to the existence of local churches.[54]

Sell was an ecumenist at heart and by conviction. He was passionately committed to attempting to heal the fragmentation and brokenness of the church. So, seventhly, we arrive at his understanding of church unity. He suggests that the Reformed stress upon the church's catholicity aided the Reformed churches involvement in the ecumenical movement, whose leadership was often found in Reformed hands.[55] Reformed ecumenists typically argue that the unity of the church is God's gift, and that, therefore, the task of all the visible outcroppings of the church is to embrace that *given* fact. Sell maintains that "an exercise of lateral thinking" would clear the logjam at the center of ecumenical discussion: he asks that "instead of focusing in ecumenical discussion upon what we have to learn from others and what we have to offer them, we probe more deeply and ask, What has the God of all grace actually done?"[56] When that is done, he insists, we are brought before an obvious truth, namely, that the gathered saints already make up "the one, holy, catholic and apostolic church of God, no matter under which denominational label they travel."[57] Ecumenists should not be lured into thinking that their task is to find ways of establishing Christian unity; rather they should be proclaiming that, through God's initiative in the Spirit, "the church of the Lord Jesus Christ is *already one*."[58] The ecumenical task, consequently, is not one of establishing unity in the church, but one of manifesting it and ordering church life accordingly.

Those who stand in the Reformed tradition naturally will be sympathetic to Sell's understanding of the church's unity being God's gift, but there is a life-time of evidence to show that his proposed pneumatological ecclesiology will not be perceived as a way of solving ecumenical problems by fellow Christians whose lives are ordered in other than Reformed ways. What Sell regarded as a radical piece of "lateral thinking" is most likely to be received as an imperialistic attempt to preference one historically contingent ecclesiology over and above other similarly contingent ones. Sell's solution to our ecumenical problems may be persuasive to those who share

---

53. *FPA*, 155.
54. See *RECT*, 93.
55. See *SVOC*, 93; *RECT*, 112; and *PHT*, 163.
56. *GE*, 222.
57. *GE*, 244–45.
58. *GE*, 250.

his commitment to a particular way of ordering the church, but, as David M. Thompson ruefully notes, it is inherently implausible that it will ever be adopted.[59] In ecclesial, as well as secular matters, politics is "the art of the possible" and it is heavily dependent upon more *bottom-up* thinking than is evident in Sell's proposal.

INADEQUATE WAYS OF UNDERSTANDING THE CHURCH

Sell highlights what he believes are three mistaken ways of understanding the church.

First, he is critical of theologians who view the church as a continuation, extension or prolongation of the incarnation, e.g., Nevin, a Mercersburg theologian;[60] Garvie, a congregationalist;[61] de Burgh[62] and Quick,[63] both Anglicans; the nineteenth-century Cambridge theologians;[64] and Nels Ferré, the United Church of Christ minister and theologian.[65] "Such language exalts the church he thunders, "and unintentionally diminishes the significance of *the* incarnation."[66] He recoils at the thought of the institutional church being "not the witness to, but the substitute for, Christ."[67] Out of first-hand experience of what he terms "the Church's creaturely status,"[68] he knew that the "Church lives between the times."[69] At best, Christians have "a foretaste and pledge of . . . a perfect reality and live out of a fullness above and beyond themselves,"[70] but they are not yet endowed with exalted status. It is important, Sell believes, that we recognize the church's proper role as a witness to the incarnation rather than high-mindedly claiming that, somehow, it is its extension. Somewhat ruefully, he suggests that, "in view of the manifest failure and sin of the Church the idea that the church is the continuation of the incarnation is a very difficult position to maintain in respect

---

59. Thompson, Review of *GE*, 263.
60. See *COM*, 262–68, and *TAT*, 207–10.
61. See *EEE*, 294–95.
62. *FPA*, 56–59.
63. *FPA*, 185.
64. *PHT*, 174.
65. *CAM*, 148–49.
66. *OMMM*, 5.
67. *SOL*, 55.
68. *SOL*, 55.
69. *REC*, 52.
70. *REC*, 52.

of the empirical Church."[71] He wants nothing to do with ideas which, he maintains, "reduce the significance of the once-for-all incarnation,"[72] and, when opposing them, he invariably introduces Forsyth as chief prosecution witness:

> It is regenerated human nature in which Christ dwells. But that cannot be a prolongation of the Incarnation, wherein there was no regeneration. . . . That which owes itself to a rebirth cannot be a prolongation of the ever sinless. . . . The Church is not the continuation of Christ, but His creation and His response[73].

Sell is correct when he says that "the notion that the Church is the continuation or prolongation of the incarnation" is at worst "a heresy as far as the empirical Church is concerned."[74] But he is also prepared to acknowledge that "at best" it may be only "an unguarded way of speaking."[75] Theologians who talk of the church as the continuation of the incarnation, however, often are indeed very guarded when making their point. The church is made up of gathered saints who are Christ's followers. The apostle Paul makes a great deal of the saints being "in Christ," thereby suggesting a fundamental sense in which the church *is* connected to Christ. Not only does Paul testify to "a mystical sense of the divine presence of Christ within and without, establishing and sustaining the individual in relation to God," but he further speaks of "a community which understood itself not only from the gospel which had called it into existence, but also from the shared experience of Christ, which bonded them as one."[76] The image of the church as "the body of Christ" underscores a sense of connectedness between Christ and the church. To be "in Christ" is to become a member of a new community which will only become fully what it is called to be at the *eschaton*. This new community called "church" is a worldly manifestation of what God intends to be the new humanity. A sinless Christ is head of a sinful church: Christ and church are distinct but never separate. So, from a conviction that, through the Spirit, the church is called to engage

---

71. *ACI*, 85.

72. *FPA*, 185.

73. Forsyth, *Church and Sacraments*, 75–76. Sell uses this quotation (or, at least, part of it) on numerous occasions to underscore his opposition to the church being called the continuation, extension or prolongation of the incarnation, thereby undercutting its pneumatological foundation, e.g., *CAM*, 149; *COM*, 271; *EEE*, 295; *FPA*, 58, 185; *OMMM*, 5; *RECT*, 52, 85; *SOL*, 54.

74. *TAT*, 208–9.

75. *TAT*, 209.

76. Dunn, *Theology of Paul*, 401.

in God's mission following the pattern displayed in Christ's life and work, it seems appropriate to talk in a suitably "general" way of the church as the continuation, extension or prolongation of the incarnation. Macquarrie, for example, argues that "the Church may properly be called the extension of the incarnation," but he prevents any misunderstanding by adding that "this must not be understood to put it on the same level as Christ or to attribute to it an exaggerated status and authority."[77] He maintains that "The incarnation *which reached its completion in* [*Christ*] is in process in the Church"; he ventures a hope "that it is moving toward completion in the Church too"; but he is realistic when admitting that "at any given time, the Church is a mixed body."[78] It is difficult to see how Sell could object to this: in no way does it exalt the church; nor does it necessarily compromise the once-for-all nature of Christ's work; and most certainly there is no substitution of Christ's work by the institutional church. Given the requisite caveats, it is perfectly possible to talk of the church as the continuation, extension or prolongation of the incarnation in a theologically appropriate way, even if the ongoing performance of the church often makes such talk incredible.

Secondly, Sell confesses that he is "somewhat reluctant to think of the Church as a sacrament."[79] He suggests that the underlying background of such an idea lies in the notion that church is a continuation of the incarnation. Not surprisingly the usual Forsythian protest is launched against that idea.[80] He adds the further point that "since the Incarnation is a mystery we have not done a great deal to elucidate the nature of the Church (also a mystery) by speaking of the latter in terms of the former."[81] Whatever we make of that—and the logical progression is in the direction of a totally *apophatic* theology—it is clear that Sell advocates the term "sacrament" be reserved for the two, dominical sacraments of the church. He reminds us that "the word 'sacrament' can (like 'love,' 'fellowship,' etc.) all too easily be devalued: the slogan 'All life is sacramental' comes to mind."[82] In typically witty fashion, he parodies W. S. Gilbert: "When everything is sacrament, then nothing's sacramental."[83] But, while it is essential to remember that any encounter with God, through either the natural world or the church, must never be allowed to confuse the Creator with creation and, hence,

---

77. Macquarrie, *Principles of Christian Theology*, 349.
78. Macquarrie, *Principles of Christian Theology*, 349. Italics mine.
79. *PHT*, 268.
80. *PHT*, 268. See also 269n.
81. *PHT*, 268.
82. *PHT*, 268.
83. See *PHT*, 269n.

collapse the God-World distinction, it remains the case that, in principle, God may be encountered "through the things he has made" (Rom 1:20). Ann Loades reminds us that "The whole cosmos teems with expressions of divine generosity and life-giving resource, and is a limitless source of wonder and gratitude, as its immensity and microscopic energies and detail are explored."[84] She calls it a "divinely constituted context which may manifest divine transformative presence."[85] If "the promise of divine grace and the transformative Spirit of God" can be received "in *human* affairs" how much more then ought that to be the case within the *Christian* community, given that that community has the calling to be a sign, expression and foretaste of God's love?[86] While attention needs to be paid to the above mentioned caveats, it seems appropriate, therefore, to speak, in principle, of the church as a sacrament. Whether it is *in practice*, of course, largely depends upon one's anthropological understanding in the light of sin. Sell's views concerning human depravity, though, suggest that *in principle* as well as *in practice* human beings are capable of encountering God's presence sacramentally. And, it can be argued, the gospel sacraments only "work" because they trade on the sacramental potential of so much in creation. Far to often, though, the Protestant tendency—often in opposition to Roman Catholic and Orthodox practice—has been to regard the "physical" as alien to the "spiritual" when, as Calvin as well as Sell knew full well, the former can often convey the latter.[87]

Sell may have over-exaggerated the obstacles to calling the church a continuation, extension or prolongation of the incarnation and a sacrament, but he was correct when, thirdly, he sought to avoid equating the church with God's kingdom. Christians are heirs to a promise which Sell describes as follows: "it is the victory of the Cross which gives us the assurance that the kingdom, or kingly rule, of God, inaugurated already, will, in God's good time, be consummated in that new heaven and new earth, the recreation of all things, the unity of the 'whole inhabited earth.'"[88] They know that "The Kingdom of God . . . is not something which we 'bring in'; it is something which God gives."[89] The church may be likened, therefore, to a kind of halfway house between an unrepentant sinful world and God's intended destiny for us. God has *inaugurated* the divine kingly rule in Christ, but nowhere

84. Loades, "Sacramentality and Spirituality," 553.
85. Loades, "Sacramentality and Spirituality," 553.
86. *GOF*, 100.
87. See Calvin, *Institutes* IV.XXIV.5.
88. *NT*, 185.
89. *GOF*, 100.

this side of eternity is it fully manifested. Accordingly, there is no place in the church for any misplaced triumphalism, for, as Sell recognizes, "the saints are saints by name if not always by nature and practice," and, hence, "the churches are earthen vessels."[90] The church must never be regarded as "co-terminus with the kingdom."[91] It should rest content in knowing its position *vis a vis* God's kingdom. And I would wish to add that sometimes the "world" may be nearer to the kingdom than the church. Recent issues concerning gender and human sexuality spring to mind.

Given Sell's utter realism concerning the fallibility of the churches and their sinful members it may come as a surprise that he rests so much faith in their ability at their gatherings to determine their mission, to exercise a relevant ministry, and to govern themselves.[92] Few theologians, though, have been so strong an advocate of "the church meeting" as him.

THE CHURCH MEETING

At the heart of Congregational ecclesiology is the role played by the Church Meeting in the life of local churches. Sell regarded it as an essential part of any adequate ecclesiology, and he shared Dale's enthusiasm for it:

> . . . to be at a church meeting—apart from any prayer that is offered—any hymn that is sung, any words that are spoken, is for me one of the chief means of grace. To know that I am surrounded by men and women who dwell in God, who have received the Holy Ghost, with whom I am to share the eternal righteousness and eternal rapture of the great life to come, this is blessedness. I breathe a Divine air. I am in the new Jerusalem . . . I rejoice in the joy of Christ over those whom He has delivered from eternal death and lifted up into the light and glory of God.[93]

Despite having attended many examples of the Church Meeting which did not live up to such a high ideal, Sell could still claim nevertheless that "such an experience, though never received without wonder and thanksgiving, ought to be normal."[94] He argues that the concept of the Church Meeting is

90. *ACT*, 87.

91. *PHT*, 234.

92. "Because they are saved expectations should be high; because they are sinners expectations should be realistic" (*ACT*, 98).

93. Quoted by Sell in *SVOC*, 75. He takes the quotation from Macfadyen, *Constructive Congregational Ideals*, 136.

94. *SVOC*, 142n20.

"a precious possession,"⁹⁵ "the ecclesiological pearl of grace,"⁹⁶ and, therefore, "of great and ecumenical significance."⁹⁷ It reflects the way in which Congregational ecclesiology seeks to complete Reformed ecclesiology "by including the ministry of the whole people of God in their deliberative aspect."⁹⁸ And it should be the model for regional and national representative church meetings. In commending this ecclesiology, Sell points out that, quite often, Christians can be found who "exalt—on paper—the ministry of the whole people of God, whilst perpetuating polities which exclude the bulk of the holy priesthood from those deliberations which are the proper concern of every local-cum-catholic church."⁹⁹ He defends the most inclusive of church polities. Difficult questions remain about the relationship between local, regional, and national church councils: overstressing the local, some argue, quickly leads to the church losing its catholicity; while others point out the way in which regional and national policy making can disempower or patronize local churches. Matters get taken out of the churches' hands somewhat when secular legislation, e.g., concerning safeguarding or employment practice, requires the national church to exercise firm oversight over what takes place at both regional and local levels.

Sell describes the Church Meeting as "a credal assembly" of the gathered saints.¹⁰⁰ It is where the Lordship of Christ is acknowledged and proclaimed, where "the mind of Christ is sought regarding the worship, service and mission of the church,"¹⁰¹ and "where those who by grace are one in him seek, by the Spirit, to be one in their decisions and judgments."¹⁰² Sell maintains that it is ecclesial "good practice" for church members to meet together regularly to pray about and deliberate upon their congregation's life and mission. It is a duty and a privilege to be able to do so. True catholicity starts when the saints gather together,¹⁰³ and the Church Meeting provides "visible evidence . . . of rootedness in the faith of the ages."¹⁰⁴ It is a natural

---

95. *TEM*, 137.

96. *PYH*, 274.

97. *EEE*, 42.

98. *TAT*, 76. Earlier, Sell tells us that "whereas Calvin stopped at elders and deacons, the Congregationalists have sought to involve the whole people of God in ministry" (*TAT*, 33).

99. *TAT*, 209.

100. See *CTF*, 196; *TAT*, 209, 288.

101. *CTF*, 196.

102. *TAT*, 288.

103. See *TAT*, 209.

104. *TAT*, 288.

continuation of the church's worship.[105] What is proclaimed when the saints gather under the Word and around the Lord's Table gets brought down to earth in Church Meeting as the following kinds of questions are asked: "'What are we to do with this gospel that we have heard in the preaching and seen enacted at the Lord's Supper? How are we to witness to it in the place where God has set us? How are we to serve our immediate community, and how, through our prayers and gifts, are we to sustain the wider ministries of the church, and play our part in the socio-political affairs of the day?'"[106] The Church Meeting, therefore, is the place where a local church does it contextual theology. Sell regards theology, accordingly, as "a communal matter" and "a churchly task."[107] The practice of theology is "too important to be left to the theologians who . . . need the checks and balances supplied by the fellowship of saints."[108] Part of the importance of the Church Meeting, therefore, rests upon its function of preserving churches "against idiosyncratic and autocratic ministries, and against individuals whether biblical, spiritualistic or liberal who, for all their differences are united in having little use for the *people* of God."[109] Equally important is the opportunity it provides for the minister "to equip the saints for the work of ministry" (Eph 4:12). That helps explain why the Reformed tradition has favored having a "learned" ministry. And, quite often, ministers require the political skill to challenge and overcome the complacency, prejudices, and power-games within church meetings. Sell places high expectations and demands upon the gathered saints. He suggests that "The ideal of every local church as a nursery of theologians is one to be striven after."[110] No doubt, but many will conclude that Sell is being unrealistic as far as most congregations are concerned.

The basis of decision making in the Church Meeting ought not to be confused with that encountered in secular political or business meetings. Sell stresses that the Church Meeting is a "Christocratic" rather than a democratic assembly.[111] The objective is not majority rule according to the pattern of one-person-one-vote; nor is the aim government by the majority. These ideas are anachronistic when applied to the originating principles of Church Meeting practices. What is being sought after, rather, is "unanimity

---

105. See *TAT*, 32–33, 340–44, and *OMMM*, 42.
106. *OMMM*, 42.
107. *TAT*, 2.
108. *TAT*, 249.
109. *DTLC*, 163. See also *CCF*, 365.
110. *CTF*, 159n44.
111. See e.g., *COM*, 175; *RECT*, 92; *SVOC*, 4; *TAT*, 33.

The Church

in Christ" stemming from thoughtful, heart-searching as the Lordship of Christ is acknowledged over the church's total life and witness.[112] The goal is that of seeking "the mind of Christ" which may or may not turn out to be identical to the will of the members. This is achieved through "prayer, discussion and consensus."[113] Sell suggests that the required outcome is achieved less by voting on motions than by adopting the Quaker approach of seeking "the sense of the meeting."[114] Any ensuing unanimity will not necessarily mean that all the members present are in 100 percent agreement; but, rather, "it means that individuals who have manageable reservations concerning a particular issue will not break fellowship."[115] The aimed-for consensus will be "the conclusion of sinner-saints who have sought the mind of Christ."[116] Sell advocates that the church members should be enabled in their deliberations by having their minister chair the Church Meeting: "the one called to lead the church to the throne of grace, and preach the Word, is the one to lead the church in reflecting upon the question, How are we to commend the gospel we have received?"[117] But ministers are not necessarily good at chairing meetings. It is not immediately obvious why the ends for which Sell is aiming cannot be achieved by an arrangement which finds the minister sitting alongside someone who is good at chairing meetings. In an era of multiple pastorates and shortages of ministers, the presence of a minister is easier to recommend than guarantee. Sell is correct, though, to suggest that the Church Meeting ought not to be conducted "by some *managerial* type who is 'good at meetings'"[118]—unless, that is, such persons are blessed with spiritual insight, theological nous, and carry the respect of the members, which, theoretically, they might do. We are ill-advised to belittle management skills in the church's life and work.

Sell had multiple experiences of the Church Meeting having become "in many places a rather dull business meeting attended by some only out

---

112. See e.g., *CAM*, 151; *COM*, 175; *CTF*, 196; *FPA*, 209–10; *HT*, 431; *RECT*, 92; *SVOL*, 4; *TAT*, 33, 248, 341.

113. *HT*, 431.

114. See *CTF*, 196. Elsewhere, Sell suggests that "Nothing constitutes a graver threat to our practice than the voting system which still prevails in some quarters," and then recommends that "what needs to be discovered through prayer and testimony, is what the Quakers call 'the sense of the meeting'" (*OMMM*, 113).

115. *HT*, 431.

116. *CAM*, 151. Ideas fundamental to the proper conduct of the Church Meeting have been adopted by some Reformed Churches in the practice of "consensus decision-making" in regional synods and national assemblies.

117. *CTF*, 196.

118. *TAT*, 33. Italics mine.

of a sense of duty."[119] He is adamant that it should not be even classed as a business meeting.[120] He believed the rot set in during nineteenth-century Congregationalism when Enlightenment individualism caused its members to sit loose on the idea that their church was a covenant community rather than "an aggregate of saved individuals,"[121] and, therefore, fostered "the notion . . . that Church Meeting was a 'one man—one vote' democratic assembly, whose goal was not the unanimity of covenanted saints in Christ, but majority rule."[122] He witnessed many examples of the Church Meeting having degenerated into democratic assemblies, but, like a voice in a wilderness, he still called for a revitalization of the Church Meeting. As he reminds us, if we are not to be branded as hypocrites, "we need to say 'Lord, Lord' in Church Meeting as well as in Sunday Worship," since "in Church Meeting we seek to know what the Lord would have us do, and to receive the strength he imparts for mission and service."[123]

It is a moot point whether the Church Meeting will ever be revitalized in the way Sell wished. Ecumenical engagement has suggested that many of the benefits it brings with it can be found in church polities which do not hold it in central place. There are commendable ways of expressing Christian identity of the "in the world but not of the world" variety, of sharing in the oversight of a local church, and of confessing faith and working out appropriate strategies of mission and service in Presbyterian, Connexional, and Episcopal churches. The appearance of the house-church movement and cell-based churches also suggest that elements of Congregational principles have been inserted into non-Congregational polities. And, in an increasingly mobile society, is there much mileage in trying to revive an emphasis upon the church as a covenant fellowship?[124] What Sell's "revitalization" agenda flags up, however, is a need to come to grips with the way in which *all* church polities are contextual, and the ongoing requirement to order the church so that it can function in a way which handles the constraints, and grasps the opportunities, of a particular time and place.

Sell alludes to the contextual factors which shape all ecclesiologies. He quotes Samuel Davidson: "Church government is a matter of expediency, and . . . it may be shaped by the spiritual consciousness of the Church,

---

119. *DTLC*, 63.
120. See *CTF*, 196, and *TAT*, 33.
121. *PHT*, 166.
122. *DTLC*, 16.
123. *DTLC*, 16.
124. Sell asks this very question himself. See *RECT*, 242.

agreeably to the circumstances and exigencies of the period."[125] We can contemplate the help to the Separatist and early Congregationalist cause that the centrality of the Church Meeting brought: it would have bound together small Christian groups living under the threat of persecution and oppression when a common identity, shared purpose, and unquenchable hope were needed. This was no time to devolve authority for who could be trusted? It made absolute sense for the gathered saints to seek the mind of Christ concerning what they as a fellowship were being called to do. We can quickly see how an ecclesiology with the Church Meeting at its center was appropriate for some Christians in a particular time and space. But, we can also ask ourselves, "What happens when a new era dawns, when threats of persecution and oppression recede, relationships between different Christian groups improve, and nonconformity is no longer required?" It would not be surprising in such circumstances for the importance of Church Meeting to wane. And, interestingly, Sell locates the start of the demise of the Church Meeting in the nineteenth century, by the end of which the decline of Nonconformity had started.

When Sell advocates a revitalization of the Church Meeting on the grounds that the church needs to be counter-cultural in providing "a check upon individualistic consumerism"[126] two thoughts spring to mind. First, the issue is not so much one of revitalizing the Church Meeting as that of revitalizing the church. It should not escape our notice that many of the most thriving churches remain in constant, interactive contact with their members through the social media. They have discovered ways of "meeting" which do not depend upon holding meetings. Stephen Orchard recognizes that "the majority prefer an informal system of delegation to coming to meetings," but in a world dominated by social media this may not necessarily result in "a spiritual deficit" in church life.[127] Leading on from this is a second question: When is it appropriate for the church to be counter-cultural, and when is it opportune for it to use the resources of culture for its own purposes? We are living in a consumer society. There is a good deal of evidence that many desire more than their society presently is offering them,[128] but the only way available for them to meet their desire is to shop around

---

125. *HT*, 255. Italics mine. The quotation is from Davidson, *Autobiography and Diary*, 24–25.

126. *COM*, 361.

127. Orchard, Review of *Nature of the Household*, 135.

128. See Davie, *Religion in Britain*. While the number of religious practitioners has nose-dived, Davie argues that "The sacred does not disappear—indeed in many ways it is becoming more rather than less prevalent in contemporary society" (*Religion in Britain*, 43).

and consider what alternatives are available. There seems little point in the church railing against the consumer society when there is not the slightest chance it is going to disappear; nor is there much mileage in expecting those who network to get excited about attending meetings. The issue for the church in this context is straight-forward: In a world now governed by information and communication technology what does it have to offer the spiritual seekers? Perhaps part of the answer involves an invitation to belong to a community built upon dynamic and informal relationships, rather than an offer of membership of an institution which has a potentially static and formal meeting at its heart? Pete Ward, consequently, asks us to conceive the church "as a series of relationship-based connections rather than as a single congregational meeting."[129] He argues that, in the future church, "Networked, informal contact between individuals and groups will replace monolithic meetings and formalized friendships."[130] If he is correct, those who share with Sell an historic attachment to the Church Meeting must face up to the hard truth that "the way we organize the church may be inherited, but it is not preordained."[131]

THE PRIESTHOOD OF ALL BELIEVERS

Another key principle of Sell's ecclesiology is "the priesthood of all believers," a subject of considerable misunderstanding. It is "undoubtedly the case," Sell argues, that the phrase means that "every believer has direct access to God through Jesus Christ the one Mediator without mediation of a priest."[132] In the Medieval church the keys to salvation were in the hands of the priest, but Reformation thinking enabled them to be taken away from a priestly caste and returned to the corporate gathering of believers. As Sell argues, "the Church, founded in the act of its great High priest, *is,* rather than *has* a priesthood."[133] This does not mean that the church can or should dispense with its ministers: they still contribute to the church's *bene esse*. The point being made is that "all Christians"—not just ministers—"*together* comprise the "royal priesthood" (1 Pet 2:19 [sic]; Heb 13)."[134] When the gathered saints meet together they exercise a "*corporate* ministry

---

129. Ward, *Liquid Church*, 45.
130. Ward, *Liquid Church*, 47.
131. Ward, *Liquid Church*, 8.
132. Sell, *OMMM*, 7. See 1 Tim 2:5.
133. *TAT*, 209.
134. *SOL*, 61. Italics mine. The biblical reference should be 1 Pet 2:9.

The Church

of confession, praise, prayer and service."[135] Not surprisingly Sell is at pains to make it clear that "the priesthood of all believers" denotes "the corporate priesthood of the gathered saints,"[136] since "we are invited to think of the priesthood of *all the people together*."[137] Correctly, he wanted to rule out the way the term has been construed "atomistically, as if each member were an isolated and insulated 'priest.'"[138]

Sell insists, therefore, that "the priesthood of all believers" is a corporate term.[139] He objects to the way in which it has been understood as a warrant to do what we like in the church, thereby behaving, as he puts it, "like unrelated atoms."[140] It does not denote "the sanctification of the aspirations, whims or prejudices of every individual member."[141] Each church member's vocation is to be carried out in a symbiotic relationship with that of the other members. What Sell refers to as "unfortunate individualism" is not to be condoned, since it is simply not the case that "every individual's opinion is as good as that of anyone else," or that "all the offices of the church are open to all."[142] All God's saints are gifted in some way. It is for the church, though, to decide the office or role that suits a person's gifts and then to set them apart for their particular ministry. Otherwise there will be a breakdown of discipline. While it is true that ministers of Word and Sacraments are part of the people of God (*laos*), it is not the case that all the members of the *laos* are such ministers. In an orderly church "those called to specific tasks are appointed thereto by the church, following whatever testing of the call and training of the person may be required."[143] It remains noteworthy that those churches which historically have practiced "the priesthood of all believers" have been known to expect their leadership to be in the hands of a *learned* ministry and therefore have prepared their ministers in rigorous and demanding ways.

Sell takes issue with those who claim that the historic episcopate is of the church's *esse*. He recognizes that contemporary Anglicans usually accept that their bishops are of the church's *bene esse* rather than *esse*; but, no doubt speaking from experience, he ruefully notes that "some of them sometimes

---

135. *COM*, 349. Italics mine.
136. *TAT*, 75.
137. *OMMM*, 7. Italics mine.
138. Sell, *GE*, 234.
139. Sell, *GE*, 234. See also *DTLC*, 16 and *REC*, 79, 166, 170.
140. *ACI*, 133.
141. *TAT*, 75.
142. *OMMM*, 7.
143. *TAT*, 34.

behave as if it were otherwise!"[144] For many a Congregationalist it is hardly less objectionable to claim that the historic episcopate belongs to the churches "fullness" than it is to say it is of its "essence." The Reformed, however, do not have an issue with episcopacy *per se*, since they have recognized the need for *trans-local* ministries. Church oversight has to be "wider" as well as "local" if true catholicity is to be maintained. The trans-local minister is particularly needed to "encourage congregations which have inherited a large portion of Enlightenment individualism . . . to understand themselves as ecclesial bodies, rather than as aggregates of saved atoms gathering under one roof," as well as to encourage and enable "local churches . . . to take their rightful place" in the regional and national church structures.[145]

Sell reveals his Reformed roots when he challenges three claims often made concerning episcopacy. First, there is the claim that episcopacy constitutes the church's continuity across the ages. Sell turns to Lovell Cocks for "the kernel of the Reformed case":

> By God's grace we already stand in the real apostolic succession, for it is in the contemporary Christ, the living Lord, that the Church's life across the centuries is summed up and secured. And as for the historical continuity—the outward succession—that is surely to be sought in the unchanging Gospel itself—the Word of God which generation after generation created and replenishes the community of believers as it is proclaimed from faith to faith.[146]

Secondly, there is the claim that the episcopate functions as the guardian of the faith. Sell says that "it ill behoves us to speak as if creeds and confessions—or, for that matter, bishops—guard the faith," since "The lesson of eighteenth-century Congregationalism is that it takes more than that to keep the faith—indeed, that without formally subscribed creeds and confessions, and in the entire absence of bishops, the faith can be kept, whilst those who have these things . . . can be doctrinally at risk."[147] He believed that the covenant ecclesiology of the Independents, with its corporate expression in the Church Meeting, helped them maintain orthodoxy. Thirdly, while Sell has no problem with the *pastor pastorum* role of the bishop, he objects to the idea that upon consecration bishops receive "powers" which they then pass on to priests at their ordination, so that they can, for example, absolve

---

144. *ACI*, 94.
145. *PHT*, 197.
146. Quoted by Sell in *RECT*, 164. See also *ACI*, 95; *CCF*, 86; *FPA*, 190; *SOL*, 58.
147. *DTLC*, 61.

sinners and conduct the sacraments. Sell endorses Robert Mackintosh's description of this as a "superstitious doctrine of sacramental grace."[148]

ESTABLISHMENT

The United Kingdom houses two Established churches. While the Anglican, episcopally-ordered Church of England is usually in Sell's sights when he writes opposing Establishment some of his arguments apply also to the Presbyterian Church of Scotland. He follows his Separatist forebears in making the case for the impropriety of the existence of Established churches.

The argument is rooted in what Paul regarded as God's command to the Corinthian church that its members should "come out from them, and be separate from them . . . and touch nothing unclean" (2 Cor 6:17).[149] They were to distance themselves from the world's sin and evil: therefore, there is a God-given requirement for Christians to be "in the world but not of the world." And, since "the apparatus of Establishment was, to the Separatists, precisely 'of the world,'" it followed that they believed that they should separate themselves from "the false state-church."[150] Among the heresies identified by the Separatists was, first, the notion that, because one happens to be born in a Christian country, one thereby automatically becomes a Christian,[151] and secondly, the Established church practice of inviting "regenerate and unregenerate alike . . . on non-biblical grounds to the sacrament of Holy Communion."[152] For Sell, a conscious decision is involved in becoming a church member, so the idea that one can become part of the regenerate as "a consequence of domicile" understandably was anathema to him.[153] As Marsh reminds us "the New Testament gives no precedent whatever for thinking of a 'nation' as a 'church.'"[154] Hence, "there is something irregular . . . about a state-established Church."[155]

All "spiritual" matters fall under the jurisdiction of "the Lord Jesus Christ, the only king and head of the Church," and are not to be meddled with by the state.[156] It follows, therefore, that the very notion of a state-

---

148. Quoted by Sell, *PHT*, 236.
149. Paul, perhaps, is referring to Isa 52:11.
150. *DTLC*, 623.
151. *TAT*, 255.
152. *TAT*, 83.
153. Sell, *GE*, 239.
154. Quoted by Sell, *TAT*, 280.
155. *TEM*, 235.
156. From *A Statement Concerning the Nature, Faith and Order of the United*

church is ruled out *in principle*. The state should not get inappropriately involved in church affairs. It is interesting though that, while the Separatists "maintained that in spiritual matters the state is not above the church," Sell points out that they often pledged loyalty to the monarch.[157] For the most part they were not republicans.[158]

Sell believes that three abiding principles emerge from the Separatist's stance. The first is that "the Christian is called a saint, and the church is a fellowship of saints."[159] Churches are made up, therefore, of "gathered, disciplined saints"[160] who are separate from the world (*qua* naughty) but of the world (*qua* geography). This distinction is easy to state but, given the "naughtiness" abroad in the church, it is seemingly impossible to make good in practice. The second principle is located in the belief that the only way of being a member of the catholic church is to be "a locally-anchored saint."[161] This entails "the voluntary making of a credible profession of faith, evidenced by a "godly walk"" and involvement in Christian mission and service with fellow church members.[162] It is not merely a matter of being part of a so-called "Christian" country. The third principle concerns what Sell refers to as "the most important point of all" in the case against Establishment,[163] namely, that "Christ alone is Head of the Church."[164] In a state-established church, Sell argues, the monarch is in danger of usurping the Lordship of Christ. He reminds us that the "Dissenters managed from time to time to make the point that the Church of England was not a true Church since it owed allegiance both to Christ and to the monarch, and not to Christ alone."[165] But, even if a monarch lives a perfect life, the question whether he or she should be the church's temporal head remains. Sell is clear that no arrangements are to be made by the state that, in any conceivable way, denies the freedom "demanded by God's grace in the Gospel"[166] for Christians "to obey God and to follow his dictates in church order and life."[167] A

Reformed Church. In Thompson, *Stating the Gospel*, 263.

157. *CTF*, 194.
158. See *TAT*, 87n173.
159. *DTLC*, 626.
160. *CTF*, 188.
161. *CTF*, 47.
162. *CTF*, 189.
163. *TAT*, 278.
164. *CTF*, 47.
165. *PDN*, 19.
166. *TAT*, 277.
167. *DTLC*, 626.

monarch should not be vested with any power which could negate Christ's sole headship of the church.[168] The bottom line is now clear: "The institution must never usurp the place of the Church's Head, the 'Crown Rights of the Redeemer' must ever be maintained within his Church."[169] Sell refers to "Jesus's God-Caesar principle," reminding us, quite correctly, that "when the chips are down, Christians are to be for God."[170] The issue being raised is of perennial importance: should Christians remain apart from the world in order to remain pure or should they get stuck in trying to make things better, even if they end up a bit dirty? It is a measure of his passion about the inappropriateness of Establishment that he confesses his hope that he would be willing "to die for the principle of the 'crown rights of the Redeemer in his Church'" even though he adds "with equal fervour" his hope "that it will not come to that."[171] And, arguably, it would never have been likely to "come to that" because Sell's liberties were protected by secular law which largely owes it origin to a drip-feed of Christian values from the Established church. But he reminds us that the case for anti-establishment is grounded not in "a secular-humanist argument for liberty of conscience, or freedom of the will," but, rather, in "the prior fact that Christ alone is Lord of the conscience."[172]

Members of the Church of England can be forgiven for thinking that some of Sell's arguments against Establishment either are no longer relevant or over exaggerate its dangers by underestimating its values. Twenty-first century Establishment is a far cry from what pertained in church-state relations in the days of the Separatists, so they will understandably ask: Who today would ever suggest that being born in England automatically makes one a Christian? At a time of synodical government is it not the case that representatives of the laity and clergy with the bishops, in effect, rule over church affairs rather than the state? And, as "Supreme Governor of the Church of England" and "Defender of the Faith" surely everyone can see that the monarch's role is procedural and ceremonial rather than determinative and legislative. As John Munsey Turner observes, Sell's treatment of Establishment "seems a little negative now," implying that Sell was fighting

---

168. See *NT*, 179: "the Church confesses Christ as the only head of the Church."

169. *SOL*, 53. See also *DTLC*, 627 and *GE*, 281, 232.

170. *COMM*, 116. His reference is to the story in which Jesus told "some Pharisees and some Herodians" to "Give to the emperor the things that are the emperor's, and to God the things that are God's" (Mark 12:17). Elsewhere, Sell says that "when the chips are down, God takes precedence over Caesar" (*CTF*, 65).

171. *CTF*, 47.

172. *CTF*, 66.

battles long since won.[173] It is also easy for members of the Free Churches to ignore the way Establishment has enabled a drip feed of Christian values into society. Sell agrees that contemporary Establishment differs greatly from yesterday's version; he rejoices in the positive changes that have come about; but he observes pointedly that Establishment has not been removed.

Twenty-first-century England is largely secular. It contains a multi-cultural, and, hence, multi-faith population. Only about 15 percent of the population claims any connection with the Church of England. It seems anachronistic, therefore, to argue a case for Establishment; but some devoted Anglicans continue to do so.[174] Sell is completely unconvinced by their arguments. He notes that the national, state church is often defended on the grounds that its parochial system enables "Church of England ministries" to be available "to all without discrimination."[175] Just why most members of our largely secular society would welcome such a gift is less than clear. Sell suggests, consequently, that, while "this claimed pastoral concern for all" may well be "well-intentioned and sincerely entertained," it "can be, and sometimes is, perceived as patronizing."[176] Just why churches need Establishment to exercise their God-given ministry to those who live in their church neighborhood remains a mystery, particularly to members of non-Established churches who take it for granted that they are called to community-based ministry, and simply get on with it. Sell is equally unconvinced by the often-made utilitarian arguments in favor of Establishment. It is claimed that Establishment provides "a voice in high places" or "a seat around the table where important decisions are made." The historical presence of bishops in the House of Lords is welcomed and the fact that other non-Anglican church representatives and leaders of non-Christian faith-communities now sit alongside them is applauded. But those of little or no religious disposition remain puzzled by such arrangements. Sell joins Townsend in noting that the Free Church argument against Establishment is "a protest against the complacency of the principle of the utility of the Establishment."[177] He suggests that, when such "pragmatic" arguments are put forward, those making them "completely bypass establishment as a theological question concerning the sole Lordship of Christ in his church."[178]

173. Turner, Review of *Protestant Nonconformity*, 88.

174. Sell refers us to Avis, "Establishment and the Mission"; Carr, "A Developing Establishment"; Edwards, *Not Angels but Anglicans*; and Habgood, *Church and Nation*. See *TAT*, 268n60 and *DTLC*, 654n.

175. *TAT*, 271.

176. *TAT*, 271.

177. *TAT*, 85. Sell quotes from Townsend, *Claims of the Free Churches*, 208.

178. *FPA*, 129.

Sell believes that it is difficult for an Established church to be suitably progressive and prophetic. An appropriate distance from the state is required if the church is to found in a position of real influence. Sell endorses Orr's view that in the nineteenth century it was "the Free Churches" rather than "the State Church" that encouraged "progress," since, "in the nature of things" an Established church has "its guns spiked."[179] Some radical Anglicans who advocate dis-establishment believe that their church has similar problems today. Giles Fraser, for example, is convinced that "the dis-establishment of the church is now both necessary and ultimately unavoidable."[180] Establishment is a heresy, he says, since the state-church "ends up forgetting who the boss is."[181] Sell would have warmed to the following:

> . . . to say that Jesus is the supreme authority is to say that no one else can be — not the Romans, not the pope, not the House of Stuart or the House of Windsor. The Church of England was specifically designed to soften that thought, to make it less dangerous.

Fraser, like Sell, honors "the crown rights of the Redeemer," and in so doing he also lays bare the problems Establishment leaves in its wake. He claims that it "weakens the church."[182] It makes it dependent: "For too long we have been made content by feeding off the crumbs left out for us by the establishment. We have become its pet. And it has made us lazy. Housetrained. Safe."[183] Fraser does not mince his words: "if the church is not vigorous enough to stand on its own two feet without a state-sanctioned-life-support system, it deserves to pass into obscurity."[184] What is more, he rails at the way Establishment "turns clerics into fawning Jeeves-like courtiers who prefer dressing up to speaking out."[185] In fairness to the Church of England, though, we should acknowledge that the latter tendencies are not the sole preserve of Established churches; they come with the religious genre.

However much, in principle, Sell remained trenchantly opposed to Establishment, he recognized that dis-establishment will only come about "when the Church of England itself seeks it."[186] It is possible, though, to en-

---

179. *DAD*, 140. Sell quotes from Orr, "Contribution of the United Presbyterian Church," 97–98.
180. Fraser, "Loose Canon," 8 September 2017.
181. Fraser, "Loose Canon," 31 January 2015.
182. Fraser, "Loose Canon," 31 January 2015.
183. Fraser, "Loose Canon," 8 September 2017.
184. Fraser, "Loose Canon," 31 January 2015.
185. Fraser, "Loose Canon," 31 January 2015.
186. *TAT*, 87.

visage an alliance of progressive Anglicans and leading secularists one day pressing for dis-establishment. The extensive parliamentary time needed to disentangle church and state in England suggests that they will not get much government support. It may be some time, therefore, before dis-establishment gets the attention that Sell believes it deserves.

8

The Means of Grace and More about the Church

THE MEANS OF GRACE

Reformed theologians have tended to follow Calvin when delineating the marks of the true church: "Wherever we see the Word of God purely preached and heard, and the sacraments administered according to Christ's institution, there, it is not to be doubted, a church of God exists."[1] At one point, Sell follows Calvin in affirming that "The true Catholicity is to recognize the Church in every community where the pure word of the Gospel is preached and the sacraments duly administered as its expressions."[2] Elsewhere we find Sell adding an additional mark of the true church. He claims that "To those in the Reformed and Dissenting traditions the characteristic marks, or notes, of the Church which, when visible, assure us that we are looking at the true Church, are that the Word is faithfully preached, the sacraments rightly administered and *discipline rightly exercised*."[3] The addition of "discipline" reflects the Separatist and Puritan stress upon the saints being called "to walk in the light in grateful response to God's grace,"[4] and the need for the gathered saints to admonish any who were falling by the wayside. To put it in modern parlance, it is crucial that Christians

---

1. Calvin, *Institutes* IV.I.9.
2. *TAT*, 279
3. *EEE*, 63. Italics mine.
4. *EEE*, 203.

"walk the walk as well as talk the talk." Sell follows the Puritan divine John Owen (1616–83),[5] "the converted Scottish Dominican," John Craig,[6] the Anabaptists, and several Reformed Confessions in adding "discipline" to the marks of the true church. We will deal with each of the three means of grace in turn.

Preaching

Preaching is not to be equated merely with the delivery of sermons in church services, since Christian proclamation is at the heart of Christian duty and a mark of authentic Christianity. Christians are told: "Always be ready to make your defense to anyone who demands from you an account of the hope that is in you" (1 Pet 3:15). They are to proclaim the gospel as representatives of the church. Sell follows Forsyth in recognizing that preaching is not simply the responsibility of ordained ministers: "it is the Church which is called to proclaim the Gospel."[7] He is aware of the way in which the faithful witness of humble saints has had a dramatic impact upon the lives of those they encounter. "It is a humbling thing for ministers," he suggests, "to reflect upon how much good can be done when they are nowhere in sight."[8] But, like Forsyth, he also knew how effective rank-and-file ministers can be: "There have been many ministers who had not pulpit gifts of a striking kind, but who, in a steady lifetime of work not only faithful but deeply spiritual, have become fountains of rich life, while meteoric hierophants slew their thousands every week."[9]

If preaching is more than sermons, not restricted to designated preachers, but the business of the church as a body and among its members, from where does the drive come to engage in it? Sell unsurprisingly takes us back to the roots of his ecclesiology for an answer: "no matter how varied the cultural, intellectual, socio-political contexts of Christian preaching may be, the *context* of preaching is the gracious work of the triune God."[10] Not only does the energy to preach derive from one's calling, but the content of

---

5. Sell quotes Owen saying that the "Chiefest acts and parts" of worship are "*preaching of the word, administration of the sacraments, and the exercise of discipline*" (*TAT*, 22).

6. *OMMM*, 122, where Craig's 1581 catechism is quoted: "the marks of the church are, 'The Word, the Sacraments, and discipline rightly exercised.'"

7. *TAT*, 43.

8. *TAT*, 44.

9. Forsyth, *Church and Sacraments*, 127.

10. *TAT*, 47.

proclamation is given in and with the gospel. Preaching is not an excuse for preachers to inflict their views on their hearers; it is rather an opportunity to witness to Christ's call on their lives. Their all-too human words can become God's Word. Hence, preaching carries a sacramental dimension. Sell shared Forsyth's view that "the preached Word of God" is not "a mere message warmly told" but "a creative sacrament by the medium of a consecrated personality."[11] The preacher is "a living oracle of God."[12]

Sell's understanding of preaching is demanding and challenging. As a minister of the gospel he aspired to be the kind of preacher Forsyth advocated, and, if his sole published sermon is anything to go by, he often succeeded.[13] He displays a fundamental belief in the necessity, power, and effectiveness of good preaching in Christian worship, and he dealt harshly with what he regarded as the lame excuses put forward by those in the church who belittle preaching. Some sit light to preaching, for example, on the grounds that congregations have lost the capacity to listen for any length of time; but Sell believes this argument runs the risk of patronizing the saints: "They may well be tired of sermons; I seriously question whether they are tired of the gospel."[14] Notwithstanding that some of the current generation may have short concentration spans, Sell holds that a higher authority can be relied upon to get our attention: "they can be held by [the gospel], and even yearn for more of it; and that not because of oratorical excellence or pulpit histrionics, but because God the Holy Spirit is addressing them, challenging them, consoling them, through it."[15] We would be wise never to doubt such possibilities, but in an era when social media grip most people's attention, the churches have to find ways of communicating the gospel which are not so dependent on the sermon. Sell also rounds on those who turn away from preaching because they do not want to be seen to be standing "six feet above criticism" or, as he puts it, "because they wish, in a feel-good, matey kind of way, to get close to the people, to whom they offer a casual word or two from the back of an envelope."[16] Preachers should operate from a pulpit or designated place, he maintains, which makes it clear to the congregation that the due distance between them and the preacher reflects something very important: "This is where one stands who has been

---

11. *TAT*, 132.
12. *TAT*, 132.
13. See *OMMM*, 118–25.
14. *OMMM*, 64. Sell echoes Forsyth: "It is not Apostles that people are tired of, but the pulpit. It is sermons that weary them, not the gospel" (*Church and Sacraments*, 134).
15. *OMMM*, 64.
16. *CTF*, 166.

much in prayer, who has studied the Scriptures, who (normally) knows the people, and who proclaims, however unworthily, God's Word to them."[17] Quite so! But cannot more informal settings also enable people to hear God's Word to them as *together* they explore scripture? A way needs to be found for holding on to all that is best in traditions of preaching, while at the same time exploring new types of proclamation. Sell's approach is worthily traditional, but it undervalues attempts to develop more interactive, less individualistic, non-hierarchical forms of Christian communication. There are different ways of skinning the homiletic cat.

He is correct, though, to remind us about two matters concerning the interface between preacher and congregation. The first, already touched on, concerns the fact that "The efficacy of preaching is by no means *wholly* dependent upon our intelligibility."[18] Preachers, of course, must do all they can to hone their communication skills and seek to present their message in an appropriate way. But, in the final analysis, what really matters is very much out of the preacher's hands. As Sell reminds us, "the sermon is given in the name of the triune God, and its efficacy depends upon the action of God's Spirit in both guiding the preacher's thoughts and words and applying the truth of the declared Gospel to the hearers."[19] This important fact takes us to the second point concerning the interface between preacher and congregation: preaching is exacting work, demanding serious effort from preacher and congregation alike. It will only be effective if church members take seriously their need to develop theologically and grow spiritually just as much as the preacher prepares for the homiletic task through biblical exploration and prayerful reflection upon the needs of the members of the congregation and the world's life. Sell believes that "Whether sermons are written or read, or delivered extempore or from notes, diligent preparation is . . . essential."[20] And part of that preparation, he argues, occurs during the course of a minister's pastoral work. In an important sense, of course, "preaching *is* pastoral work."[21] Its purpose is "the upbuilding of the saints in the faith as they face the particular issues of life that confront them."[22] As Sell puts it elsewhere, "It is designed to move, instruct, encourage, console,

---

17. *CTF*, 165.

18. *FPA*, 198.

19. *FPA*, 198. Sell tells us that "Ministers should preach expectantly not, indeed, because they think that by their oratory they will raise the multitude or prod the remnant, but because they know that when the gospel is faithfully preached, however humbly and falteringly, it is followed by the Holy Spirit's blessing" (*OMMM*, 52).

20. *OMMM*, 54.

21. *CTF*, 164; *OMMM*, 65: *SOL*, 66.

22. *OMMM*, 65.

and rebuke those who hear it."[23] On the other hand, unless preachers know those they address it is doubtful whether their message will penetrate to the heart of their hearers' lives. The nub of the matter is that ministers need to be diligent in their preparation for preaching, and those who sit in the congregation must recognize that "really to hear a sermon is hard work; and the work begins before Sunday comes and continues after it has passed."[24] On both sides, the effectiveness of preaching is governed largely by the amount of attention given to catechetical and spiritual development by preacher and congregation alike.

Sell was generous in the advice he offered to preachers. First, those who are called to preach God's Word to others should attend to their own spiritual condition. Prayer is a necessary prelude to preaching. Preachers should not put themselves in a position where they earnestly call others to do what they are not trying to do for themselves. Sell quotes Spurgeon: "We may not be butchers at the block chopping off for hungry ones the meat of which we do not partake."[25] Secondly, preaching should be biblically-based. Sell believed passionately that "the faithful preaching of the gospel of God's grace in Christ, rooted in clear, solid (but not stodgy), non-patronizing biblical exposition, is the right place to begin."[26] Thirdly, preachers must be honest: they cannot afford to invite others to believe what they doubt, or ask them to commit to courses of action they are not prepared to follow. Sell reminds us that this amounts to "more than telling the truth and refraining from telling lies," since "in preaching we are testifying to what we have seen and heard. Personal integrity . . . is at stake here."[27] Fourthly, preachers should be as comprehensive as possible in the subjects they tackle. The Christian Year ought to be covered. Towards the end of his life, Sell maintained that he did not wish "to belong to a church which required slavish use of a lectionary,"[28] but he still pleaded that preachers acquaint their congregations "with the main arteries of that 'body of divinity' about which some of our forebears unburdened themselves at such great length."[29] The primary purpose of lectionaries is to ensure that an orderly set of biblical readings, free of repetition, and maximizing coverage of the canon of scripture, is read in church during the Christian year. If ever they operate as a

---

23. *CTF*, 164.
24. *CTF*, 67.
25. *TAT*, 44. The quotation comes from *An All-Round Ministry*, 66
26. *CAC*, 180.
27. *OMMM*, 51.
28. *TAT*, 46.
29. *TAT*, 46.

straight-jacket, it only concerns what is to be *read* in the church. They need not unduly be prescriptive for preachers. Fifthly, following on from this, Sell pleads that preachers address the core content of the gospel and avoid becoming side-tracked with topics seemingly more relevant to them. He spoke from experience of hearing preachers address, for example, peace and justice issues, the rights of homosexuals, and concerns about the hungry, abused, and bullied.[30] And he asks: "But if this is not to be bland humanism, where is the convictional basis, and where comes the necessary power?"[31] He was not suggesting that such topics should not become the subject of sermons, only that they are given a proper theological underpinning; but he did wonder whether the frequency with which he was hearing sermons on such topics meant that the more central topics were being "conveniently" avoided by preachers. His rhetorical question rings bells: "I cannot help wondering where, for example, have gone the sermons on adoption, regeneration, justification by grace through faith, sanctification, and even on the cross?"[32] Where indeed?

Sacraments

Sacraments are signs or symbols used in Christian worship to help Christians have the gospel brought home to them. Sell calls them "signs and seals of the covenant of grace" and "reminders of the Saviour's love."[33] While the Lord's Supper is generally taken to have been instituted by Christ himself, there is little evidence that he also instituted the sacrament of adult baptism let alone infant baptism.[34] Hence Sell is unwise perhaps to describe the sacraments as Christ's "personalized, inscribed love tokens given to his friends."[35] Sell insists that the meaning of sacraments "derives from a prior hearing of the Word."[36] Sacraments confirm and, hence, seal the gracious

---

30. See *NT*, 166; *OMMM*, 66.

31. *OMMM*, 60.

32. *OMMM*, 60.

33. *SOL*, 68.

34. The only explicit command of Jesus to baptize occurs at Matthew 28:19 within a passage which is generally believed to represent the tradition of the author's Christian community. Concerning infant baptism, Barth's verdict is sharp but to the point: "nowhere in the New Testament is infant baptism either permitted or commanded" (*Church Dogmatics* IV.4.179).

35. *SOL*, 68.

36. *RECT*, 161.

promises of God. We are reminded that, while sacraments are seals, it is the Holy Spirit who does the sealing (2 Cor 1:22; Eph 1:13; 4:30).[37]

Sell calls sacraments "the badges of membership of the Church."[38] Important though badges are, it cannot be said that the church is *constituted* by her sacraments.[39] Nor do sacraments effect salvation: "They witness to the gospel of God's prevenient grace, and they testify to what God has already done or . . . can do, by the Spirit in the lives of those who are gathered and covenanted in his name."[40] Sell's position entails affirming that sacraments are of the church's *bene esse* but rejecting any claim to their being of her *esse*. Claims that sacraments are constitutive of the church, he maintains, "may be but a short step to *ex opere operato* views of the sacraments and to a minimizing of that catholic-evangelical claim . . . that God constitutes his church by the Spirit through the Word on the basis of the once-for-all reconciling work of Christ."[41] Sell went to his death proclaiming to all who would listen that nothing—certainly not priests, an episcopate or sacraments—is constitutive of the church other than the triune God.

Sacraments are not necessary for salvation: it is the Word which saves; the sacraments ratify it. At their heart is God's gracious activity: "They do not turn upon what we do—partaking, remembering, confession [sic] our faith—but upon what he has done."[42] What the gathered saints do when participating in the sacraments is important since, through them, they are declaring their faith in God's redeeming work in Christ. The onus is placed upon the whole church, not just the president, to ensure that the sacraments are presided over in an orderly fashion. Sell makes a great deal of the fact that "it is the Church (and not the ministry) which celebrates the sacraments."[43] He was opposed to all forms of sacerdotalism. What is vital in sacraments is not the president, but what God has already done in Christ.

Sell also maintained that it is in a local church's gift to decide who should preside at the sacraments in their church. Normally, their choice is a given in so far as the ordained minister they call will be their president. But Sell courted ecumenical controversy with his insistence that, in the absence

---

37. Sell is very close to Calvin when defining a sacrament: "It seems to me that . . . [a sacrament is] an outward sign by which the Lord seals on our consciences the promises of his good will towards us in order to sustain the weakness of our faith" (*Institutes* IV.XIV.1).

38. *SOL*, 68.

39. See *GE*, 258; *RECT*, 142; *TEM*, 234.

40. *GE*, 258.

41. *RECT*, 142.

42. *SOL*, 68.

43. *TAT*, 43.

of an ordained minister, a local church may appoint a lay-person to preside. "I suspect that we may be holding to very un-Reformed doctrine," he tells us, "if we think that God will not meet with his people if the Lord's Supper is conducted by a faithful lay person who has been called by the Church to officiate."[44] It is a persuasive argument honoring "the ministry of all who are called by God to serve," as well as reminding "the ministers that they, along with all other members, are part of the *laos* of God, and not members of a priestly caste."[45] If churches are willing to advance the practice of lay preaching, it is very difficult to make out a case against lay presidency. As Sell rightly says: "Both Word and sacrament testify to the Gospel, and the latter is 'dumb' without the preached word;" but, nevertheless, he notes that "some drive a wedge between these two which the liturgiologists say belong together, by allowing almost anyone to preach and being very opposed to the lay 'administration' (ugly word) of the sacraments."[46] There is nothing disorderly in a church solemnly at Church Meeting setting apart a lay person to preside *if or when the need arises*.

The pre-Reformation church operated with seven sacraments (baptism, confirmation, penance, eucharist, holy orders, matrimony and anointing of the sick). At the Reformation the list was reduced to baptism and the Lord's Supper on the grounds that supposedly only the two so-called "dominical" sacraments were specifically instituted by Jesus. We now turn to consider those sacraments. It is worthwhile at the outset to recognize that Sell follows Calvin in maintaining that, since they are *church* sacraments, baptism is reserved for the family of the covenant and Holy Communion set aside for professed believers.[47] We will consider each sacrament in turn.

Baptism

Sell's understanding of baptism flows from his view of the church being God's covenant people. He places the emphasis not upon the context of a person's conversion but upon that person's church membership. He claims that "Baptism is the standing objection to that individualistic view of the Church which regards the Church as an aggregate of saved atom-souls."[48] It is part of initiation into the covenant community, being one part of a process through which the Holy Spirit draws people into full membership

---

44. *TAT*, 34. See also *RECT*, 172.
45. *TAT*, 34.
46. *HT*, 549.
47. See *CTF*, 161.
48. *SOL*, 71.

The Means of Grace and More about the Church

of the church. The process involves baptism, nurture, profession of faith and reception/confirmation,[49] though not necessarily in that order. In adult baptism traditions, for example, baptism immediately follows profession of faith.[50] But whether we are thinking of infant or adult—so-called "believer's"—baptism we are dealing with one element involved in becoming enrolled as "a covenant signatory in the local church understood as a manifestation of the one Church catholic."[51] Unless baptism is placed within its proper covenant context, Sell believes that it is susceptible to being surrounded by unfortunate superstition.

Augustine taught that the waters of baptism wash away original sin. Sell correctly observes that this pipe-line view of grace "muddied the waters and made baptism into something which could be, and sometimes was, thought of as a magical rite."[52] Indiscriminate baptism is sometimes justified on the grounds that unless persons are baptized they fall outside the sphere of God's saving love. And, as Sell observes, by "the free admission to baptism of children of all comers" churches collude with this unfortunate theology.[53] We are wise to remember that our union with Christ is never dependent upon sacraments. What *is* necessary for it is hearing and accepting the gracious good news of the gospel. A divine blessing is given at infant baptism—"part of that grace which in a little while they shall enjoy to the full,"[54] but Sell draws back from saying that baptism is always and necessarily the occasion for regeneration: "infants are baptized into future repentance and faith, and even though these have not yet been formed in them, the seed of both lies hidden within them by the secret working of the Spirit."[55] In fact, Sell argues, "the majority of Protestants . . . have not normally understood the gift of regeneration—*the* operative factor in the translation to new life—as being necessarily received on the occasion of

---

49. See *COM*, 345.

50 It is important to remember that, in belonging to the URC, Sell was part of a church which "includes within its membership both persons whose conviction it is that baptism can only be appropriately administered to a believer and those whose conviction it is that the infant baptism is also in harmony with the mind of Christ"; and which, in an ecumenical spirit, attempts to honor both convictions in the belief that "both forms of baptism are understood to be used by God in the upbuilding of faith" ("Basis of Union of the United Reformed Church"; in Thompson, *Stating the Gospel*, 252).

51. *CCC*, 76n24.

52. *SOL*, 70.

53. *RM*, 50.

54. Calvin, *Institutes* IV.XVI.19.

55. Calvin, *Institutes* IV.XVI.20.

baptism."[56] He notes the arguments supporting their case: first, the doctrine of baptismal regeneration is not warranted by the New Testament; secondly, scripture does not suggest that God cannot regenerate persons at any time outside of baptism, even if they are totally unaware of when the gift is given; and, thirdly, God is not totally confined to acting through sacraments.[57] Sell thereby arrives at a commendable conclusion: "The truth would seem to be that all require to be regenerated, that this may or may not happen at baptism, that we cannot accurately specify the moment when it occurs, and, hence, that godly agnosticism is the most appropriate stance to adopt."[58]

During Sell's lifetime Pentecostalism was on the increase and the so-called "Charismatic Movement" was advancing. With this came an emphasis upon "signs and wonders" and "baptism in the Spirit," along with an accompanying inference that only those who could show evidence of having received the Spirit could be considered authentic Christians. A principal idea in such thinking is that we receive Christ at our conversion and the Spirit later at our baptism. Setting to one side the plight of those who are in the seemingly unfortunate position of having grown up in Christian families and joined the Church without ever being able to claim that they were converted, we share Sell's concerns about the ensuing appearance of "first-class and second-class varieties of Christians."[59] The implied separation of Christ's work and that of the Spirit rouses Sell to thunder: "The Spirit does nothing apart from or additional to what Christ does; nor is Christ subordinate to the Spirit."[60] And he then accuses "some Pentecostals" for "not being Pentecostal enough" due to their reticence to talk about the Spirit's work "in relation to creation, the world or even the Church."[61]

When discussing baptism, Sell offers us the following sentence: "God, the community, the individual: the order is highly significant."[62] For either infant or believer's baptism "the primary thing is the activity of God."[63] This underscores "the gospel truth that God's grace goes before us, and that before we can do anything, God does everything."[64] Above all else, therefore, baptism is a witness to the prevenient grace of God, not only in the case of

56. FPA, 156.
57. FPA, 268.
58. CTF, 189n45.
59. SOL, 76.
60. SOL, 76.
61. SOL, 76.
62. SOL, 70.
63. SOL, 70.
64. OMMM, 8.

infants who are not of an age to speak for themselves, but also in believer's baptism. Those who practice believer's baptism do well to remember that, "if any sinner anywhere is at all inclined to repent, God has already been there"![65] The most important things about the sacrament of baptism, consequently, concern God's action and the church's witness. Sell maintains, therefore, that, in the case of believer's baptism, the role of the baptismal candidate is "important" but "not paramount."[66] And "the question of the time in a person's life when baptism occurs is of secondary importance."[67]

Sell holds that paedobaptism is consistent with the idea of the covenant church. The baptized infant is placed within the church family who witness to the covenant God has made with them. A process of Christian initiation has then started; the baptized child becomes a catechumen.[68] A journey of faith has commenced which, hopefully, will lead to that person coming to her or his own profession of faith and being received as a full church member. It follows that the child's parents, as well as the church, play an important role in the initiation process. The entire logic of paedobaptism therefore presupposes that the parents are church members—or, at the very least, that one of them is. As Sell tells us: "The parents do not make promises on behalf of, or in place of, the child; but they undertake to bring their child up to know and love the Lord—and that means within the family of the Church."[69] Notwithstanding the prevalent practices of many churches, he believes that "unless there is a strong grasp of the covenant idea, and a real attempt to teach and receive as members parents who have not professed their faith, it would seem that the justification that baptism provides an evangelical opportunity for outreach to unchurched parents rings hollow."[70] Outside the doctrine of the covenant the case for paedobaptism falls: we are left with "a service of dedication, a rite of passage or a naming ceremony."[71] Sell makes it crystal clear that "infant baptism is for children of the covenant."[72] When "parents are not themselves members of the church then the first thing which must take place is that "the Church's evangelical and educative mission should be purposefully undertaken."[73]

65. *HT*, 63.
66. *SOL*, 70
67. *SOL*, 72.
68. See *CCC*, 76; *CTF*, 189n45.
69. *SOL*, 71.
70. *TAT*, 34.
71. *EEE*, 44.
72. *CTF*, 162.
73. *CTF*, 162; see also 189.

The hope is that the parents are "received as members on the day their child is baptized."[74] What Sell never tells us is whether the baptismal service would go ahead if that hope is not fulfilled. In the age of "believing but not belonging" many churches and ministers cry out for a credible, if perhaps pragmatic, answer to that question.

The Lord's Supper

Several terms are used to describe the second dominical sacrament: Mass, Eucharist, Holy Communion and Lord's Supper. Sell favors the latter for two reasons: first, it carries biblical precedence (1 Cor 11:20), and, secondly, "it clearly marks the distinction between the Last Supper of the first Maundy Thursday and the post-Easter Lord's Supper."[75] This sacrament recalls the Last Supper within the context of Easter affirmation. Both theologically and liturgically preaching (God's audible Word) and the Lord's Supper (God's visible Word) belong together. As Sell says, "when the Lord's Supper is kept we have the enacted witness to the gospel which was verbally proclaimed."[76] However, since the sacrament of the Lord's Supper "strikes to the heart of God's eternal purposes," Sell acknowledges that at the Lord's Table we encounter "inevitable mystery" but not "utter incomprehensibility."[77]

In attempting to elucidate Sell's understanding of the Lord's Supper it is useful to consider certain key terms. First, the Lord's Supper is an act of remembrance or a memorial (*anamnesis*). It brings home to us the event, costs, and benefits of our salvation. More than simple recollection is in view. We must never forget the Hebrew background of this ordinance. In Semitic cultures "remembering" involves bringing something from the past into the present in such a way that it "lives" again. The heart of what we "re-member" around the Lord's Table is the life, death, and resurrection of Jesus Christ, with the sacrament becoming effective through the act of remembering. Secondly, the sacrament of the Lord's Supper is an ordinance which seals Christ's benefits to the gathered saints. As Sell says, "The broken bread is to the believer the body of Christ; the poured out wine his blood."[78] They re-present to us Christ's sacrifice for us and set us alight with faith, hope, and love. Thirdly, at the Lord's Supper we receive spiritual food for life's journey. Christ is truly present with his people around the communion table.

74. *OMMM*, 42.
75. *OMMM*, 38.
76. *OMMM*, 27.
77. *COL*, 68.
78. *COL*, 73.

The Means of Grace and More about the Church

But what actually takes place when the communion bread is broken and the wine is poured and blessed during the Lord's Supper, has been a great bone of contention and cause of divisive disagreement.[79] Sell follows the Reformed tradition by rejecting two sacramental theories: the medieval idea of "transubstantiation" given in the theology of Aquinas, and the Lutheran notion of "consubstantiation." The presence of Christ during the Lord's Supper is not located in the *outward* visible elements, but rather it is an *inward*, invisible presence personally known to those gathered around the Lord's Table, both individually and corporately. The sacramental signs belong to what they represent: "bread and wine" are associated objectively with "body and blood." The connection is not simply made in the worshipper's head. Forsyth maintains that the "mere memorialism" view, often attributed to Zwingli, is "a more fatal error than the Mass, and a far less lovely."[80] But Sell knows that Zwingli was no "mere memorialist." He shares with White the view that "Zwingli was stating in a new way the reality of Christ's presence as a transubstantiation of the congregation rather than of the elements."[81] He was emphasizing the *corporate* dimension of the spiritual presence of Christ among those gathered at the Lord's Supper. With Calvin, however, the stress is on the *individual* dimension; Christ becomes spiritually present to the individual when he or she takes part in the Lord's Supper.[82] Sell seeks to hold together both the *individual* and *corporate* dimensions of Christ's real presence with the gathered saints. The Lord's Supper is indeed a "holy communion." It gives rise to fellowship (*koinonia*) with God and fellow Christians. As Sell affirms, "The risen, ever-living Christ, is there in the midst. He is not imagined to be there, he is there with his people."[83] Fourthly, thanksgiving is also a dimension of the Lord's Supper. As we remember what Christ has done for us we give thanks. We are thus involved in a "eucharist."[84] Fifthly, at the Lord's Supper an eschatological note is sounded when those gathered around the Lord's Table look to the future coming of God's kingdom. Involved in this is one of the earliest Christian prayers: *Maranatha*, Lord Come! Finally, the Lord's Supper is a means through which the church offers itself to God in worship and service. Sell would have us remember that "what we offer is our imperfect best, while what Christ offers is the one, full,

---

79. On the various theories of sacramental action, see my *Reforming Theology*, 212–15.

80. Forsyth, *Church and Sacraments*, 8.

81. *PHT*, 290. Sell, quoting from White, *Protestant Worship*, 59.

82. See Calvin, *Institutes* IV.XVIII.10.

83. *SOL*, 73.

84. The word "eucharist" comes from the Greek word *eucharistia*, meaning "thanksgiving."

perfect, and sufficient sacrifice for sin."[85] And he insists that "any notion that at the Lord's Supper Christ is sacrificed again is ruled out."[86]

The Lord's Supper "is not 'done to' the saints by members of a priestly caste," since "it is the church, the corporate priesthood of believers, which keeps the Supper."[87] The president is the church's ordained minister, or, in his or her absence, a lay person (often a lay preacher who may or may not be an elder). Sell tells us that "The majority opinion in the Reformed family has been . . . that the Lord's Supper . . . is for those whose Christian initiation is complete."[88] Those eligible to partake, consequently, are the enrolled saints. Sell insists, though, that "the Lord's table is open to all who are his."[89] He shudders at the thought that any church would fence off the Lord's Table from the members of other church traditions. In the Reformed tradition three types of person would typically be expected to be present around Christ's table: first, church members; secondly, "those who would like to believe, and for whom the sacrament, since it witnesses to the gospel, may be a converting ordinance";[90] and, thirdly, "those who would receive the elements prior to making their profession of faith," and are allowed to do so because their action indicates "a desire for that closer fellowship which completed initiation implies and would have brought the pastoral forces of the church into play."[91] Sell is very reluctant to countenance the addition of children and young people to that list. He acknowledges that "the reception of children at the Lord's table is becoming increasingly common, and the reception of infants is not unknown."[92] But he dismisses the grounds for so doing, namely, that "all the baptized are of the family of Christ."[93] While wishing to deny them the opportunity to participate until after they become church members upon profession of faith (or, as some say, upon confirmation), he accepts nevertheless that it is good that "children are present at the sacrament, for they can be moved by the sense of reverence and awe, and . . . a measure of understanding is more likely to follow if they have been within eye-and-earshot of the service than if they had not."[94] Although he raises

---

85. *RECT*, 159.
86. *RECT*, 159.
87. *OMMM*, 7.
88. *RECT*, 155.
89. *OMMM*, 38.
90. *RECT*, 154.
91. *RECT*, 155.
92. *RECT*, 155.
93. *RECT*, 155.
94. *OMMM*, 39.

The Means of Grace and More about the Church

here the matter of "understanding" he admits that "none of us ever attains to" a position of understanding "the full significance" of the Lord's Supper.[95] Nevertheless, Sell over-intellectualizes the matter. He is certainly in danger of asking of children and young people more than the church actually in practice asks of adults. As Donald Hilton notes, this implies that "Children . . . must have a cerebral understanding of the table event, and enjoy a faith which they can articulate before they share fully at the table whereas, week by week, we break bread and drink wine with adults who acknowledge that they do not yet fully understand, and are still in the early stages of a faith they cannot yet, and may never, articulate."[96] Given recent research into children's spirituality there are increasing grounds for encouraging children and young people to share fully at the Lord's Table. Hilton asks a poignant question: "Are not those children who by action, worship and mutual friendship clearly belong to the local Christian community, already members with a right to share fully in the church's total worship life?"[97] As we discover new meanings of membership in liquid modernity, we may come to realize that the all-determining moment in a person's Christian initiation is not necessarily when faith is formally confessed. Many regard themselves as "members" before becoming enrolled saints.

The different names used to describe this sacrament point to complementary emphases in our understanding of it.[98] In a similar way the "mechanics" of the Lord's Supper, the manner in which it is administered and the types of bread and wine used, convey different and sometimes even alternative messages about the sacrament. The background of the Last Supper is generally taken to be a Passover meal (*seder*). Hence the liturgical choreography of the Lord's Supper in its purest form is drawn towards participants breaking pieces off a common loaf and sharing a common cup. Both practices become difficult to carry out in large congregations. Sell is very defensive, though, about the practices of his own tradition, in which small pieces of bread and wine contained in small glasses are given to participants in their seats by a Deacon or an Elder. He is more concerned that those who require gluten-free bread are catered for than that "we become liturgically precious concerning the "one loaf,"[99] and he laments that "When communicants proceed to the Lord's table in groups to receive the chalice the idea of all eating and drinking together, which is preserved when the

---

95. *OMMM*, 39.
96. Hilton, *Table Talk*, 124.
97. Hilton, *Table Talk*, 126.
98. See Hilton, *Table Talk*, 5–17 for a thought-provoking account of this fact.
99. *OMMM*, 40.

bread and wine in individual glasses are received by the people in their seats, is lost."[100] But, of course, eating and drinking in that formulaic way is nowhere apparent in a Jewish *seder*—and with no loss of *koinonia*. Sell states sensitively that a similar attitude to the requirement to have gluten bread available entails making non-alcoholic wine available for "those who on principle or for health reasons" need to be catered for.[101]

But the bottom-line for Sell is that "the primary objective should be the reverent keeping of the Supper."[102] While few would take issue with that, Hilton reminds us of the dangers involved in allowing what we do sacramentally to obscure the meaning it is intended to serve:

> Fragments of bread and minuscule glasses of wine, or wafer and a shared cup of wine lose their point unless they affect the way we live together in the Church and the World. The food we all need for our everyday Christian journey is not a drink of non-alcoholic fruit juice from a tiny glass nor 12° proof wine from a costly chalice, but companionship, support, and shalom; rebuke, challenge, and inspiration.[103]

The Lord's Supper actually is the meal of a counter-cultural community. It involves "a statement about the politics of caring and sharing in a national and world community."[104] Sell does not discuss the political implications of the Lord's Supper. But, at its heart, it "offers a vision of women and men, all races, all colours, sitting around the world's table which is filled with the Lord's gifts."[105] It is nothing less than the foretaste of God's kingdom prefigured in Jesus' table-fellowship during his ministry.

Discipline

Sell's ecclesiology hinges upon there being a clear distinction between those who are enrolled in the covenant community and those who are not. Some form of discipline is required, not only to maintain this distinction, but also to ensure that church members are living up to their calling. Sell knows that, since "the saints are also sinners," there will be occasions "when, in the interests of honouring God and maintaining the peace and integrity

---

100. *OMMM*, 41.
101. *OMMM*, 40.
102. *OMMM*, 41.
103. Hilton, *Table Talk*, 50.
104. Hilton, *Table Talk*, 58.
105. Hilton, *Table Talk*, 58.

of the church discipline is needed."[106] But, among people who "proclaim inclusivity as a virtue and exclusivity as a vice"[107] it is a brave person who suggests today that the church should re-discover "the well-nigh lost art of discipline."[108] Sell, though, was never afraid to swim against the tide when faithfulness to the gospel was at stake. Questions of who belongs to the gathered saints, and who does not, arise all the more urgently at a time when many Western churches appear to be "so identified with the surrounding culture as to be almost indistinguishable from it."[109]

According to Sell, discipline is a means of grace which aids the church in three areas. First, it helps determine who is or is not a church member: Is the person offering a credible profession of faith? Is there evidence of a determination to practice a Godly walk? Secondly, it is helpful in doctrinal matters, differentiating between orthodoxy and heresy: Is it really appropriate for a person with Unitarian beliefs to be enrolled as a member of a Trinitarian church? Thirdly, it helps maintain moral standards in the church, even though, in practice, some of those standards have been shown to be culturally dependent, with practices ruled out in one era becoming acceptable in future ones. Without discipline, however, churches find themselves sliding into the habits of their culture; they end up without anything distinctive to offer; and their evangelical witness is blunted.

Sell offers four introductory comments to his discussion of church discipline. First, lest he be thought of as rubbing his hands in enjoyment at the very thought of exercising discipline, he reminds us that "the 'policing' of the saints is an awesome responsibility, not a hobby to be enjoyed."[110] If disciplinary processes happen to give a person a "buzz," then it is arguable that such a person should not be entrusted with administering them. Secondly, he tells us that "church discipline is discipline under the Gospel."[111] This rules out "legalism" (Christianity is not "a new set of rules") as well as "antinomianism" (Christianity is not "an inducement to free-wheeling license").[112] Thirdly, he argues that "the will of the Lord of the Church is paramount and this should sincerely be sought."[113] That takes place in Church Meeting—or one of the other (regional and national) church coun-

---

106. *EEE*, 347.
107. *EEE*, 347.
108. *HT*, 545.
109. *OMMM*, 44,
110. *CAM*, 152.
111. *EEE*, 342.
112. *EEE*, 342.
113. *EEE*, 342.

cils where mutual episcopacy is exercised. Fourthly, he warns against using discipline as an opportunity to be vindictive; its purpose is more adequately understood as being corrective.

When discussing the objectives of church discipline Sell largely follows Calvin, who says that, "as the saving doctrine of Christ is the soul of the church, so does discipline serve as its sinews, through which the members of the body hold together, each in its own place."[114] For Sell there are four purposes served by church discipline.[115] First, the all-encompassing aim is one of glorifying God. Secondly, discipline helps up-hold the church's integrity: "The primary objective is that Christ, the Head of the Church, be not dishonoured by immoral or hypocritical behavior (Romans 2:23)."[116] A third objective is that of ensuring "that the weaker brothers and sisters [will] not be harmed."[117] This is the "one bad apple can affect the whole barrel" principle.[118] The fourth objective is the restoration of repentant offenders and their rehabilitation in the church's fellowship.[119] Unless there exists adequate discipline in the church, Sell maintains, the primary functions of the church will not be fully carried out and, hence, the gathered saints will fail the Lord they are set apart to worship and serve. In a broad church living in a plural, multicultural society, such ideals are easier to state than carry out. The boundaries of Christian belief and practice are more fluent today than in the eighteenth-century world so loved by Sell.

THE PRIMARY FUNCTIONS OF THE CHURCH

When we remember that the primary mode of Christian service is found in the service of others and that a fundamental way of serving God is in the service of others,[120] any undue concerns about the inward-looking nature of ecclesiology begin to recede. Nevertheless, we are minded that, when it comes to understanding the church's nature, due attention ought to be paid

---

114. Calvin, *Institutes* IV.XII.1.

115. See *EEE*, 341–42 and *OMMM*, 43.

116. *EEE*, 341–42. Calvin describes the objective as follows: "that they who lead a filthy and infamous life may not be called Christian, to the dishonour of God" (*Institutes* IV.XII.4)

117. *OMMM*, 43. See also *EEE*, 342.

118. As stated by Calvin, the objective is "that the good not be corrupted by the constant company of the wicked" (*Institutes* IV.XII.4).

119. Sell provides a list of biblical warrants in connection with the objective, as Calvin puts it, "that those overcome by shame for their baseness begin to repent" (*Institutes* IV.XII.4), e.g., Matt 18:15; 1 Cor 2:5; 2 Cor 2:6–8; Gal 6:1; 2 Thess 3:14.

120. See Matt 25:31–46.

to the way in which it should benefit the lives of its members as well as those beyond the membership. Only as the church exists to further God's mission (*missio Dei*) is it theologically legitimate to say that it has been established for God's benefit. Sell assigns the church two primary duties: worship and mission.

Worship

To the question: "What, then, is the true work of the church?" Sell answers that he accords "priority to the worship of God."[121] And he is convinced that "The primary thing in the worship of God is the worship of God."[122] He challenges, therefore, all anthropocentric understandings of worship, which start with "what we may or may not experience during the service"[123] and seldom pay due attention to the proper object of Christian worship, namely, the transcendent God. How we worship—the liturgies we use and the way worship is conducted—reveals what we have in mind concerning the God we worship. Sell is right, therefore, to acknowledge that "worship is a theological *locus*";[124] or, as he notes elsewhere: "As your doctrine is, so will your worship be."[125] As we shall see, he was concerned about what he perceived to be a lack of reverence before the Almighty in many supposedly modern worship patterns. But there is a note of even-handedness in his witty observation that "There is a reverential medium between a happy hour and an hour sitting in a freezer."[126]

Sell's discussion of worship reminds us of the primary grounds upon which the Independents developed their pattern of "free" worship: "they were against the 'vain repetition' to which they thought set forms could lead; they objected to some of the content of the *Book of Common Prayer*; and they denied that it was the monarch's prerogative to prescribe the worship of Christ's Church."[127] Over three hundred years on, Sell accepts that set patterns of worship have their place in any contemporary diet of Free Church worship. So prevalent have they become, though, that he wonders whether "for all the benefits to be derived from drawing upon the liturgical inheritance of the ages, the pendulum has nowadays swung too far in the direc-

---

121. *CAM*, 152. See also *EEE*, 236 and *OMMM*, 26.
122. *TAT*, 319.
123. *TAT*, 319.
124. *TAT*, 244.
125. *EEE*, 163.
126. *OMMM*, 29.
127. *PHT*, 291.

tion of liturgical scriptedness?"[128] He partly has the practice of extempore prayer in mind, but, perhaps, he overestimates the number of people who are gifted in it. Personal opinion about the content of worship will undoubtedly reflect preferences in worship styles, but establishing a balance between "freedom" and "order" in worship is crucial. Sell provides us with helpful guidance: "the freer the worship the more imperative it is that those leading it be disciplined and unselfish, resisting the temptation to fasten exclusively upon their favourite hymns, their favourite biblical passages and, in prayer, their passing moods."[129] Worship leaders are public persons whose task is leading the worship of the saints. Their "high calling" is not one of performing their private devotions in public.[130]

Sell recognizes that public worship can become routine and lackluster. When this occurs he asks us to remind ourselves that "it is well-nigh miraculous that sinners are called by the God of holy and pursuing love to commune with him in concert."[131] Worship is a privilege. The liturgy we follow will be adequate if it enables us "to offer [our] praise to God and to hear and respond to his Word."[132] It needs to cater for "a wide range of human emotions and needs (such as we find in the Psalms)."[133] A major reason for Sell's dislike of a great deal of "modern" worship is that the sole mood it captures before God is that of being "constantly jolly."[134] He asks the "happy-clappy types . . . to remember that their very gaiety can alienate those who need to hear good news," before whimsically noting that in church we must recognize that "some Christians are in pain, and that other Christians can be a pain in the neck."[135] It is very clear that Sell's preferred worship style is not that of the "praise service" with its central diet of "worship songs." In fact, he can hardly contain his delight when recalling an American mantra associated with such services: "Somebody has characterized this practice as 'four words, three notes, and two hours.'"[136] All of which leads us neatly on to the place of hymns in worship.

---

128. *TAT*, 32.
129. *TAT*, 322.
130. *CTF*, 284.
131. *OMMM*, 26.
132. *TAT*, 32.
133. *OMMM*, 32.
134. *OMMM*, 32.
135. *TAT*, 328.
136. *TAT*, 327. Sell received the mantra from D. G. Hart. See Hart's "Post-modern Evangelical Worship," 451–59.

During the seventeenth century there was resistance to the use of hymns in public worship, though some like Baxter were experimenting at the time with hymn writing. But, as Sell reminds us, "It was only in the eighteenth century that hymns could really begin [sic] play their impressive community-cementing role in English Dissent."[137] Prior to this metrical psalms and paraphrases dominated the congregational singing of the Independents. But, due to the innovations of, most notably, Doddridge and Watts, a new dimension opened up in worship. Through their hymnody Congregationalists were able to offer "some of their best gifts to the world Church."[138] And they have continued to do so through the hymns of, for example, Alan Gaunt, Fred Kaan, Caryl Micklem and Brian Wren. Sell rightly maintains that hymn writers have "a high calling."[139] He has the "worship song" brigade clearly in mind when he tells us that "there is a distinction to be drawn between the 'strangely warmed' heart and heartburn; and between nourishing doctrinal food and hard polemical rusks on the one hand or sentimental blancmange on the other."[140] Many modern worship songs, Sell believes, are not worth singing on either musical or theological grounds. He put it as follows:

> . . . when one has entered all appropriate caveats, and been as gracious as possible, there remains a significant problem. It is that so many of the songs are banal, self-serving, and boringly repetitive They should be sparingly used, if used at all; otherwise any hope that Nonconformists will continue to learn their doctrine from their hymns (as could once be said with some justification) is vain indeed.[141]

We are dealing with more than matters of taste here, since significant *theological* issues are at stake, for example, whether we view God as "a heavenly friend" or "a dear old pal."[142] Sell is concerned that justice is done to God's transcendence. It worries him that many Christians are awash with sentimentality since they are only being fed a diet of such songs.

Innovation in worship is never easily achieved. A balance must always be struck between what Sell calls "proper issues of the heritage of praise" and "liturgical adventurousness."[143] Pastoral issues are never far below the

---

137. *CTF*, 47.
138. *TAT*, 22.
139. *FPA*, 262.
140. *FPA*, 262.
141. *OMMM*, 31–32.
142. *TNM*, 243.
143. *TAT*, 31.

surface when liturgical revisions are on the agenda. We get a sense of Sell's conservative stance on these matters when he suggests that "The rhythm of the familiar is not altogether to be despised."[144] Sometimes we find ourselves having not only to be pastorally sensitive when considering innovation but also needing to maintain our theological integrity. Sell believes that the way Congregationalists were able to bring Word and Sacrament together inside the one service, for example, was an example of good innovation: it makes *theological* sense.[145] But the modern custom of the worship leader beginning worship "in 'wake-up-happy-campers-style' with a jolly 'Good morning everybody: how are you feeling today?'" Sell argues, is bad innovation. He maintains that "it is possible to infer something of the minister's doctrine of God from the way in which he or she arrives, or bounds, into the church."[146] It is true that some modern ways of commencing worship "[direct] the congregation to their own feelings and away from the majesty of God."[147] Sell also regrets the way in which *extempore* prayer has almost disappeared from contemporary services. Set, written prayers have their value, he believes, but their use need not, nor should not, entail the total omission of "free" prayer. Sell believes that we should continue to "honour our rich heritage of free prayer and practice the art and craft faithfully."[148] That, of course, involves recognizing "the correlation between what comes out in free prayer and what has previously gone in, in terms of the devotional life and the pastoral concern of the one leading the prayers."[149] Worship and pastoral care go hand in hand.

Mission

David Bosch reminds us that "Christianity is missionary by its very nature, or it denies its very *raison d'être*."[150] The church, therefore, is not only called to worship God, but also to participate in the *missio Dei*. Bosch defines God's mission as follows: "God's self-revelation as the One who loves the world, God's involvement in and with the world, which embraces both the church and the world, and in which the church is privileged to participate."[151] As a

---

144. *TAT*, 31.
145. See *CTF*, 157 and *TAT*, 23.
146. *OMMM*, 29.
147. *TNM*, 243.
148. *TAT*, 323.
149. *TAT*, 323.
150. Bosch, *Transforming Mission*, 9.
151. Bosch, *Transforming Mission*, 10.

participant in the *missio Dei*, the church is involved in two clear tasks. The first is *evangelism*, which Bosch describes as "the proclamation of salvation in Christ to those who do not believe in him, calling them to repentance and conversion, announcing forgiveness of sin, and inviting them to become living members of Christ's earthly community."[152] The second, which we shall call *service*, flows out of the church as both its "yes" and "no" to the world. It expresses the way the church is in "solidarity with society" as well as its "opposition to and engagement with the world."[153] Before we consider what Sell says about the twin components of mission, it is worthwhile pausing to reflect upon how the word "mission" recently has been hijacked by the corporate world and thoroughly secularized; and also to recall that the world the term now inhabits is exercising a significant influence upon the church.

Sell's exposure to North American church culture made him acutely aware of the way in which the church's mission can become diluted when it adopts the *corporate* world view. He wonders whether Western churches may have "poached the terms of the corporate world and shown no inclination to rebaptize them."[154] His rhetorical question drives to the heart of the issue: "Can we imagine that Baxter or Forsyth would think of ministry as a 'job,' that they would be impressed by talk of 'ministerial career patterns' or the 'hiring and firing' of pastors; that they would rate the person in a four-point charge lower than one in a 'tall steeple church,' or think of the latter as having been 'promoted'?"[155] He insists that we never should forget that "The Church is a fellowship of believers, called by grace, before it is a corporation bound by trust deeds,"[156] and points to five examples of a corporate mentality hindering the church. First, where "calls" to ministerial service are concerned, Sell believes that "more business-like" sometimes means "less theological."[157] He is horrified that in some churches "the profound distinction between the calling of a pastor and the hiring of staff is all but obliterated."[158] A mindset holds sway which does not see the *theological* significance of considering one candidate at a time.[159] Related to this is, secondly, the way in which "deployment" is tending to undermine "vocation" in the settlement of ministers. Sell is right to suggest that "no church should

---

152. Bosch, *Transforming Mission*, 10.
153. Bosch, *Transforming Mission*, 11.
154. *TAT*, 46.
155. *TAT*, 46.
156. *CTF*, 14.
157. *OMMM*, 16 n32.
158. *COM*, 176
159. See *OMMM*, 13–17

be regularly served by one whom they have not called; and every minister is entitled to know that he or she has been called by the people whom they regularly serve."[160] Thirdly, we should not to arrive at the position whereby the minister is viewed as "a master of ceremonies" or "a managing director" in the church.[161] Nor, fourthly, is Sell happy with the idea that elders or deacons become regarded as "the executive committee of a democratic assembly" rather than "God's appointees in a Christocratic body" who "serve with (not below) the minister in the exercise of their duties."[162] Fifthly, as we have noted,[163] Sell holds that the "Church meeting should be revitalized as a check upon individualistic consumerism and the corporate model of churchly life."[164] Sell is not adverse to the church using corporate insights and practices—provided they do not undermine essential features of the church's God-given nature and its fundamental *raison d'être*.

Sell argues that, to be the church is to be involved in God's mission: it is to be sent by God "into the world."[165] Mission is not the church's invention; its origin is located "in eternity itself."[166] And "we need to remember . . . that the final outcome turns not upon what we do, but upon what God in Christ has already done."[167] Mission is decidedly crucicentric. Sell declares that there is no reason to believe that the reception the church receives will be different from that which befell Jesus. "The blood of countless missionary martyrs," he suggests, "testifies to this."[168] He most likely has his Separatist and Dissenting forebears in mind when venturing the opinion that "the Church has usually been at its most faithful when it has been at its most oppressed and confined."[169] It is a pity, however, if it takes such social and political constraints to bring the best out of the church. Everywhere and always, Sell tells us, "the crusade must be for genuine Churches composed of genuine Christians who are rejoicing in the Gospel; who will really forsake all (even their Church buildings!) if this should be God's will; who are learning their faith; and who, under the guidance of the Spirit, own the Lordship of Christ in all their affairs, and not least in connection with their

---

160. *OMMM*, 16–17.
161. *EEE*, 237.
162. *RECT*, 173.
163. See chapter 7, "The Church Meeting."
164. *COM*, 361.
165. *ACI*, 113.
166. *ACI*, 113.
167. *TAT*, 349.
168. *ACI*, 121.
169. *ACI*, 111.

The Means of Grace and More about the Church 227

mission."¹⁷⁰ We may doubt the wisdom of using the word "crusade" in any connection with Christian mission, given past history, but Sell captures very well the awesome nature of engaging in the *missio Dei*. It is a calling that some, though not all, are able to manage. He likens the faithful in the contemporary church to the biblical "remnant" assuring us that "the Bible has more to say concerning the faithful remnant than in [sic] does about packing everyone in before it is too late."¹⁷¹ Triumphalism this side of eternity is ill-placed in missiology.

Nevertheless, whenever Christian mission is discussed, the elephant in the room is the problem which numerical decline provides for Western churches. Is the image of "remnant" as realistic as it appears appropriate? Or, perhaps, the image of "exile" is more helpful to interpret the present situation? Whatever way we choose to understand the Western church's position in its increasingly secular world, Sell is quite sure that the relationship between "evangelism" and "service" needs reconfiguring. He is not against "community service"¹⁷² or "good works in the world";¹⁷³ rather, he accepts such Christian activity as a very important part of the church's mission. He points out, however, that such service is not exclusively Christian; it can be undertaken by non-Christians; and, Sell argues, neither is it even "the church's distinctive task"¹⁷⁴ nor "the best that [Christians] have to offer."¹⁷⁵ Prior to "service" he claims, is "the proclamation of the gospel" which creates among Christians "the service which the church offers to society in terms of peacemaking, the quest of justice, feeding the hungry, and much also besides."¹⁷⁶ Evangelism, therefore, is at the fore-front of mission. Sell insists that only the saints are going to proclaim the gospel; so he pleads that they get on with it. He argues that "community service will not compensate for a truncated message";¹⁷⁷ he points out that if Christians "do not *speak* the gospel" those outside the church are left with having "to infer what Christians believe . . . from what they do";¹⁷⁸ and he refers to "those cowardly silences which occur when Christ would have the use of our vocal folds and

---

170. *TNM*, 253
171. *CTF*, 227. See also *TAT*, 349.
172. *DTLC*, 472.
173. *SOL*, 77.
174. *OMMM*, 45.
175. *SOL*, 77.
176. *OMMM*, 45.
177. *DTLC*, 472.
178. *SOL*, 77.

we will not let him."[179] He simply cannot understand why those who are supposedly "consumed by the love of God in Christ" are not just saddened by the presence of others who "do not know him" but also not motivated by a desire to engage in evangelism to do something about it."[180]

There is, quite clearly, a strong evangelical thrust to Sell's theology. On the subject of "mission" he has little to say about what falls under the umbrella of "service." Most of his statements concern "evangelism" presumably because he was addressing what he took to be the weaknesses of the contemporary churches, in general, and liberal Christians, in particular. After all, what point is there in encouraging people to do what they are already doing—and often very well? Sell is addressing what he regards as, at worst, sins of omission, or, at best, an over-emphasis on "service" to the detriment of "evangelism." But, interestingly, his career spanned the era of liberation theology, with its call to attend more than hitherto to issues of "emancipation." Some Western theologians found it motivated them to reconfigure their doctrines of salvation so they gave significant attention not only to "redemption" but also to "emancipation." Sell's response was rather different: Segundo (like many others before him) is criticized for his "lack of attention to Christ's atoning work, and . . . to the regenerating work of God the Holy Spirit."[181] Sell refers to "the classic question with which the *Westminster Shorter Catechism* opens: 'What is the chief end of man'?" and its well-known answer: "'Man's chief end is to glorify God, and to enjoy him for ever.'"[182] He wonders how this relates to Segundo's view that "Turning ourselves into *persons*, in the fullest sense of the term, was the end goal of hominization. And turning ourselves into *persons* also seems to be the end goal of our elevation, our divinization."[183] A more appropriate answer involves the recognition that "persons" are not fully persons until viewed from the perspective of their relationship with their fellow human beings *as well as* their relationship with God. Sell questions whether liberation theologians like Segundo do justice to the latter; but, actually, there is evidence that Sell does not do justice to the former. To return to the *Westminster Shorter Catechism*: Is it not the case that an important subsidiary "end" of human beings is to love their fellow human beings, and to do all that can be done to promote their flourishing? At one point Sell acknowledges this:

179. SOL, 78.
180. SOL, 78.
181. PHT, 263.
182. PHT, 263.

183 Segundo, *Theology for Artisans*, 2:70. Interestingly, when quoted by Sell (*PHT*, 263) the words "in the fullest sense of the term" are deliberately missed out. Perhaps they point to the kind of answer Sell would welcome?

"In Christian theology the end is beatitude. . . . The means to the end is . . . a reconciled life of praise *and service* enabled by the sanctifying grace of God the Holy Spirit."[184] Our complaint, though, concerns the one-sided way Sell stresses "redemption" and, thereby, belittles concerns about "emancipation" in the totality of God's liberation.

Sell quotes McAfee Brown: "the minute we Christians begin to *sound* just like everyone else, we've lost the ball game."[185] But what notes should Christians be sounding to make their distinctive voice heard? Sell suggests that "We are called to proclaim the inexhaustible riches of God's grace; to declare that in Christ God has visited and redeemed his people; to announce that by his cross and resurrection God in Christ has won the victory over all that could keep us from him—sin and the grave are vanquished—and all because of God's free and overflowing grace, and not because of our merit or status."[186] The basis of the church's evangelistic message, therefore, is quite clear. Sell maintains that what the church is called to proclaim is indeed what the world needs to hear. He agrees with Orr that it is not "the preaching of this old Gospel of the grace of God—old, yet ever new—which is alienating the modern world from the Churches," but, rather, it is the fact that it is not being preached "which is emptying the churches."[187] What is needed is that the *full* gospel is proclaimed and its implications worked out "for life in today's threatened and dangerous world."[188] At a time of seismic, numerical decline it would be tempting "to tone down the Gospel, to reduce the challenge of the way of the Cross, and to tempt people into the Church by all possible means."[189] But, Sell argues, "nothing is gained by reducing the challenge of church membership."[190] He refuses to countenance sacrificing the gospel to the church's program. There are here clear echoes of Forsyth: "We must not empty the Gospel in order quickly to fill the Church."[191] Sell was also particularly fond of quoting the following: "Too many are occupied in throwing over precious cargo; they are lightening the ship even of its fuel."[192] However, while Sell insisted that there should be no paring down

---

184. *MOG*, 107. Italics mine.

185. See *ACI*, 74, quoting Brown, "Discoveries and Dangers," 13. See also *OMMM*, 44.

186. *COM*, 170.

187. *DAD*, 171.

188. *COM*, 170.

189. *TNM*, 252.

190. *OMMM*, 40.

191. Forsyth, *Theology in Church and State*, 25. Quoted by Sell at *TAT*, 155n97.

192. Forsyth, *Principal of Authority*, 261. Quoted by Sell at *OMMM*, 62.

of the gospel in the church's evangelism, he recognized the need "to address the honest intellectual concerns of 'outside' critics whether hostile or benign."[193] Indeed, he even went so far as to argue that one cause for numerical decline in the church is the failure of its members, the front-line evangelists, in competently giving a straight-forward account of their faith. Their tongue-tied-ness reflects "a crisis of faith of significant proportions" in the churches.[194]

Sell believes that there is a need for "a thoroughgoing theology of evangelism which will arouse the slumbering and remind any who may need to be reminded that there is more to it than the invocation and application of marketing techniques."[195] He does not provide, however, a bespoke "thorough going theology of evangelism," though what he tells us about evangelism lays down some bedrock upon which one can be built. First, it is crucial to remember that "the fulfillment of God's purposes" does not depend "on our being successful as missionaries."[196] As Sell says, "The Church is the advance party of the kingdom, God's outpost, ever witnessing and working, but always realizing that the harvest is with him."[197] And, of course, faithfulness to God has sometimes entailed the church becoming marginalized, and hence deemed to be a failure in the world's eyes. Secondly, evangelism carries an order of priority: we are to "protest *for* the gospel of grace" before we get embroiled in the "protests *against* the manifold evils around us."[198] Sell here underlines his belief that "evangelism" should start with the gospel, "the pearl of price."[199] Thirdly, evangelism is directed at the whole person. Sell reminds us that "wills must be won over as well as minds convinced"[200]—and, we might argue, hearts also moved. Holistic evangelism will be directed at people's feelings, intellect, and practical activity. Fourthly, the contextual factors involved in sharing God's good news need to be recognized. As Sell says, "those who sow seed must have some regard to the soil."[201] We must, therefore, "take account of the intellectual climate in each successive, changing, age if communication is to take place."[202] But,

---

193. *TAT*, 247.
194. *OMMM*, 71. See also *TAT*, 165.
195. *HT*, 635.
196. *SOL*, 79.
197. *SOL*, 79.
198. "John Wyclif," 299.
199. "John Wyclif," 299.
200. *CCF*, 16.
201. *DAD*, 13.
202. *DAD*, 13.

it might be pressed, does this mean that the content of the gospel changes over time? At one point, Sell tells us that "the message which was addressed to an age which readily associated anxiety with guilt and morality with the Ten Commandments literally construed will require radical modification if it is to be heard by people for whom God is but a memory, anxiety no more than a human condition, and morality only a matter of individual taste."[203] What does he mean though by "modification" of "the message"? Has he basic content in mind? Sell's orthodoxy suggests a negative answer. The language in which the gospel is expressed may be subject to contextual variation; some of the peripheral elements of the gospel are not set in stone; but, according to Sell, the gospel centralities remain fixed. Fifthly, following the contours of his theology, Sell argues that evangelism's objective is "the engrafting of believers into God's servant body" and not "the salvation of individual souls who will continue in isolation from all others."[204] It remains to be seen whether this objective can continue to be met in our "believing without belonging" culture. Sixthly, evangelism, as Sell views it, is predicated upon Christians being "in a proper sense" fundamentally "exclusive."[205] It is concerned about the fate of non-Christians, and, necessarily, contains what, pejoratively, is described as "a hell and damnation" element. Sell suggests that "To be eternally separated from God, and to know it, would be hell indeed."[206] He maintains that any church "which is so complacent, introverted, and unmissionary-minded as not to care for the fate of others" is in "a sorry state."[207] After all, he reminds us, part of the inspiration for the nineteenth-century missionary movement was the sending churches' concern about the heathen.

SECTARIANISM IN THE CHURCH

Sell's life spanned a period of high hope concerning church unity in England, followed by major disappointments regarding the catalytic role the URC felt called to play in bringing the churches together.[208] The deep divisions within the church were for him not only a betrayal of the way God has sought to bring all people together, but also a contradiction of the church's role in being a sign, expression, and foretaste of "the coming unity of the

203. *COM*, 88.
204. *COM*, 87.
205. *SOL*, 79.
206. *SOL*, 90.
207. *SOL*, 90.
208. For an account of the URC's role, see Camroux, *Ecumenism in Retreat*.

whole inhabited earth."[209] It is not surprising that he "sometimes felt . . . that strife within the household of faith has done more harm to the cause of Christ then all the assaults of the godless;"[210] but he also knew that the ecumenical movement had brought advances. He had seen levels of cooperation among the churches increase, and there was evidence of greater mutual understanding. And we find him noting genuine theological gains:

> There should be no need in these latter days to argue a case that pipe-line theories of grace unwarrantably "mechanize" grace, the personal, unmerited favour of the personal God; nor to show that a continuous succession of ministers from Peter onwards is impossible to demonstrate from history. It should not even be necessary any longer to oppose the views of [those] who . . . make episcopacy the *esse*, not simply the *bene esse* of the church . . . .[211]

There is no need today to fight battles already won.

Sell believes that it should be the case that "Christians—among whom are all sorts and conditions of people—hear God's voice and respond to it, and they recognize one another as belonging to the same household of faith."[212] But, as we know, things are not that simple! Almost in desperation, Sell asks: "We have been accepted by Christ just as we are; and he has accepted all of us; why, then, can we not accept one another completely and joyfully?"[213] If Christians are "called by God and given grace to acknowledge Christ as Lord and Saviour," he maintains, they "are already in communion whether [they] know it, agree with it, or like it, or not."[214] Surely, the decent thing would be to acknowledge and manifest it? But, sadly, Sell knows that Christians often fail to allow what God has done for them to "take precedence over [their] feeble grasp of the truth and [their] imperfect understanding and practice of polity."[215] While Christians, in principle, "cannot

---

209. *CTF*, 154. Elsewhere Sell affirms that "The motivation in all our conversations with other Christian world communions is the desire to manifest that unity in Christ into which God has, by grace, already called us, so that the Church truly becomes a sign of the ultimate reconciliation of all things ('the whole inhabited earth'—not just the churches) in God" (*EEE*, 260-61).

210. *SOL*, 44.

211. *GE*, 259.

212. *CCF*, 87.

213. *CTF*, 228-29.

214. *COM*, 48.

215. *CTF*, 100.

The Means of Grace and More about the Church

break the fundamental unity into which they have been called by God's grace" in practice, they can "render it opaque by sectarianism."[216]

A central motif in Sell's ecclesiology concerns "the obligation to eschew sectarianism."[217] He equates the grounds contemporary Christians use to justify why they are not in full communion with other Christians with those put forward in first-century Galatia to marginalize Gentile Christians. Although Jewish himself, Paul rejected the idea that the path to Christianity involved as a first step following the entire Torah. He insisted, instead, that in Christ different people have been drawn into a newly created unity: "There is no longer Jew or Greek, there is no longer slave or free, there is no longer male and female; for all of you are one in Christ Jesus" (Gal 3:28). Differences remain between church members, but they have been drawn into one fellowship through their allegiance to Christ: "in Christ Jesus you are all children of God through faith" (Gal 3:26). The ethnic, social, and gender differences do not vanish, but the barriers, hostility, and the sense of superiority or inferiority between people are removed. And, what is more, Christians have to treat one another accordingly both inside and outside the church. This innovation constituted a social revolution.

All Christians share in common one basic fact: they have been drawn together in unity as they have started to respond to God's graciousness towards them in Christ. Sell asserts that their "saintly status is given."[218] What is also a reality, though, is that their theological interpretations of what being a Christian involves, their understanding of the ethical requirements it expects, and their way of organizing themselves as a church, all are likely to exhibit some measure of difference. Sell believes that those differences should never be allowed to trump the unity already given in Christ; otherwise new examples of the Galatian heresy will be born. Theological interpretations, ethical requirements, and church polity all too easily become "terms of fellowship" or "badges of sectarian exclusion."[219] Or, to put it another way, Sell insists that of "primary importance for Christians" is "their shared basic assurance"; but the "superstructures they erect upon it" are always "provisional and subject to modification" and, hence, "should not be elevated into fortresses of sectarianism."[220] Finally, and fully, our salvation is by grace through faith—period; it is heresy to suggest that, as Sell puts it,

---

216. *COM*, 32.
217. *EEE*, 203. See also *TNM*, 249.
218. *GE*, 269.
219. *GE*, 269.
220. *CCF*, 361.

"salvation is by Christ *plus*."[221] As soon as we add "pluses" a new form of the Galatian heresy is created.[222] New "circumcisions" get introduced; "human interpretations" end up being "elevated above God's action in Christ";[223] and, hence, God's inclusive intentions are turned to "exclusion" due to "the obdurate, rebellious, abuse of human freedom."[224]

Sell maintains that the introduction of new "circumcisions" is the cause of most of the "neuralgic"[225] issues which dominate the ecumenical dialogue. Once they concerned matters of ministry, sacraments, and polity, but today they also involve the acceptable means of reading the Bible, appropriate ways of doing theology, and approaches to resolving ethical challenges.[226] Let us, first, refer to Sell's concerns about the barriers which have been erected to prevent full-participation at the Lord's Supper. He reminds us that "there are still Anglicans who would not accept the Lord's invitation to communion in a Reformed church, and some who would deny that such churches have true sacraments at all."[227] By so doing, he accuses them of elevating "sectarian denominational small print . . . above the gospel of God's grace."[228] Legalism is being allowed to trump grace.[229] As Sell says, in such cases "the grace of God is controlled by the structure of the church."[230] The structure in question, of course, is either episcopal (Anglican or Orthodox) or episcopal headed by a papacy (Roman Catholic). It rules that unless the sacraments are conducted by someone authorized by a bishop and administered in the "correct" manner they are invalid. The theological background to this is found in Augustine, and the rule goes back to the Middle Ages, when it was maintained that episcopal ordination conferred upon priests

---

221. *COS*, 108. See also *GE*, 254–55.

222. In *GE*, Sell tells us that "In whatever form it comes, [the Galatian heresy] boils down to the insistence that unless and until you believe as we believe, order your church as we order ours, or subscribe to our ethical code, we will not have fellowship with you" (251). See also *ACI*, 92; *EEE*, 283; *TAT*, 337.

223. *CTF*, 218.

224. *EEE*, 329.

225. One of Sell's favourite words. See *CCC*, 77 and *CTF*, 218.

226. In *TAT*, Sell says that "in our own time we have caucuses and politicized pressure groups within the churches which can seem on occasion to elevate their particular way of doing theology, or their preferred set of ethical stances above the Gospel which has made us one, so that if we do not all look exactly up their periscope we are somehow traitors to the cause or less than bona fide believers. This is the Galatian heresy, and it is sad" (240).

227. *CTF*, 193.

228. *CTF*, 193

229. See *CAM*, 97.

230. *RECT*, 164.

the *potestas ordinis*, which enabled them to conduct sacraments and absolve sinners.[231] Only those who receive such ordination, some argue, can perform valid sacraments. Sell rebels against what he regards as *sacerdotal sectarianism*, quoting Manning in his cause: "we decline still, as we have always declined, to have Episcopalian ordination of ministers . . . made into a sort of new circumcision within the limits of which alone is there the full and valid and regular operation of God's grace."[232] Manning then takes us to the heart of the matter:

> The entire conception of *validity* and *regularity*, *invalidity* and *irregularity*, applied to the means of grace and to the action of the Body of Christ, is both ludicrous and blasphemous. If God acts at all He cannot act invalidly or irregularly; and if God be not acting in the Church there is no action; for the Church has no meaning whatever as a human society apart from God's action. . . . We simply do not know what an irregular or an invalid celebration is. We do not deal in percentages with the grace of God.[233]

Sell confesses that "it has always seemed ironical" to him that "among those most apt to invoke the category of mystery are some who are quickest to say 'lo here' and 'lo there' where questions of validity are concerned."[234] Both the ministry and the sacraments are God's gift to the church, and Sell eschews any church-generated rules, save those concerning discipline, which unnecessarily fence off the Lord's Table from any of God's gathered saints.

Secondly, it is common for a favored system of theology to become a new circumcision in a fresh version of the Galatian heresy. Sell regards this as "arrogant, 'Pelagian' and divisive."[235] It is "inherently sectarian" to maintain that the only proper way of being a Christian is to hold a particular theological outlook.[236] As Sell notes, "if we insist upon peddling our expositions as if they were [sic] condition of salvation or terms of fellowship, we have landed once more in sectarianism."[237] In practice, of course, many individual congregations have evolved to represent a theological brand. But such inevitabilities need not become the excuse for one congregation to unchurch another. Sell makes a distinction between the "basic Christian

231. See *JW*, 296, and *PHT*, 235.
232. Manning, *Essays*, 133. Quoted in *REC*, 165.
233. *REC*, 75, 116. Quoted by *CTF*, 220.
234. *ACI*, 95.
235. *CCF*, 26.
236. *CCF*, 26.
237. *TAT*, 191.

testimony" required of candidates for church membership and "formal doctrinal assent" to the propositions of a theological system. He then argues that strict theological tests should not be employed to judge who is or not a *bona fide* Christian.[238] When such tests are used, sectarianism is never far away, and "openness to the Holy Spirit's subsequent guidance" may also be discouraged.[239] It remains a moot point, however, where the line is to be drawn between "Christian testimony" and "doctrinal assent." What should be the commonly agreed "testimony" required for a candidate for church membership? A definite answer to that question is nowhere agreed.

A third example of a new circumcision comes into view when we recall those who have said things like, "Because you are not a woman you cannot really understand where I am coming from theologically"; "Because you are white you cannot grasp the point I am making"; "Because you are not "born again" you really are not a full Christian." Such statements reflect elitism: we are only a step away from elevating our gender, race or experience into "a privileged norm of interpretation" or a criterion to judge who are true Christians."[240] Sell maintains, however, that it is a "sectarian step to deny that those who do not manifest one's favoured experiential criterion are genuine Christians."[241] Through empathy men can get near to where women "are coming from"; through the close listening of cross-cultural encounter whites can gain understanding of what blacks are saying; and there are no mandatory grounds for making any person's religious experience the predominant criterion for their church membership. As Sell says, "None of us may regard other Christians as "second class" because their route to Christ has been different from ours."[242] He also notes that "contextual theologies which are supposed to critique the imposition of theological imperialisms from elsewhere" often tend to "become imperialistic in attitude."[243] No-one's personal experience should be allowed to become "the sole norm of biblical or theological interpretation."[244] We are wise, then, to recall that God "has spoken a Word which judges all our partial experiences."[245] If we forget that, we also may find ourselves falling into some form of sectarian heresy.

238. *GE*, 253.
239. *GE*, 253.
240. *COM*, 54.
241. *EEE*, 233.
242. *SOL*, 23.
243. *EEE*, 323.
244. *EEE*, 323.
245. *COM*, 55.

The final example of a new circumcision comes from the Protestant camp. It concerns a misuse of the Bible that flourishes when the text is treated as inerrant and infallible. Many a Protestant sectarian has made it a condition of Christian believing and church membership that the Bible be understood in this way. The Bible, then, is treated legalistically; and, as Sell puts it, "as if grace required the protection of law" thereby reducing faith to "giving assent to propositions supernaturally received."[246] But the sectarianism which emanates from such bibliolatry joins the other examples of the Galatian heresy in generating Sell's utter condemnation. He wants to rebrand the convictions underpinning all such sectarianism as "differing expressions of views in a family united in Christ within which . . . absolute uniformity of belief and practice cannot properly be imposed by either ecclesial or secular powers, and, if the attempt is made, it is doomed to fail."[247]

246. *CTF*, 222.
247. *GE*, 271.

9

Salvation

Yesterday, Today, and Tomorrow

Sell believes that Christians during their earthly lives are always working out their salvation (Phil 2:12). Through their "Godly walk"—their life of praise and service to God—they are being drawn nearer to God. On the journey to sanctification, believers engage in a process whereby they receive new life in the Spirit and are set free from sin's captivity. While a justified person is involved in sanctification, Sell reminds us that that person remains a sinner. The believer is both justified and a sinner (*simul iustus et peccator*). It follows that salvation also contains a future dimension, a looking forward to the time when God's promises will be fully realized. As Sell puts it, "Eternity has broken into time, and love's victory, already won, will be fully worked out."[1] We have arrived, consequently, in the realm of eschatology.

Sell recognizes that eschatology "has never been central in academic theology" and he acknowledges that "sometimes it has been tacked on as a rather half-hearted appendix."[2] In the latter part of the twentieth century, however, it has been given greater prominence due to the work of Moltmann and Pannenberg. We have been reminded, therefore, of Sell's belief that "The eschatological theme surrounds and cements the whole course of Christian doctrine."[3] Nevertheless, Sell is very suspicious of those who wax at great lengths on eschatological themes. He reminds us that "if it be true that eternity has broken into time we must not be surprised if human

---

1. *SOL*, 83.
2. *SOL*, 83.
3. *SOL*, 83.

language is strained in trying to express the results."[4] Once again, he invites us to exercise a modicum of Godly agnosticism, this time concerning what God has in store for us in the future. Sell neither wants to, nor believes he can, in words echoing Reinhold Niebuhr, "describe the furniture of heaven . . . take the temperature of hell . . . predict when the 'End' will be."[5] He prefers to dwell on what is certain: "Our hope is grounded in something that has happened; and if we have new life now, if our fellowship with God through Christ by the Spirit is real now, why need we doubt that it will grow closer and deeper hereafter?"[6] Sell believes that, in one sense, there will be no *new* life to come: the saints already have that life now, if only in a flawed state. At the end of days, though, he tells us that "it will be made perfect."[7]

According to Sell, heaven is "a matter of harmony with the Father through the Son."[8] Sell, therefore, avoids conceiving "heaven" in spatial terms, preferring to flesh out the idea in terms of relationships. It is as relevant to the "here and now" as it is to any *post mortem* existence. One aspect of heaven, consequently, is the knowledge that we have been brought to the point where we "acknowledge God's kingly reign" and become aware that we "cannot be parted" from the One who has called us in Christ and adopted us by the Spirit.[9] The other aspect, though, does concern a life beyond the grave. Sell avoids conceiving *post-mortem* existence in terms of "immortality." This Greek doctrine, he claims, "is highly speculative and unanchored in history."[10] Further, it only deals with part of the person: the body is devalued and preference is given to the soul. Sell reminds us, however, that "in Christian thought the whole person is raised with Christ (1 Cor 15)," and that "there is nothing in Christian teaching to prompt us to despise God's created matter."[11] He further believes that "the saddest feature of the Greek doctrine of immortality is the shadowy, unspecific nature of its future life."[12] But, it might be pointed out, what else can one expect when one is speculatively imagining what essentially is *other*-worldly? Religious thinkers may actually find "immortality" easier to handle than "resurrection" since the migration of souls to a *post-mortem* world is an arguably less

4. *SOL*, 84.
5. *SOL*, 84.
6. *SOL*, 86.
7. *SOL*, 87.
8. *SOL*, 86
9. *SOL*, 86.
10. *SOL*, 85.
11. *SOL*, 85.
12. *SOL*, 85.

problematic idea than the re-assembly of erstwhile dead bodies in a new living form. Skeptics, of course, will not be overly enthusiastic about either idea. Sell, meanwhile, is utterly confident that at the cross, death was, once and for all, overcome. For Christians, therefore, death is "the last occasion of earthly praise and testimony."[13] But will it only be Christians who enjoy the *post-mortem* life? And will there be some who taste a less than enjoyable life hereafter?

THE DOCTRINE OF ELECTION

The doctrine of election has been a focus of a great deal of the criticism launched at Reformed theology. Its genesis is found in scripture (Rom 8:20, 29–30; Eph 1:3–4), but we owe the initial formative treatment of it to Augustine.[14] Augustine argues that God elects sinners to salvation not because of any merit they possess but solely due to an inscrutable divine decision. His doctrine of predestination involves God being gracious to some but not all sinners. Although Augustine holds back from saying specifically that the non-elect are damned, the inescapable logic of the doctrine suggests that they are, and not just, as he puts it, passed by. Many theologians have not been so reticent about landing themselves in a situation where they allow their awareness of God's boundless, saving love to be compromised unnecessarily by a fixation upon God's elective, sovereign power.

While such a charge can be leveled at many a Calvinist with total justification it does not fairly represent Calvin's position. As Sell recognizes, predestination is not the primary doctrine in Calvin's theology. It is "a derivative of his doctrine of God's sovereignty;"[15] and Calvin deals with it in connection with how people receive the divine grace needed for salvation rather than in a discussion of God's nature. Nevertheless, Calvin does not hesitate to argue that God, "according to his secret plan" freely chooses whom God pleases, while rejecting others.[16] As Sell points out, however, "Calvin throws the emphasis upon election to salvation, and treats the decree of reprobation with wholesome reserve."[17] Calvin undoubtedly goes beyond Augustine's notion of God passing by the non-elect in stressing God's election of some to salvation, and he does not draw back from acknowledging the logical conclusion that others are predestined to damna-

13. *SOL*, 89.
14. See my *Reforming Theology*, 159.
15. *GD*, 3.
16. *Institutes* III.XXIII.7.
17. *GD*, 19.

Salvation

tion. Sell maintains that, given human sin, God would have been justified in condemning the entire human race; but God chose to save some, if not all: a *double* predestination was involved. Regarding reprobation, Calvin is "awestruck but unrelenting."[18] He admits that "The decree is dreadful indeed, I confess";[19] but he believes it is not in our gift to penetrate God's wisdom. That may be the case, but what also ought not be denied is that Calvin's discussion of election bequeathed to theology a picture of God in which "the character of God-in-Christ appears to be underplayed in the Trinitarian redemption transaction" to such an extent that "we are left with a God who can *as willingly* consign his creatures to one final destiny as to the other."[20] It is a picture that Sell repudiates.

Sell recognizes the truth in Calvin's starting point: he also wants to be realistic about the gravity of human sin and he emphasizes the gracious divine initiative which has been taken to remedy it. In *that* sense Sell is a Calvinist—he is as concerned as Calvin to hold "accurate views of man's state—views which [require] sovereign grace as the only remedy—and to ascribe all the glory of salvation to God."[21] But, in other important senses, he is far from a Calvinist: he regrets the way in which "the *Westminster Confession* and its Congregational and Baptist successors fostered a pattern of study and reflection in which God's grace did not assume primacy, and in which convictions concerning God's sovereign power were inadequately balanced by those concerning his grace and mercy."[22] He joins the "moral protest" within the Reformed world "against expressions of Christian doctrine which [turn] God into a tyrant or human beings into automata."[23] Not only does he want to dissociate himself from those who reduce the Triune God to "an absolute, capricious, inscrutable will, from whose deliberations even the Son is excluded,"[24] but he also refuses to join those who denigrate human beings by removing from them *their* freedom to repent and believe or to decline so to do.[25] Despite what he calls, rather flatteringly, "Calvin's best efforts," he regrets that, "the moral objection to the unbiblical notion that a God of all grace would decree the reprobation of specific individuals

---

18. Calvin, *Institutes* III.XXIII.7n17.
19. Calvin, *Institutes* III.XXIII.7.
20. *GD*, 22.
21. *GD*, 18.
22. *EEE*, 164.
23. *EEE*, 107.
24. *GD*, 18.
25. See *GD*, 98.

from eternity was not removed."[26] Hence he could understand "the Wesleyan protest against a God of capricious partiality"[27] as well as why Wesley objected to "the idea that there is unconditional election, for this implies unconditional reprobation."[28] In Sell's opinion, it is as profoundly un-biblical to ground one's idea of God in God's inscrutable sovereign will rather than in God's love as it is to render human beings wholly unaccountable for their destiny. The Christian gospel, he believes, "is primarily concerned with . . . an overflowing sovereign *grace* that fulfills but does not overturn the law."[29] Those who belong to the Reformed heritage, therefore, need to hold together God's "justice and power" with God's "love and mercy" in such a way that the former does not become "capricious and arbitrary"; only then will they do justice to the doctrine of "God-*in-Christ*."[30] Sell advises us, further, to understand "predestination" and "election" as *religious* rather than philosophical, concepts. He believes that many of the problems surrounding election actually stem from understanding its central idea "in a deterministic way."[31] When predestination is aligned to philosophical necessity human freedom is inevitably threatened.

One of the benefits of Enlightenment criticism of theology has been the way in which, as Sell puts it, "it brought a moral critique to bear upon some unwholesome ways of speaking and thinking about God."[32] It questioned, for example, caricatures within the doctrine of election, such as "God as arbitrary will" and "predestination needlessly and devastatingly entangled with philosophical determinism."[33] But what does the doctrine of election involve when liberated from such caricatures? Sell is too orthodox to do away with it. He tells us that "The idea of election is ineradicable from the Bible and from the various types of writing flowing down from orthodox Dissenters and Nonconformists."[34] He claims that it arises inevitably from reflection upon Christian experience. It seeks to do justice to a Christian's awareness that God has an eternal purpose prepared for the saints. They have been called to a life of praise and service. The doctrine arose, Sell argues, when Paul tried to account for not having come to new life "under his

26. *EEE*, 330.
27. *GD*, 76.
28. *EEE*, 97.
29. *RECT*, 29.
30. *GD*, 98.
31. *TAT*, 136. Sell also *HT*, 413 and *EEE*, 159, 275.
32. *NT*, 166.
33. *NT*, 166.
34. *GE*, 224.

own steam."[35] Christians, upon reflection, realized that they "did not arrive at their present position unaided."[36] Sell asserts, therefore, that "it was the personal experience of unmerited grace enjoyed by Paul, Augustine, and Calvin which historically constituted the route by which the doctrine of 'eternal Predestination to life' came into the Reformed Churches."[37] The origin of what Sell calls "the good news"[38] of predestination resides, therefore, in reflection upon Christian experience rather than any remote philosophical speculation. The doctrine is "a testimony to God's prevenient grace";[39] its language belongs to "the vocabulary of grateful testimony";[40] but it is a step too far to claim that we know "the "mechanics" of eternity."[41] Once again we find Sell playing the "mystery" card. What is crucial for him is that we affirm two facts: first, that we know that we are saved by grace; and, secondly, that we are free, responsible human beings. Just how the two facts are "ultimately reconciled," he informs us, "we do not know."[42]

Sell defines "the essential truth" underlying the doctrine of predestination as "God from eternity [desiring] to have a people for his praise" and "in Christ" doing "all that is necessary to secure this end in every generation by the Spirit."[43] Christians are saints because they have been called. Therein resides the doctrine of election.[44] But, we must ask, "What about the vexed matter of reprobation?" Sell's answer begins with scripture. He tells us that "there is no New Testament justification for the view that God from eternity predestined some to damnation."[45] The Bible, he claims, speaks of "election by grace" but not "predestination to damnation."[46] The former is an assured fact; the latter is mere speculation. According to Sell, Christians can know that they have been called to be saints, but "They quite literally know nothing at all about the eternal status of those who *seem* not to have been so called."[47] The saints, then, are well-advised not to draw "negative

35. *EEE*, 159, 337. See also *HT*, 577 and *PHT*, 300.
36. *CCC*, 73.
37. *RECT*, 28.
38. *PHT*, 300.
39. *HT*, 577.
40. *COS*, 17.
41. *COS*, 17.
42. *COS*, 17.
43. *DTLC*, 63.
44. See *CTF*, 180.
45. *GOF*, 105.
46. *SOL*, 91.
47. *SOL*, 91.

implications" regarding the ultimate status of those outside (or inside?) the Christian fold.[48]

Christians may hope that those who die in unbelief may somehow finally find a saving faith, but whether they ever will is impossible for us to know. And, further, Sell damps down any burgeoning hopes we might hold concerning everyone one day being saved. He does not deny, of course, that "there is ground for hope that God's undefeatable love will at last win over the hardest rebel."[49] However, he demurs at the adoption of "uncritical universalism with judgment drained away."[50] He advises us that "There are sufficient warnings in the New Testament to preclude universalism."[51] He admits, though, to hoping that universalism is correct, but confesses that "godly agnosticism" once again overtakes him.[52]

In his discussion of election, Sell is attempting to hold together two convictions central to the dispute over Arminianism within the Reformed tradition. With the Calvinists he is "seeking to honour God's sovereignty in salvation" and with the Arminians he is seeking "to uphold human responsibility before God."[53] He sums up his position as follows: "God's electing grace is not to be construed fatalistically, but in the context of God's undiscriminating love whereby all are called to salvation, to which all may make their own, enabled response."[54] Sell calls his position "an amelioration of Calvinism."[55] He is disturbed that, in recent years, "predestination—even as good news—is conspicuous by its absence from many statements and affirmations of faith published by Reformed churches."[56] That fact, no doubt, has been due to many people's sensitive reactions to *un*-ameliorated Calvinism understandably driving them towards forms of Arminianism.

---

48. *HT*, 577.

49. *NT*, 185.

50. Turner quoted by Sell in *PHT*, 165.

51. *NT*, 185. See also *CTF*, 251. In *SOL*, Sell says, "God neither forces us to be saved or to be damned; and we should think more then twice before we deny that by what F. W. Robertson called 'God's terrible permission' a person may remain obdurate to the end" (90).

52. *CAM*, 160.

53. *EEE*, 275. Arminianism refers, strictly speaking, to the doctrines of Jacob Arminius (1560–1609) but, more generally, to views which emphasis the ability of human beings to respond to God's grace.

54. *EEE*, 275.

55. *GD*, 23, 98.

56. *PHT*, 209.

THE LAST THINGS

Throughout his life the Christian gospel was Sell's driving force, so it was important that it be proclaimed whole-heartedly at his funeral. Robert Pope preached the sermon, and declared: "In the shadow of death, we glimpse the living hope which the gospel offers, a hope by which Alan lived and through which he courageously faced his own death in the faith that because his Lord had gone before him and prepared a place for him, there was a place for him in the Father's 'many mansions' of which the Jesus of John's Gospel speaks (14:1–3)."[57] We turn to elucidate further what Sell understood by this "living hope."

We begin with a typical statement from Sell concerning the Christian hope:

> The One into whose fellowship we are called by grace is the God and Father of our Lord Jesus Christ, and that relationship means a new life which begins in the present and continues after death, and joy and peace that know no end; and all of this because Jesus Christ was raised, and those who are united to him are raised with him. Death has no power over them, for it was defeated one-for-all at the cross.[58]

Central is Sell's conviction that becoming a Christian involves entering now upon a new life which will be fully completed in a life beyond death. To use familiar biblical terms, we can say that *eternal* life begins in this life and is *fully* experienced beyond death. Sell maintains that "our *post-mortem* life is not bound or measured by time so "we no longer have to think that "eternal" means "never-ending.""[59] We are actually referring to a *quality* of life received from being in a saving relationship with God. Those living outside of such a relationship, Sell suggests, can be said to be living in hell. At one point, we find Sell allowing us access to his deepest thoughts: "If I were to tell you what would really make me afraid it would be this: to be willfully and knowingly at odds with Christ; to spurn his love, to reject his mercy. That would make death an enemy: the possibility of a Christ-less eternity is one I do not care to contemplate."[60] The possibility that some people are in such a state, in Sell's opinion, ought to drive the church's evangelism. He declares forcefully: "That church is in a sorry state which is so complacent, introverted, and unmissionary-minded as not to care for the fate of

57. From a privately circulated manuscript.
58. CTF, 253.
59. *SOL*, 90.
60. *SOL*, 88–89.

others."⁶¹ It follows that our eyes must not be so fixed upon a post-mortem future that we are diverted from earthly requirements. "If the End is implicit in the beginning," Sell asserts, "the present matters enormously."⁶² Whether or not we—and others—are in harmony with God *now* is crucial.

Sell knows how speculative some Christian thinkers become when discussing eschatological themes. We are confronted with what he calls a "most important yet most treacherous area of doctrine."⁶³ It needs a cool, calm head to enter an arena often inhabited by enthusiasts, fanatics, and fatalists, who act as though futurology is an exact science. Nowhere is Sell's recourse to "godly agnosticism" more needed than when considering the Final Advent. He offers us seven opinions concerning the End based upon "a consideration of the biblical teaching as a whole":⁶⁴

1. "God will bring his mighty redemptive purposes to completion, and all will know it."⁶⁵

2. "His manner will be that of holy love, and Christ will be his agent."⁶⁶ This means that judgment is involved. In a certain sense, the Easter event proclaims that the last judgment is over. It is also certainly the case that we are being judged daily on the basis of how we exercise our stewardship. But Sell maintains with tradition that there will be "the consummation" which includes "the final judgment."⁶⁷ He admits that he does not know what all this involves "exactly."⁶⁸ But, nevertheless, a final judgment "is too prominent in the New Testament to be ignored."⁶⁹

3. "We do not know, and have no means of knowing, when the End will be. Our task is not to pry but to prepare."⁷⁰

4. "The final advent must not be conceived in such a way as to blunt the truth that the risen Christ is present with his people now."⁷¹

---

61. *SOL*, 90.
62. *SOL*, 93.
63. *SOL*, 93.
64. *SOL*, 91.
65. *SOL*, 91.
66. *SOL*, 91.
67. *SOL*, 92.
68. *SOL*, 92.
69. *CTF*, 250.
70. *SOL*, 91.
71. *SOL*, 91.

5. "There is insufficient evidence to permit definite views on the so-called millennial reign of Christ. . . . Indeed, undue emphasis upon a millennial reign between our history and the eternal kingdom of God severs the inseverable: the kingdom is now."[72]

6. "The End will involve the whole inhabited earth in such a way that the only appropriate way of speaking of it is in terms of a new heaven and a new earth (Rev 21)."[73]

7. "We are living in the last times now, and we cannot exclude the idea of judgment from our thinking."[74]

From a human perspective, the End is "beatitude" and the way to receive it is to engage in "a reconciled life of praise and service enabled by the sanctifying grace of God the Holy Spirit."[75]

When discussing eschatology, theologians are faced with two major problems. First, they are dealing with a future, which, save for speculative extrapolations from present data, is largely unknown. This fact ought to send a cautionary note to them concerning the limitations they confront when dealing with eschatology. Then, secondly, theologians have to deal with a tradition generated largely from the biblical texts. This involves treating with seriousness the stories the earliest Christians told to kindle and proclaim their ultimate hope. These stories are anchored in the first-century world of Jewish apocalyptic thought, which is at odds with current cosmological thinking. What is required, consequently, is that the eschatological stories are unraveled to lay bare whatever truth they have to convey to us. It is a mistake to treat those stories literally, thereby opening up space for the fatalists and fantasizers to flourish. Sell carefully steers clear of treating the biblical stories concerning the End in a wooden way. He plays his "godly agnosticism" card at those points where less careful theologians wax eloquently. But some will argue that he ought to go further and openly acknowledge that stories rooted in a redundant apocalyptic worldview are no longer helpful. Perhaps a touch of "reverent atheism" needs to replace his "godly agnosticism"? What the situation requires, they will say, is the telling of new stories to convey credibly what we want to say about our Christian hope. They have a point. What is needed is a revisionary account of God's creative and redemptive activity which, while still centered upon the Christ event, places the moment-by-moment life of the universe—not just planet

72. *SOL*, 91.
73. *SOL*, 92.
74. *SOL*, 92.
75. *MOG*, 107.

Earth and *homo sapiens*—within the framework of that activity. Eschatology needs releasing from its first-century, teleological strictures. Our hope lies totally in a *present* fact: God's unconditional love, which is both the source and the goal of our lives and the entire cosmos. We have no *empirical* knowledge concerning what lies beyond death, but what we know *theologically* is all we need to know: "For I am convinced that neither death, nor life, nor angels, nor rulers, nor things present, nor things to come, nor powers, nor height, nor depth, nor anything else in all creation, will be able to separate us from the love of God in Christ Jesus our Lord." (Rom 8:38–39). To want to know anymore is a pointless act of *un*-faith.

10

Conclusion

Alan was a Christian who knew that theology is an essential aspect of discipleship. At every point in his life—enquiring youth, ministerial candidate, minister of word and sacraments, ecumenical bureaucrat and administrator, university professor, and actively retired—he attempted to work out his Christian self-understanding as well as articulate a theological under-pinning for his Christian commitments.[1] At the heart of his theological work was an attempt to defend what he regarded as a classical theological tradition located in Puritanism, Dissent, and Nonconformity. The eighteenth century became his intellectual home.[2] He felt called to retrieve a theological tradition which he believed had been marginalized. In many respects, therefore, he was a *historical* rather than systematic theologian. His British focus, perhaps, left him with insufficient time to do justice to Continental Reformed thinkers like Moltmann and Jüngel, thereby leaving him open to the charge of being parochial. Some also felt that sometimes his "back to the future" approach did not pay sufficient attention to current theological debates and particularly those which were responding to the way recent knowledge has thrown huge question marks against some traditional theological formulations. Alan ought to have asked more often the following question: "What must the truth be *now*, if our faithful forebears

---

1. Pope tells us that Alan considered "his academic work as the fulfilment of his calling to Christian ministry which, of course, was rooted in him being one of God's gathered saints" (Pope, "Alan Philip Frederick Sell," 525).

2. It is interesting to note that the hymns Alan chose for his funeral service all came from eighteenth-century writers: Gellert (1715–69), Watts (1674–1748), and Doddridge (1702–51).

expressed it *then*, in their culture and time, as they did?" To make the point in another way: I do not think Alan allowed enough for the way in which theology evolves as Christians seek to express their faith in different intellectual paradigms and cultural settings. We certainly need to be "generous" with our orthodoxy, but, since what counts as *adequate* theology changes over time, we must also face the need, when required, to be less conservative and more revisionary.

In theory Alan was far from a theological backwoodsman. Unlike many theologians he insisted upon fulfilling his apologetic responsibilities. Theologians, after all, must not only present an understanding of the Christian faith which displays due congruence with the earliest Christian witness. They also need to construct one that is credible in the contemporary world. Alan's take on Christian apologetics certainly reflects the need to *translate* the faith handed down to us into a language that enables it to be *commended* to contemporary people in ways they can understand. But he failed to see how his stance on apologetics was often undermined by his habit of making the apologetic task secondary to that of confession. What is missing is a wholehearted acceptance that the handed-down faith may sometimes require *revision*. He was correct to share with Forsyth a fear that in inter-changes with different cultures or new intellectual frameworks some "precious cargo" will get lost. That risk, though, has to be measured against something equally problematical, namely, the danger that without revision the handed-down faith will get dismissed as irrelevant and/or incredible. Willshaw is close to the mark when he suggests that "apologetics cannot be content merely to defend the tradition."[3] He argues that it must be "more open" than Alan suggests, "more concerned with dialogue and a mutual seeking after truth, recognizing, more thoroughly . . . the extra-ecclesial work of the Holy Spirit. . . . Apologetics should be a much more *creative* enterprise."[4] Quite often, Alan criticizes revisionary theologians in a way which shows little appreciation for their attempts to make the gospel credible for contemporary people.[5] In his reviews of modern theology he sometimes gives the impression that such theologies are "only a willful piece of self-assertion."[6] Meanwhile, when assessing the merits of utilizing idealist philosophies to articulate the Christian faith, he is prone to failing to acknowledge the orthodoxy which some of those who used them were

---

3. Willshaw, Review of *CCF*, 81.

4. Willshaw, Review of *CCF*, 81. Italics mine.

5. This is noted by Michael J. Townsend (see his reviews of *TIT* and *SVOC*) and Ruth Page (see her review of *TIT*).

6. Page, Review of *TIT*.

Conclusion

actually trying to display,[7] and he does not always do justice to the way our understanding has been enhanced by some of their achievements.[8]

Alan tried to walk a tightrope: if he fell to one side he would sacrifice Christian identity; if he fell to the other he would land in contextual irrelevance and incredibility. He wanted theology to be "as coherent as we can make it," but he expressed the hope that it would "not be too foreign to the truth of him who is Lord and Saviour."[9] He was adamant that "walking a tightrope is not equivalent to sitting on the fence."[10] He wanted to face up to addressing both the "identity" and "involvement" crises.[11] It led to a tension in his theology. He tried to avoid Barthian tendencies to annex theological claims from public debate. He was not one of those confessional theologians who set out intentionally to take traditional Christian beliefs as a "given" from which to develop further their theological reflections, and then, as Wiles puts it, hold up their heads "boldly in the contemporary cultural scene, because in a post-modern world you cannot be called on to justify the foundational beliefs from which to choose to begin."[12] He had little time for the anti-foundationalism of post-modernism.[13] Lindbeck, particularly, comes under his scrutiny.[14] He accuses Lindbeck's post-liberalism of so tying God's revelation "to the Christian community" that it prompts "fears of the intellectual 'ghetto.'"[15] But Alan's conviction that theology must have an apologetic dimension was always being countered by his fear that too liberal an approach risks reducing the Christian faith to what happens to be currently believable or acceptable. His ultimate commitment to a crucicentric starting point, therefore, led him to be dismissive of theologies which had what he characteristically called "cross-shaped blanks."[16] But, regrettably, that commitment was made in such a way that sometimes he could not avoid proceeding "by assertion . . . rather than by argument."[17]

---

7. See Kendal, Review of *PICB*.
8. See Matthews, Review of *PICB*.
9. *CCF*, 370.
10. *CCF*, 372.
11. See Moltmann, *Crucified God*, 7.
12. Wiles, "Theology in the Twenty-First Century," 408.
13. See *CTF*, 133; *HT*, 1; and *NT*, 168.
14. See Lindbeck, *Nature of Doctrine*.
15. *CCF*, 145.
16. *CAM*, 146.
17. Kendal, Review of *PICB*, 122. Kendal is turning words that Alan uses against the Idealists against him instead.

Theologians must have a starting-point: the pertinent issue concerns what the starting point is to be. As I argued earlier, Alan's choice is controversial. The problem with it is three-fold: first, whilst eschewing the notion of total depravity, he puts forward an extremely negative account of human nature when a more nuanced view is called for. At times he appears obsessed by how sinful we are. Secondly, and perhaps as a result of his emphasis on sin, he places a disproportionate emphasis upon the atonement, thereby marginalizing the significance of Jesus' life and teaching. This all leads, thirdly, to his becoming heavily dependent upon Forsyth's particular soteriological framework. Alan saddled himself, therefore, with all the criticism which has been turned upon Forsyth: "The primacy of revelation ad [sic] redemption and the lack of any systematic doctrine of creation in [Forsyth's] work opens him up to the criticism that he ignores the created order."[18] And, given that "creation" has been a battleground upon which the fight for the credibility of Christianity has been conducted, that is a very serious matter.

I was trained as a scientist before I became a Christian minister. By the time I had become a chemistry undergraduate I was aware of key challenges being posed to traditional theology. First, the theory of evolution suggests revisions need making to traditional doctrines of creation. The nature of the way things have come into being necessitates less emphasis being placed upon God's initiative "once upon a time" and more attention being paid to God's ongoing creative involvement in the world. From once speaking of the one divine creative act we are now required to conceive of a stream of divine initiatives taking place in the creative process—or succumb to Deism. Secondly, we must re-assess our place in creation. Such is the enormous age of our planet that, if we equate its life to a clock-face, then we have to recognize that *homo sapiens* arrived on the scene just before the hands reach twelve. This suggests, therefore, that *anthropocentric* understandings of the origin and destiny of the world are hubristic. They do not give sufficient account of the significance of nature, either to God or us. To understand God's redemptive activity solely in terms of its benefits to human beings leaves out of account the significance of the rest of creation to God. Willshaw is correct to say that "the doctrine of creation must be given as much attention as that of redemption, so that all experience is seen as religious and the continuing activity of God in a world full of suffering and imperfection, as well as beauty and goodness, may be discerned."[19] When that is done it becomes apparent that the key theological problem is "the perpetual perish-

---

18. Cornick, "P. T. Forsyth's Doctrine of the Church," 167.
19 Willshaw, Review of *CCF*, 81.

Conclusion

ing" (Whitehead) of the entire created order, rather than the finiteness of human beings. Thirdly, if evolution puts *homo sapiens* firmly in its place, then astrophysics achieves something similar regarding the planet itself. It renders it akin to a speck in the cosmos. Life on other planets cannot be ruled out. Traditional conceptions of God, consequently, are made to seem like descriptions of the tribal deity of one particular planet. This leads, fourthly, to the need to respond to an increased awareness of Christianity being just one of several world religions, and to face up to the ensuing puzzle concerning the relationship between them. To put the issue crudely: Where does the God of Abraham, Sarah and Jesus fit in with the other deities worshipped by our brothers and sisters?

Christians, as a matter of integrity, need to go public with a narrative which speaks about the significance of God—as God has been glimpsed in Jesus—for all living things in a way that the above issues are addressed. Alan's theology does not provide such a narrative. Not only does he fail, as John Taylor puts it, to do justice to "the influences of secular ideas on our traditions,"[20] but he also begs the issue of the adequacy of his crucicentric emphasis. He never fully appreciated, perhaps, the way in which his given theological starting point comes with its own cultural and metaphysical clothing. That said, there were occasions when Alan came near to contributing to the narrative for which I am calling. First, we find him asking: "But what exactly is the Spirit doing directly in and through animals and inanimate creation?"[21] His cautious answer is understandable: "I see no option but godly agnosticism at this point,"[22] and his additional comment is commendable: "Since . . . everything we know about God suggests that he loves all that he has made, it is a justified, and not simply a pious, hope that for the whole created order it will be well."[23] But he never offered us a metaphysical framework within which such divine activity can be conceived. In turning his back on process thought he rejected a possible candidate for such a framework. Secondly, concerning the relationship between Christianity and the other world religions, we find him discussing *logos* christology, which some have used as a stepping stone towards a theology of world religions. Alan accepts that "a *logos* theology can be the basis for a compelling theology of universal faith and world religions, *provided that we give precedence to the fact that the logos has acted redemptively and once for all at the cross*

---

20. Taylor, Review of *SVOC*.
21. *EEE*, 298.
22. *EEE*, 298.
23. *EEE*, 298.

of Christ."[24] Seemingly nothing could shake the exclusivist convictions he had concerning Christ's work on the cross. He spurned all temptation to move from his christocentric view of God's redemptive activity, never coming near to crossing Hick's Rubicon.[25] But he did believe that Jesus' followers should be neighborly towards members of the non-Christian faiths. While he might have drawn back from saying explicitly that the church's missionary aim concerning them is conversion, his position's logic suggests implicitly that Christians should still witness to the truth and hope within them. What is really required, theologically, in response to the evidence, is a much more *theo*centric approach. God's revelation in Jesus Christ is not *constitutive* of our salvation, though it *decisively re-presents* its possibility to those who stand in the stream of consciousness flowing from Jesus. Unless more attention is paid to *general* as well as special divine revelation and to the Spirit blowing where the Spirit wills, we run the risk of suggesting that God invites other faiths to the soup kitchen, but only Christians to the feast.

I belong to the same ecclesial tradition that Alan graced, so it is hardly surprising that I warm to his statements concerning ecclesiology. I am not convinced that the Congregational Way is heaven-sent, but I do believe that it promotes ecclesial values of great merit, e.g., non-hierarchical approaches to ordering church life; equality between women and men at all points of church life; the priesthood of all believers (properly conceived); consensus decision-making based upon patiently listening to one another and sensing the movement of the Holy Spirit; and an emphasis upon the local congregation borne out of a sense of freedom which does not result in isolation from the wider church. Alan was aware, though, that very often Reformed churches do not live up to the ideals represented by those values, but he rejoiced when he found them taken up by churches outside the Reformed world. At a time in England when the standing of the mainline churches is exceedingly low—due to them often being perceived to be on the wrong side of the argument and beset by lurid sex scandals—it is arguable that any church exhibiting such values will have a fighting chance of gaining traction in a society which favors "localism" and is in a rebellious mood concerning the authoritarian figures of its major institutions. Nevertheless, champions of Congregational-style ecclesiology need to remember that its emphasis upon "visible sainthood" can lead to what Trevor Hart calls an emphasis upon "the experience of the saved in an attempt to discover the evidences of belonging" and "an exclusivist outlook such as that represented

---

24. *CAM*, 206.
25. See chapter 5, "Sell's Doctrine of Atonement."

in the practice of fencing the Lord's Table so that only 'enrolled saints' may participate in the sacrament."[26]

I end with three observations. First, I have been overjoyed to find the man I knew coming through in what he wrote. We can benefit from "meeting" him again as we read him afresh. And what we will find has been perceptively encapsulated by Binfield: "dry humour . . . sharp eye, the written equivalent of the real-life shrewd twinkle in his eye, the sense of a critical acumen carefully . . . reined in."[27] Secondly, I share Brierley's opinion that "Sell's greatest gift and service to the discipline of theology" has been his ability "to provide detailed portraits of [the "hinterland"] theologians, as well as remain abreast of the more prominent ones."[28] Alan describes the hinterland theologians as follows:

> They are seldom dignified, or fossilized, in lists of 'set texts,' but their writings sometimes stimulate those of their better-known contemporaries and successors either positively or negatively. Even when they did not, the ways in which the hinterland people adjusted to, or the reasons why they ignored, what better-known authors were saying is in itself interesting. It may even be argued that we have not fully understood the Lockes and Barths of this world until we have investigated what the hinterland people made of them.[29]

I believe that Alan now graces the exalted company of those hinterland theologians. And, thirdly, with one eye on this book's title, I offer the following three-fold judgment about Alan's "generous orthodoxy." First, it is unnecessarily *crucicentric* when what is required is for "creation" and "redemption" to be held together as distinct, if never separate, elements in a *theo*centric account of God's ongoing, salvific activity. Second, it is thoroughly *congregational* and, thereby, presents us with an ecclesiology capable of displaying a range of much-needed ecclesial values. Third, it is intentionally *catholic* but does not engage sufficiently in the "wider" ecumenism concerning the world's religions which is required to bring unity and peace to the *óikoumene*.[30]

26. Hart, Review of SVOC, 363.
27. Binfield, Letter to the author, 10 February 2017.
28. Brierley, Review of PHT, 401.
29. HT, 2.
30. Hans Küng's mantra springs to mind: "No peace among the nations without peace among the religions. No peace among the religions without dialogue between the religions. No dialogue between the religions without investigation of the foundation of the religions" [*Christianity*, 2].

One critic describes Alan's position as "liberal orthodoxy";[31] an establishment Anglican defines it as "an orthodoxy which is radical but intelligible";[32] while an irenic Unitarian calls it "impeccably orthodox"[33] and "moderately conservative."[34] My major regret is that Alan was not more "generous" towards liberal ideas that would have led him to construct the kind of revisionary theology required today. But, as was usually the case, Alan must have the last word: "Under whatsoever auspices they travel, I hope that theologians of the future will hold high the Cross, declare the gospel of the triune God of all grace, and combat those sectarianisms which deny the unity which in Christ by the Spirit the Father has already given his church."[35]

---

31. Stewart, Review of *TAT*, 26.
32. Edwards, Review of *CCF*, 287.
33. Long, Review of *ACI*, 67; Long, Review of *RECT*, 69.
34. Long, Review of *RECT*, 69.
35. *NT*, 192.

Bibliographies

A. THE WRITINGS OF ALAN P. F. SELL

1. Authored Books

Alfred Dye, Minister of the Gospel. London: Fauconberg, 1974.
Aspects of Christian Integrity. Louisville: Westminster John Knox, 1991.
Christ and Controversy: The Person of Christ in Nonconformist Thought and Ecclesial Experience, 1600-2000. Eugene, OR: Pickwick, 2012.
Christ Our Saviour. Shippensburg, PA: Ragged Edge, 2000.
Church Planting: A Study of Westmorland Nonconformity. Reprint. Eugene, OR: Wipf & Stock, 1998.
Commemorations: Studies in Christian Thought and History. Reprint. Eugene, OR: Wipf & Stock, 1998.
Confessing and Commending the Faith: Historic Witness and Apologetic Method. Reprint. Eugene, OR: Wipf & Stock, 2006.
Confessing the Faith Yesterday and Today: Essays Reformed, Dissenting and Catholic. Eugene, OR: Pickwick, 2013.
Content and Method in Christian Theology: A Case Study of the Thought of Nels Ferré. Cambridge: James Clarke, 2014.
Convinced, Concise and Christian: The Thought of Huw Parri Owen. Eugene, OR: Pickwick, 2012.
Defending and Declaring the Faith: Some Scottish Examples 1860-1920. Exeter: Paternoster, 1987.
Dissenting Thought and the Life of Churches: Studies in an English Tradition. Lewiston, NY: Mellen, 1990.
Enlightenment, Ecumenism, Evangel: Theological Themes and Thinkers 1550-2000. Carlisle: Paternoster, 2005.
Four Philosophical Anglicans: W. G. de Burgh, W. R. Matthews, O. C. Quick, H. A. Hodges. Farnham: Ashgate, 2010.
God Our Father: Doctrine and Devotion. 2nd ed. Shippensburg, PA: Ragged Edge, 2000.
The Great Debate: Calvin, Arminianism and Salvation. Reprint. Eugene, OR: Wipf & Stock, 1998.

Hinterland Theology: A Stimulus to Theological Construction. Milton Keynes: Paternoster, 2008.
John Locke and the Eighteenth-Century Divines. Reprint. Eugene, OR: Wipf & Stock, 2006.
[Owen, Isaac, pseud.] *A Land of Pure Delight. Elijah Morgan and the Saints of Bethel*. Reprint. Eugene, OR: Resource, 2013.
Mill and Religion: Contemporary Responses to Three Essays on Religion. Bristol: Thoemmes, 1997.
Mill on God: The Pervasiveness and Elusiveness of Mill's Religious Thought. Reprint. Eugene, OR: Wipf & Stock, 2012.
Nonconformist Theology in the Twentieth Century. Milton Keynes: Paternoster, 2006.
One Ministry, Many Ministers: A Case Study from the Reformed Tradition. Eugene, OR: Pickwick, 2014.
Philosophical Idealism and Christian Belief. Reprint. Eugene, OR: Wipf & Stock, 2006.
Philosophy, Dissent and Nonconformity 1689–2020. Reprint. Eugene, OR: Wipf & Stock, 2009.
Philosophy, History, and Theology: Selected Reviews, 1975–2011. Eugene, OR: Wipf & Stock, 2012.
The Philosophy of Religion 1875–1980. Reprint. Bristol: Thoemmes, 1996.
A Reformed, Evangelical, Catholic Theology. The Contribution of the World Alliance of Reformed Churches 1875–1982. Reprint. Eugene, OR: Wipf & Stock, 1998.
Robert Mackintosh: Theologian of Integrity. Reprint. Eugene, OR: Wipf & Stock, 2012.
Saints: Visible, Orderly and Catholic: The Congregational Idea of the Church. Princeton Theological Monograph Series 7. Allison Park, PA: Pickwick, 1986.
The Spirit Our Life. Shippensburg, PA: Ragged Edge, 2000.
Testimony and Tradition: Studies in Reformed and Dissenting Thought. Aldershot: Ashgate, 2005.
The Theological Education of the Ministry: Soundings in the British Reformed and Dissenting Traditions. Eugene, OR: Pickwick, 2013.
Theology in Turmoil: The Roots, Course and Significance of the Conservative-Liberal Debate in Modern Theology. Reprint. Eugene, OR: Wipf & Stock, 1998.

2. Edited Books

i Sole Editor

The Bible in Church, Academy and Culture: Essays in Honour of the Reverend Dr. John Tudno Williams. Eugene, OR: Pickwick, 2011.
The Great Ejectment of 1662: Its Antecedents, Aftermath and Ecumenical Significance. Eugene, OR: Pickwick, 2012.
Protestant Nonconformists and the West Midlands of England. Keele: Keele University Press, 1996.
P. T. Forsyth: Theologian for a New Millennium. London: United Reformed Church, 2000.
Reformed Theology and The Jewish People. Studies from the WARC 9. Geneva: WARC, 1986.

Bibliographies

ii Joint Editor

Baptism, Peace and the State in the Reformed and Mennonite Traditions. Waterloo, Ontario: Wilfred Laurier University Press, 1991.
The Church in the Reformed Tradition. European Studies from the WARC 1. Geneva: WARC, 1995.
Dictionary of Nineteenth-Century British Philosophers. Bristol: Theommes, 2002.
Protestant Nonconformity in the Twentieth Century. Carlisle: Paternoster, 2003.
Protestant Nonconformist Texts, Vol. 2: The Eighteenth Century. Reprint. Eugene OR: Wipf & Stock, 2015.
Towards a Common Testimony. Geneva: John Knox International Centre, 1989.

iii Series Editor

Nonconformist Texts. 4 vols. Reprint. Eugene OR: Wipf & Stock, 2015.

3. Articles and Pamphlets (except letters, obituaries, and pieces written for dictionaries, encyclopedias, and church magazines/journals)

"250th Anniversary of John Wesley's Conversion." *Canada Lutheran*, September 1988.
"*Agape*, Atonement and Christian Ethics." *The Downside Review* 91.303 (April 1973) 83–100.
"Alfred Dye: A Postscript." *Grace Magazine*, February 1985.
"The Alliance in Dialogue, 1970–2002: Retrospect and Reflections." *Reformed World* 53.4 (December 2003) 210–28.
"Anabaptist-Congregational Relations and Current Mennonite-Reformed Dialogue." *The Mennonite Quarterly Review* 61.3 (July 1987) 321–34.
"Andrew Fuller and the Socinians." *Enlightenment and Dissent* 19 (2000) 91–115.
"An Approach to College Counselling." *Learning for Living* 12.4 (March 1973) 11–15.
"Approaches to Moral Philosophy among the Eighteenth-Century Dissenters of England and Wales." *Jahrbuch für Recht und Ethik* 8 (2000) 263–313.
"Arminians, Deists and Reason." *Faith and Freedom* 33.1 (Autumn 1979) 19–31.
"Athens and Jerusalem: Facing Both Ways to Calgary." In *Christian Thought in the Twenty-first Century: Agenda for the Future*, edited by D. H. Schantz and T. Ruparell, 150–55. Eugene, OR: Cascade, 2012.
"Augustine *verses* Pelagius: A Cautionary Tale of Perennial Importance." *Calvin Theological Journal* 12.2 (November 1977) 117–43.
"Augustinian and Pelagian Variations from Cassian to Luther." *Theolgia Evangelica* 11.2-3 (July–September 1978) 79–100.
"Autonomy, Immanence and the Loss of Authority." *Churchman* 96.2 (1982) 123–41.
"The Background of the Current RE/ME Debate in Britain: An Historical Sketch." *Religious Education* 68.1 (January–February 1973) 42–56.

"A Bold Baptist, an Intrepid Independent and a Pithy Presbyterian: Sketches of Three Ejected Ministers of the 'B' Team." London: Association of Denominational Historical Societies and Cognate Libraries, 2013.

"By the Spirit, through the Word, within the Fellowship." *Touchstone* 7.3 (September 1989) 32–41.

"Calvin's Challenges to the Twenty-First Century Church." *Sárospataki Füzetek* 1 (2010) 79–98.

"The Centenary of Flint's Theism." *Philosophical Studies* 26 (1979) 167–90.

"Christian and Secular Philosophy in Britain at the Beginning of the Twentieth Century: A Study of Approaches and Relationships." *The Downside Review* 93.311 (April 1975) 122–43.

"Christian Ethics and Moral Philosophy: Some Reflections on the Contemporary Situation." *Scottish Journal of Theology* 16 (December 1963) 337–51.

"Christianity, Secularism and Toleration: Liberal Values and Illiberal Attitudes." In *Literature, Culture and Tolerance*, edited by A. R. Murphy et al., 71–90. Frankfurt: Lang, 2009.

"The Christian's Great Interest—and the Preacher's." *Evangelical Quarterly* 46.2 (April–June 1974) 72–80.

"Christians, Humanists and Common Ground." *Journal of Moral Education* 1.3 (June 1972) 177–85.

"Chrześcjiaństwo, Sekularyzm I Tolerancja: Liberalne Wartości I Nieoświecone Postawy." In *Literature, Kultura, Tolerancja*, edited by Grzegorz Gazda et al., 267–91. Kraków, 2008.

"Church and Chapel in the Eighteenth and Nineteenth Centuries." In *The Impact of Christianity on Life in the Dales*, 7–8. Sedbergh: Sedbergh and District History Society, 2001.

"Clarity, Precision, and on Towards Comprehension: The Intellectual Legacy of N. H. G. Robinson (1912–1978)." In *Border Crossings: Explorations of an Interdisciplinary Historian, Festschrift for Irving Hexham*, edited by Ulrich van der Heyden and Adreas Feldtkeller, 267–85. Stuttgart: Franz Steiner, 2008.

"Confessing the Faith and Confessions of Faith." In *Christian Identity (Studies in Reformed Theology, XVI)*, edited by Eduardus Van der Borght, 151–67. Leiden: Brill, 2008.

"Confessing the Faith in English Congregationalism." *JURCHS* 4.3 (October 1988) 170–213.

"Confessing the Faith in the Intellectual Context." *Journal of Reformed Theology* 1.2 (2007) 132–52.

"Conflicting Loyalties: Some Anglo-Canadian Reflections." *Uniting Church Studies* 1.1 (March 1995) 20–21.

Congregationalism at Worplesdon 1822–1972. Birmingham, 1972.

"*Conscience* in Recent Discussion." *Theology* 66 (December 1963) 498–504.

Conservation and Exploration in Christian Theology [The Inaugural Lecture from the Chair of Christian Doctrine and Philosophy of Religion]. Caernarfon: Gwasg Pantycelyn, 1993.

"Conservatives, Liberals and the Gospel." *Faith and Thought* 105.1–2 (Autumn 1978) 62–118.

"Cradley Chapel: from Independency to the Establishment." *JURCHS* 3 (1984) 120–31.

"Decision-making in our Churches, including Matters of Faith." *One in Christ* 32.1 (1996) 70–84.
The Dissenting Witness, Yesterday and Today. London: Protestant Dissenting Deputies of the Three Denominations, 2002.
"*The Doctrinal and Ecumenical Significance of the Great Ejectment.*" In *The Great Ejectment of 1662: Its Antecedents Aftermath and Ecumenical Significance*, 183–282. Eugene, OR: Pickwick, 2012.
"Doctrine, Polity, Liberty: What do Baptists Stand For?" In *Pilgrim Pathways: Essays in Baptist History in Honour of Barrington R. White*, edited by William H. Brackney et al., 1–46. Macon, GA: Mercer University Press, 1999.
"Dubious Establishment? A Neglected Ecclesiological Testimony." *Mid-Stream* 24.1 (January 1985) 1–28.
"Ecclesiology in Perspective: Conversations with Anglicans and Baptists." *Reformed World* 38 (September 1984) 168–76.
"English Dissent: Dissoluble or Dissolute?" *Baptist Quarterly* 33.5 (January 1990) 243–46.
"An Englishman, an Irishman and a Scotsman . . ." *Scottish Journal of Theology* 38.1 (1985) 41–83.
"Epilogue." In *The Church in the Reformed Tradition*, edited by C. E. Gunton et al., 54–56. European Studies from the WARC 1. Geneva: WARC, 1995.
"An Epiphany Charge to Wise Men." *Reformed World* 308.4 (December 1984) 216–19.
"Eschatology: Some Theological, Apologetic and Pastoral Reflections." In *Strangers and Pilgrims on the Earth. Essays in Honour of Abraham van de Beek*, edited by E. Van der Borght and P. van Geest, 357–69. Leiden: Brill, 2012.
"Establishment as a Theological Issue: the Dissenting Witness." *Theology* 106 (July/August 2003) 237–49.
"Evolution: Theory and Theme." *Faith and Thought* 104.3 (Winter 1977–78) 202–20.
"Fear God and Pay Him Homage." In *An Eastern European Liberation Theology*, edited by J. Pungur, 320–28. Calgary: Angelus, 1994.
"Foreword." In *Methods in the Madness: Diversity in Twentieth-Century Christian Social Ethics*, by Anna M. Robbins, xii–xiv. Carlisle: Paternoster, 2004.
"Friends and Philosophy." *The Friends' Quarterly* 18.2 (April 1973) 72–82
"Friends and Philosophy." *The Friends' Quarterly* 18.3 (July 1973) 111–22.
"From Union to Church: Autobiographical Recollections on [sic] Congregational Ecclesiology in the 1960s." In *Modern Christianity and Cultural Aspirations, a Festschrift for Clyde Binfield*, edited by David Bebbington and Timothy Larson, 309–44. London: Sheffield Academic Press, 2003.
"From Worms to Sunbeams: The Dilution of Calvinism in English Congregationalism 1830–1930." *JURCHS* 7.4 (May 2004) 253–74.
"General Editor's Preface and Introduction." In *Henry Grove: Ethical and Theological Writings*, by Henry Grove, v–xxxix. 6 vols. Bristol: Thoemmes, 2000.
"Geoffrey Nuttall in Conversation." *JURCHS* 8.5 (November 2009) 266–90.
"George Burder and the Lichfield Dissenters." *South Staffordshire Archaeological and Historical Society Transactions* 13 (1971–72) 52–60.
"George Tavard on Lewis S. Mudge: a Congregational Comment." *Mid-Stream* 34.1 (January 1995) 75–76.
"God, Grace and the Bible in Scottish Reformed Theology: A Review Article." *Irish Theological Quarterly* 54.1 (1988) 66–71.

"Gospel Discipline and Church (Dis)unity in the Reformed Tradition." In *The Unity of the Church*, edited by E. Van der Borght, 169–85. Leiden: Brill, 2010.

"The Gospel Its Own Witness: Deism, Thomas Paine and Andrew Fuller." In *You Will Be My Witnesses: A Festschrift for Allison A. Trites*, edited by Glenn Wooden et al., 188–229. Macon: Mercer University Press, 2003.

Guidelines on Church Discipline. London: United Reformed Church, 1983.

"The Heart of the Christian Gospel." *The Indian Journal of Theology* 28.1 (January–March 1979) 15–32.

"Henry Grove: A Dissenter at the Parting of the Ways." *Enlightenment and Dissent* 4 (1985) 53–63.

"Henry Rogers and *The Eclipse of Faith*." *JURCHS* 2.5 (May 1980) 128–43.

"The Holy Spirit and Ecumenism: Some Catholic Ruminations of a Reformed Theologian." In *The Holy Spirit, The Church and Christian Unity: Proceedings of the Consultation held at the Monastery of Bose, Italy (14–20 October 2002)*, edited by D. Donnelly et al., 75–92. Bibliotheca Ephemeridum Theologicarum Lovaniensium 181. Leuven: Peeters, 2005.

"Honouring John Tudno Williams: Minister, Scholar, Welshman." In *The Bible in Church, Academy and Culture: Essays in Honour of the Reverend Dr. John Tudno Williams*, edited by Alan P. F. Sell, 1–19. Eugene, OR: Pickwick, 2011.

"Immanentism and the Theological Enterprise." *Faith and Thought* 104.2 (Autumn 1977) 119–45.

"In the Wake of the Enlightenment: The Adjustments of James Martineau and A. Campbell Fraser." *Enlightenment and Dissent* 9 (1990) 63–92.

"Is Geoffrey Also Among The Theologians? Part 1." *JURCHS* 8.9 (November 2011) 558–86.

"Is Geoffrey Also Among The Theologians? Part 2." *JURCHS* 8.10 (May 2012) 624–39.

"Jerusalem *verses* Athens?" *Irish Theological Quarterly* 49.2 (1982) 75–90.

"J. H. A. Bomberger (1817–1890) *versus* J. W. Nevin: A Centenary Reappraisal." *The New Mercersburg Review* 8 (Autumn 1990) 3–24.

"John Baillie and Christian Epistemology." *The London Quarterly and Holborn Review* 33 (July 1964) 224–31.

"John Chater: From Independent Minister to Sandemanian Author." *Baptist Quarterly* 21.3 (July 1985) 100–117.

"John Howe's Eclectic Theism." *JURCHS* 2.6 (October 1980) 187–93.

"John Locke's Highland Critic." *Scottish Church History Society Records* 30.1 (1987) 65–76.

"John Wyclif (d.1384): Anniversary Reflections." *Reformed World* 38.5 (March 1985) 290–300.

"A Liberated Churchman." *The Philosophical Journal* 10.2 (July 1973) 85–96.

"The Life and Work of Robert Mackintosh (1958–1933)." *JURCHS* 1.3 (May 1974) 79–90.

"A Little Friendly Light: The Candour of Bourn, Taylor and Towgood: Part 1." *JURCHS* 4.9 (December 1991) 517–40.

"A Little Friendly Light: The Candour of Bourn, Taylor and Towgood: Part 2." *JURCHS* 4.10 (May 1992) 580–613.

"Living in the Half Lights: John Oman in Context." In *John Omen: Fresh Perspectives*, edited by Adam Hood, 3–63. Milton Keynes: Paternoster, 2012.

"Locke and Descartes through Victorian Eyes." *Philosophical Studies* 30 (1984) 220–29.

"The Lord's Supper in the Reformed Family." *Reformed World* 39.2 (June 1986) 518–27.

The Message of the Erkines for Today: An Address Delivered on February 10, 1987 to Commemorate Erskine Theological Seminary's 150th Anniversary. Due West, SC: Erskine Theological Seminary, 1987.

"New Departures in Baptist Theology: A Review Article." *Modern Believing* 56.4 (October 2015) 445–54.

"No Doctrinal Obstacles: Reformed Dialogue with Disciples and Methodists." *Reformed World* 39.8 (December 1987) 821–22.

"Nonconformists and the Person of Christ." In *T&T Clark Companion to Nonconformity*, edited by Robert Pope, 163–84. Edinburgh: Bloomsbury, 2013.

"Parables, Propositions and Information." *Journal of Theology for Southern Africa* 37 (December 1981) 38–49.

"The Pembrokeshire Congregational Magazine." *JURCHS* 4.2 (May 1988) 98–103.

"The Peril of Reductionism in Christian Thought." *Scottish Journal of Theology* 28 (1974) 48–64.

"*Philosophical Studies* and Philosophical Frontiers." *Philosophical Studies* 23 (1975) 7–21.

"Philosophy in the Eighteenth-century Dissenting Academies of England and Wales." *History of Universities* 11 (1992) 75–122.

"Platonists (Ancient and Modern) and the Gospel." *Irish Theological Quarterly* 44.3 (1977) 153–74.

"Preface." In *Reformed and Methodists in Dialogue: Report of the Reformed/Methodist Conversations 1985 and 1987*, 3–4. Studies from the WARC 12. Geneva: WARC, 1988.

"Preface." In *Towards Closer Fellowship: Report of the Dialogue between Reformed and Disciples of Christ*, 3–4. Studies from the WARC 11. Geneva: WARC, 1988.

The Preparation and Delivery of Sermons. London: The United Reformed Church, 1983.

"Presbyterianism in Eighteenth-century England: the Doctrinal Dimension." *JURCHS* 4.6 (May 1990) 352–86.

"Priestley's Polemic Against Reid." *The Price-Priestly Newsletter* 3 (1979) 19–31.

"Priestley's Polemic Against Reid: An Additional Note." *Enlightenment and Dissent* 2 (1983) 121.

"P. T. Forsyth as Unsystematic Systematician." In *Justice the True and Only Mercy. Essays on the Life and Theology of Peter Taylor Forsyth*, edited by Trevor A. Hart, 110–45. Edinburgh: T. & T. Clark, 1995.

"P. T. Forsyth: Theologian for a New Millennium." *Réformatus Szemle* 92 (November–December 1999) 470–76.

"The Public Worship of God: Memories and Challenges." *Sárospataki Füzetek* 1 (2003) 4–14.

"Rectifying Calvin's Ecclesiology: The Doctrinal and Ecumenical Importance of Separatist-Congregational Catholicity." In *John Calvin's Ecclesiology: Ecumenical Perspectives*, edited by Gerard Mannion and Eddy van der Borght, 143–68. London: T. & T. Clark, 2011.

"A Református Teológia Gyökerei, Fejlődése És Jövője." *Sárospataki Füzetek* 2 (2008) 12–19.

"The Reformed Family: A Profile." In *Mennonites and Reformed in Dialogue*, edited by Hans Georg vom Berg et al., 23–32. Studies from the WARC 7. Geneva: WARC, 1986.

"The Reformed Family Today: Some Theological Reflections." In *Major Themes in the Reformed Tradition*, edited by Donald K. McKim, 433–41. Grand Rapids: Eerdmans, 1992.

"Reformed Identity: A Non-Issue of Catholic Significance." *Reformed Review* 56.1 (Autumn 2000) 17–27.

[With Ross T. Bender.] "Reformed-Mennonite Dialogue: Phase Two." *Journal of Mennonite Studies* 8 (1990) 9–10.

"Reformed Reflections on Spirituality." *Reformed Review* 56.2 (Winter 2002/2003) 139–61.

"Reformed Theology and Worship: A Revision Course form Mercersburg." In *JURCHS* 9.2 (May 2013) 123–27.

"Reformed Theology in Britain in the Twentieth Century: A Bibliographical Survey." In *Vicissitudes of Reformed Theology in the Twentieth Century*, edited by G. Harinck and D. van Keulen, 130–46. Studies in Reformed Theology 9. Zoetermeer: Meinema, 2004

"Reformed Theology: Whence and Whither?" In *Theology Reformed and Reforming*, edited by Peter McEnhill, 65–87. St Andrews: Theology in Scotland, 2008.

Reminiscence, Reflection, Reassurance. Caernarfon: Pantycelyn, 2002.

"A Renewed Plea for 'Impractical' Divinity." *Studies in Christian Ethics* 8.2 (1995) 68–91.

"The Resolution on Racism and South Africa: 2 Years on." *Reformed Press Service* 228 (September 1984) 10–12.

"Responding to Baptism, Eucharist and Ministry: A Word to the Reformed Churches." *Reformed World* 38.3 (September 1984) 187–200.

"Retirement Denied: The Life and Ministry of Noah Jones (1725–1785)." *Transactions of the Unitarian Historical Society* 18.2 (April 1984) 91–105.

Rhetoric and Reality: Theological Reflections upon Congregationalism and its Heirs. The Congregational Lectures. London: Congregational Memorial Hall Trust, 1991.

"The Rise and Reception of Modern Biblical Criticism." *Evangelical Quarterly* 52.3 (July–September 1980) 132–48.

"Ritschl Appraised, Then And Now." *Reformed Theological Review* 38.2 (May–August 1979) 33–41.

"Robert Barclay (1648–1690), the Fathers, and the Inward Universal Saving Light: A Tercentenary Appraisal." *Journal of the Friends' Historical Society* 56.3 (1992) 210–26.

"Robert Mackintosh, A Neglected Theologian." *The Modern Churchman* 20.3 (Spring 1977) 95–108.

"Robert Travers and the Lichfield-Longdon Church Book." *JURCHS* 3.7 (October 1985) 268–78.

"Roger Williams, 1603–1683." In *Des Hommes Une Idée: la Réforme*, 39–41. Geneva: Fondation des Clefs de Saint Pierre, 1985.

"The Role of Bilateral Dialogues in the One Ecumenical Movement." *Ecumenical Review* 46.4 (October 1994) 453–60.

"The Samoan White Sunday." *Journal of Pacific History* 26.1 (1991) 94–97.

"Samuel Clark on the Existence of God." *Enlightenment and Dissent* 3 (1984) 65–75.

"Separatists and Dissenters Amidst the Arguments For And Against Toleration: Some Soundings 1550–1689." *Enlightenment and Dissent* 28 (2012) 89–118.

"Should the Presbyterian Church in Wales become a Peace Church?" *Reconciliation Quarterly* (Autumn 1996) 25–27.

"So Last Century? A Response." *JURCHS* 8.1 (January 2008) 55–59.
"The Social and Literary Contribution of Three Unitarian Ministers to Nineteenth-century Walsall." *Transactions of the Unitarian Historical Society* 15.3 (October 1973) 77–97.
"Some Contemporaries." *JURCHS* 3.8 (May 1986) 362–65.
"Some Reflections on Reformed-Methodist Relations." *Epworth Review* 12.1 (January 1986) 30–40.
"Some Reformed Approaches to the Peace Question." In *The Fragmentation of the Church and its Unity in Peacemaking*, edited by Jeffrey Gros and John D. Rampel, 119–36. Grand Rapids: Eerdmans, 2001.
"Some Reformed Responses to *Baptism, Eucharist and Ministry.*" *Reformed World* 39.3 (September 1986) 549–65.
"Some Sermons of Gilbert White." *The Philosophical Journal* 11.1 (January 1974) 10–18.
"Some Theological Aspects of the English Enlightenment Calmly Consider'd." *Eighteenth-Century Thought* 2 (2004) 255–98.
"Some Theological Responses to the First World War in the Reformed Churches of England and Wales." In *Der Erste Weltkrieg und die reformierte Welt*, edited by Hans-Georg Ulrichs, 237–53. Forschungen zur Reformierten Theologie 3. Neukirchen-Vluyn: Neukirchener, 2014.
"Striving for an Educated Ministry Then—and Now? A Review Article." *Baptist Quarterly* 41 (January 2005) 53–57.
"Telling the Story: Then and Now." In *Story Lines: Chapters on Thought, Word and Deed for Gabriel Fackre*, edited by Skye Fackre Gibson, 146–56. Grand Rapids: Eerdmans, 2002.
"The Theological Contribution of Protestant Nonconformists in the Twentieth-Century: Some Soundings." In *Protestant Nonconformity in the Twentieth Century*, edited by Anthony R. Cross and Alan P. F. Sell, 33–62. Carlisle: Paternoster, 2003.
"Theological Education by Degrees." *The Expository Times* 75.7 (April 1964) 196–200.
"Theology and the Philosophical Climate: Case Studies from the Second Century AD (Part 1)." *Vox Evangelica* 13 (1983) 41–66.
"Theology and the Philosophical Climate: Case Studies from the Second Century AD (Part 2)." *Vox Evangelica* 14 (1984) 53–64.
"Theology in Canada: Random Reflections from Afar." *Canadian Theological Society Newsletter* 13.2 (April 1994) 1–4.
"Through Suffering to Liberty: 1689 in the English and Vaudois Experience." In *Dall' Europa Alle Valli Valdesi*, edited by Albert De Lange, 215–36. Turin: Claudiana, 1990.
"Transcendence, Immanence and the Gospel." *Journal of Theology for Southern Africa* 26 (March 1979) 56–66.
"The Translocal Ministry of Moderators: David R. Peel, *The Story of the Moderators*." In *Friends of the Congregational Library Newsletter* 4.6 (Autumn 2013) 8–11.
"The Unsung Ministers of Congregationalism's Union List B." *JURCHS* 9.6 (May 2015) 339–57.
"The Use, Abuse and Relevance of Religion: Some Reflections on Professor Abraham von de Beek's Proposal." In *Religion Without Ulterior Motive*, edited by Eddy A. J. G. Van der Borght, 89–100. Studies in Reformed Theology 13. Leiden: Brill, 2006.
"A Valued Inheritance of New Testament Scholarship." *Studia Doctorum Theologiae Protestantis* 1 (2011) 57–76.

"Varieties of English Separatist and Dissenting Writings, 1550–1689." In *Writing and Religion in England, 1558–1689: Studies in Community-Making and Cultural Memory*, edited by Roger D. Sell and Anthony W. Johnson, 25–46. Farnham: Ashgate, 2009.

"The Walsall Riots, the Rooker Family and Eighteenth-Century Dissent." *South Staffordshire Archaeological and Historical Society Transactions* 25 (1983–84) 50–71.

"What has P. T. Forsyth to do with Mercersburg?" *The New Mercersburg Review* 22 (Autumn 1997) 8–45.

"The Witness and Legacy of Congregationalism." *Historic Sites and Archives Journal* 6.1 (May 1993) 16–19.

"The Witness of Reformed Theology and Theologians Today." *The Near East School of Theology Theological Review* 7.2 (November 1986) 91–105.

"The Worship of English Congregationalism." In *Christian Worship in Reformed Churches Past and Present*, edited by Lukas Vischer, 83–106. Grand Rapids: Eerdmans, 2003.

4. Contributions to Reference Works

Biographical Dictionary of Twentieth-Century Philosophers. London: Routledge, 1996. (Entries on "A. J. Balfour," "K. Barth," "E. Brunner," "R. Bultmann," "R. Eucken," "J. Macquarrie," "E. Mascall," "B. Mitchell," "J. W. Oman," "T. Penelhum," "K. Rahner," "H. Scholz," "R. N. Smart," and "E. Troeltsch.")

Biographical Encyclopedia of British Idealism. London: Continuum, 2010. (Entries on "W. G. De Burgh" and "Robert Flint.")

Britannica Book of the Year. Chicago: Encyclopaedia Britannica, 1986 (Entry on "Reformed, Presbyterian and Congregational Churches.")

The Cambridge Dictionary of Christianity. Cambridge: Cambridge University Press, 2010. (Entry on "John Locke.")

Dictionary of Biblical Interpretation. Nashville: Abingdon, 1999. (Entries on "J. Orr," "P. T. Forsyth," "M. Dods," "A. S. Peake," and "C. H. Spurgeon.")

Dictionary of the Ecumenical Movement. 2nd ed. Grand Rapids: Eerdmans, 2002. (Entries on "Anglican-Reformed Dialogue" and "Congregationalism.")

Dictionary of Eighteenth-Century British Philosophers. Bristol: Thoemmes, 1999. (Entries on "Henry Grove" and "John Taylor.")

Dictionary of Historical Theology. Carlisle: Paternoster, 2000. (Entries on "A. B. Bruce," S. Cave," and "R. S. Franks.")

Dictionary of Nineteenth-Century British Philosophers. Bristol: Thoemmes, 2002. (Entries on "W. L. Alexander," "Richard Alliott," "Henry Allon," "Elkanah Armitage," "Robert Aspland," "Henry Batchelor," "James Bennett," "E. R. Conder," "W. L. Courtney," "A. M. Fairbairn," "Robert Flint," "Benjamin Godwin," "J. H. Godwin," "J. T. Gray," "J. M. Hodgson," "James Iverach," "James Lindsay," "Samuel McAll," "Robert Mackintosh," "Edward Miall," "William Parry," "George Payne," "George Redford," "Henry Rogers," "Joseph Sortain," "Samuel Spalding," "John Stoughton," "J. R. Thomson," "Robert Vaughan," "Gilbert Wardlaw," and "Ralph Wardlaw.")

A Dictionary of Religious Education. London: SCM, 1984. (Entry on "Rationality.")

Dictionary of Scottish Church History and Theology. Edinburgh: T. & T. Clark, 1993. (Entries on "D. W. Forrest," "A. Campbell Fraser," "J. Fraser," "J. Iverach," "J. Kennedy," "H. R. Mackintosh," "R. Mackintosh," and "World Alliance of Reformed Churches.")

Dictionary of Seventeenth-Century British Philosophers. Bristol: Thoemmes, 2005. (Entries on "R. Barclay," "J. Goodwin," "J. Howe," "P. Nye," T. Rowe," and "M. Warren.")

Dictionary of Twentieth-Century British Philosophers. Bristol: Thoemmes, 2005. (Entries on "W. G. De Burgh," "W. R. Matthews," "H. P. Owen," "F. J. Powicke," "N. H. G. Robinson," and "J. Heywood Thomas.")

Encyclopedia of the Reformed Faith. Louisville: Westminster John Knox, 1992. (Entries on "J. H. A. Bomberger," "R. Browne," "J. Caird," "Congregationalism—British," "R. W. Dale," "Dissenting Academies," "A. M. Fairbairn," "R. Flint," "Nonconformity," "J. Oman," "Savoy Declaration," "A. M. Toplady," and "World Alliance of Reformed Churches.")

Evangelisches Kirkenlexikon. Göttingen: Vandenhoeck & Ruprecht, 1996. (Entry on "The Westminster Assembly and Confession of Faith.")

Handbook of Theological Education in World Christianity. Oxford: Oxford University Press, 2004. (Entry on "Reformed Theological Education Networks.")

Historical Dictionary of Reformed Churches. Lanham: Scarecrow, 1999. (Editorial and biographical contributions)

Ökumene Lexikon. Frankfurt: Lembeck, 1985. (Entry on "Reformierte Kirchen" with K. Halaski).

Oxford Dictionary of National Biography. Oxford: Oxford University Press, 2004. (Entries on "W. H. Bennett," "S. Bourn," "S. Bourn III," "H. F. L. Cocks," "A. M. Fairbairn," "R. Flint," "J. Fraser," "W. J. F. Huxtable," "N. Ladner," "J. Kennedy," "R. Mackintosh," "J. Reynolds," "W. G. Robinson," "J. Taylor," and "J. S. Whale.")

The Oxford Handbook to Nineteenth-Century British Philosophy. Oxford: Oxford University Press, 2014. (Entry on "Scottish Religious Philosophy, 1850-1900.")

The Reformed Family Worldwide. Grand Rapids: Eerdmans, 1999. (Entry on "The International Congregational Fellowship.")

The Westminster Dictionary of Theology. Louisville: Westminster John Knox, 1983. (Entry on "Apologetics.")

The Westminster Handbook to Reformed Theology. Louisville: Westminster John Knox, 2001. (Entry on "Savoy Declaration of Faith and Order.")

Who They Were in the Reformed Churches of England and Wales 1901-2000. Donnington: Tyas, 2007. (Entries on "C. J. Cadoux," "H. F. Lovell Cocks," "P. T. Forsyth," "N. Goodall," "W. B. Selbie," and "H. S. Stanley.")

Wörterbuch des Christentums. Zurich: Benzinge, 1988. (Entry for "Presbyterianer.")

5. Book Reviews (not including short book notes)

Review of *The Actuality of Atonement*, by Colin E. Gunton. *Irish Theological Quarterly* 57.1 (1991) 82-84.

Review of *Analytic Philosophy of Religion*, by James E. Harris. *Philosophical Books* 64.3 (July 2003) 285-89.

Review of *Anticipations of the Enlightenment in England, France and Germany*, edited by Alan Charles Kors and Paul J. Korshin. *Faith and Freedom* 42.3 (Autumn 1989) 150–51.

Review of *Aquinas, Calvin and Contemporary Protestant Thought*, by Arvin Vos. *Philosophical Studies* 32 (1988–1990) 377–79.

Review of *Art, Modernity and Faith*, by George Pattison. *Irish Theological Quarterly* 44 (1999) 83–84.

Review of *The Assembly of the Lord*, by Robert S. Paul. *Irish Theological Quarterly* 54.4 (1988) 324–25.

Review of *Assurance of Faith: Calvinism, English Puritanism, and the Second Dutch Reformation*, by Joel R. Beeke. *European Journal of Theology* 2.1 (1993) 81–82.

Review of *Atonement and Imagination*, by V. White. *Irish Theological Quarterly* 58.2 (1992) 158–59.

Review of *Atonement and Justification*, by Alan C. Clifford. *Proceedings of the Huguenot Society* 25.3 (1991) 293–94.

Review of *Baillie, Oman and Macmurray: Experience and Religious Belief*, by Adam Hood. *Heythrop Journal* 46.4 (October 2005) 554–55.

Review of *Baptist Church Covenants*, by Charles W. DeWeese. *Baptist Quarterly* 34.3 (July 1991) 142–43.

Review of *Baptist Theologians*, edited by Timothy George and David S. Dockery. *Calvin Theological Journal* 27.1 (April 1992) 121–25.

Review of *Beginning to Read the Fathers*, by Boniface Ramsay. *The Furrow* 37.10 (October 1986) 673–74.

Review of *Being and Truth: Essay in Honour of John Macquarrie*, edited by Alistair Kee, and Eugene T. Long. *Irish Theological Quarterly* 56.1 (1990) 68.

Review of *The Bible and Epistemology: Biblical Soundings on the Knowledge of God*, edited by Mary Healy and Robin Parry. *Journal of Reformed Theology* 3 (2009) 219–26.

Review of *The Bible in Theology and Preaching*, by Donald K. McKim. *Irish Biblical Studies* 18 (October 1996) 217–18.

Review of *The Blackwell Companion to Nineteenth Century Theology*, edited by David A. Fergusson. *Journal of Ecclesiastical History* 62 (2011) 638–39.

Review of *The Blackwell Companion to the Enlightenment*, edited by John W. Yolton et al. *Irish Theological Quarterly* 53.4 (1998) 415–16.

Review of *The Blackwell Dictionary of Evangelical Biography*, edited by Donald M. Lewis. *Baptist Quarterly* 37.3 (July 1997) 150–52.

Review of *The Blackwell Encyclopedia of Modern Christian Thought*, edited by Alister E. McGrath. *European Journal of Theology* 4.2 (1995) 182–83.

Review of *The Brethren Encyclopedia*, edited by Donald F. Durnbaugh et al. 3 vols. *JURCHS* 4.2 (May 1988) 161–65.

Review of *Brothers Unite*, edited and translated by the Hutterian Brethren. *Mid-Stream* 28.4 (October 1989) 441–42.

Review of *Butler: The Arguments of the Philosophers*, by Terence Penelhum. *Philosophical Studies* 33 (1991–92) 398–401.

Review of *A Call for Continuity: The Theological Contribution of James Orr*, by Glen Scorgie. *Canadian Theological Society Newsletter* 9.1 (October 1989) 12–13.

Review of *Calvin and Scottish Theology: The Doctrine of Assurance*, by M. Charles Bell. *Irish Theological Quarterly* 54 (1988) 66–71.

Review of *Calvinism and Communion in Victorian England: Studies in Nineteenth-Century Strict-Communion Baptist Ecclesiology*, by Geoffrey R. Breed. *JURCHS* 8.5 (November 2009) 306–7.
Review of *Calvinism in Europe: 1540–1620*, edited by Andrew Pettegree et al. *Calvin Theological Journal* 33.2 (1997) 517–19.
Review of *Calvin's Concept of the Law*, by I. John Hesselink. *European Journal of Theology* 3.2 (1994) 175–76.
Review of *Calvin's Ecclesiastical Advice*, translated by Mary Beaty and Benjamin W. Farley. *Reformed Review* 45.3 (Spring 1992) 234.
Review of *The Cambridge Companion to Christian Ethics*, edited by Robin Gill. *Modern Believing* 42.3 (October 2001) 68–70.
Review of *The Cambridge Companion to Locke*, edited by Vere Chappell. *Faith and Freedom* 49.1 (Spring–Summer 1996) 84–86.
Review of *Cambridge Theology in the Nineteenth Century*, by David Thompson. *JURCHS* 8.4 (June 2009) 236–39.
Review of *The Case for Christian Humanism*, by Joseph M. Shaw and R. William Franklin. *Calvin Theological Journal* 27.2 (November 1992) 431–33.
Review of *Catholicity and Secession*, by Henry Zwaanstra. *Eerdmans Academic Catalogue* (1992) 3.
Review of *Celebrating Life: A Book of Special Services*, edited by A. Hill. *Faith and Freedom* 46.2 (Autumn 1993) 132.
Review of *A Century of Moral Philosophy*, by Donald Hudson. *Reform* (January 1981) 26.
Review of *A Century of Protestant Theology*, by Alasdair I. C. Heron. *Reform* (January 1981) 26.
Review of *Challenges to the Enlightenment*, edited by Paul Kurtz and Tim J. Madigan. *Faith and Freedom* 51.2 (Autumn and Winter 1998) 174–75.
Review of *Charles Grandison Finney*, by Keith J. Hardman. *Baptist Quarterly* 33.2 (April 1989) 99–100.
Review of *Charles Hodge Revisited: A Critical Appraisal of His Life and Work*, edited by John W. Stewart and James H. Moorhead. *Modern Believing* 44 (July 2003) 74–76.
Review of *Christ and Prometheus? A Quest for Theological Identity*, by Jan Milic Lochman. *Mid-Stream* 31.1 (January 1992) 69–71.
Review of *Christ in Our Place*, edited by Trevor A. Hart and Daniel Thimell. *Reformed Review* 46.1 (Autumn 1992) 56–57.
Review of *Christian Ethics: A Historical Introduction*, by J. Philip Wogaman. *Modern Believing* 35.2 (April 1994) 64–66.
Review of *Christian Faith and Society*, by Gordon Harland. *Touchstone* 7.1 (January 1989) 51–53.
Review of *The Christian Story: A Pastoral Systematics, Vol. II*, by Gabriel Fackre. *Scottish Journal of Theology* 43.1 (1990) 117–19.
Review of *Christian Theism and Moral Philosophy*, edited by Mary Beaty et al. *Studies in Christian Ethics* 13.1 (2000) 108–12.
Review of *Christian Theology: An Introduction*, edited by Alister E. McGrath. *Irish Theological Quarterly* 63.2 (1998) 204–5.
Review of *Christianity and the Hellenistic World*, by Ronald H. Nash. *Philosophical Studies* 33 (1988–90) 341–42.

Review of *The Chronicle of Hutterian Brethren, Vol 1*, edited and translated by the Hutterian Brethren. *The Ecumenical Review* 40.1 (1998) 112–13.

Review of *Church and Confession: Conservative Theologians in Germany, England and America 1815–1866*, by Walter H. Conser Jr. *Calvin Theological Journal* 28.2 (November 1993) 449–51.

Review of *The Church of England, c. 1689–c. 1833: From Toleration to Tractarianism*, edited by John Walsh et al. *British Journal for the History of Philosophy* 4.1 (March 1996) 197–98.

Review of *C. J. Cadoux, Theologian, Scholar and Pacifist*, by Elaine Kaye. *Faith and Freedom* 43.3 (Autumn 1990) 150–51.

Review of *Coena Mystica: Debating Reformed Eucharistic Theology*, edited by Linden J. DeBie. *JURCHS* 10.1 (November 2017) 41–42.

Review of *Companion Encyclopedia to Asian Philosophy*, edited by Brian Carr and Indira Mahalingam. *Modern Believing* 39.4 (October 1998) 58–59.

Review of *A Companion to Philosophy of Religion*, edited by Charles Taliaferro et al. *Calvin Theological Journal* 34.1 (April 1999) 251–54.

Review of *The Concept of Church*, by Herwi Rikhof. *Philosophical Studies* 30 (1984) 362–63.

Review of *A Concise Encyclopedia of the Philosophy of Religion*, by Anthony Thiselton. *Theology Today* 60.1 (April 2003) 145.

Review of *Confessions and Catechisms of the Reformation*, edited by Mark A. Noll. *Reformed Review* 45.3 (Spring 1992) 235–36.

Review of *Conflict and Reconciliation: Studies in Methodism and Ecumenism in England, 1740–1982*, by John Munsey Turner. *Mid-Steam* 27.1 (January 1988) 82–85.

Review of *Confusions in Christian Social Ethics*, by Ronald H. Preston. *Modern Believing* 36.3 (July 1995) 63–67.

Review of *Congregational Independence in Lowland Scotland, Vol. 2*, by William D. McNaughton. *JURCHS* 8.2 (May 2008) 121–23.

Review of *Congregationalism in Wales*, by R. Tudor Jones. *Friends of the Congregational Library Newsletter* 2.2 (Autumn 2005) 16–18.

Review of *Continental Philosophy: An Introduction*, by David West. *Modern Believing* 39.1 (January 1998) 53–54.

Review of *The Correspondence of Richard Price, Vol. III*, edited by William Bernard Peach. *International Journal of Philosophical Studies* 3.1 (March 1995) 213–15.

Review of *The Correspondence of Richard Price, Vol. 1: July 1748–March 1778*, edited by D. O. Thomas and William Bernard Peach. *Philosophical Studies* 31 (1986–87) 432–35.

Review of *The Correspondence of Richard Price, Vol. 2*, edited by D. O. Thomas. *International Journal of Philosophical Studies* 3.1 (March 1995) 213–15.

Review of *Criticism and Faith in Late Victorian Scotland: A. B. Davidson, W. R. Smith and G. A. Smith*, by Richard A. Riesen. *Irish Theological Quarterly* 54 (1988) 66–71.

Review of *Dark Satanic Mills? Religion and Irreligion in Birmingham and the Black Country*, by Geoff Robson. *Proceedings of the Wesley Historical Society* 54.4 (February 2004) 135–37.

Review of *Darwinism and Divinity*, edited by John Durant. *Irish Theological Quarterly* 55.3 (1989) 251.

Review of *Darwinism and the Divine in America*, by Jon H. Roberts. *Reformed Review* 43.1 (Autumn 1989) 77–78.

Review of *A Dictionary of Biblical Interpretation*, edited by David L. Jeffrey. *Reformed Review* 47.1 (Autumn 1993) 56–57.
Review of *Dictionary of the Eighteenth-Century British Philosophers*, edited by John W. Yolton et al. *International Journal of Philosophical Studies* 18.2 (2000) 266–69.
Review of *A Dictionary of Methodism in Britain and Ireland*, edited by John A. Vickers. *Proceedings of the Wesley Historical Society* 52.6 (October 2000) 77–79.
Review of *The Dictionary of Seventeenth-Century British Philosophers*, edited by Andrew Pyle. *International Journal of Philosophical Studies* 9.4 (2001) 553–55.
Review of *Dilemmas: A Christian Approach to Moral Decision Making*, by Richard Higginson. *Reformed Review* 43.3 (Spring 1990) 221–22.
Review of *Disruption to Diversity: Edinburgh Divinity, 1846–1996*, edited by David F. Wright and Gary D. Badcock. *JURCHS* 6.2 (May 1998) 147–48.
Review of *The Dissolution of Dissent 1850–1918*, by Mark D. Johnson. *Baptist Quarterly* 33 (1990) 243–46.
Review of *Divine Providence and Human Suffering*, by John Walsh and P. G. Walsh. *The Furrow* 37.10 (October 1986) 674.
Review of *Dr. Taylor of Norwich: Wesley's Arch Heretic*, by G. T. Eddy. *Journal of Ecclesiastical History* 54.4 (October 2003) 780–81.
Review of *Early Congregational Independence in the Highland and Islands of North-East Scotland*, by William D. McNaughton. *JURCHS* 7.6 (May 2005) 398–401.
Review of *Early Congregational Independence in Lowland Scotland, Vol. 1*, by William D. McNaughton. *JURCHS* 7.8 (June 2006) 513.
Review of *Early Congregational Independence in Shetland*, by William D. McNaughton. *JURCHS* 7.8 (June 2006) 513.
Review of *Education for Peoplehood*, by Ross T. Bender. *Epworth Review* 25.3 (July 1998) 109–10.
Review of *Eighteenth-Century Hermeneutics*, by Joel C. Weinsheimer. *British Journal for Eighteenth-Century Studies* 19.1 (Spring 1996) 93.
Review of *Election and Predestination*, by Paul King Jewett. *Reformed Review* 41.1 (Autumn 1987) 55.
Review of *The Enlightenment*, by Roy Porter. *British Journal for the History of Philosophy* 1.2 (September 1993) 160–61.
Review of *The Enlightenment and Religion: Rational Dissent in Eighteenth-Century Britain*, edited by Knud Haakonssen. *International Journal of Philosophical Studies* 5.1 (1997) 142–43.
Review of *The Enlightenment World*, by Martin Fitzpatrick et al. *Enlightenment and Dissent* 21 (2005) 198–209.
Review of *The English Baptists of the Nineteenth Century*, by John H. Y. Briggs. *Evangelical Quarterly* 48.2 (April 1996) 180–82.
Review of *English Philosophy in the Age of Locke*, edited by M. A. Stewart. *Transactions of the Unitarian Historical Society* 23.1 (April 2003) 480–82.
Review of *The English Sabbath*, by Kenneth L. Parker. *Calvin Theological Journal* 24.2 (November 1989) 354–57.
Review of *English Students at Leiden University: 1575–1650*, by Daniela Prögler. *JURCHS* 9.7 (November 2015) 450–52.
Review of *The Eucharistic Service of the Catholic Apostolic Church*, by Gregg A. Mast. *JURCHS* 6.5 (November 1999) 377–79.

Review of *Evangelicalism in Modern Britain*, by D. W. Bebbington. *Enlightenment and Dissent* 10 (1991) 115–18.
Review of *The Experience of God: An Invitation to Do Theology*, by Dermot A. Lane. *Philosophical Studies* 30 (1984) 363–65.
Review of *Faith*, by Keith W. Clements. *Reform* (September 1981) 25.
Review of *Faith and the Life of Reason*, by John King-Farlow and William N. Christensen. *Philosophical Studies* 24 (1976) 280–83.
Review of *Faith, Scepticism and Personal Identity: A Festschrift for Terence Penelhum*, edited by John James Macintosh and Hugo Anthony Meynell. *International Journal of Philosophical Studies* 4.2 (September 1996) 363–65.
Review of *The Faith We Confess: An Ecumenical Dogmatics*, by Jan Milic Lochman. *Irish Theological Quarterly* 56.2 (1990) 150–51.
Review of *The Faith We Hold*, by James Arne Nestingen. *Reformed Review* 38 (1984) 76.
Review of *A Fantasy of Reason: The Life and Thought of William Godwin*, by Don Locke. *Philosophical Studies* 30 (1984) 325–27.
Review of *Fields of Faith*, by David F. Ford et al. *Anvil* 22.4 (2005) 323–24.
Review of *Fire in the Thatch*, by Elfion Evans. *Cylchgrawn Hanes* 20 (1996) 77–81.
Review of *Forgiveness is a Work as Well as a Grace*, by Edna Hong. *Reformed Review* 39 (1985) 64–65.
Review of *The Free Church in Victorian Canada, 1844–1861*, by Richard W. Vaudry. *Canadian Theological Society Newsletter* 10.1 (November 1990) 8–9.
Review of *Freedom for Obedience*, by Donald G. Bloesch. *The Reformed Journal* 37.11 (November 1987) 26–27; *Irish Theological Review* 57.4 (1991) 331–32.
Review of *Freedom or Order: The Eucharistic Liturgy in English Congregationalism 1645–1980*, by Bryan D. Spinks. *Journal of Ecclesiastical History* 37.1 (January 1986) 176–77.
Review of *From Form to Transformation: A Study in the Philosophy of Plotinus*, by Frederic M. Schroeder. *International Journal of Philosophical Studies* 1.1 (March 1993) 168–69.
Review of *Glanvill: The Uses and Abuses of Scepticism*, by Sascha Talmor. *Philosophical Studies* 30 (1984) 323–24.
Review of *Hazlitt the Dissenter: Religion, Philosophy and Politics, 1766–1816*, by Stephen Burley. *Baptist Quarterly* 47.4 (October 2016) 179–80.
Review of *A History of the Evangelical and Reformed Church*, by David Dunn et al. *JURCHS* 5.2 (July 1993) 117–19.
Review of *The History of the Unity of Brethren*, by Rudolf Rican. *JURCHS* 5.10 (June 1997) 642–43.
Review of *History, Religion and Culture: British Intellectual History 1750–1950*, edited by Stefan Collini et al. *British Journal for the History of Philosophy* 11.1 (February 2003) 161–64.
Review of *Holding the Fort: Studies in Victorian Revivalism*, by John Kent. *Reform* (June 1979) 27.
Review of *The Honest Mind: The Life and Work of Richard Price*, edited by D. O. Thomas. *Philosophical Studies* 26 (1979) 305–10.
Review of *Implications of the Gospel*, edited by William A. Norgren and William G. Rush. *Mid-Stream* 28.3 (July 1989) 326–28.
Review of *The Incarnate Word: Selected Writings on Christology*, edited by William B. Evans. *JURCHS* 10.1 (November 2017) 43.

Review of *The Individual and World Need*, by Eberhard Arnold. *Baptist Quarterly* 35.6 (April 1994) 293.
Review of *The Inquirer: A History and Other Reflections*, by Alan R. Ruston et al. *Faith and Freedom* 46.2 (Autumn 1993) 129.
Review of *Instruments of Unity*, edited by T. F. Best. *Mid-Stream* 28.2 (April 1989) 218.
Review of *An Introduction to Counselling Psychology*, by Richard Nelson-Jones. *West Midlands Journal of Teacher Education* 1.2 (September 1982) 63–64.
Review of *Is Christianity True?*, by Hugo Anthony Meynell. *Faith and Freedom* 48.2 (Autumn–Winter 1995) 172–73.
Review of *James McCosh and the Scottish Intellectual Tradition*, by J. David Hoeveler Jr. *Philosophical Studies* 31 (1986–87) 435–37.
Review of *John and Donald Baillie: Transatlantic Theology*, by George M. Newlands. *Irish Theological Quarterly* 68.4 (2003) 400–402.
Review of *John Gill and the Cause of God and Truth*, by George M. Ella. *Evangelical Quarterly* 71.1 (1999) 81–82.
Review of *John Locke*, by W. M. Spellman. *Enlightenment and Dissent* 18 (1999) 270–75.
Review of *John Locke and Christianity*, edited by Victor Nuovo. *The Locke Newsletter* 29 (1998) 181–83.
Review of *John Locke and the Problem of Depravity*, by W. M. Spellman. *Enlightenment and Dissent* 9 (1990) 134–37.
Review of *John Locke: Selected Correspondence*, edited by Mark Goldie. *The Scriblerian* 30.1 (Autumn 2004) 95–96.
Review of *John Locke: The Reasonableness of the Christian Religion as Delivered in the Scriptures*, edited by John C. Higgins-Biddle. *Journal of Ecclesiastical History* 52.4 (2001) 756–57.
Review of *John Locke: Resistance, Religion and Responsibility*, by John Marshall. *Enlightenment and Dissent* 15 (1996) 112–16.
Review of *John Locke, Toleration and Early Enlightenment Culture*, by John Marshall. *Enlightenment and Dissent* 27 (2011) 208–12.
Review of *John Locke: Writings on Religion*, edited by Victor Nuovo. *British Journal for the History of Philosophy* 11.2 (May 2003) 345–47.
Review of *John Owen, Richard Baxter and the Formation of Nonconformity*, by Tim Cooper. *Journal of Reformed Theology* 1 (2013) 119–20
Review of *John Smyth's Congregation*, by James R. Coggins. *Baptist Quarterly* 38.3 (1999) 155–56.
Review of *John Stuart Mill and the Religion of Humanity*, by Linda C. Raeder. *International Journal of Philosophical Studies* 11.3 (2003) 356–58.
Review of *John Wesley: A Personal Portrait*, by Ralph Waller. *Journal of Ecclesiastical History* 54.4 (October 2003) 780–81.
Review of *John Wesley and the Anglican Evangelicals of the Eighteenth Century*, by Albert Brown-Lawson. *Baptist Quarterly* 36.6 (April 1996) 310–11.
Review of *John Williamson Nevin, American Theologian*, by Richard E. Wentz. *JURCHS* 6.4 (July 1999) 303–5.
Review of *Joseph Butler's Moral and Religious Thought*, edited by Christopher Cunliffe. *Ethics* 104.3 (April 1994) 668.
Review of *Joseph Priestly, Scientist, Philosopher and Theologian*, edited by Isabel Rivers. and David L. Wykes. *Journal of Ecclesiastical History* 60.2 (April 2009) 408–9.

Review of *Keeping the Faith: Essays to Mark the Centenary of Lux Mundi*, edited by Geoffrey Wainwright. *JURCHS* 4.6 (May 1990) 397–99.

Review of *Kierkegaard's Critique of Reason and Society*, by Merold Westphal. *Faith and Freedom* 45.3 (Autumn 1992) 130–31.

Review of *Letting God be God: The Reformed Tradition*, by David Cornick. *JURCHS* 8.3 (December 2008) 155–60.

Review of *The Liberation of Theology*, by Juan Luis Segundo. *Philosophical Studies* 26 (1979) 302–5.

Review of *The Life and Thought of John Gill (1697-1771)*, edited by Michael A. G. Haykin. *Baptist Quarterly* 38.4 (October 1999) 203–4.

Review of *Locke and Burnet*, by S. A. Grave. *Philosophical Studies* 31 (1986–87) 439–40.

Review of *A Locke Dictionary*, edited by John W. Yolton. *British Journal for Eighteenth-Century Studies* 19.1 (Spring 1996) 93–94.

Review of *Locke, Wesley and the Method of English Romanticism*, by Richard E. Brantley. *Enlightenment and Dissent* 8 (1989) 140–44.

Review of *Locke's Enlightenment: Aspects of the Origin, Nature and Impact of His Philosophy*, by G. A. J. Rogers. *The European Legacy* 4.4 (1999) 102–5.

Review of *Love is Like Fire: The Confession of an Anabaptist Prisoner*, by Peter Riedemann. *Baptist Quarterly* 35.6 (April 1994) 293.

Review of *Lovers of Discord*, by Keith Clements. *Irish Theological Quarterly* 58.4 (1992) 322–23.

Review of *Luther: Theologian for Catholics and Protestants*, edited by George Yule. *Reformed World* 39.2 (June 1986) 546–47.

Review of *The Magdalen Metaphysicals: Idealism and Orthodoxy at Oxford, 1901-1945*, by James Patrick. *Philosophical Studies* 32 (1988–90) 350–52.

Review of *The Making of a Northern Baptist College*, by Peter Shepherd. *Baptist Quarterly* 41 (2005) 53–57.

Review of *Making Sense of Christian Faith*, by Victor A. Shepherd. *Studies in Religion* 18.2 (1989) 249–50.

Review of *Making Sense of Life*, by Andrew D. MacRae. *Touchstone* 8.1 (January 1990) 55.

Review of *Mansfield College, Oxford*, by Elaine Kaye. *Journal of Ecclesiastical History* 48.3 (July 1997) 596–97.

Review of *The Margins of Orthodoxy*, edited by Roger D. Lund. *British Journal for the History of Philosophy* 6.3 (October 1998) 498–99.

Review of *The Meaning of Mission*, by Jose Comblin. *Philosophical Studies* 29 (1983) 378–81.

Review of *Medieval Thought*, by David Luscombe. *Faith and Freedom* 51.1 (Spring–Summer 1998) 77–78.

Review of *The Mercersburg Theology and the Quest for Reformed Catholicity*, by W. Bradford Littlejohn. *New Mercersburg Review* 44 (Spring 2011) 22–30.

Review of *Method in Ecumenical Theology: The Lessons So Far*, by Gillian R. Evans. *Scottish Journal of Theology* 52.3 (1999) 401–2.

Review of *Methodists in Dialog*, edited by Geoffrey Wainwright. *Ecumenical Review* 51.2 (April 1999) 224–27.

Review of *Models of the Church*, by Avery Dulles. *Philosophical Studies* 27 (1980) 348–51.

Review of *The Modern Theologians*, edited by David F. Ford. *Modern Believing* 39.2 (April 1998) 38-40.

Review of *Mysticism in the Wesleyan Tradition*, by Robert G. Tuttle Jr. *Proceedings of the Wesley Historical Society* 48.3 (October 1991) 103.

Review of *Natural Law and Toleration in the Early Enlightenment*, edited by Jon Parkin and Timothy Stanton. *Enlightenment and Dissent* 29 (2014) 150-54.

Review of *New Dictionary of Christian Ethics and Pastoral* Theology, edited by David J. Atkinson et al. *Modern Believing* 37.1 (January 1996) 61-62.

Review of *New Essays in the Philosophy of Education*, by Glenn Langford and D. J. O'Connor. *Philosophical Studies* 12 (1974) 301-4.

Review of *A New Handbook of Christian Theology*, edited by Donald W. Musser and Joseph L. Price. *Irish Theological Quarterly* 53.4 (1998) 403-4.

Review of *New Perspectives on Old-Time Religion*, by George Schlesinger. *Critical Review of Books in Religion* 3 (1990) 398-400.

Review of *Nonconformist Communion Plate and Vessela*, by Christopher Stell. *Friends of the Congregational Library* 3.3 (Spring 2009) 1-2.

Review of *Nonconformity's Romantic Generation: Evangelical and Liberal Theologies in Victorian England*, by Mark Hopkins. *Journal of Ecclesiastical History* 57.4 (October 2006) 791-92.

Review of *Oliver Quick and the Quest for a Christian Metaphysic*, by Alexander J. Hughes. *Modern Believing* 57.2 (2016) 191-93.

Review of *On Being the Church: Essays on the Christian Community*, edited by Colin E. Gunton and Daniel Hardy. *Ecumenical Review* 41.4 (October 1989) 626-29.

Review of *On Religious Freedom*, by Jay Newman. *Modern Churchman* 34.2 (1992) 49-50.

Review of *On the Nature and Existence of God*, by Richard M. Gale. *International Journal of Philosophical Studies* 1.1 (March 1993) 143-46.

Review of *Origin: The Bible and Philosophy in the Third Century*, by Joseph W. Trigg. *Philosophical Studies* 32 (1988-90) 370-71.

Review of *Our Natural Knowledge of God*, by Ned Wisnefske. *Modern Churchman* 34.5 (1993) 143-44.

Review of *Oxford Dictionary of the Christian Church* (3rd ed.), edited by Elizabeth A. Livingstone. *Faith and Freedom* 50.2 (Autumn-Winter 1997) 156-57.

Review of *The Oxford Movement in Context*, by Peter B. Nockles. *Enlightenment and Dissent* 15 (1996) 128-30.

Review of *Particular Baptists in Victorian England*, by Geoffrey R. Breed. *Baptist Quarterly* 40.8 (October 2004) 500-501.

Review of *The Personal Life of the Christian*, by A.W. Robinson. *Reform* (September 1981) 25.

Review of *The Philadelphia Baptist Tradition and Church Authority, 1707-1814: An Ecumenical Analysis and Theological Interpretation*, by Francis W. Sacks. *Calvin Theological Journal* 26.1 (April 1991) 227-31.

Review of *Philip Schaff: Christian Scholar and Ecumenical Prophet*, by George Shriver. *Ecumenical Review* 41.1 (January 1989) 141-42.

Review of *Philip Schaff: Historian and Ambassador of the Universal Church*, by Klaus Penzel. *Scottish Journal of Theology* 49.2 (1996) 257-58.

Review of *The Philosophical Frontiers of Christian Theology: Essays Presented to D. M. MacKinnon*, edited by Brian Hebblethwaite and Stewart Sutherland. *Philosophical Studies* 30 (1984) 357–62.

Review of *Philosophy and Religion in Enlightenment Britain*, edited by Ruth Savage. *Enlightenment and Dissent* 28 (2012) 221–34.

Review of *Philosophy for Understanding Theology*, by Diogenes Allen. *Faith and Freedom* 44.3 (Autumn 1991) 140–41.

Review of *Philosophy, History and Civilization*, edited by David Boucher et al. *International Journal of Philosophical Studies* 6.2 (June 1998) 302–4.

Review of *The Philosophy of Education*, edited by Richard Stanley Peters. *Philosophical Studies* 23 (1975) 255–60.

Review of *Philosophy, Religion and Science in the 17th and 18th Centuries*, edited by John W. Yolton. *International Journal of Philosophical Studies* 7.2 (June 1999) 279–80.

Review of *Picking up a Pin for the Lord: English Particular Baptists from 1688 to the Early Nineteenth Century*, by Peter Naylor. *Baptist Quarterly* 35.5 (January 1994) 257–58.

Review of *Political Writings*, edited and translated by David Wootton. *British Journal for Eighteenth-Century Studies* 19.1 (Spring 1996) 93–94.

Review of *Postmodern Theologies*, by Terrence W. Tilley et al. *Heythrop Journal* 39.4 (October 1998) 470–71.

Review of *Post-Reformation Reformed Dogmatics: The Rise and Development of Reformed Orthodoxy, ca. 1520 to ca. 1725*, by Richard A. Muller. 4 vols. *Reformed Review* 42.2 (Winter 1988) 174–75.

Review of *Practical Ethics*, by Thomas Reid, edited by Knud Haakonssen. *British Journal of Eighteenth-Century Studies* 15.1 (Spring 1992) 89–90.

Review of *The Presbyterian Predicament: Six Perspectives*, edited by Milton J. Coalter et al. *Reformed Review* 65.1 (Autumn 1991) 70.

Review of *The Principles of the Most Ancient and Modern Philosophy*, by Anne Conway. *Philosophical Studies* 30 (1984) 327–28.

Review of *Probing the Foundations: A Study in Theistic Reconstruction*, by David A. Pailin. *Calvin Theological Journal* 33.1 (April 1998) 215–16.

Review of *The Problem of Evil and the Problem of God*, by D. Z. Phillips. *Anvil* 22.3 (2005) 237–38.

Review of *Protestant Worship: Traditions in Transition*, by James F. White. *National Bulletin on Liturgy* 23.123 (December 1990) 253–55.

Review of *Pulpit, Table, and Song: Essays in Celebration of Howard G. Hageman*, edited by Edward C. Zaragoza and Heather Murray Elkins. *JURCHS* 6.5 (November 1999) 379.

Review of *Puritan Christianity in America*, by Allen Carden. *Reformed Review* 44.3 (Spring 1991) 263.

Review of *The Quest for Eternity: An Outline of the Philosophy of Religion*, by J. C. A. Gaskin. *Philosophical Studies* 31 (1986–87) 400–401.

Review of *Radical Christian Voices and Practice*, edited by Zoe Bennett and David B. Gowler. *The Journal of Theological Studies* 65.1 (April 2014) 378–82.

Review of *A Radical Hegelian: The Political and Social Philosophy of Henry Jones*, by David Boucher and Andrew Vincent. *British Journal for History of Philosophy* 3.1 (February 1995) 201–4.

Review of *Ramism in William Perkins' Theology*, by Donald K. McKim. *Evangelical Quarterly* 64.1 (1992) 81–82.
Review of *Readings in Christian Ethics: A Historical Sourcebook*, edited by J. Philip Wogaman and Douglas M. Strong. *Modern Believing* 40.3 (1999) 77–78.
Review of *Reason and Religious Belief*, by Michael L. Peterson et al. *Philosophical Studies* 33 (1991–92) 401–2.
Review of *Reason, Grace and Sentiment, Vol. 2: Shaftesbury to Hume: A Study of the Language of Religion and Ethics in England, 1660–1780*, by Isabel Rivers. *Epworth Review* 27.4 (October 2000) 77–79.
Review of *Reasonable Enthusiast: John Wesley and the Rise of Methodism*, by Henry D. Rack. *Baptist Quarterly* 33.8 (October 1990) 396–97.
Review of *Reasonable Faith*, by Winfried Corduan. *Calvin Theological Journal* 32.1 (April 1997) 177–78.
Review of *Recognition: Advancing Ecumenical Thinking*, by Gerard Kelly. *Ecumenical Review* 51.3 (July 1999) 315–17.
Review of *Reformed Confessionalism in Nineteenth- Century America*, edited by Sam Hamstra Jr. and Arie J. Griffioen. *JURCHS* 6.1 (October 1997) 61–63.
Review of *Reformed Theology: Identity and Ecumenicity*, edited by Wallace M. Alston Jr. and Michael Welker. *Theology* 107 (September/October 2004) 376–77.
Review of *Reformed Theology in America*, edited by David F. Wells. *Reformed World* 39.6 (June 1987) 738–39.
Review of *Reformed Thought and Scholasticism*, by John Platt. *Philosophical Studies* 31 (1986–87) 429–32.
Review of *The Relevance of Natural Science to Theology*, by William H. Austin. *Philosophical Studies* 25 (1977) 378–79.
Review of *Religion and Imagination*, by John Coulson. *Philosophical Studies* 29 (1983) 300–303.
Review of *"Religion" and the Religions in the English Enlightenment*, by Peter Harrison. *British Journal for Eighteenth-Century Studies* 16.1 (Spring 1993) 145–46.
Review of *The Religion of the Heart*, by Ted A. Campbell. *Baptist Quarterly* 35.5 (January 1994) 256–57.
Review of *Religion, Politics and Dissent 1660–1832*, edited by Robert D. Cornwall and William Gibson. *Journal of Ecclesiastical History* 62.1 (January 2011) 189–90.
Review of *Religious Belief: The Contemporary Debate*, by William Sweet. *International Journal of Philosophical Studies* 12.2 (2004) 228–29.
Review of *Religious Life and the Poor*, edited by Alejandro Cussiánovich. *Philosophical Studies* 29 (1983) 381–83.
Review of *Reluctant Saint? A Theological Biography of Fletcher of Madeley*, by Patrick Streiff. *Modern Believing* 43.2 (April 2002) 54–56.
Review of *The Rise and Decline of Anglican Idealism in the Nineteenth Century*, by Timothy Maxwell Gouldstone. *British Journal for the History of Philosophy* 13.4 (2005) 811–15.
Review of *Science, Reason and Religion*, by Derek Stanesby. *Religious Studies and Theology* 7.3 (1988) 49–51.
Review of *The Scottish Congregational Ministry 1794–1993*, by William D. McNaughton. *JURCHS* 5.5 (November 1994) 303–4.
Review of *Scottish Theology from John Knox to John McLeod Campbell*, by Thomas F. Torrance. *Heythrop Journal* 39.1 (January 1998) 84–85.

Review of *Secularizing the Faith in Canada: The Protestant Clergy and the Crisis of Belief 1850-1930*, by David B. Marshall. *Literary Review of Canada* 1.9 (September 1992) 11-12.

Review of *So Rich a Soil: John McLeod Campbell on Christian Atonement*, by George M. Tuttle. *Irish Theological Quarterly* 54 (1988) 66-71.

Review of *The Shaping of American Congregationalism, 1620-1957*, by John Von Rohr. *Congregational History Circle Magazine* 3.5 (Spring 1997) 50-52.

Review of *Should a Christian Support Guerillas?*, by Richard Harries. *Reform* (July-August 1982) 27.

Review of *The Social Uplifters: Presbyterian Progressives and the Social Gospel in Canada 1875-1915*, by Brian J. Fraser. *Studies in Religion* 18.4 (1989) 495-96.

Review of *Sources for the History of English Nonconformity 1660-1830*, by Michael Mullett. *Proceedings of the Huguenot Society* 25.5 (1993) 518.

Review of *Speculative Theology and Common-Sense Religion: Mercersburg and the Conservative Roots of American Religion* by Linden J. DeBie. *The New Mercersburg Review* 40 (Spring 2009) 52-56.

Review of *Spinoza*, by R. J. Delahunty. *Philosophical Studies* 32 (1988-90) 299-301.

Review of *Spires and Meeting Houses*, by Mark Hopkins. *Friends of the Congregational Library Newsletter* 4.2 (Spring 2012) 6-8.

Review of *Spiritual Pilgrim: A Reassessment of the Life of the Countess of Huntingdon*, by Edwin Welch. *Welsh History Review* 18.1 (1996) 164-65.

Review of *Spirituality in Adversity*, by Raymond Brown. *Bunyan Studies* 17 (2013) 162-67; *Friends of the Congregational Library Newsletter* 4.5 (Spring 2013) 4-6; *Welsh Journal of Religious History* 7.8 (2013) 232-37.

Review of *Subverting the System: D'Aubigné and Calvinism*, by Catharine Randall Coats. *Reformed Review* 53.2 (1999-2000) 161.

Review of *Talking About Welfare: Readings in Philosophy and Social Policy*, edited by Noel Timms and David Watson. *Philosophical Studies* 25 (1977) 358-60.

Review of *Taunton Dissenting Academy*, by Brian Kirk. *JURCHS* 8.1 (January 2008) 64.

Review of *Telling Another Generation*, edited by Michael Plant and Alan Tovey. *Reformed Quarterly* NS 2.2 (Autumn 1994) 14.

Review of *Themes in Theology: The Three-fold Cord: Essays in Philosophy, Politics, and Theology*, by Donald M. MacKinnon. *King's Theological Review* 11.2 (Autumn 1988) 71-72.

Review of *Theology and Integration: Four Essays in Philosophical Theology*, by Anders Jeffner. *Faith and Philosophy* 9.3 (July 1992) 400-402.

Review of *A Theology for Artisans of a New Humanity*, by Juan Luis Segundo. *Philosophical Studies* 28 (1981) 270-73.

Review of *Theology for Pew and Pulpit*, by Joseph A. Bassett. *Epworth Review* 24.1 (January 1997) 126-27.

Review of *Theology of the Reformers*, by Timothy George. *Mid-Stream* 28.1 (January 1989) 142-44.

Review of *Theology through the Theologians*, by Colin E. Gunton. *Scottish Journal of Theology* 52.2 (2000) 262-64.

Review of *Thinking Matter: Materialism in Eighteenth-Century Britain*, edited by John W. Yolton. *Philosophical Studies* 31 (1986-1987) 438-39.

Review of *Thinking the Faith: Christian Theology in a North American Context*, by Douglas John Hall. *Reformed Review* 43.3 (Spring 1990) 233.

Review of *Thomas Chalmers: Enthusiast for Mission*, by John Roxborough. *Evangelical Quarterly* 74.3 (July 2002) 287–88.
Review of *Thomism in John Owen*, by Christopher Cleveland. *JURCHS* 9.3 (November 2013) 202–4.
Review of *To Confess the Faith Today*, edited by Jack L. Stotts and Jane Dempsey Douglass. *Reformed Review* 45.1 (Autumn 1991) 72–73.
Review of *Torches Rekindled: The Bruderhof's Struggle for Renewal*, by Merrill Mow. *Journal of Mennonite Studies* 8 (1990) 223–34.
Review of *The Transformation of Congregationalism, 1900-2000*, by Alan Argent. *Faith and Freedom* 67 1 (Spring/Summer 2014) 52–54.
Review of *The Transformation of Congregationalism, 1900-2000*, by Alan Argent. *JURCHS* 9.5 (October 2014) 330–36.
Review of *The Transformation of New England Theology*, by Robert C. Whittemore. *Evangelical Quarterly* 61.4 (1989) 366–68.
Review of *The Trinitarian Theology of Dr. Samuel Clarke*, by Thomas C. Pfizenmaier. *Enlightenment and Dissent* 18 (1999) 270–75.
Review of *Truth, Liberty and Religion: Essays Celebrating Two Hundred Years of Manchester College*, edited by Barbara Smith. *JURCHS* 4.5 (October 1989) 339–40.
Review of *The Turn to Experience in Contemporary Theology*, by Donald L. Gelpi. *Heythrop Journal* 38.3 (July 1997) 327–28.
Review of *Twentieth-Century Western Philosophy of Religion 1900-2000*, by Eugene Thomas Long. *Philosophical Books* 63.1 (January 2002) 74–76.
Review of *The Two Intellectual Worlds of John Locke*, edited by John W. Yolton. *The Scriblerian* 39.1 (Autumn 2006) 82–83.
Review of *Under God's Good Hand*, by David Cornick. *Congregational History Circle Magazine* 4.1 (Spring 1999) 71–74.
Review of *Understanding the Atonement for the Mission of the Church*, by John Driver. *Irish Theological Quarterly* 57.1 (1991) 82–84.
Review of *Unitarian to the Core*, edited by Leonard Smith. *Faith and Freedom* 57.2 (Autumn/Winter 2005) 175–79.
Review of *The Unitarians: A Short History*, edited by Leonard Smith. *Transactions of the Unitarian History Society* 24.1 (April 2007) 44–46.
Review of *Universes*, by John Leslie. *Studies in Religion* 20.2 (1991) 240–41.
Review of *What are They Saying about Papal Primacy?*, J. Michael Miller. *Reformed Review* 38 (1984) 91.
Review of *What Can God Do?*, by Fredrick Sontag. *Reformed Review* 33.3 (1980) 188.
Review of *What Did the First Christians Believe?*, by Leslie Houlden. *Reform* (July–August 1982) 27.
Review of *What the British Found When they Discovered the French Vaudois in the Nineteenth Century*, by W. S. F. Pickering. *Proceedings of the Huguenot Society* 26.5 (1997) 683–84.
Review of *Who is Jesus?*, by J. Beer. *Reform* (July–August 1982) 27.
Review of *Why Bother with Adam and Eve?*, by Henry McKeating. *Reform* (July–August 1982) 27.
Review of *Word and Church: Essays in Christian Dogmatics*, by John Webster. *International Journal of Systematic Theology* 5.3 (November 2003) 332–37.
Review of *Worldly Saints: The Puritans as They Really Were*, by Leland Ryken. *Reformed Review* 42.2 (Winter 1988) 177–78.

Review of *William Brewster, "The Father of New England": His Life and Times 1567–1644*, by Harold Kirk-Smith. *Evangelical Quarterly* 66.4 (1994) 358–59.

Review of *Wittgenstein and Religious Belief*, by Donald Hudson. *Philosophical Studies* (1977) 390–92.

Review of *You Are My Witnesses: The Waldensians Across 800 Years*, by Giorgio Tourn et al. *JURCHS* 4.7 (October 1990) 455–56.

B. THE WRITINGS OF ALAN SELL PRESENTED THEMATICALLY

1. Christian Doctrine and Theology
GOF; *COS*; *SOL*; *RM*; *GD*; *ACI* (chapter 2); *COM* (chapters 1, 7, 11, 13); *TNM* (chapter 9); *TAT* (chapters 1, 3, 7, 8, 10, 13); *EEE* (chapters 5, 6, 12, 13); *NT*; *HT*; *PHT* (Part 3); *CTF* (chapter 10, 11); *TEM* (chapter 4); *CAM*.

2. Philosophy and Ethics
RM; *TIT*; *PR*; *ACI* (chapters 1, 3, 6); *DTLC* (chapters 2, 3, 4, 8, 15, 18, 19); *COM* (chapter 10); *MAR*; *PDN*; *MOG*; *TAT* (chapters 1, 9); *EEE* (chapters 3, 7); *FPA*; *CCC*; *PHT* (Part 1); *TEM* (chapters 3, 5).

3. Apologetics
DAD; *PICB*; *JL*; *CCF*; *CTF* (chapters 4, 5, 6).

4. Studies in English and Welsh Dissent and Nonconformity
(reserving the Establishment question to ecclesiology under "Ecumenism" below)
SVOC; *CAM*; *AD*; *RM*; *CP*; *DTLC* (chapters 1, 5, 6, 7, 9, 10, 11, 12, 13, 14, 16, 17, 19); *COM* (chapters 3, 6, 8, 9, 12); *PN* (chapter 2); *PDN*; *TAT* (chapters 2, 4, 5, 6); *EEE* (chapters 1, 2, 4, 5); *NT*; *HT*; *BIC* (chapter 1); *CAC*; *PHT* (Part 2); *CTF* (chapters 2, 3); *TEM* (chapters 1, 6, 7, 8).

5. Ecumenism, Ecclesiology and Reformed Tradition
SVOC; *RECT*; *ACI* (chapters 4, 5); *DTLC* (chapters 20, 21, 22); *COM* (chapters 2, 4, 5, 14); *TAT* (chapters 10, 11); *EEE* (chapters 9, 10, 11); *BPS*; *HT*; *NT* (chapter 3); *GE* (Part 2); *CTF* (chapters 1, 7, 8, 9); *OMMM*.

C. WORKS CONSULTED IN WRITING THIS BOOK

Anderson, Arnold A. *The Book of Psalms, Vol. 2*. London: Marshall, Morgan & Scott, 1972.

Anselm of Canterbury. *St. Anselm: Basic Writings*. Translated by S. W. Deane. La Salle, IL: Open Court, 1962.

Argent, Alan. *The Transformation of Congregationalism 1900-2000*. Nottingham: Congregational Federation, 2013.

Avis, Paul. "Establishment and the Mission of a National Church." *Theology* 103 (January–February 2000) 3–12.

Bibliographies

Baillie, D. M. *God Was in Christ: An Essay on Incarnation and Atonement*. London: Faber & Faber, 1956.

Barr, James. "Abba Isn't Daddy!" *Journal of Theological Studies* 39 (1988) 28–47.

———. *The Bible in the Modern World: The Croall Lectures Given in New College, Edinburgh in November 1970*. London: SCM, 1973.

Barth, Karl. *Church Dogmatics*. Vol. IV, 1. Edinburgh: T. & T. Clark, 1956.

———. *Church Dogmatics*. Vol. IV, 4. Edinburgh: T. & T. Clark, 1969.

Bauman, Zygmunt. *Liquid Modernity*. 2nd ed. Cambridge: Polity, 2013.

Bebbington, David, et al., eds. *Protestant Nonconformist Texts, Vol. 3: The Nineteenth Century*. Reprint. Eugene, OR: Wipf & Stock, 2015.

Berger, Peter L. *A Rumour of Angels: Modern Society and The Rediscovery of the Supernatural*. Harmondsworth: Penguin, 1970.

Berry, Thomas. "The Spirituality of the Earth." In *Liberating Life: Contemporary Approaches to Ecological Theology*, edited by Charles Birch et al., 151–58. Maryknoll: Orbis, 1990.

Bettenson, Henry. *Documents of the Christian Church*. 2nd ed. London: Oxford University Press, 1963.

Binfield, Clyde. "Geoffrey Fillingham Nuttall 1911–2007." *Biographical Memoirs of Fellows of the British Academy* 14 (2015) 441–65.

———. "P.T. Forsyth As Congregational Minister." In *Justice the True and Only Mercy*, edited by Trevor A. Hart, 168–96. Edinburgh: T. & T. Clark, 1995.

Birch, Charles, et al., eds. *Liberating Life: Contemporary Approaches to Ecological Theology*. Maryknoll: Orbis, 1990.

Bonhoeffer, Dietrich. *Letters and Papers from Prison*. Enlarged edition. London: SCM, 1971.

Bosch, David J. *Transforming Mission: Paradigm Shifts in the Theology of Mission*. Maryknoll: Orbis, 2001.

Brierley, Michael. Review of *PHT*, by Alan P. F. Sell. *Modern Believing* 56.3 (2015) 399–401.

Brown, R. McAfee. "Discoveries and Dangers." *New Christian*, April 2, 1970.

Bruce, F. F. *The Books and the Parchments: Some Chapters on the Transmission of the Bible*. London: Pickering & Inglis, 1950.

———. *The New Testament Documents*. London: InterVarsity, 1943.

Brueggemann, Walter. *Genesis*. Atlanta: John Knox, 1982.

———. *The Prophetic Imagination*. 2nd ed. Minneapolis: Fortress, 2001.

Bultmann, Rudolf. *Existence and Faith: Shorter Writings of Rudolf Bultmann*. Selected, translated, and introduced by Schubert M. Ogden. London: Hodder & Stoughton, 1961.

———. *The History of the Synoptic Tradition*. Oxford: Blackwell, 1963.

———. "The Idea of God and Modern Man." In *Translating Theology into the Modern Age, Journal for Theology and the Church, Vol. 2*, translated by Robert W. Funk, 83–95. New York: Harper & Row, 1965.

———. *New Testament and Mythology and Other Basic Writings*. Selected, edited, and translated by Schubert M. Ogden. London: SCM, 1985.

Burrell, David B. *Aquinas, God and Action*. Notre Dame: University of Notre Dame Press, 1979.

———. Review of *The Reality of God*, by Schubert M. Ogden. *Theological Studies* 3.28 (6 September 1967) 605–9.

Calvin, John. *Institutes of the Christian Religion*. Edited by John T. McNeill. Translated and indexed by Ford Lewis Battles. Philadelphia: Westminster, 1960.

Campbell, John McLeod. *The Nature of Atonement*. Cambridge: Macmillan, 1956.

Camroux, Martin. *Ecumenism in Retreat: How the United Reformed Church Failed to Break the Mould*. Eugene OR: Wipf & Stock, 2016.

Carr, Wesley. "A Developing Establishment." *Theology* 103 (January–February 1999) 2–10.

Carter, David. Review of *JL*, by Alan P. F. Sell. *Epworth Review* 26.2 (April 1999) 122–23.

Chapman, Mark. Review of *Justice the True and Only Mercy: Essays on the Life and Theology of Peter Taylor Forsyth*, edited by Trevor A. Hart. *Modern Believing* 36.4 (October 1995) 57–58.

Clements, Keith. *Lovers of Discord: Twentieth Century Theological Controversies in England*. London: SPCK, 1988.

Cobb, John B., Jr., and David Ray Griffin. *Process Theology: An Introductory Exposition*. Belfast: Christian Journals, 1977.

Cornick, David E. "P. T. Forsyth's Doctrine of the Church." In *P. T. Forsyth: Theologian for a New Millennium*, edited by Alan P. F. Sell, 153–70. London: United Reformed Church, 1999.

Cranfield, C. E. B. *The Apostles' Creed: A Faith to Live By*. Edinburgh: T. & T. Clark, 1993.

———. *The Gospel According to Saint Mark: An Introduction and Commentary*. Cambridge Greek Testament Commentary. Cambridge: Cambridge University Press, 1959.

Cunliffe-Jones, Hubert. *Christian Theology Since 1600*. London: Duckworth, 1970.

Curtin, Maurice. "Process Philosophy and its Metaphysical Implication." *The Irish Theological Quarterly* 44 (1977) 232–42.

Davidson, Ann J. *The Autobiography and Diary of Samuel Davidson*. Edinburgh: T. & T. Clark, 1899.

Davie, Grace. *Religion in Britain Since 1945: Believing without Belonging*. Oxford: Blackwell, 1994.

Denny, James. *The Christian Doctrine of Reconciliation*. London: Hodder & Stoughton, 1917.

———. *Jesus and the Gospel*. London: Hodder & Stoughton, 1909.

Dillistone, F. W. *The Christian Understanding of Atonement*. 2nd ed. London: SCM, 1984.

Dunn, James D. G. *The Theology of Paul the Apostle*. London: T. & T. Clark, 1998.

Edwards, David L. *Not Angels but Anglicans*. London: SCM, 1958.

———. Review of *CCF*, by Alan P. F. Sell. *Theology* 106.832 (July–August 2003) 286–88.

Evans, C. F. *Saint Luke*. Reprint. London: SCM, 1990.

Fabricius, Kim. Review of *CTF*, by Alan P. F. Sell. *JURCHS* 9.6 (May 2015) 383–85.

Fiddes, Paul S. *Past Event and Present Salvation: The Christian Idea of Atonement*. London: Darton, Longman & Todd, 1989.

Floyd, Richard L. "The Work of Christ in the Thought of P. T. Forsyth, Kenosis and Plerosis Revisited." In *P. T. Forsyth: Theologian for a New Millennium*, edited by Alan P. F. Sell, 131–52. London: United Reformed Church, 1999.

Ford, Lewis S., ed. *Two Process Philosophers: Hartshorne's Encounter with Whitehead*. Tallahassee: American Academy of Religion, 1973.

Forsyth, Peter T. *The Cruciality of the Cross*. 2nd ed. London: Independent, 1948.

―――. *Faith, Freedom and the Future*. Reprint. London: Independent, 1955.
―――. "A Holy Church, the Moral Guide to Society." In *The Church, the Gospel and Society*, 5–64. Reprint. London: Independent, 1962.
―――. *The Justification of God: Lectures for War-Time on a Christian Theodicy*. London: Independent, 1948.
―――. *Lectures on the Church and Sacraments*. London: Longmans, Green & Co., 1917.
―――. *The Person and Place of Jesus Christ*. London: Hodder & Stoughton, 1910.
―――. *Positive Preaching and the Modern Mind*. London: Independent, 1907.
―――. *The Principal of Authority*. Reprint. London: Independent, 1952.
―――. *Rome, Reform and Reaction: Four Lectures on the Religious Situation*. London: Hodder & Stoughton, 1899.
―――. *Theology in Church and State*. London: Hodder & Stoughton, 1915.
―――. *The Work of Christ*. Reprint. London: Independent, 1938.
Franks, Robert S. *The Atonement: The Dale Lectures for 1933*. London: Oxford University Press, 1934.
Fraser, Giles. "Loose Canon." *The Guardian*, January 31, 2015.
―――. "Loose Canon." *The Guardian*, September 8, 2017.
Frei, Hans W. *Types of Christian Theology*. Edited by George Hungsinger and William C. Placher. New Haven: Yale University Press, 1992.
Garvie, Alfred E. *The Christian Belief in God*. London: Hodder & Stoughton, 1932.
―――. *The Christian Certainty and the Modern Perplexity*. London: Hodder & Stoughton, 1910.
―――. *The Christian Doctrine of the Godhead*. London: Hodder & Stoughton, 1925.
―――. *The Christian Ideal for Human Society*. London: Hodder & Stoughton, 1930.
―――. "The Limits of Doctrinal Restatement." In *Volume of Proceedings of the Third International Congregational Council*, 90–98. London: Congregational Union of England and Wales, 1908.
―――. "Placarding the Cross." *The Congregational Quarterly* 21 (October 1943) 343–52.
Gilkey, Langdon B. "A Theology in Process: Schubert Ogden's Developing Theology." *Interpretation* 21 (1967) 447–59.
Green, Michael, ed. *The Truth of God Incarnate*. London: Hodder & Stoughton, 1977.
Groves, Peter. "Atonement." *Theology* 104.817 (January/February 2001) 26–33.
Gunton, Colin E. *The Actuality of Atonement: A Study of Metaphor, Rationality and the Christian Tradition*. Edinburgh: T. & T. Clark, 1988.
―――. *Becoming and Being: The Doctrine of God in Charles Hartshorne and Karl Barth*. Oxford: Oxford University Press, 1978.
―――. *Christ and Creation*. The Didsbury Lectures, 1990. Carlisle: Paternoster, 1992.
―――. *Enlightenment and Alienation: An Essay towards a Trinitarian Theology*. Basingstoke: Marshall, Morgan & Scott, 1985.
―――. *Father, Son and Holy Spirit: Towards a Fully Trinitarian Theology*. London: T. & T. Clark, 2003.
―――. *The One, the Three and the Many: God, Creation and Culture of Modernity*. Bampton Lectures, 1992. Cambridge: Cambridge University Press, 1993.
―――. "Process Theology: A Reply." *Expository Times* 85.7 (April 1974) 215.
―――. "Process Theology's Concept of God: An Outline and Assessment." *Expository Times* 84.10 (July 1973) 292–96.

———. *The Promise of Trinitarian Theology*. 2nd ed. Edinburgh: T. & T. Clark, 1997.
———. "The Real as Redemptive: Forsyth on Authority and Freedom." In *Justice the True and Only Mercy*, edited by Trevor A. Hart, 37–58. Edinburgh: T. & T. Clark, 1995.
Guttierrez, Gustavo. *A Theology of Liberation: History, Politics and Salvation*. Maryknoll: Orbis, 1973.
Habgood, John. *Church and Nation in a Secular Age*. London: Darton, Longman & Todd, 1983.
Hampson, Daphne. *Theology and Feminism*. Oxford: Blackwell, 1990.
Hardy, Daniel W., and Colin E. Gunton, eds. *On Being the Church: Essays on the Christian Community*. Edinburgh: T. & T. Clark, 1989.
Harrison, Ted. *The Durham Phenomenon*. London: Darton, Longman & Todd, 1985.
Hart, D. G. "Post-modern Evangelical Worship." *Calvin Theological Journal* 30.2 (November 1995) 451–59.
Hart, Trevor A., ed. *Justice the True and Only Mercy*. Edinburgh: T. & T. Clark, 1995.
———. Review of *SVOC*, by Alan P. F. Sell. *Evangelical Quarterly* 59.4 (October 1987) 262–63.
Hartshorne, Charles. *Creative Synthesis and Philosophic Method*. London: SCM, 1970.
———. *The Divine Relativity*. New Haven: Yale University Press, 1948.
———. *The Logic of Perfection*. La Salle, IL: Open Court, 1962.
———. *Man's Vision of God and the Logic of Theism*. Hamden, CT: Archon, 1964.
———. *A Natural Theology For Our Time*. La Salle, IL: Open Court, 1967.
———. *Omnipotence and Other Theological Mistakes*. Albany: State University of New York Press, 1984.
———. *Reality As Social Process: Studies in Metaphysics and Religion*. New York: Hafner, 1971.
Harvey, A. E., ed. *God Incarnate: Story and Belief*. London: SPCK, 1981.
Harvey, Van A. *The Historian and the Believer*. London: SCM, 1967.
Hick, John. *Death and Eternal Life*. London: Collins, 1976.
———. *Evil and the God of Love*. London: Macmillan, 1966.
Hick, John, ed. *The Myth of God Incarnate*. London: SCM, 1977.
Hick, John, and Paul F. Knitter, eds. *The Myth of Christian Uniqueness*. London: SCM, 1987.
Hilton, Donald H. *Table Talk: Looking at the Communion Table from the Outside and Inside*. London: United Reformed Church, 1998.
Hughes, T. Hywel. "Dr. Forsyth's View of the Atonement." *Congregational Quarterly* 28 (January 1940) 30–37.
Jamison, Trevor. Review of *CTF*, by Alan P. F. Sell. *Reform* (March 2014) 34.
Jenkins, Daniel T. *The Nature of Catholicity*. London: Faber & Faber, 1942.
Jenkins, David E. *The Glory of Man*. London: SCM, 1967
———. *God, Miracle and the Church of England*. London: SCM, 1987.
Jeremias, Joachim. *The Prayers of Jesus*. London: SCM, 1967.
Jones, R. Tudur, et al., eds. *Protestant Nonconformist Texts, Volume 1: 1550–1700*. Reprint. Eugene, OR: Wipf & Stock, 2015.
Kelly, J. N. D. *Early Christian Creeds*. 2nd ed. London: Longmans, Green & Co., 1960.
Kendal, Gordon. Review of *PICB*, by Alan P. F. Sell. *Journal of Theological Studies* 47.2 (October 1996) 770–77.
Küng, Hans. *Christianity: Its Essence and History*. London: SCM, 1995.

Lessing, Georg E. *Theological Writings*. Edited and translated by Henry Chadwick. London: Black, 1956.
Lindbeck, George. *The Nature of Doctrine: Religion and Theology in a Postliberal Age*. London: SPCK, 1984.
Loades, Ann. "Sacramentality and Spirituality." In *The New SCM Dictionary of Christian Spirituality*, edited by Philip Sheldrake, 553–55. London: SCM, 2005.
Locke, John. "A Second Vindication of the Reasonableness in Christianity." In *The Works of John Locke, Vol. 7*, 191–424. London: Otridge, Leigh & Sotheby, 1812.
Long, Arthur. Review of *ACI*, by Alan P. F. Sell. *Faith and Freedom* 45.1–2 (Spring/Summer 1992) 65–68.
———. Review of *RECT*, by Alan P. F. Sell. *Faith and Freedom* 46 (Part 1) 136 (1993) 68–69.
Macfadyen, Dugald. *Constructive Congregational Ideals*. London: Allenson, 1902.
Macquarrie, John. *Jesus Christ in Modern Thought*. London: SCM, 1990.
———. *The Principles of Christian Theology*. London: SCM, 1966.
Manning, Bernard Lord. *Essays in Orthodox Dissent*. London, Independent, 1939.
Marsh, John M. *A Particular Church of Christ at Worcester*. Worcester: Worcester United Reformed Church, 1987.
Matthews, E. Gwyn. Review of PICB. In *Efrydiau Athronyddel* 60 (1997) 95–98.
McGrath, Alister E. *Christian Theology: An Introduction*. Oxford: Blackwell, 1994.
McGrath, Alister E., ed. *The Christian Theology Reader*. Oxford: Blackwell, 1995.
Moberly, R. C. *Atonement and Personality*. London: John Murray, 1917.
Moltmann, Jürgen. *The Crucified God: The Cross of Christ as the Foundation and Criticism of Christian Theology*. London: SCM, 1974.
———. *God in Creation: An Ecological Doctrine of Creation*. London: SCM, 1985.
———. *The Spirit of Life: A Universal Affirmation*. London: SCM, 1992.
———. *The Trinity and the Kingdom of God: The Doctrine of God*. London, SCM, 1981.
Niebuhr, Reinhold. *The Children of Light and the Children of Darkness: A Vindication of Democracy and a Critique of its Traditional Defenders*. London: Nisbet, 1945.
———. *Moral Man and Immoral Society: A Study in Ethics and Politics*. New York: Scribner's, 1932.
———. *The Nature and Destiny of Man: A Christian Interpretation, Vol. 1: Human Nature*. London: Nisbet, 1941.
Nineham D. E. *Saint Mark*. Harmondsworth: Penguin, 1963.
Norwood, Donald W. Review of *Ecumenical and Eclectic, the Unity of the Church in the Contemporary World: Essays in Honour of Alan P. F. Sell*. Edited by Anna M. Robbins. In *JURCHS* 9.2 (May 2013) 138–40.
Nuttall, Geoffrey F. *The Holy Spirit in Puritan Faith and Experience*. Oxford: Blackwell, 1946.
———. *Visible Saints: The Congregational Way, 1640–1660*. Oxford: Blackwell, 1957.
Ogden, Schubert M. "Christian Theology and Neoclassical Theism." *The Journal of Religion* 9.2 (April 1980) 205–209.
———. "Evil and Belief in God: The Distinctive Relevance of a 'Process Theology.'" *The Perkins School of Theology Journal* 41.4 (Summer 1978) 29–34.
———. *Faith and Freedom: Toward a Theology of Liberation*. Nashville: Abingdon, 1979.

———. "Faith and Secularity." In *God, Secularization and History: Essays in Memory of Ronald Gregor Smith*, edited by Eugene Thomas Long, 26–43. Columbia: University of South Carolina Press, 1974.

———. *Is There Only One True Religion or Are There Many?* Dallas: Southern Methodist University Press, 1992.

———. *On Theology*. San Francisco: Harper & Row, 1986.

———. "On the Trinity." *Theology* 83.692 (March 1980) 97–102.

———. *The Point of Christology*. London: SCM, 1982.

———. *The Reality of God and Other Essays*. New York: Harper & Row, 1963.

———. *To Teach the Truth: Selected Courses and Seminars*. Eugene, OR: Cascade, 2015.

———. *The Understanding of Christian Faith*. Eugene, OR: Cascade, 2010.

Orchard, S. C. Review of *The Nature of the Household of Faith*, by Alan Argent. *JURCHS* 9.2 (May 2013) 134–35.

Orr, James. "The Contribution of the United Presbyterian Church to Religious Thought." In *Memorial of the Jubilee Synod of the United Presbyterian Church*, edited by William Blair, 88–97. Edinburgh: Publications Office, 1897.

Owen, H. P. *The Christian Knowledge of God*. London: Athlone, 1969.

———. *Christian Theism: A Study in Its Basic Principles*. Edinburgh: T. & T. Clark, 1984.

———. *Concepts of Deity*. London: Macmillan, 1971.

———. "Letter." *Theology* 70.569 (November 1967) 513.

———. *Revelation and Existence: A Study in the Theology of Rudolf Bultmann*. Cardiff: University of Wales Press, 1957.

———. Review of *The Reality of God*, by Schubert M. Ogden. *Theology* 70.566 (August 1967) 359–60.

Page, Ruth. Review of *TIT*, by Alan P. F. Sell. *Expository Times* 99.2 (November 1987) 56–57.

Pailin, David A. *The Anthropological Character of Theology: Conditioning Theological Understanding*. Cambridge: Cambridge University Press, 1990.

———. *God and the Processes of Reality: Foundations of a Credible Theism*. London: Routledge, 1989.

———. *Groundwork of Philosophy of Religion*. London: Epworth, 1986.

———. *Probing the Foundations: A Study in Theistic Reconstruction*. Kampen: Pharos, 1994.

Paul, Robert. "P. T. Forsyth: Prophet for the Twentieth Century." In *P. T. Forsyth: The Man, The Preachers' Theologian, Prophet for the 20th Century*, edited by Donald G. Miller et al. Pittsburg: Pickwick, 1981.

Peel, David R. "Alfred Ernest Garvie: Early Scottish Congregationalist Process Theologian?" *King's Theological Review* 12.1 (Spring 1989) 18–22.

———. *Encountering Church*. London: United Reformed Church, 2006.

———. "Is Schubert M. Ogden's 'God' Christian?" In *Journal of Religion* 70.2 (April 1990) 147–66.

———. *Reforming Theology*. London: United Reformed Church, 2002.

Pittenger, Norman. "Letter." *Theology* 70.568 (October 1967) 456–57.

———. *Picturing God*. London: SCM, 1982.

———. "Process Theology." *Expository Times* 85.2 (November 1973) 56–57.

Pope, Robert. "Alan Philip Frederick Sell (15 November 1935—7 February 2016)." *JURCHS* 9 (November 2016) 519–26.

Quick, O. C. *Doctrines of the Creed: Their Basis in Scripture and their Meaning Today.* London: Collins, 1971.

———. *The Gospel of the New World: A Study in the Christian Doctrine of Atonement.* London: Nisbet, 1944.

Rahner, Karl. *Theological Investigations.* Vol 5. London: Darton, Longman & Todd, 1966.

———. *Theological Investigations.* Vol 6. London: Darton, Longman & Todd, 1969.

———. *Theological Investigations.* Vol 14. London: Darton, Longman & Todd, 1976.

———. *Theological Investigations.* Vol 16. London: Darton, Longman & Todd, 1979.

Regan, Tom. "Christianity and Animal Rights: The Challenge and Promise." In *Liberating Life: Contemporary Approaches to Ecological Theology*, edited by Charles Birch et al., 73–87. Maryknoll: Orbis, 1990,

Richmond, James. "God, Time and Process Philosophy." *Theology* 68.539 (May 1965) 234–41.

Robbins, Anna M., ed. *Ecumenical and Eclectic, the Unity of the Church in the Contemporary World: Essays in Honour of Alan P. F. Sell.* Milton Keynes: Paternoster, 2007.

Russell, Stanley H. Review of *P. T. Forsyth: Theologian for a New Millennium*, edited by Alan P. F. Sell. *Epworth Review* 27.2 (April 2000) 95.

Sacks, Jonathan. *Not in God's Name: Confronting Religious Violence.* London: Hodder & Stoughton, 2015.

Schleiermacher, Friedrich. *The Christian Faith.* Edited by H. R. Mackintosh and J. S. Steward. Edinburgh: T. & T. Clark, 1928.

———. *On Religion: Speeches to its Cultured Despisers.* New York: Harper & Row, 1978.

Schumacher E. F. *Small is Beautiful: A Study of Economics as if People Mattered.* London: Blond & Briggs, 1973.

Segundo, Juan L. *A Theology for Artisans of a New Humanity.* 5 vols. Maryknoll: Orbis, 1973.

Sobrino, Jon. *Christology at the Crossroads.* London: SCM, 1978.

Spurgeon C. H. *An All-Round Ministry: Addresses to Ministers and Students.* Reprint. London: Banner of Truth, 1960.

Stewart, Kenneth J. Review of *GE*, edited by Alan P. F. Sell. *Scottish Bulletin of Evangelical Theology* 33.1 (2015) 109–11.

Stewart, M. A. Review of *TAT*, by Alan P. F. Sell. *Friends of the Congregational Library Newsletter* (Spring 2006) 25–26.

Taylor, John H. Review of *SVOC*, by Alan P. F. Sell. *JURCHS* 4.1 (October 1987) 91–92.

Taylor, John H., and Clyde Binfield, eds. *Who They Were In The Reformed Churches of England and Wales, 1901–2000.* Donnington: Tyas, 2007.

Taylor, Vincent. *The Gospel According To St. Mark.* London: Macmillan, 1996.

Thomas, T. A. "The Kenosis Question." In *Evangelical Quarterly* 42 (July–September 1970) 142–51.

Thompson, Colin P. Review of *OMMM*, by Alan P. F. Sell. *JURCHS* 9.9 (November 2016) 566–69.

Thompson, David M. Review of *DTLC*, by Alan P. F. Sell. *JURCHS* 5.8 (May 1996) 504–5.

———. Review of *GE*, edited by Alan P. F. Sell. *Ecclesiology* 9.2 (2013) 263–65.

Thompson, David M., ed. *Stating the Gospel: Formulations and Declarations of Faith from the Heritage of the United Reformed Church.* Edinburgh: T. & T. Clark, 1990.

Thompson, David M., et al., eds. *Protestant Nonconformist Texts, Vol. 4: The Twentieth Century*. Reprint. Eugene, OR: Wipf & Stock, 2015.

Tillich, Paul. *Systematic Theology, Vol. 3*. Chicago: University of Chicago Press, 1963.

Townsend, Henry. *The Claims of the Free Churches*. London: Hodder & Stoughton, 1949.

Townsend, Michael J. Review of *TIT*, by Alan P. F. Sell. *Epworth Review* 14.3 (September 1987) 108.

———. Review of *SVOC*, by Alan P. F. Sell. *Epworth Review* 14.3 (September 1987) 108.

Tracy, David. *The Analogical Imagination: Christian Theology and the Culture of Pluralism*. London: SCM, 1981.

———. *Blessed Rage For Order: The New Pluralism in Theology*. New York: Seabury, 1979.

Turner, John M. Review of *Protestant Nonconformity in the Twentieth Century*, edited by Alan P. F. Sell and Anthony R. Cross. *Epworth Review* 31.4 (October 2004) 88–89.

United Reformed Church. *Rejoice and Sing*. Oxford: Oxford University Press, 1991.

Vermes, Geza. *Jesus in his Jewish Context*. London: SCM, 2003.

———. *Jesus the Jew: A Historian's Reading of the Gospels*. 3rd ed. London: SCM, 2001.

———. *The Religion of Jesus the Jew*. London: SCM, 1993.

von Rad, Gerhard. *Genesis*. London: SCM, 1961.

Ward, Keith. *Divine Action*. London: Flame, 1990.

———. *The Living God*. London: SPCK, 1984.

———. *Rational Theology and the Creativity of God*. Oxford: Blackwell, 1982.

Ward, Pete. *Liquid Church*. Peabody: Hendrickson, 2002.

Watson, Brenda. "To Know Or Not To Know? Re-Assessing Historical Scepticism." *Theology* 103.813 (May/June 2000) 190.

Webster, John. *Holiness*. London: SCM, 2003.

Westermann, Claus. *Creation*. Translated by John J. Scullion. London: SPCK, 1974.

———. *Genesis 1–11*. Translated by John J. Scullion. London: SPCK, 1984.

White, James F. *Protestant Worship: Traditions in Transition*. Louisville: Westminster John Knox, 1989.

Whitehead, A. N. *Process and Reality*. Edited by David Ray Griffin and Donald W. Sherburne. London and New York: Free Press, 1978.

Wiles, Maurice. *God's Action in the World*. London: SCM, 1986.

———. "Theology in the Twenty-First Century." *Theology* 103.816 (November/December 2000) 403–11.

Williams, T. Rhondda. *How I Found my Faith*. London: Cassell, 1938.

Willshaw, Mervyn. Review of *CCF*, by Alan P. F. Sell. *Epworth Review* 30.2 (April 2003) 80–81.

Wiseman, David, ed. *Colleagues*. Self-published, 2007.

General Index

Abelard, Peter, 136-38
Acadia Divinity School, 25
adoption, 208
Allegro, John, 7n25
American Academy of Religion, 21, 27
American Theological Society, 21
Anabaptist/s, 59, 204
analogy, 44, 98
analytic philosophy; *see* philosophy
anamnesis, 214
Anderson, Arnold A., 90
Angel Street Congregational Church, 10, 12-14
Anglican, 195, 197, 201-2, 234
Anselm of Canterbury, 133, 134
antinomianism, 219
apologetics; *see* theology
apostolicity, 39-41
Aquinas, 30, 52, 81-83, 86, 102, 215; *see also* Thomism/Thomist
Argent, Alan, xiii, 14
Aristotle, 52, 101
Arminian/ism, 29, 169, 244
Association of Denominational Historical Societies and Cognate Libraries, 24
atonement, theories of, 80, 131-56
 confession of God's holiness, 142-45
 moral influence, 136-38, 142, 147, 167-68
 penal substitution, 134-36, 138, 144-45, 150
 sacrifice, 131, 134, 137, 139, 141, 144, 148, 150-52
 satisfaction, 133, 139, 142, 148, 150, 151, 152
 vicarious repentance 139-40
 see also Christ
Augustine, 30, 211, 234, 240, 243
Avis, Paul, 200

Baillie, Donald, 166
baptism; *see* sacraments
baptism in the Spirit; *see* Spirit
Baptist, 241
Barne, J., 27
Barr, James, xiin16, 41
Barth, Karl, 31, 33, 52, 111, 112, 208, 255
Barthian/s, 30, 36, 251
Basis of Union; *see* United Reformed Church
Bauman, Zygmunt, 181; *see also* liquid modernity; Ward, Pete
Baxter, Richard, 223, 225
Bell, Donald, 21
Berger, Peter L., 45n62
Berry, Thomas, 109
Bettenson, Henry, 159n13
Bible, 37, 48-50, 61, 81, 157, 161, 206, 237, 242
 biblical, 190, 206, 207
 fundamentalism, 49
 sola scriptura, 50
Binfield, Clyde, xiii, 19n79, 26n124, 31n156, 255
bishops; *see* episcopate

General Index

Brandon, S. G. F., 7n25
Bonhoeffer, Dietrich, 96
Bosch, David, 224
Boyce, Max, 2
Book of Common Prayer, 221
Brierley, Michael, 255
Broadway Congregational/United Reformed Church, 15
Brown, Robert McAfee, 229
Bruce, F. F., 49n86
Brueggemann, Walter, 107-8, 110-11, 155
Brunner, Emil, 112
Bucklow Hill Congregational Church, 8
Bultmann, Rudolf, 43-44, 49, 90, 123, 124
Bunyan, John, 14
Burnham, Anthony G. xiii
Burrell, David B., 81

Calgary McLeod Presbytery, 22
Calvin, John, 13, 30, 33, 46, 65, 111, 133, 134-36, 139n119, 161, 187, 189n98, 203, 209, 211, 215, 220, 240-42, 243
Calvinism, 33, 169, 244
Calvinist/s, 29, 30, 57, 65, 113, 136, 139, 240, 241, 244
Cambridge Platonists, 68, 184
Campbell, John McLeod, 138-41, 143
Campbell, R. J., 68
Camroux, Martin F., xiii, 231
Canadian Theological Society, 21
Carr, Wesley, 200
Carter, David, xi
catholicity; *see* Church
Cave, Sydney, 5
Chalcedon, Council of; *see* Creeds
Chapman, Mark, 150, 152
Charismatic Movement, 212; *see also* Pentecostalism
Christ, Jesus, 122-56
  atoning work, 55, 96, 97, 104, 114, 117-18, 124, 127, 128, 131-56, 208, 209, 247
  crucifixion, 45, 118, 124, 137, 138, 144, 155, 246

  historical knowledge, 38-47
  life and teaching, 149, 152, 252
  lordship, 189, 197-99, 201, 226
  person, 123-31
  resurrection, 44, 62, 119, 124, 125-27, 129
  sinlessness, 130-31, 135, 140
  virgin birth, 129-30
  see also christology; cross
Christ Church Presbyterian Church, 13n54
christology, 47, 103-4, 122, 124-25
  kenotic, 94, 102-4, 119-20, 127
  re-presentative, 70, 149, 152-53, 167-68, 254
Christ the Cornerstone Church, 26
Church, 124, 125-26, 141, 145, 149, 151, 154-55, 157, 175, 176-202
  catholicity, 177, 182, 189, 203, 209, 255
  cell-based, 192
  Church Meeting, 11, 188-94, 210, 219, 225
  continuation of incarnation, 184-6
  councils, 50-51, 159, 189, 219-20
  ecclesiology, 176-237
  Episcopal, 192
  Establishment, 197-202
  Free, 200, 221
  gathered, 177-84, 189, 209, 225, 231
  government, 192
  Independency/Independents, 182, 221
  marks of true, 203-4
  medieval, 194
  priesthood of all believers, 189, 194-7, 216
  primary functions, 220-31
  relation to God's kingdom, 187-88, 230
  sectarianism, 56, 231-37, 255
  see also covenant; worship; mission
church members; *see* saints
Church of England, 197-99, 201; *see also* Anglican; Establishment
Church of Scotland, 197

General Index

children at the Lord's Supper; *see* worship
Clements, Keith, 31n156
Cocks, H. F. Lovell, 46, 196
confessions; *see* Creeds
Congregational Library, Boston, xiii
Congregationalism, 14–15, 150, 176, 177, 178, 182, 188, 192, 193, 196, 254, 255
Congregationalist/s, 31, 32, 180, 223, 224, 241
Connexional, 192
Cook, Graham J., xiii
confirmation; *see* baptism
consubstantiation, 215; *see also* Lord's Supper
conversion, 164–66
Cope, Martin, xiii, 9
Coppleston, F. C., 80
Cornick, David, 252
corporate world, 225–26
councils; *see* Church
covenant, 110, 111, 146, 179, 181, 192, 210, 213, 218; *see also* Church, gathered
Craig, John, 204
Cranfield, C. E. B., 124, 130
Cranleigh Infant School, 3
creation, 68–9, 100–121, 186, 252–53
 creatio ex nihilo, 68–69, 86–91, 100, 102
 stewardship, 107–10
Creed/s, 196
 Calcedon, 52, 127–31
 confessions, 204
 Nicaeno-Constantinopolitan, 159
 subscription, 51–52
Cressey, Martin T., 18
cross, theology of, 38, 45, 62, 118, 122, 187, 208
 scandal of particularity, 42, 47, 70, 148, 168
 see also Christ
Cunliffe-Jones, Hubert, 140
Curtin, Maurice, 80
Czegledy, Sandor, 23

Dale, Robert William, 133, 188

Darwin, Charles, 100; *see also* evolution
Davidson, Samuel, 192–93
Davie, Grace, 193
Deacon, 217, 226
de Burgh, W. G., 184
deism, 101, 252
Denney, James, 125, 128n43
Dent Congregational Church, 2, 9
Dillistone, F. W., 136–7
discipline, 203, 218–20
Dissent, 30, 54, 176, 223, 249
 dissenter/s 29, 226, 242
 see also Congregationalism
divine activity; *see* God
Doctrine, Prayer and Worship Committee; *see* United Reformed Church
Doddridge, Philip, 223, 249
Donald Tract Fund, xiii
Dr. Williams's Library, xiii, 2, 19, 24
 Friends of, 26n117
dualism; *see* philosophy
Dugmore, C. W., 7n25
Dunn, James D. G., 185
Durber, Susan, xiii, 26
Duthie, Charles S., 95

ecclesiology; *see* Church
Ecumenical Movement, 231–32
ecumenism/ecumenical, 29, 177, 183–84, 192, 234
Eddowes, Chris, xiii
Edwards, David L., 200
Elder, 217, 226
election, 93, 178, 240–44
 universalism, 244
Elstow Preparatory School, 3
Emmet, Dorothy, 7n25
empiricism; *see* philosophy
Enlightenment, 37, 56, 139, 192, 242
environmental threat, 107–9
episcopate, historic, 195–97, 234
 bishops, 196, 200
 episcope, 196, 220
 mutual, 14–15
eschatology, 238–40
 Final Advent/Judgment, 246–47

eschatology *(continued)*
  heaven, 239
  life after death, 245–48
  immortality, 239–40
  resurrection, 239–40; *see also* Christ
eschaton, 185
Establishment; *see* Church
Eucharist; *see* Lord's supper
evangelical/s, 29, 129, 209
evangelism, 166, 225, 227–31
Evans, Christopher F., 134
Evans, O. E., 7n25
evil, 116–17, 118
  problem of, 116–21
evolution, 76, 101, 102, 104, 105, 252, 253; *see also* Darwin
Ewhurst Congregational Church, 5
exile, 227
extempore prayer; *see* prayer

Fabricius, Kim C., 40–41
Fackre, Gabriel, 33
Fairfield High School for Girls, 9
faith, 168–69
Family Worship; *see* Worship
Fall, the; *see* sin/sinner
Farr, George, 7n25
feminist, 114–15
Fergusson, David, 22n93
Ferré, Nels, 68, 70, 80–92, 184
filioque, 159–61
Final Advent/Judgment; *see* eschatology
Flint, Robert, 57
Floyd, Richard L. 103n17 & n18
forgiveness, 164–66
Forsyth, Peter Taylor, 10, 11, 31–33, 38–39, 52, 103, 118, 122, 128, 128n44, 129, 132, 136, 138, 140, 141–45, 146, 147, 149, 150–51, 152, 153–54, 155–56, 185, 186, 204, 205, 215, 225, 229, 250, 252
foundationalism; *see* philosophy
Franks, R. S., 31, 140
Fraser, Giles, 201
Free Church; *see* Church

Friends of the Congregational Library, 25n117
Friends of the Dr. Williams's Library; *see* Dr. Williams's Library
fruits of the Spirit; *see* Spirit
fundamentalism; *see* Bible
Fung, Raymond, 153
Galatian heresy; *see* sectarianism
Galileo Galilei, 100–101
Garvie, Alfred Ernest, 67, 96, 103, 155, 184
gathered church; *see* Church
Gaunt, Alan, xiii, 6, 223
Gellert, C. F., 249
Gilbert, W. S., 186
Gilkey, Langdon B. 80–81
Gilman, E., 7n25
God, 64–99
  activity, 65–66
  attributes, 75, 92–96
  creativity, 85, 104, 247
  dipolar structure, 71, 74–80
  holy love, 64–65, 88–89, 92, 116–18, 129, 131, 136–38, 139–49, 158, 162, 187, 222
  immanence, 68, 69–70, 72, 76, 91–92
  impassibility, 95–96
  omnipotence, 94, 116, 118, 120–21
  omniscience/foreknowledge, 93–94
  proofs for the existence of, 42–57
  providence, 117–18
  relationship to the world, 66–71, 102, 187
  sovereignty, 117, 241, 244
  transcendence, 69–70, 72, 76, 91–92, 221, 223
  triune/Trinity, 95–96, 96–99, 104, 127–28, 135, 146–47, 157, 178, 179, 204, 206, 209, 219, 241
  ultimacy/perfection, 83–85, 102
  see also election; theism; pantheism; panentheism
Godalming Congregational Church, 3
Goodwin, A., 7n25
grace, 114, 135, 136, 140, 141–42, 152, 162–70, 178, 189, 191, 208, 209, 211, 219, 229, 230, 234, 241–44

General Index

means of, 203–20; *see also* preaching; sacraments; discipline
prevenient, 209, 243
Great Ejectment, 28
Green, Michael, 128n42
Griffin, David Ray, 78
Graves, Peter, 150
Gunton, Colin E., 23, 31n156, 44, 72, 86, 87, 88, 96–97, 98–99, 103, 104, 145, 154–55, 160
Guttierrez, Gustavo, 54n117

Habgood, John, 200
Hallow Congregational Church, 12
Hampson, Daphne, 115
Hardy, Daniel T., 12, 99n201
Harrison, Jonathan, 10n37
Harrison, Ted, 126n32
Harrod, John, xiii
Hart, D. G., 222
Hart, Trevor A., 152, 254
Hartshorne, Charles, 72, 73, 74, 76, 77, 78, 79, 82, 85–86, 89, 94, 120–21
Henry, D. P., 7n25
Harvey, A. E., 128n42
Harvey, Van A, 42–43, 44–45
heaven; *see* eschatology
Hegel, Georg William Friedrich, 68
Hepburn, Ronald W., 10n37
Heywood-Thomas, John, 7, 7n25, 20, 22, 30
Hick, John, 93, 119, 128n42, 153n218, 254
Highland Theological College, xiii
Hilton, Donald, 217, 218
Holy Communion; *see* Lord's supper
homosexuals, 208
Horne, Charles Sylvester, 31n156
Hope Congregational Church, 9
house-church movement, 192
Human beings
  nature of, 105–7
  vocation of, 107–10; *see also* stewardship
  see also sin/sinner
hymns, 223

imago Dei, 42, 46, 57, 105–7, 111–13, 163
immortality; *see* eschatology
incarnation, 94, 103, 128; *see also* Christ; Church
inclusive language, xi–xiii
idealism; *see* philosophy
independency; *see* Church
individualism, 195, 210; *see also* covenant
Irenaeus, 112, 119

James, the Apostle, 170
Jamison, Trevor, 41
Jenkins, David E., 70, 126
Jenkins, Daniel T., 17, 182
Jeremias, Joachim, xii
Jewish, *see* Semitic
John Knox College, 22
John Rylands Library, xiii
John the Baptist, 158
Jones, Edgar, 17
Judaism, 126; *see also* Semitic
Jump, J. D., 7n25
Jüngel, Eberhard, 23, 249
justification, 166–70, 208, 238

Kaan, Fred, 223
Kelly, J. N. D., 159n14
Kendall, Gordon, 102, 251
kenosis/kenotic; *see* christology
kingdom of God, 187–88, 218; *see also* Church
Knitter, Paul F., 153n218
Knowles, V., 7n25
koinonia, 215, 239
Küng, Hans, 96, 255n30

Lampeter School of Theology, 23
laity, 210, 216
Lancashire Independent College, 5, 6
Leahy, D, 7n25
lectionaries, 207–8
Lees, Janet, xiii
legalism, 219, 234, 237
Leslie, R. F., 7n25
Lessing, Georg, 45–47
liberal/ism; *see* theology

liberation theologians, 52, 54, 155; *see also* theology
life after death; *see* eschatology
Lindbeck, George, 251
liquid modernity, 181, 195, 217; *see also* Bauman; Ward, Pete
Littlejohn, W. Bradford, 60
liturgy, 221–22
    liturgiologists, 210
Loades, Ann, 187
Locke, John, xi, 49, 75, 255
Lord's supper; *see* sacraments
Luther, Martin, 30
Lutheran/s, 30, 215

Macedonia Congregational Church, 9
Macfadyen, Dugald, 188
Mackintosh, Robert, 30n147, 31, 57n137, 134–35, 197
Macquarrie, John, 139n118, 186
Manning, Bernard Lord, 235
Mansfield College, 17
Manson, Thomas W., 7, 7n25
Maranatha, 215
Marquis Fund, xiii
Marlow, A.N., 7n25
Marsden, Carole R., xiii, 26
Marsh, John, 17, 197
Marsh, John Malcolm, xiii, 12n49, 13n55, 13n56
Martensen, H. L., 88
Mass; *see* Lord's Supper
Matthews, E. Gwyn, 251
McKelvey, Robert John, 17
metaphysics; *see* philosophy
Micklem, Caryl, 223
Miller, Richard, 21
Mill Hill School, 17
Mill, John Stuart, xi, 93
Ministerial Offices, 12–13
Minister/s, xi, 191, 195, 204, 209–10, 216
    pastoral work, 206–7
    see also preaching
ministry; *see* Church
mission, 198, 213, 214–31
    missio Dei, 221, 224–25, 227
Moberly, R. C., 137

Moltmann, 23, 96, 108, 160, 161, 238, 249, 251
Moore, G. E., 10
Morgan, George Stanley, 5
myth/mythology, 130, 247

neoclassical metaphysics; *see* process philosophy
neo-orthodoxy, 52
Nevin, J. W., 184
New College, London, 5
Newlands, George, 26–27
Nicaeno-Constantinopolitan Creed; *see* Creeds
Niebuhr, Reinhold, 113–14, 115–16, 154, 239
Nineham, Dennis E., 124n20
Nonconformity/Nonconformist, 29, 102, 182, 193, 242, 249
Northern College (United Reformed and Congregational), 17–18, 27; *see also* Lancashire Independent College
Norwood, Donald W., ix, x, xiii
Nuttall, Geoffrey Fillingham, 19–20, 24

Ogden, Schubert M., xiin18, 40–41, 55, 63, 65n13, 71, 72, 73, 74, 78, 79, 81, 82, 83–84, 85, 86, 87, 89, 104, 120, 121n117, 123, 130, 153n217
Ombersley Congregational Church, 12
Open University, 16
Orchard, Stephen, 193
ordination, 234–35
Origen, 30
original sin; *see* sin/sinner
Orthodox/y, 187, 234
orthodoxy; *see* theology
Orr, James, 201, 229
Owen, Hugh Parry, 7n25, 44, 60, 72, 73, 76–80, 88, 95
Owen, John, 204

Page, Heidi K., xiii
Page, Ruth, 17n69, 250

General Index

Pailin, David A., 1, 46, 47, 65, 66, 67, 72, 74, 101, 151
panentheism, 66–67, 71, 72, 73, 75–76; *see also* God; process philosophy; process theology
Pannenberg, Wolfhart, 238
pantheism, 66–67, 72, 73, 75–76
Passover, 217; *see also seder*
pastoral work; *see* minister/s
patripassianism; *see* God, impassibility
Paul, Robert, 154
Paul, the Apostle, 106, 110, 113, 125, 164, 166, 169, 170, 171–75, 185, 197, 233, 242, 243
peace and justice, 208
Peel, Andrew D., xiii
Peel, Patricia E., xiii
Pelagian/ism, 168, 235
Pembroke College, 16
penitence, 163–65, 178–79
Penn Club, 20
Pentecost, 159
Pentecostal/ism, 162, 212; *see also* Charismatic Movement
Perkin, H., 7n25
Perry Hill Congregational Church, 5
Pewley School, 4
Phillips, George, 7n25
philosophy, 57–9
  analytic, 57
  dualism, 117
  empiricism, 96
  foundationalism, 61
  idealism, 31, 58, 96
  metaphysics, 47, 58–59, 71, 72–73, 97, 253
  of religion, 57
  positivism, 61
  process, 58–59, 71–92, 253; *see also* process theology
Pickering, David A., xiii
Pittenger, Norman, 72, 87, 90
Plaskow, Judith, 115n84
Pollard, A, 7n25
Pope, Robert, ixn3, xiii, 4, 8, 23n99, 27, 28, 151, 245, 249
positivism; *see* philosophy

prayer, 206, 207
  extempore, 221–22, 224
preaching, 166, 190, 203, 204–8, 210
predestination; *see* election
Presbyterian/s, 180, 192
Presbyterian Church of Wales, 22
Preston, Ronald H., 7n25, 7n29
priesthood of all believers; *see* Church
process theology; *see* theology
process philosophy; *see* philosophy
Protestant, 29, 187
providence; *see* God
Puritan/ism, 98, 203, 249

Quaker, 191
Queen Mary Court, 19
quest for the 'historical' Jesus; *see* Christ
Quick, O. C., 112, 184

Rahner, Karl, 153
real presence, 215; *see also* the Lord's Supper
Reformation, 37, 52, 166, 194, 210
reformed church/tradition, 29, 103, 111, 174, 176, 181, 182, 189, 190, 196, 216, 242, 243, 244, 254; *see also* reformed theology
reformed theology/theologians; *see* theology
Regan, Tom, 109
regeneration; *see* Spirit
remnant, 227
repentance, 164–66
re-presentation/re-presentative; *see* christology
reprobation; *see* election
republican, 198
resurrection; *see* Christ; eschatology
revelation, 42, 68, 101, 104
Richards, Elwyn, xiii
Richmond, James, 10n37, 72, 83, 84
Ritschl, Albrecht B., 65
Robbins, Anna M., xiii, 23–24
Robinson, W. Gordon, 5, 7n25
Roman Catholic/ism, 161, 187, 234
Rowley, H. H., 7n25
Royal Historical Society, 25n116

Rupp, Gordon E., 7n25
Russell, Stanley H., 155–56

sacerdotalism, 209
Sacks, Jonathan, 45
sacraments, 186–87, 203, 208–10, 234
    dominical sacraments, 210
        baptism, 208, 210–14
        Lord's Supper, 176, 190, 197, 208, 214–18, 235
        presidency, 209–10
    seven sacraments, 210
sacrifice; *see* Christ, atoning work; atonement
sainthood; *see* Spirit
saints, 178, 198, 219, 242, 243
salvation, 209, 238–48; *see also* atonement; Christ; conversion; cross; justification; regeneration; sanctification
sanctification, 171–72, 208
satisfaction; *see* atonement
scandal of particularity; *see* cross
Schleiermacher, F. D. E., 30, 31, 33, 52, 60
Schumacher, E. F., 3
science/scientist, 100–102, 252
Scripture; *see* Bible
sectarianism; *see* Church
Sedbergh Congregational Church, 2, 9, 10–12
seder, 217, 218; *see also* Passover
Segundo, Juan Luis, 54n117, 228
Sell, Alan P. F. biographical, 2–28
    colleague, 24
    minister, 26
    person, 27, 255
    teacher, 23–24
    theologian, 27, 29–33, 48, 59, 178, 256
    wider church, 26
Sell, Arthur Philip, 3
Sell, Bridget Rebecca Karen, 9, 16
Sell, Freda Marion, née Bushen, 3
Sell, Jonathan Patrick Alan, 9, 16
Sell, Judith Bronwen Amanda, 9, 16
Sell, Karen Elisabeth née Lloyd, xiii, 9, 16, 20, 21, 28

Sell, Roger David 3
Semitic, 214, 247
sensus divinitatis, 42, 106
Separatism/Separatist, 51, 176, 180, 193, 197, 198, 199, 203, 226
sermons; *see* preaching
service, 227–29
Simpson, Sarah C., xiii, 23
Simpson, William E., 10n38
sin/sinner, 54, 57, 110–16, 130–31, 131–56, 162–66, 171, 187, 218, 238, 241, 251
    Fall, 110–11
    original sin, 211
Skelton, R., 7n25
Smith, D. H., 7n25
Sobrino, Jon, 54n117
social justice, 149, 153–54
social media, 205
Society for the Study of Theology, 21
Society of Antiquaries of London, 25n116
sola scriptura; *see* Bible
soteriology; *see* cross
Spence, Dorothy C., xiii
Spirit, Holy, 49–50, 59, 135, 138, 147, 148, 157–75, 177–78, 185, 187, 189, 205, 206, 209, 210, 212, 229, 236, 239, 250, 253, 254
    baptism in the Spirit, 212; *see also* Charismatic Movement
    fruits of the Spirit, 173–75
    regeneration, 162–69, 208, 211–12
    sainthood; life in the Spirit, 170–75
spiritualist/spiritualism, 190
Spurgeon, C. H., 207
St Andrew's Hall, 17
Stevenson, D. J. G., 31n156
stewardship; *see* creation
Sub Rosa, 25
subscription; *see* Creeds
supernatural, 59, 70, 112, 127, 148

Tatem, David W., xiii, 26
Taylor, Michael, H., 8n33
Taylor, John H., 253
Taylor, Vincent, 124n20
Ten Commandments, 231

theism, 66, 72–73, 76, 80–83, 85, 89
Thistleton, Anthony, 22n96
theology 34–63
    apologetics, 30, 60–63, 66, 155–56, 250
    apophatic, 186
    compartmentalization within, 28–29
    confessional, 251
    contextual nature of, 1, 52–56, 177, 236
    final authority for, 60
    labels, 29
    liberal, ix, 64–65, 110, 133, 137, 141, 144, 146, 228, 256
    liberation, 228–29; see also liberation theologians
    natural, 42, 57
    orthodoxy, 101, 116, 128, 219, 231, 242, 250, 256
    practioners of, 35–37, 190
    process, 71–92, 96, 253; see also process philosophy
    reformed, 33, 50, 57, 114, 176, 183–84, 196, 203, 210, 215, 240
    revisionary, ix, x, 249–50, 256
    roll of experience in, 59–60
    roll of reason in, 56–59
    resources for, 48–56
    starting point of, 37–48, 62, 94
    task of, 38
Thomism/Thomist, 75, 79, 80–83; *see also* Aquinas
Thompson, Colin P., 49n87
Thompson, David M., xiii, 159n13, 180, 184, 198, 211n50
Townsend, Michael J., 250
Tillich, Paul, 67, 70
Torah, 233
Torrence, Thomas F., 23
Townsend, Henry, 200
Tracy, David, 36–37, 81
tradition, 50-2, 62
transubstantiation, 215
Trinity; *see* God
truth, 58
Turner, John Munsey, 199–200

Unitarian/ism, 98, 180, 219
United Reformed Church, 22
    Basis of Union, 49–50
    Doctrine, Prayer and Worship Committee, 26
United Theological College, 23–23, 25
universalism; *see* election
University of Alcala, 16
University of Aberdeen, 22
University of Birmingham, 12
University of Calgary, 20, 21
University of Chester, 25n115
University of Edinburgh, 17
University of Manchester, 7–8, 10, 23, 30, 72
University of Nottingham, 10, 22, 26, 72
University of St Andrews, 17
University of Sussex, 17
University of Wales Trinity Saint David, 25n115
United Church of Christ, 184
universalism; *see* election

Varsity Acres Presbyterian Church, 21
Vermes, Geza, xii
Vine, Aubrey Russell, 98
Virgin birth; *see* Christ
von Rad, Gerhard, 90, 110

Ward, W. R., 7n25, 93
Ward, Keith, 66, 102, 104–5, 119–20
Ward, Pete, 181, 194; *see also* Baumen; liquid modernity
Watson, Brenda, 1
Watson, Thomas, 163, 171
Watts, Isaac, 223, 249
Webster, John, 37
Wesley, Charles, 136
Wesley, John, 242
Wesleyan, 242
Westermann, Claus, 90–91, 107–8
Western, R., 7n25
West Midland's College of Higher Education, 13, 15–16
Westminster Chapel, 5
Westminster College Library, xiii
Westminster Confession, 241

Westminster Shorter Catechism, 55, 228
White, James F., 215
Whitehead, Alfred North, 76, 78, 81, 96, 106, 253
Whitehead, Donald, xiii, 7
Wiles, Maurice, 53, 65n13, 251
Williams, John Tudno, xiii
Williams, T. Rhondda, 31n156
Willshaw, Mervyn, 250, 252
Wilson, A. J. N., 7n25
Wiseman, David, ixn3
Worcester United Reformed Church, 13n54
Word; *see* preaching
World Alliance of Reformed Churches, 18–19, 21
World Council of Churches, 19
World Faiths, Christianity's relation to, 148, 149, 153, 162, 253–54, 255
Worship, 192, 205, 221–24
  children at the Lord's supper, 216–17
  conduct of, 221
  Family, 11, 13
  see also hymns; liturgy; prayer; preaching
Wren, Brian, 223
Wykes, David L., xiii

Young, Frances M., 128

Zwingli, Huldrych, 215